Uneasy in Babylon

RELIGION AND AMERICAN CULTURE

SERIES EDITORS

David Edwin Harrell Jr.
Wayne Flynt
Edith L. Blumhofer

Uneasy in Babylon

Southern Baptist Conservatives and American Culture

BARRY HANKINS

The University of Alabama Press
Tuscaloosa and London

Copyright © 2002
The University of Alabama Press
Tuscaloosa, Alabama 35487-0380
All rights reserved
Manufactured in the United States of America

Typeface: ACaslon

∞

The paper on which this book is printed meets the minimum requirements of
American National Standard for Information Science–Permanence of Paper for
Printed Library Materials, ANSI Z39.48–1984.

Library of Congress Cataloging-in-Publication Data

Hankins, Barry, 1956–
  Uneasy in Babylon : Southern Baptist conservatives and American culture /
Barry Hankins.
      p. cm. — (Religion and American culture)
Includes bibliographical references and index.
  ISBN 0-8173-1142-4 (cloth : alk. paper)
  1. Southern Baptist Convention—History—20th century. 2. Conservatism—
Religious aspects—Southern Baptist Convention—History—20th century.
I. Title. II. Religion and American culture (Tuscaloosa, Ala.)
  BX6462.3 .H36 2002
  286'.132—dc21

                                                                    2001006526

Parts of chapter 1 originally appeared in different form in "Southern Baptists and
Northern Evangelicals: Cultural Factors and the Nature of Religious Alliances,"
Religion and American Culture: A Journal of Interpretation 7 (summer 1997): 271–98;
and "'How Ya Gonna Keep Em Down on the Farm?': Southern Baptist Conservatives and Neo-Evangelicals," *Mid-America: An Historical Review* 82 (fall 2000): 325–
53.

British Library Cataloguing-in-Publication Data available

This book is dedicated to Robert and Shirley Hankins

Contents

Acknowledgments

Among institutions that supported this project, I would first like to thank the University Research Committee at Baylor University for four consecutive summers of grant support. The funding allowed me to travel about interviewing Southern Baptist conservatives and doing archival research, without which I would have been unable to complete this project. Baylor's Institute for Oral History, under the direction of Rebecca Sharpless, also awarded me two summer fellowships and, perhaps more importantly for future scholars, transcribed all of the interviews; they are bound in volumes and housed in the Baylor University Texas Collection. The tapes and transcripts will be available for other researchers in perpetuity. The Southern Baptist Historical Library and Archives in Nashville also provided a grant. Archive director Bill Sumner proved to be a good sounding board as he listened to my musings on Southern Baptists and offered his own considerable insights on a variety of topics. The videotaped interviews he did with SBC conservatives were also very helpful.

The following people read parts of the manuscript and offered invaluable insights: Peggy Bendroth, Brad Creed, David Gushee, Michael Hamilton, Scott Moore, and Carey Newman. David Morgan, Wayne Flynt, and Bill Leonard read the entire manuscript, the latter twice. All three provided helpful criticism that saved me embarrassment. Leonard offered the most extensive critique of the manuscript; he and I debated back and forth via e-mail. I accepted much of his criticism and found all of his insights worthy of consideration, but the flaws that remain are mine.

I had the energetic aid of three graduate assistants during the nearly four years this book came together. Al Beck, Brett Lattimer, and Marshall Johnston made endless forays into archives and libraries, tracking down citations and generally chasing all kinds of rabbits that kept scurrying to and fro across the path the research took.

At The University of Alabama Press, series editors Wayne Flynt, Edith Blumhofer, and David Edwin Harrell Jr.; former press director Nicole Mitchell; and assistant acquisitions editor Dan Waterman were extremely patient, supportive, and encouraging. In addition, copyeditor Kevin Brock saved me from many a gaffe.

Parts of chapter one appeared originally in a different form in two articles. The journals *Mid-America: An Historical Review* and *Religion and American Culture: A Journal of Interpretation* graciously granted permission to reuse the material.

While acknowledging all these friends and colleagues, I, of course, accept full responsibility for the book.

UNEASY IN BABYLON

Introduction

In 1967 historian Rufus Spain published a social history of late-nineteenth-century Southern Baptists entitled *At Ease in Zion*. In that book Spain showed how Southern Baptists were comfortable in a culture they had largely built. This did not necessarily mean that Southern Baptists had succeeded in making the South distinctly Christian, let alone Baptist, just that they had come to identify with southern culture and feel comfortable in their role of supporting and perpetuating its norms and mores.[1] Throughout much of the twentieth century, the easy identification of Southern Baptists and southern culture persisted, so much so that church historian Martin Marty once referred to the Southern Baptist Convention (SBC) as the "Catholic Church of the south." He argued that southern Protestants in general, along with African American Protestants and Mormons, had the most intact religious subcultures in America.[2] As the SBC grew, its dominance over the South only increased, especially as other mainline denominations in the region ceased to identify so closely with southern culture. And as the SBC became ever more dominant, the historic Baptist tradition of dissent was largely lost, at least at the highest levels of denominational life.[3] It was left to a minority on the fringes of SBC life to carry that dissenting tradition forward. During the last quarter of the twentieth century, however, the time was largely passed when an intact Southern Baptist Convention could dominate a largely homogenous southern culture. It is neither as clear nor as easy as it was once to know exactly what it means to be a southerner or a Southern Baptist.[4]

In the late twentieth century, a group of Southern Baptists quite different from Spain's subjects came to control the Southern Baptist Convention, but they do not dominate the South like their Baptist forebears of a century ago.

They are not at ease in their Zion. Rather, Southern Baptist conservatives, as they prefer to be called, are convinced that American culture has turned hostile to traditional forms of faith and that the South has become more like the rest of the United States than ever before. This being the case, they are seeking to put America's largest Protestant denomination at the head of what they perceive to be a full-scale culture war. This book is an attempt to understand and explain who Southern Baptist conservatives are, how they became evangelical culture warriors, and what they intend to do with their considerable influence. Although this is not a study about the Southern Baptist controversy, it is impossible to discuss SBC conservatives without some reference to the denominational clash that brought them to power. It is important at the outset, therefore, to give a brief overview of the conflict in order to set the stage for understanding the conservatives.

THE SBC CONTROVERSY

Historian David Morgan, in his history of the SBC controversy, asked, "Why did the idea of inerrancy capture the imagination of so many Southern Baptists in 1979 and throughout the 1980s when it failed to do so in 1969 and during the early 1970s?" His shorthand answer is "that it took time for society to react in an organized fashion to the disturbing revolutionary decisions of the Supreme Court under Chief Justice Earl Warren and to the excesses of student protesters and others during the Vietnam War."[5] Morgan makes a connection between the theological controversy over the inerrancy of scripture that rocked the SBC and the changes in the culture that preceded the controversy. The current study is a more extended answer to a question very similar to Morgan's. Put most simply, how did the conservative leaders of America's largest Protestant denomination come to hold cultural views that put them at odds with the moderates who had preceded them in the leadership positions of their denomination? The short answer is that these leaders, as young men, moved outside the South intellectually, and in some cases even geographically, and began to adopt an evangelical critique of American culture. They became convinced that the South was no longer immune to diversity, pluralism, and secularism, and they began to mobilize. The first stage of mobilization would be within the SBC as they organized to take control of their denomination.

Beginning in 1979, the Southern Baptist Convention experienced one of the most contentious and significant denominational battles in American religious history. It is best known now as the Southern Baptist controversy, and it resulted in the conservative faction completely ousting the moderates from power and taking control of all denominational agencies, including the six SBC seminaries. This was only the second time that the conservative side had won a major denominational battle for power (the other being the Lutheran Church Missouri Synod in the 1970s). In the major battles of the early twentieth century in the Presbyterian and Northern Baptist denominations, the liberal side emerged largely victorious.

There have always been conservatives in the Southern Baptist Convention. In fact, the vast majority of Southern Baptists are solidly evangelical in belief and conservative in matters of theology. Nevertheless, for most of the twentieth century the group of elites that controlled the denominational machinery were positioned in the middle of the Southern Baptist theological spectrum. Arrayed on either side of them were dissenters who prodded and goaded these moderate leaders. On the left was what David Stricklin has recently called a "genealogy of dissent" made up of activists who tried to move moderates on issues of race, women in the ministry, and social justice.[6] For the most part the left wing was satisfied to remain on the fringes of the denomination, serving as a prophetic voice.

Right-wing dissenters of the SBC were often called the fundamentalists of the denomination. Their patriarch was W. A. Criswell of First Baptist Church, Dallas, for many years the denomination's largest congregation. Certain individuals from the fundamentalist wing occasionally found their way into positions of power. Criswell, for example, served as the president of the convention for the standard two one-year terms in the late sixties (1968–70). Still, the conservatives had little representation on boards of denominational agencies or on the faculties of the six seminaries. In this regard the conservatives were in many ways like the left-wing dissenters. Stricklin makes a plausible case that those on the left and the right had more in common with each other as quasi-outsiders than either had with the moderates who controlled the SBC. The presence of the left and right wings shows how much diversity existed within the SBC, but even among the moderates there was considerable theological diversity: some were biblical inerrantists, others appropriated features of neo-orthodoxy, still others were influenced by the Social Gospel, some were Calvinist, and many others simply pietistic Baptist Christians whose primary concern was living a holy life and evangelizing their neighbors.

Such diversity should not be surprising for anyone who studies evangelicals in various settings. The broad umbrella that is evangelicalism has been defined in different ways, but the two primary features are belief that the sole or ultimate authority for the Christian life is the Bible and that salvation comes only by an experience with a risen Christ.[7] Within this broad definition there is plenty of room for variation. Eminent historian of southern culture Sam Hill once identified four distinct parties just within southern evangelicalism: the truth party, which was dedicated to correct belief; the conversion party, committed primarily to missions and evangelism; the spirituality party, which emphasized the experience of God and His intimate presence; and the service party, which stressed the need for service to humanity.[8] Many Southern Baptist individuals and congregations, whether moderate or conservative, would embody one or more of these emphases.

For most of the twentieth century these diverse constituencies of the SBC had been held together by what Southern Baptist church historian Bill Leonard and others have called the "Grand Compromise." This was a tacit agreement not to let the right, left, or any other ideological party take control of the denomination. Instead, the SBC would be held together by centrists, and ideological diversity would be tolerated for the sake of missions and evangelism. This was a compromise, not a synthesis. As Leonard writes, "There was less a synthesis than a Grand Compromise based in an unspoken agreement that the convention would resist all attempts to define basic doctrines in ways that excluded one tradition or another, thereby destroying unity and undermining the missionary imperative."[9]

The right-wing dissenters, however, began in the 1970s to plan a strategy for taking control of the denomination and bringing an end to the Grand Compromise. They believed that the denomination should be unified doctrinally, and they were convinced that the SBC was becoming too liberal—that is, by allowing latitude in matters of theology, it was going the way of other mainline denominations. Only a course correction would keep Southern Baptists in the orthodox, evangelical fold. Their rallying cry became the inerrancy of scripture as conservatives set out to take control of the institutions of the SBC. They believed that if denominational employees were required to be inerrantists, the SBC would be protected from theological drift to the left.

Inerrancy is often a problematic term. Used in populist fashion, as it was during the SBC controversy, it simply means that the Bible is without error in all matters on which it touches, including science and history. In scholarly circles, however, it is often acknowledged that there are several different theories as to just what inerrancy means. For example, just to cite one area of diversity, while many inerrantists believe in a literal interpretation of the Genesis creation account, an inerrantist would not necessarily have to hold to such a view. The Genesis account could be interpreted as true but more mythic than literal. In the mid-1980s, sociologist Nancy Ammerman surveyed Southern Baptist pastors as to their beliefs on several issues. On inerrancy, 85 percent agreed with the statement "[T]he scriptures are the inerrant word of God, accurate in every detail," but more than half of the respondents agreed with the statement, "The Genesis creation stories are there more to tell us about God's involvement than to give us a how and when." Only 38 percent disagreed or strongly disagreed with the second statement. Moreover, even among the avowed inerrantists, less than half insisted on a literal interpretation of the creation stories. Ammerman concluded, "While inerrancy may be the dominant view in Southern Baptist life, then, literalism is not."[10] That said, in popular theological disputes, those who are the strongest proponents of inerrancy often insist on a high level of literalism as well and as a result are quite intolerant of the view that some portions of scripture are more mythic than literal. Sociologist James Davison Hunter calls inerrancy a hermeneutic that "is essentially literalistic, meaning that the Bible should be interpreted at face value whenever possible."[11] Hunter's definition fits Southern Baptist conservatives quite well. What this means, in effect, is that the term "inerrancy," which is a theory about the Bible, is often conflated with a certain hermeneutical approach to the Bible, meaning that under conservative rule, only those with very similar interpretations will be eligible for office in the SBC.

"Inerrancy," however defined, became a very effective tool in the hands of SBC conservatives as they attempted to convince rank-and-file Southern Baptists that their moderate leaders and denominational employees were too liberal. Many moderates refused to accept or use the term precisely because they saw it as so problematic and unclear, but conservatives insisted that one must hold to inerrancy to be an orthodox Southern Baptist. Conservative activist Paul Pressler put the case very well when he said, "Once you have crossed the theological Rubicon of saying that the Bible is sufficiently man's work so that it can be in error and make mistakes, then you have opened the floodgates for the individual to determine the categories which are truth, and that is [an] extremely presumptuous thing for a man to do." Similarly, popular preacher Adrian Rogers put the battle into neat, either-or categories, saying that either the Bible is inerrant or errant, infallible or fallible. As many conservative preachers began to put the issue, if one did not believe in the inerrancy of scripture, one was a "heretic and disbeliever."[12] One conservative SBC president articulated the slippery-slope argument employed by many conservatives. "The view that the Bible contains error is worth fighting against. That's the first domino to fall. Then you move into areas like the resurrection of Christ, the deity of Christ, soteriology, the whole works—all stem from your view of scripture."[13] Using these rhetorical measures, conservatives were able to force rank-and-file Southern Baptists to make a choice, and when forced to choose, the majority sided with the conservatives.

The architects of the conservative drive to take control of the denomination were biblical scholar Paige Patterson, aforementioned appeals court judge Paul Pressler, and pastor Adrian Rogers. As one interpretation goes, this was a three-leader movement with Patterson serving as theologian, Pressler as organizing tactician, and Rogers as the visible popular preacher.[14] Together they were successful where other activists on the right had failed. In 1979, under the guidance of Pressler and Patterson primarily, the conservative party won its first SBC presidency at the convention meeting in Houston with Rogers's election to the presidency. The denomination has a presidential vote each summer at its annual meeting, known as the Southern Baptist Convention. Messengers from congregations across the country gather and engage in what could be characterized as a very large plebiscite. While messengers are in many ways like delegates, there is one important difference. Each messenger, though credentialed by his or her congregation, attends the convention as an individual, with no responsibility to vote in accordance with the home church, an example of the high degree of individualism that Baptists have emphasized throughout their history.

Customarily at convention meetings, there would usually be several men nominated for president, and their names would be placed before the messengers. There was no preconvention campaigning, and the votes were usually rather routine with little controversy. The convention of 1979 was no different except for one important change: conservatives had a clear choice for president, and they had apparently been able to rally their troops to stand behind Rogers. He received 51 percent of the vote in a field of six candidates. The conservative strategy, unknown to most at the time and denied by conservatives until years later, was to use the appointive powers of the SBC presidency to remake the boards of the denominational agencies and seminaries. Pressler and Patterson at some point realized that if conservatives could hold the presidency for ten years, they could achieve a majority on all the boards. The power of the SBC presidency lies primarily in appointments. The president appoints members of a body that then appoints the trustees for the denominational agencies and seminaries. If he makes his appointments carefully and those appointees in turn use their power in accordance with his will, over time the agencies would reflect the tenor of the conservative movement. The next step was for the trustees of the agencies to hire conservative executive directors or presidents who run the daily operations of the agencies and seminaries. Viewed by many at the time as a temporary interruption in the Grand Compromise that had kept moderates in control, the 1979 conservative victory proved to be the beginning of the conservative takeover of the denomination.

The 1979 convention meeting touched off more than a decade of intense denominational warfare between conservatives and moderates. Because of the organizational structure of the SBC, conservatives needed to retain control of the presidency in order to use the office's appointive powers to remake all agency and seminary boards. Moderates, therefore, committed themselves to breaking the momentum of the conservative resurgence in order to retain control, or at worst to ensure a balance between the two camps. What ensued after 1979 were intense battles for the presidency. Each side began to recruit, organize, and mobilize for the annual convention meetings, especially those every other year, when the presidency was considered open per tradition.[15] As one would guess, the size of the annual meetings grew as each side rallied its troops, peaking in 1985 when forty-five thousand messengers attended the meeting in Dallas.

As the battle unfolded in the yearly SBC meetings, the fight was also carried into the agency and seminary boards of the denomination as conservatives began to take their places there. During the 1980s both sides engaged in efforts to delegitimize the other. Conservatives accused moderates of being liberals who had drifted away from the evangelical faith and taken the denomination with them. In many cases, very conservative and orthodox Southern Baptist moderates were tarred with accusations that would have made Joseph McCarthy blush. On the other side, most moderates never accepted that conservatives were really interested in theology. They charged repeatedly that conservative theology was being used as a cover for the rawest and crudest grab for power. Moderates also charged that conservative insistence on inerrancy amounted to an un-Baptist form of creedalism. Historically, many moderate Southern Baptists had held to the dictum "no creed but the Bible," which is somewhat oversimplified in that the denomination has had a confession of faith since 1925. Admittedly, however, conservatives were determined to make doctrinal tests for denominational positions far more stringent and defined than before. It is almost impossible to overstate the mutual mistrust that resulted from these accusations. Sociologists sometimes argue that people from opposing ideological camps usually cool their rhetoric and come to appreciate their opponents' point of view when they meet them face to face, unless the issues are religious. With religious disputes the level of conflict and intensity seems to increase as the opposing camps come into proximity to one another. During the 1980s it was as if Southern Baptists had deliberately set out to prove that this was true.

After 1979, moderates never won another presidency. By the early 1990s the denomination was in the hands of the right wing, as all agency and seminary boards had conservative majorities and were on their way to having only conservative inerrantist members. The 1990s, therefore, saw the transformation of all agencies and, perhaps most importantly, the SBC seminaries into conservative evangelical, inerrantist institutions. During the decade the battle between conservatives and moderates shifted from the national denomination to the state Baptist conventions, where it continues to this day.

While the vast majority of the early twenty-first century's sixteen million Southern Baptists are the same people who were counted in the denomination before conservatives took control, the public character and personality of the SBC is very different today than it was twenty years ago. This is possible because the leadership of a religious organization is not necessarily reflective of rank-and-file members of the churches that make up the denomination. While this is true of mainline denominations like the Presbyterians and Methodists, where the leadership is decidedly more liberal than most congregants, it is even more likely to be the case in a denomination that allows for congregational autonomy. Within the Southern Baptist Convention there are many churches that care little about what happens at denominational headquarters in Nashville. In keeping with Baptist history, members believe that they are the local and gathered body of Christ running their own affairs democratically in light of what they believe to be the will of God. Since Baptist churches choose their own pastors, they do not have to worry about the possibility of being assigned a leader who does not fit.

Likewise, they decide as a congregation whether or not to send money to the national body and how much. Historically, the only requirement for being a Southern Baptist church in good standing has been that the congregation send a nominal sum to the denomination's Cooperative Program, which disperses funds for all denomination-wide enterprises. In the 1990s there was a change in the SBC bylaws stipulating that churches that bless homosexual unions or ordain gay ministers would not be eligible to send messengers to SBC meetings. Oddly, then, all a Baptist church has to do to affiliate with the SBC is send a few hundred dollars to Nashville and refrain from ordaining or marrying homosexuals. Even under the leadership of conservatives, with their heightened concern for doctrinal purity, congregational autonomy continues.

All this being the case, many Southern Baptist churches make a point of ignoring the larger denominational structure except when it comes to utilizing the services that structure can provide. When moderates were in control of the SBC, many conservative churches stood aloof from denominational institutions. In fact, some larger churches such as First Baptist, Dallas, where Criswell pastored, even started their own schools and seminaries to better reflect their own theological positions while continuing to consider themselves Southern Baptists. Other conservative churches sent only a very small percentage of their annual receipts to Nashville, using the bulk of their monies to fund enterprises more in keeping with their beliefs. With conservatives now in charge nationally, many moderate churches are reducing the amount they send to Nashville, and moderates have formed new seminaries as alternatives to the six SBC schools.

In addition to the issues that might interest only church historians, there are also very important cultural considerations at stake in the SBC controversy. These features were formerly confined largely to the South, but it is not going too far to say that Southern Baptists are rapidly becoming the most visible and influential force on the conservative side of what many perceive to be a culture war. Conservatives were able to win the Southern Baptist Controversy by tapping into basic conservative instincts that existed among rank-and-file Southern Baptists who did not identify with their moderate leaders. Before 1979 these rank-and-file Baptists were largely unmobilized, accustomed as they were to being culturally dominant in their own region. Conservative leaders were able to develop and articulate a new Southern Baptist public personality or posture that resonated with the majority of Southern Baptists. As will be argued in the chapters that follow, a certain stance toward culture was the major component in this new public personality.

This is not to deny that theology played a major role in the SBC conservative movement. But, why did these leaders decide that theology was so important, and why did so many Southern Baptists agree that if the theology of the denomination were not narrowed and more clearly defined, the denomination would lose its ability to function as an instrument of God in this world? The short answer is that conservative leaders came to believe that America, including the South, was in the throes of a cultural crisis that necessitated a warlike struggle against the forces that were hostile to evangelical faith. The first step in the process of engaging the popular culture was to reestablish a theological foundation for resistance. The second step was to win control of the denominational machinery that would be put into the service of cultural warfare. The third step was to fight and win that culture war—which is what Southern Baptist conservatives are attempting to do today. They seek nothing less than to lead the right wing of this national struggle, and if appearances on *Larry King Live* and other news programs are any indication, they are succeeding in this effort to become the most visible and influential of America's cultural conservatives. This does not mean that they only took over the SBC so they could more effectively join the culture war. Rather, it is to say that theological warfare and cultural warfare are in this case related. Once they won the battle within the denomination, conservatives commenced their efforts to lead the secular battles. This includes, but is not limited to, winning souls for the kingdom. In addition to that effort aimed at individuals, Southern Baptist conservatives also believe they are called to permeate and help mold the institutions of their society in an effort to stem the tide of cultural decay. It was as if millions of Southern Baptists, formerly at ease in Zion, had by the 1980s become very uneasy about the cultural trajectory of their region and needed only to have their worst fears articulated by a new group of elites. The first half of this book considers how these leaders became who they are and the difficulties inherent in the transition to a more explicitly evangelical and countercultural personality. The second half examines how they are now fighting their cultural battles on the issues most important to them.

Before advancing to the discussion of SBC conservatives, it might be helpful to include a brief discussion of the perspective of this book. In a day when notions of objective scholarship are either rejected out of hand or, at the least, viewed very skeptically, it seems reasonable, perhaps requisite, for authors to say something of their perspective. This can be considered a kind of truth-in-marketing exercise. On a topic that has been as controversial as the Southern Baptists, it seems especially important to be forthcoming at the beginning as to where I stand in relationship to my subjects.

I grew up neither southern nor Baptist. Rather, I was reared in the holiness Free Methodist denomination in Michigan. In short, I grew up a northern evangelical. In 1976 I transferred from my own denominational college, Spring Arbor College, to Baylor University. From that time forward, with the exception of three years at Kansas State University, I have been somewhat within the Southern Baptist orbit either by church attendance or, for the past decade, on the faculty of a Baptist college or university—first Louisiana College and now Baylor. As a member of a moderate-liberal Southern Baptist church in the late 1980s, then on the faculty of Baptist colleges in the 1990s, I have been a participant-observer in the Southern Baptist controversy, and when the lines are drawn and the battle engaged, I have sided with the moderates. Still, having come from outside both the denomination and the South, my perspective is quite different from that of a true insider. While I understand the deep sense of loss that many moderates feel as a result of the conservative takeover of the SBC, I cannot feel that loss because my identification as a Baptist has always been localized to particular congregations and/or colleges and not to the national SBC. I have never identified myself as a Southern Baptist. As Sam Hill once mentioned in conversation, one can never be fully Southern Baptist if he or she was not reared in that tradition. There is a "cultural ethnicity" that outsiders will never fully share.

All that said, I do not claim objectivity. If postmodernism has taught us anything, it is just how important perspective is in nearly every scholarly endeavor. I fully acknowledge that I have a particular perspective that informs this book. That perspective was shaped by northern evangelicalism of a holiness sort combined with the rigors of academic training in the history profession that brought me to an appreciation of Baptist history, especially its emphasis on congregational autonomy, the priesthood of believers, and religious liberty. My location has allowed me to see Southern Baptist life up close, indeed from the inside, without actually being an insider. I hope that I can appreciate certain features of both the conservative and moderate factions in Southern Baptist life while at the same time being detached enough from both to be critical yet fair. I do not think this book will fit the typical moderate view of the SBC conservative movement, and I fully expect some of my moderate friends and colleagues who have spent their lives in the SBC to take issue with my interpretations. I can only say that my goal in this book is to understand and explain the conservatives and not to refute them. To argue that the SBC conservative movement has a certain coherency about it and to demonstrate that moderate interpretations of the conservative movement were often off the mark is not necessarily to agree with the positions conservatives hold or the achievements they have attained in taking control of the denomination. Moderate and conservative Southern Baptists do not understand each other very well. Each side seems to focus on the worst-case-scenario caricature of the other. I am merely trying to break through the moderate caricature of the conservatives and explain who they are from a different perspective. In most cases, even where I may disagree with them, I still find their views to be largely coherent—at least as coherent as moderate Baptist views as well as those of most other religious groups in America. This book, then, will be one interpretation of SBC conservatives, the first book-length, scholarly work about them. Others will follow that will challenge my interpretations, and the conversation will move forward. If I can jump-start that scholarly discussion, even as the interpreter others will seek to refute, I will be pleased to have put something forward that moves the discussion.

Most authors who have dealt recently with Southern Baptists refer to the conservatives as fundamentalists. I eschew the F-word for two reasons. First, this is not the term they prefer. The word "fundamentalist" has taken on pejorative connotations. Conservatives bristle at its use in much the same way that moderates who are genuinely evangelical in their theology resist being called liberals. Second, the term "fundamentalist," in its usage among historians, is not quite accurate for the SBC conservatives. As will be shown in chapter one, by 1960 or so, it was a term embraced primarily by those who continued to take a separatist stance toward American culture. Southern Baptist conservatives reject this in favor of cultural engagement. There are certainly ways in which "fundamentalist" fits SBC conservatives—primarily in their militant defense of evangelical orthodoxy. This book, however, is about SBC conservatives and American culture, and it is precisely with regard to cultural engagement that the conservatives do not act like classical fundamentalists.

I would like to thank all those who agreed to interview with me for this project. As the footnotes will reveal, most of these individuals are Southern Baptist conservatives; after all, the book is about them. In addition, however, I have also interviewed several evangelicals who tried to be a part of the Southern Baptist conservative movement and found it impossible, and I have spent time with many moderates to ensure that I have their perspective as well. While there is a good bit about moderate Southern Baptist views that is necessary to an understanding of where and how conservatives differ from them, I have not placed a moderate counterargument at every turn. Again, the book is primarily about the conservatives. At times it is impossible to understand their views without reference to the moderates, but at other times the conservatives' positions must be evaluated in a broader context and critiqued on their own merits.

As I stated in the footnote to the first article I wrote after starting to interview SBC conservatives, they have without exception been gracious and forthcoming in our conversations. They never once gloated about winning control of the SBC, and I never once gloated about the moderates hanging on to Baylor.

I
Moving off the Plantation

Southern Baptist Conservatives become
American Evangelicals

Throughout most of the twentieth century, moderate Southern Baptists who controlled the Southern Baptist Convention cared much less about challenging and critiquing their culture than did progressives on the left wing of the denomination or conservatives on the right. While most moderates were comfortable within southern culture, progressives pestered them on issues of race, peace and justice, and women in ministry. Certainly, many moderates agreed with the basic principles of the progressives, but as a group the moderates were dedicated to the maintenance of a smoothly functioning denomination that measured its success in terms of conversions, baptisms, and numbers of missionaries in the field. On the right wing of the denomination, there developed a group of conservative leaders who, like the progressives, had a socio-political program for reforming American culture. While disagreeing on almost all social and political issues, progressives and conservatives had more in common with each other than either had with the moderates. Both the right and the left of the SBC were more interested in advancing principle, even at the risk of disrupting the denomination, but both were held on the margins of SBC life until the 1980s by the moderates at the center. In addition to their disagreements on theology and politics, the primary difference between the progressives and conservatives was that the latter decided it was not enough to exist on the fringes. Instead, the conservatives decided to take over the denomination and become its new insiders.[1]

Southern Baptist conservatives might well have come to their cultural views on their own by simply observing and responding to cultural change, but it actually did not happen that simply. Rather, the most influential shapers of conservative opinion in the denomination had help from northern evangelicals in developing their views, and some also had experiences outside the South in their pre- or early-adult years that alerted them to the secularizing tendencies rife in American culture. This exposure to nonsouthern culture and to evangelicals who were interpreting that culture shaped conservatives in powerful ways.

SBC Moderates and Evangelicals

The question of relationship between evangelicals and Southern Baptists has garnered the attention of several scholars. Two books emerged in the 1980s addressing this issue. The first was *Are Southern Baptists "Evangelicals"?* It took the form of a debate between Southern Baptist theologian James Leo Garrett and Southern Baptist historian Glenn Hinson, with James Tull weighing in as a moderator of sorts. Garrett, of Southwestern Baptist Theological Seminary in Fort Worth, argues the affirmative case. He begins cautiously with a discussion of the possible reasons that Southern Baptists have not thought of themselves as evangelicals. First, Southern Baptists did not want to be identified with fundamentalism during the fundamentalist-modernist controversy of the early twentieth century. Second, Southern Baptists exhibit a strong denominational independence that does not allow for very much interdenominational affiliation. Third, Southern Baptists have always preferred the terms "conservative," "evangelistic," and "missionary" to "evangelical."[2] The second point seems most critical. Garrett believes that early in the twentieth century, the Southern Baptist Convention, while supportive of some ad hoc interdenominational activity, was already deeply separatist. This was partly a result of the Landmark movement that peaked in the 1890s and taught that only Baptist churches were true churches. In addition to this, Garrett argues, Southern Baptists in the early part of the twentieth century still had rather vivid memories of persecution at the hands of the denominations usually called evangelical. When one considers also that these other denominations were usually pedobaptistic (that is, they baptized infants), it is understandable why Southern Baptists were wary of pursuing common causes with them.[3]

Hinson employs these same facts to argue that Southern Baptists are not evangelicals, but Garrett merely acknowledges the basis for the question as he prepares to argue that they are. After carefully examining what evangelicals have been historically, Garrett concludes that while Southern Baptists may not be considered part of a common movement of evangelicals, there is really no other place for them on the theological spectrum. Therefore, Southern Baptists are "denominational evangelicals," by which he means that they were theologically but not institutionally part of a broad movement of Christians who share beliefs in the authority of Scripture, a life-transforming encounter with a risen Christ, and a strong missionary impulse. These three identifiers are often used as a way of defining evangelicals broadly.[4]

Hinson, who was at the time of publication of *Are Southern Baptists Evangelicals?* on the faculty of Southern Baptist Seminary in Louisville, counters Garrett's argument, working vigorously to show that Southern Baptists are not "denominational" or any other kind of evangelicals. Hinson claims that arguing the negative on this question is a painful experience for him because he has endeavored throughout his distinguished career as a church historian and theologian to move Southern Baptists toward ecumenical relationships. He goes so far as to suggest that few in SBC circles "come closer in meriting the title 'ecumaniac' than I." Admittedly, Hinson's vigor in differentiating Southern Baptists from evangelicals stems in large part from the fact that the two groups are so similar. He states that evangelicals are "dangerous" to Southern Baptist distinctiveness because "[t]hey are too much like us in too many ways, or, conversely, we are too like them in too many ways."[5]

Just who were these "dangerous" evangelicals that Hinson fears? He cited three ways in which the term "evangelical" has been used historically: (1) as a synonym for Lutherans, (2) to designate Protestants who emphasize personal conversion or heart religion, and (3) as a name for Protestants who are preoccupied with orthodoxy. Since the third group has laid special claim to the term, he chooses to focus on it. Hinson is here limiting "evangelical" to those who want to fight about theology. To the extent that theological fights have often led to the formation of creeds, he views evangelicalism as a threat to the Baptist emphasis on voluntarism in religion. Hinson here emphasizes the strong moderate Southern Baptist disdain for creedalism. Many moderates, while accepting confessions of faith geared toward defining what Baptists do believe, are wary of creeds used to articulate what a person must believe. One of the historic rallying cries for Baptists has been "no creed but the Bible." Hinson uses an analogy to press the importance of maintaining a distinction between evangelicals and Southern Baptists: the Christian faith is like an electrical conduit containing many wires insulated from one another.[6] He wants to be sure that the Southern Baptist wire, with its emphasis on voluntarism and liberty, is well insulated from the evangelical wire containing its creedal concern for orthodoxy.

Hinson's antagonism toward evangelicals is not some sort of personal idiosyncrasy. It is shared by other Southern Baptist moderates, dating from before the Southern Baptist controversy erupted in 1979. Perhaps the most belligerent example of Southern Baptist reluctance to be classed as evangelicals came from Foy Valentine of the SBC Christian Life Commission during the 1976 presidential campaign. With references to Jimmy Carter's Southern Baptist evangelicalism swirling everywhere, Valentine groused to *Newsweek* magazine: "Southern Baptists are not evangelicals. That's a Yankee word. They want to claim us because we are big and successful and growing every year. But we have our own traditions, our own hymns, and more students in our seminaries than they have in all theirs put together. We don't share their politics or their fussy fundamentalism, and we don't want to get involved in their theological witch-hunts."[7]

More recently, Southwestern Baptist Theological Seminary historian Leon McBeth has exhibited the inability of many Southern Baptist moderates to shake the negative image of evangelicals. He told a joint conference of Southern Baptists and northern evangelicals, "If you are a narrow, 'card-carrying,' militant, antidenomination, antiecclesiastical, organized evangelical, then leave me alone."[8] McBeth here failed to distinguish between evangelicals and fundamentalists, and even among fundamentalists, not all would fit his description. The most famous Southern Baptist fundamentalist, J. Frank Norris, however, would, and McBeth admitted that Norris is what many Southern Baptists would have in mind when they think of either fundamentalism or evangelicalism. Norris was pastor of First Baptist Church, Fort Worth, Texas, from 1909 to 1952. He was an often-belligerent and militant critic of the SBC as he attempted to import northern fundamentalism into the denomination. In addition to his frequent attacks on Southern Baptist leaders and institutions, Norris was also tried for murder after shooting and killing a man in his own church office.[9] Assuming that Norris was typical of fundamentalists, McBeth's statement also misconstrued historian George Marsden's term "card-carrying evangelical." McBeth seemed to think that a "card-carrying evangelical" is someone who is more militant than a regular evangelical. Marsden, however, employs this term to designate those who think of themselves as evangelicals first and members of a particular denomination second. While Marsden allows that those who have a "directly fundamentalist background" often exhibit the strongest identification with evangelicalism, the "card-carrying" label has nothing to do with how militant one is.[10] Nevertheless, the negative view of evangelicals held by Valentine, McBeth, Hinson, and other moderates is fostered by Marsden's references to neoevangelicals since 1950 as the "heirs of fundamentalism."[11]

McBeth rightly classified himself outside the "card-carrying" group even if for the wrong reasons. In reflecting on his own upbringing as a Southern Baptist, he wrote, "Not one of my family, friends, Sunday School teachers, or pastors ever mentioned the word [evangelical], much less claimed to be one."[12] For McBeth, and nearly all in his denomination, being Christian and Southern Baptist were quite enough. There was no need to designate oneself as anything else. Evangelicals were some other kind of Christians who had their own concerns. This feeling of differentiation between Southern Baptists and evangelicals was heightened considerably by the SBC controversy of the 1980s. Both McBeth and Hinson came under heavy attack from the conservatives, the wing of the denomination most willing to make common cause with northern evangelicals and fundamentalists. In the existential reality of the controversy, it is perhaps understandable that these two scholars came to view evangelicals as not only different from Southern Baptists but as a threat as well.

The year after *Are Southern Baptists Evangelicals?* appeared, Leonard I. Sweet, in a footnote in a book by the publisher (Mercer) of Garrett, Hinson, and Tull's volume, writes that the Garrett-Hinson debate was "[o]ne of the stranger exchanges about whether a denomination is 'evangelical.'"[13] Sweet does not say why he views the book as strange, but one can speculate that it is because the question in the title is of such importance to Southern Baptists that one of their presses would devote an entire book to it. A non–Southern Baptist might well respond to such a book by asking, "who cares?" Even more likely, Sweet may have thought the book strange because, outside the Southern Baptist Convention, there is no debate over whether or not Southern Baptists are evangelicals. It has been universally accepted that they are.[14]

Deep into the identity crisis that the Southern Baptist controversy became, however, members wrangled over their relationship to evangelicals; so much so that in 1993 Broadman-Holman published a continuation of this debate, *Southern Baptists and Evangelicals: The Conversation Continues,* an edited volume that emanated from the conference at which McBeth uttered his evangelical disclaimer. This time, eleven Southern Baptists weighed in on the discussion, and six non–Southern Baptists entered the fray as well. While a review of all the many positions represented cannot be undertaken here, this book was unable to securely establish the place of Southern Baptists within American Protestantism. There seemed to be a growing sense, however, that Southern Baptists are evangelicals, but different.

There have been several attempts to identify just how Southern Baptists are different and to explain why the moderates who controlled the denomination for so long never aligned completely with the broader evangelical world. One standard explanation is that the SBC was a full-service denomination needing no alliances. By contrast, northern evangelicalism is a parachurch movement out of necessity. No evangelical denomination in the North has the resources necessary to meet all the needs of the many such churches and individuals. This being the case, there are interdenominational publishing houses, missionary agencies, colleges, periodicals, and even churches in that region. Joel Carpenter has called this phenomenon the "evangelical united front," while George Marsden has likened it to a feudal kingdom and Timothy Smith a mosaic.[15] By contrast, Southern Baptists constructed a massive empire that has services and materials for everything. By the 1970s the denomination's Baptist Sunday School Board was the largest publisher of religious literature in the world, and the SBC Foreign Mission Board sent out more missionaries than any other denomination. Southwestern Baptist Theological Seminary was the largest in the world, and there were five other SBC seminaries with enrollments that dwarfed the schools of most other denominations. There were also more than forty-five SBC colleges and universities and a handful of secondary schools. Retreat centers and camps abounded across the South, while denominational agencies occupied offices in downtown Nashville, addressing everything from home and foreign missions to political action. Moderates simply felt little need to align with what were by comparison fledgling enterprises in the northern evangelical world. Indeed, when the National Association of Evangelicals (NAE) was formed in 1942 in St. Louis, two prominent Southern Baptists attended the organizational meetings, but the SBC declined affiliation. As one of the Southern Baptists present at the St. Louis meeting put it, the denomination already had the basic values of the NAE and "need not further organizational set-up to possess them."[16]

Another reason often argued for why SBC moderates did not align with northern evangelicals, the belief that the two groups were just fundamentally different theologically, is somewhat less plausible. Many conservatives favor this interpretation, believing that moderates, for the most part, are not traditional enough to qualify as evangelicals. Ironically, as Hinson and McBeth show, many moderates, knowing little about the variety of northern evangelicalism, also accepted this interpretation. Especially after conservatives began to reach out to other inerrantist northerners, moderates took the view that the friends of our enemies are indeed our enemies. In reality, the diversity of both SBC moderates and northern evangelicals meant that, with little effort, most in either camp could have found counterparts in the other had they bothered to do so.

A third interpretation is that the southern-ness of SBC moderates kept them from aligning with northerners. There certainly is something to this view. For at least the first half of the twentieth century, the North and South were dissimilar enough that religious alliances were unlikely. Relatively speaking, the South was backward educationally and industrially and harbored a residual wariness of all things northern. This was exacerbated by the race issue, which eventually brought northerners, federal government agents, and ultimately federal troops into the South to help destroy segregation. It is not hard to see why alliances across the Mason-Dixon line would have been difficult for many Southern Baptists, but it does seem that those most likely to seek out northern evangelicals during the period from the 1950s through the 1970s would be the moderate elites in the SBC who were more progressive on issues such as race than their rank-and-file brethren. This was not the case. In fact, some who were most progressive, Valentine for example, were also the most hostile to evangelicalism.

Certainly, several factors played a part in moderate reluctance to forge ties with northern evangelicals. Moreover, this reluctance was just part of the insular nature of a Southern Baptist Convention whose leaders largely remained aloof from most other Christians as well. As one former Southern Baptist seminary professor was quoted as saying in 1998, "We Southern Baptists were not conscious of ecumenical points of view when I began teaching 42 years ago."[17]

While Southern Baptist moderates did not align with northern evangelicals, conservatives did, particularly with neoevangelicals. Neoevangelicalism developed in the 1940s and 1950s as certain leaders emerged from the fundamentalist movement. Fundamentalism is usually defined as the early-twentieth-century movement of traditional Protestants who battled against the development of theological modernism, later called theological liberalism. Modernism was the attempt to harmonize Protestant theology with modern ways of thinking, particularly higher textual criticism of Scripture and evolutionary thought. During the first few decades of the century, there existed a broad coalition of conservative Protestants who defended traditional points of theology such as the Virgin Birth and the bodily resurrection of Christ against modernists who were reinterpreting and redefining those doctrines. After World War I, this broad coalition of conservatives began to harden into the militant defense of Protestant orthodoxy, and the term "fundamentalist" was coined around 1920. The Scopes trial of 1925, or more accurately the way it was interpreted in the 1930s, signified to many that fundamentalists had lost the fight. This was, in fact, the case in some denominations, particularly the Northern Baptists and among northern Presbyterians, where modernists won key denominational battles with conservatives, leaving the fundamentalists to either separate or remain as a minority within the denomination. In the 1930s and 1940s, it appeared that fundamentalists were defeated and had withdrawn from the mainstream of American culture. In reality, we know now that many of them were in a period of realignment and institution building that would prepare them to reenter American life during the 1950s and 1960s. Those who did attempt to reenter and reengage American culture came to be known as the neoevangelicals.

Essentially, the neoevangelicals became disenchanted with the militancy and, especially, the separatism of fundamentalists. Sometime after the Scopes trial, many fundamentalists had adopted a doctrine of separation from any facet of American life that was tainted with modernism. This included everything from mainline denominations to the entertainment industry to politics. In short, fundamentalist separatism sought to escape culture and save people from it rather than engage it. Marsden argues that by 1960 or so only the most extreme fundamentalists who continued to emphasize separatism and the end-times doctrine known as dispensational premillennialism were comfortable with the name "fundamentalist." Those who wanted to critically reengage culture in an effort to have a broader influence in American life took the name "neoevangelical," or simply "evangelical."[18]

CONSERVATIVE EXPERIENCES OUTSIDE THE SOUTH

It was this brand of evangelicalism that would resonate with SBC conservatives, and their introduction to it came as they moved out of their Southern Baptist context. This happened in two ways: first, they actually moved geographically outside the South in order to attend college or graduate school; and second, after they moved into new areas, they began to read northern evangelical literature. These two experiences combined to develop a mindset that was distinctly evangelical and Baptist instead of just Baptist. The most prominent among the nonsouthern intellectual influences were Carl F. H. Henry and Francis Schaeffer, two northern evangelical thinkers who stressed cultural crisis in a way that resonated with SBC conservatives. It would not be going too far to say that Henry has been a mentor for nearly the entire SBC conservative movement. Indeed, he helped officiate at the installation of Richard Land at the Christian Life Commission, Albert Mohler as president of Southern Seminary, Timothy George as dean of the Beeson Divinity School, and Mark Coppenger as president of Midwestern Baptist Seminary in Kansas City.

Henry has been one of the guiding lights of northern evangelicalism since the 1940s. As a founding professor of Fuller Seminary, the first editor of *Christianity Today,* and a prolific writer, he has probably done more than anyone, save Billy Graham, to shape twentieth-century evangelicalism. Conservatives claim him as a Southern Baptist, which is factually true and misleading at the same time. Although a longtime member of a dually aligned Baptist church (American and Southern Baptist) in Washington D.C., Henry was reared and educated in the North and Midwest and spent his entire career in non–Southern Baptist institutions outside of the South. Understandably, then, the entry for Henry in the *Dictionary of Christianity in America* does not even mention the SBC.[19] In the advanced stages of his life and career, however, Henry and SBC conservatives have embraced each other.

Schaeffer has also been immensely influential in evangelical circles, as a 1997 *Christianity Today* issue entitled "Our Saint Francis" attests. A product of Presbyterian fundamentalism, in the 1950s he and his wife, Edith, established a retreat center in the Swiss Alps called L'Abri (the shelter). From that lofty perch, Schaeffer began to write books and pamphlets critiquing the present state of western culture and challenging American evangelicals to adopt a more rigorous, activist, and culturally engaged theology. For many budding Christian intellectuals in the 1960s, a trip to Schaeffer's L'Abri was an intellectual pilgrimage. Unfortunately for Schaeffer's own reputation as an intellectual leader of the first rank, many young evangelicals accepted his challenge and became serious scholars, eventually coming to recognize the inaccuracies and inadequacies of Schaeffer's historical analysis. These evangelical thinkers, nevertheless, credit him with alerting them to the need for serious intellectual engagement with culture.[20]

Richard Land's experience is typical of most SBC conservative elites in that he was reared in the South but was exposed extensively to nonsouthern culture while still a young man. He was from Houston, Texas, where he attended segregated public schools, worshipped at a segregated church, and lived in an all-white neighborhood. After high school graduation, Land went off to Princeton University. Having never even met a black person his own age, he soon found that he had more in common with an African American classmate from the South than he did with white northerners. Land recalls with a chuckle that his black friend and he were the only ones in the Princeton dorm who did not have accents. Looking back at that experience, he believes that he was beginning to realize that Southern Baptists were culturally dominant and therefore culturally comfortable and captive, especially on the issue of race. As he puts it, "[Southern Baptists] could never say, 'Let righteousness roll down' as long as we were living in our segregation captivity."[21] Following graduation from Princeton, Land returned to the South. He earned a master of divinity degree at New Orleans Baptist Theological Seminary, then left the South again for several years of doctoral work at Oxford University.

While living outside the South, Land came into contact with the thinking of Henry and Schaeffer, and they remain high on his list of formative influences. He had been exposed to Schaeffer's early books by the time he reached New Orleans. Those works convinced Land that there was "a real attempt to suppress the religious free speech and the religious free exercise rights of the people in the public square in general and in public schools in particular." On church-state issues, Schaeffer convinced Land that violations of the U.S. Constitution's Free Exercise Clause were far more pervasive and important than violations of the Establishment Clause. Beyond this, reading Schaeffer helped Land move beyond the pietistic withdrawal from politics that marks so many Southern Baptists. For Land, Schaeffer's was the "confrontational, uneasy conscience of evangelicalism" willing to engage and battle culture. Land echoes the 1997 *Christianity Today* article by saying that it would be hard to imagine Schaeffer being enough at ease in American culture to play golf with presidents, an obvious allusion to Billy Graham.[22]

Henry also played a major and early role in shaping Land's thought on cultural issues, especially through his book *The Uneasy Conscience of Modern Fundamentalism*, something of a classic in northern evangelical circles. In it,

Henry argues that the sectarian withdrawal from culture that had marked fundamentalism during the first half of the twentieth century was unacceptable biblically. The book helped inspire midcentury neoevangelicals to reenter the cultural conversations that were taking place in politics and in seminaries and universities nationwide.[23] Ironically, just as Schaeffer's challenge to young scholars resulted in critiques of his own work, Henry's challenge to evangelicals to reenter politics also had unforeseen consequences. Although he seems to have envisioned a moderate, moralistic, and broadly Republican approach to political activity, any such consensus broke apart during the era of the Vietnam War, with left-wing evangelicals founding *Sojourners* magazine and calling for a very different and more radical form of engagement with culture. Southern Baptist conservatives, however, were among those who found Henry's vision quite satisfactory.

In 1996 Land wrote, "Carl F. H. Henry is undeniably the 20th-century's greatest evangelical theologian, and arguably its most important theologian of any perspective."[24] The Ethics and Religious Liberty Commission under Land's direction has published one of Henry's books entitled *Has Democracy Had Its Day?* Land enthusiastically promoted this book, for in his words it shows "how representative self-government that we call democracy in America is inextricably tied to the basic, fundamental values of a Judeo-Christian world view and that our form of government with the liberties that it guarantees will work only when the vast majority of the people share a common world view."[25] This view, combined with Schaeffer's belief that there is "a real attempt to suppress religious free speech," has become the cultural mantra of SBC conservatives.

Henry was the academic theological version of Southern Baptist conservative patriarch W. A. Criswell, Land believes, arguing that Criswell's life refuted the notion that one could not be theologically trained and still believe in the literal veracity of Scripture and traditional views for the dating and authorship of various biblical books. He was the pastoral model of conservatism, while Henry became the academic model. Land can speak with equal passion about his Southern Baptist and evangelical heritages. In addition to his steady diet of E. S. James and the *Texas Baptist Standard* newspaper, Land also came to intellectual maturity via the nourishment of Schaeffer and Henry, which happened in conjunction with his forays outside the comfortable confines of the South. Most importantly, Schaeffer and Henry helped Land expand his sense of engagement with secular culture. Northern evangelicals were always outsiders, while southerners were culturally dominant, too often content with the status quo, and therefore uninvolved in politics. Schaeffer and Henry showed him that this was un-biblical.[26]

Like Land, Al Mohler also fed at the evangelical table. As a youngster, he left the relatively intact southern culture of central Florida for more cosmo-politan southern Florida. In this far more diverse, pluralistic, and secular setting, he developed serious questions about the big cultural issues that evangelicals in the North had already begun to consider. He found few re-sources among Southern Baptists and quite naturally turned to Schaeffer, who had become the most visible cultural critic among conservative Chris-tians. Southern Baptist intellectuals in the late 1960s and early 1970s, accord-ing to Mohler, had not yet begun to consider the types of cultural issues that evangelicals were encountering.[27] Conservative pastor D. James Kennedy's Coral Ridge Presbyterian Church, which was just down the road from Mohler's own Baptist church, facilitated his move into the broader evangeli-cal world. (Kennedy has been an influential voice among the conservative wing of evangelicalism and a primary player in the New Religious Right of the last two decades of the twentieth century.) The youth groups at Coral Ridge and First Baptist had a good deal of contact. Moreover, Mohler was not alone as he began to appropriate evangelical influences in the mid-1970s. His own pastor had also just discovered Schaeffer as well.[28]

Mohler grew up in a community that was more like other parts of the country than it was a part of the South, and he was exposed to evangelical ideas during the formative years of his youth. Later, as a student at Southern Seminary, Mohler "intellectually graduated" from Schaeffer the popularizer to the more scholarly Henry. Then, while working on his doctorate, Mohler and Henry became friends and scholarly compatriots. The two have lectured and written together, engaged in extensive correspondence, and as of 1997 were jointly authoring a book. Mohler was also a prime mover behind the republication of Henry's six-volume magnum opus, *God, Revelation, and Authority,* and he has edited other Henry works as well.[29]

Mohler was attracted to the evangelical critique of American culture. For him, Henry was addressing issues that pertained to an older evangelical pe-riod, but without even knowing it, he was also addressing issues that were current to the South in the 1970s.[30] In other words, the kind of cultural crisis that evangelicals in the North faced in the first half of twentieth century, Southern Baptists began to face a few decades later. The culture stayed in-tact longer in the South than in the North, and Southern Baptists were insiders in that culture. Beginning as early as the 1920s, northern evangelicals were forced to deal with their status as outsiders in a culture that was becoming rapidly more diverse, pluralistic, and secular.[31] Southern Baptists of Mohler's generation began to face the same sort of fractured culture, and his own experiences in pluralistic south Florida gave him a jump on even his contemporaries' understanding of where America was heading. Most Southern Baptists were relatively unaware of the forces pressing in on the South until conservatives began to argue that issues like prayer in schools and abortion were important to the region's identity.

Mohler sees the whole situation as partly generational, pitting post–World War II Southern Baptist progressives against the "post-Sputnik" conservatives. For the former, the war was the great nationalizing event that allowed moderates to see the South as provincial, especially on race. These moderates, therefore, appropriated northern progressive impulses on the issue, not realizing that the progressive impulse was also the great secularizer of culture. Mohler's generation, especially those who had experiences outside the South, were much less enamored by change, seeing in it the secularizing element that was quite sinister. Beginning in the 1970s, these two camps came into direct conflict with each other theologically, and differing perceptions of culture were very important in that debate, even if relatively unnoticed at the time. The denomination experienced a fundamentalist-modernist controversy a half century after the Northern Baptists and Presbyterians had experienced their own struggles. Conservatives in the SBC, Mohler argues, spoke a clear "no" to both theological liberalism and fundamentalism and instead appropriated the neoevangelical position outlined in Henry's scholarly work. They rejected the progressive spirit and all that went with it except on the race question. So, just as Henry led midcentury neoevangelicals in the North, he became a mentor for a whole generation of Southern Baptist conservatives who have reengaged their culture, taking positions that oppose what they believe is the secular progressive spirit that captured too many moderates.[32]

Certainly, Mohler's critique of Southern Baptist moderates can be challenged at several points. The important point here, however, is that his perception, correct or not, of moderates as having drunk too deeply from the secular progressive well and his own contact with evangelical influences resulted eventually in his move to the conservative camp. Mohler's own switch from moderate to conservative was precipitated by his experiences at Southern Seminary as a masters and then doctoral student. Moderates often interpret his shift as rank opportunism. That he ended up president of his alma mater after it had been captured by conservatives lends to such an interpretation. Some even say that he decided before he ever got to Southern that he wanted to be president of the school and would do everything in his power to make that happen. As this explanation goes, he became a conservative when he saw that this would be his ticket for achieving that dream.[33] Former Southern Seminary president Roy Honeycutt, Mohler's predecessor, puts this argument in its strongest terms. Mohler traveled extensively with Honeycutt while serving as assistant to the president in the early 1980s. The former president says that in all their time together, he never got any inkling of Mohler's hard-line right-wing beliefs, calling him during this period a "closet conservative." "He did a 180-degree turn on us," Honeycutt says in retrospect, "I think he saw where the direction was going and got out in front of the parade."[34]

Not surprisingly, Mohler has a rather different view of his metamorphosis from moderate to conservative. After beginning to concern himself with cultural issues during high school, he recalls that matters like abortion and homosexuality were hardly discussed at Samford University while he was an undergraduate there in the seventies—further evidence that Southern Baptists in places like Birmingham, Alabama, the home of Samford, were still rather insulated from the cultural transformation America was experiencing. At Southern Seminary, however, these were hot topics by the time Mohler arrived as a masters of divinity candidate in 1980. He immediately fell in love with Southern and tried to fit into the academic culture there. He even became something of a moderate activist, leading student protests against the incipient conservative movement when it first began. Over time, as Mohler became disenchanted with his professors, he began to reach out to the larger evangelical world just as he had in high school. It is as if he expected that he could harmonize the evangelical impulses he had felt as a youngster with the culture of Southern Seminary, though he eventually found this to be impossible. His experience in helping bring Carl Henry to Southern Seminary played a crucial culminating role in Mohler's transformation.

Henry visited Southern Seminary while Mohler was a doctoral student and serving as assistant to President Honeycutt. Henry had been invited by an evangelical student fellowship, and Mohler ended up being his host. In Mohler's view this was because no one in the Southern administration or on the faculty wanted to have much to do with the evangelical theologian. The administration knew that Mohler was involved in the evangelical fellowship on campus and therefore viewed him as the seminary's conduit to that movement. Still in his early twenties, Mohler had custody of the person he believed was the paradigmatic evangelical theologian. This in itself was a tall order, but compounding the awkwardness of the situation was the treatment Henry received, treatment that humiliated Mohler. As Mohler tells the story, the faculty permitted Henry to attend a doctoral colloquium, but the professor leading it clearly indicated in his introduction that the theologian would not be allowed to speak. This was customary; visitors usually did not participate in class discussions. The student who presented his paper for discussion that day barely recalled the incident, but it had a significant affect on Mohler, who believed there was no need to announce that Henry would not be allowed to speak. As Mohler recalled many years later: "Can you imagine if Wolfhart Pannenberg or Jürgen Moltmann had come in. . . . Is it imaginable that they would have been introduced by saying 'they won't be allowed to speak'? Even if they wouldn't [be allowed to speak], what a way to treat someone."[35]

Compounding the embarrassment was the subject of the colloquium that day. The students were discussing readings by James Barr and Henry Childs. Mohler found out later that Henry had recently been at Cambridge debating Barr and then at Yale debating Childs. Although he had personally engaged in debate with the principle subjects of the colloquium, Henry was nevertheless not allowed to weigh in on the discussion.[36] This experience helped solidify in Mohler's mind a disconnect between elite moderate Southern Baptist intellectual life and the larger evangelical world, and he believed that the evangelicals had the more developed and sophisticated weapons needed to battle a culture increasingly hostile to Christian faith.

Honeycutt, who was Southern's president at the time, has no recollection of this particular visit by Henry, possibly because student groups at Southern had fairly wide latitude in inviting individuals to visit campus. Indeed, student invitations to guest speakers did not go through the president's office. This being the case, Henry's visit was not an official seminary function, and, therefore, the professor was under no obligation to allow Henry to participate in the class discussion. Still, though, the importance of this event for Mohler was that it left him with the impression that his Southern Seminary professors were hostile toward evangelicalism. The clear impression the then graduate student took from this experience was that America's leading evangelical theologian could not get the sort of respect at Southern Seminary that more liberal theologians would receive. While hostile may be too strong a word, Honeycutt agrees that with the exception of those who studied contemporary theology, the faculty members at Southern were not very familiar with the evangelical world. "They still thought of [evangelicalism] as old fundamentalism, and that was a serious mistake," Honeycutt reflects. In his view, there were responsible scholars coming out of neoevangelicalism who were not very different from many of the professors at Southern. "I've had an appreciation for the New-Evangelicalism, but I don't think we gave enough attention to it," Honeycutt recalled later. As a result, he believes, moderates paid a price during the controversy.[37] Part of that price was that Baptists like Mohler, who were attracted to evangelicalism, felt they had to make a choice between SBC moderates and evangelicals.

Timothy George's experience as a professor at Southern Seminary before going to Beeson Divinity School corroborates Mohler's experience with Henry. Most moderate intellectuals seemed to George to be oblivious to the larger evangelical world. Such was the case when George had to identify evangelical theologian Kenneth Kantzer, at that time editor of *Christianity Today*, for one well-known Southern Baptist moderate. George also claims that Duke McCall, who was Southern Seminary's president before Honeycutt, once told him that he tried to bring Henry to the seminary on five occasions but could not garner enough faculty support.[38] Surely, many in the evangelical world were as oblivious to Southern Baptist moderates as moderates were to evangelicals, but when SBC conservatives began to reach out to the larger evangelical world, they felt welcomed and embraced, which only exacerbated their feelings that moderate hostility to evangelicalism had been a mistake.

George's introduction to evangelicalism, like that of Mohler and Land, came through both reading and geography. By the time he reached college, he was already well prepared to negotiate the two worlds because he had grown up in both independent fundamentalism and the SBC. George had even preached a youth revival at Jerry Falwell's Thomas Road Baptist Church at a time when Falwell considered himself a fundamentalist far too conservative for the SBC. At the University of Tennessee at Chattanooga, George studied with professors who were products of the University of Chicago at the tail end of the "Death of God" movement of the 1960s. The young student experienced something of a crisis of faith but ended up rejecting most of the theology his UTC professors presented. Nevertheless, they did teach George to read widely and to respect the opinions of others. Embarking on an independent studies program, George encountered

Schaeffer, who helped the young preacher boy understand that he could believe traditional theology such as the Resurrection of Christ without sacrificing his intellect. George came to accept the old saw, "You can believe in an empty tomb without having an empty head." Like so many evangelical scholars, George now recognizes Schaeffer's limitations, but at a crucial time in the young man's life, Schaeffer's influence was decisive on some points.[39] Stories like this are very common among northern evangelicals. Historians Mark Noll at Wheaton College, George Marsden and Nathan Hatch of Notre Dame, and Ronald Wells of Calvin have all discussed at length both the strengths and weaknesses of Schaeffer's views, but they, like so many other northern evangelical intellectuals, acknowledge the influence he had in inspiring a whole generation of young Christians to take the world of ideas seriously without compromising their faith.[40] By contrast, Schaeffer's influence among SBC moderates has been practically nonexistent, with many Southern Baptists having only the most vague idea of who he was.[41]

After graduating from the University of Tennessee at Chattanooga, George went to Harvard Divinity School for his doctoral studies under the well-known Reformation scholar George Hunston Williams. There was little evangelical influence at Harvard, probably less then than there is today, George mused. Still, it was after he got to Harvard that George began to read Carl Henry. Just as important for his development as an evangelical, however, was Harvard's geographic location. For seven years while in doctoral studies, George lived and worked among New England evangelicals, pastoring a Baptist church under the auspices of the SBC Home Mission Board and working within the welter of the evangelical world. He was part of the New England Evangelical Fellowship and came into frequent contact with the renowned evangelical Park Street Church. Park Street was Harold Ockenga's pastorate during the 1940s through 1960s, when he was one of the leading neoevangelicals in the country and first president of Fuller Seminary. George also worked with Billy Graham's ministry, Gordon-Conwell Theological Seminary, and other evangelical organizations.[42]

When George returned to the Southern Baptist subculture as a professor at Southern Seminary, he was thus well aware of the larger evangelical world and began to advocate a rapprochement with evangelicals. This was in the late 1970s and early 1980s, however, when the SBC controversy was beginning to take shape. George's trafficking in evangelicalism eventually drew him into the Southern Baptist debate. Still, he never became a "down-and-dirty partisan," to use his own terminology. He was never a precinct captain in the conservative political movement, so to speak, and some of his colleagues at Southern were surprised that he actually sided with the right wing. They perceived him to have made every effort to fit in at Southern Seminary. But like Mohler, who was one of his students at Southern, George found Southern Baptist moderates to be quite resistant to evangelicalism, which was odd to him. Among conservatives, he has been a scholarly voice for reeducating Southern Baptists in an attempt to convince them that they are evangelicals.[43]

Mohler and George differ somewhat on the question of why moderates resisted evangelical alliances. Mohler attributes this largely to theological differences. In his view, moderates opposed evangelicals because they just disagreed with them and were on the opposite side of the salient issues. Henry, Mohler points out, was a proponent of biblical inerrancy; moderates by and large were not, especially at the elite levels.[44] George goes easier on moderates, emphasizing the self-sufficiency of the SBC discussed earlier in this chapter. Moderates just had little need to reach out. This is now changing, George believes, as even some moderates are recognizing how much they have in common with evangelicals. This difference in viewpoint can be attributed partly to the difference in temperament between Mohler and George. George eschews the culture warrior mantle whenever possible and has had the luxury of being out of the fray by virtue of his appointment at the interdenominational Beeson Divinity School. George is careful to make clear that he is not speaking ill of moderates when he analyzes their failure to capitalize on potential evangelical alliances in the past. "They weren't malicious," George says of moderates. "They were pious; most were Bible-believing, conservative people. They just didn't have a vision for the convention that could win the day."[45] Clearly, the vision that did win the day was evangelical to the core.

Like George, former Midwestern Baptist Theological Seminary president Mark Coppenger also sojourned in the wider evangelical world at a critical time of his scholarly career. And like Mohler, Coppenger switched from the moderate to the conservative side of the controversy as the issues became clear to him. Coppenger was the product of a moderate Baptist upbringing in Arkansas, growing up on the campus of Ouachita Baptist University, where his father was a philosophy professor. After graduation from OBU, he took a Ph.D. in philosophy at Vanderbilt University and then became a professor at Wheaton College, a bastion of northern evangelicalism. At Wheaton he had the reputation of being something of a campus liberal, but this was primarily because he taught a course in aesthetics that was required for fine-arts majors. In the course, controversies arose over nudity in sculpture, profanity in drama, and a variety of moral problems with the films his classes analyzed along with jazz and rock-and-roll music. As late as the mid-1960s, just ten years before Coppenger arrived, Wheaton had a rule forbidding students and faculty from even attending movies, so it is not surprising that there were alumni and trustees who were troubled by the idea of students watching films in class. When Coppenger's classes viewed and discussed *The Deer Hunter* or *One Flew over the Cuckoo's Nest*, certain constituents of the Wheaton community were sure to protest. In most respects, however, Coppenger was far from radical and fit in quite well at Wheaton, even winning a teaching award among the junior faculty. The honor had to be approved by the college president, which seems to suggest that whatever controversy his courses precipitated was not enough to put him crosswise with the administration.[46]

Like George, Coppenger stresses how different the evangelical community he experienced at Wheaton was from his Southern Baptist roots. "Wheaton's a whole different world," he says. "It's a para-church world. Bible churches, Wycliffe [Bible Translators], InterVarsity, and Eerdmans. It's just a whole different universe up there."[47] While at Wheaton, Coppenger was somewhat out of the loop when the SBC controversy erupted. He began to hear of the "troublemakers" in the SBC and learned that one of his own congregation was among them. Coppenger attended Glenfield Baptist Church in Glen Ellyn, Illinois, also the church of Harold Lindsell, who in 1976 had authored the well-known book *The Battle for the Bible.* In a chapter on Southern Baptists, Lindsell charged that the denomination was drifting away from biblical infallibility and therefore in danger of slipping out of the evangelical fold. He predicted a conflagration if something was not done to stem the tide of biblical infidelity. By almost everyone's reckoning on both sides of the SBC wars, this book helped launch the controversy by emboldening conservatives.[48] When Lindsell received a nomination to be a messenger from Glenfield Baptist Church to a Southern Baptist Convention meeting, Coppenger protested at a Wednesday night business meeting and was able to get the appointment tabled. Coppenger's views of the SBC had been shaped by moderate friends and family members, so his first inclination was to oppose the conservative movement. All he knew, he later recalled, was that people he trusted thought the conservatives were intent on

upsetting the smooth workings of the SBC. His own in-laws were supporters of the moderate SBC and viewed conservatives as troublemakers.[49]

Coppenger began to reconsider his tentatively held position when he
heard old-guard moderates imply that to be a biblical inerrantist was to be
something of a moron. That Coppenger would bristle at moderate counter-
offensives is somewhat ironic, for throughout the Southern Baptist controversy, moderates were on the defensive; most of the scathing charges were
made by conservatives about moderates. Yet given his social location in the
evangelical world, where he knew inerrantist intellectuals, such charges elicited a strong reaction. Coppenger recognized that at Wheaton he worked
with several avowed inerrantists who were, in fact, astute intellectuals who
did not fit the critique being made by moderates. "These guys were sharper
than the ones I knew in the Southern Baptist world," he remembers thinking. Indeed, Wheaton at this time hosted an annual philosophy conference
that regularly brought in some of the heavy hitters of Christian thought—
George Mavrodes from the University of Michigan, Keith Yandell from the
University of Wisconsin, Alvin Plantinga from Calvin College and later
Notre Dame, Bob and Marilyn Adams from UCLA, and Phil Quinn from
Brown. Coppenger knew of no one in the Baptist colleges and universities
who was equal to this group. He came to believe that Wheaton had a level
of energy and substance absent at most Southern Baptist schools. This led
him to question the moderate line of argument that suggested that inerrantists and other evangelicals were somehow second rate intellectually.[50]

At about the same time that Coppenger began to have doubts concerning
what moderates were saying about conservatives in the SBC, he began to
feel somewhat disillusioned with philosophy as a profession. Accompanying
this, he experienced a growing enthusiasm for Bible teaching in the Sunday
School class he led at Glenfield Baptist Church. This culminated in a career
shift in the early 1980s, when at the age of thirty-three he left a secure faculty position at Wheaton and enrolled as a student at Southwestern Baptist
Theological Seminary in Fort Worth, Texas, to begin training for the ministry. At Southwestern he heard more digs at inerrantists. As he recalls, "I
was getting kind of miffed because I was thinking, 'Look, you're jabbing at
guys like [J. I.] Packer, and you couldn't carry their lunchbox." Some of the
moderate critics of inerrancy relied heavily on a book authored by scholars
Jack Rogers and Donald McKim entitled *The Authority and Interpretation of
the Bible: An Historical Approach*. The authors sought to provide an evangeli-

cal alternative to the inerrantist point of view. But theologian David Woodbridge answered this critique in his book *Biblical Authority: A Critique of the Rogers/McKim Proposal* and was quite successful in laying bare the inadequacies of Rogers and McKim's work, according to Coppenger. The new student was surprised, therefore, when Southwestern president Russell Dilday used Rogers and McKim as part of a doctrinal study at the seminary, making all the same errors they had. "I started to have a growing sense that the inerrantists were being cheap shotted."[51]

While at Southwestern, Coppenger also began to question moderate rhetoric on another level. Many moderates charged that the SBC conservative movement was going to endanger the great mission enterprise of the SBC. There was some plausibility to this line of reasoning in that the denominational-missions effort had been built on the Grand Compromise, the belief that the unity of the denomination would be organizational and institutional instead of confessional.[52] Those who supported this particular vision recognized that the confessionalism desired by the conservatives would end the compromise. Nevertheless, to say that the conservative movement would wreck evangelism and missions was also to assume that the moderate vision was doing an adequate job of bringing in the converts, which had, in fact, been quite true for the middle third of the century, when the SBC became the largest Protestant denomination in the United States. Coppenger, however, questioned whether the moderate vision of the 1980s was still producing results. When his own moderate pastor charged that the conservatives would ruin evangelism, Coppenger decided to do his own informal study. He measured his own Fort Worth church's baptismal rate against that of First Baptist, Euless, where the newly elected conservative SBC president James Draper pastored. Coppenger discovered that his own church baptized 1 new member per year for each 115 members already on the rolls, while at Draper's church the ratio was 1 to 15. Coppenger asked rhetorically, who was really succeeding in evangelism?[53]

Coppenger's own theological and biblical studies sealed his decision to plant his flag with the conservative movement. Before shifting from college philosophy professor to Southern Baptist preacher, he had reflected very little on the important issues of the SBC controversy. When he applied for the position at Wheaton, for example, he received a standard questionnaire that included a query about the plenary inspiration of scripture; Coppenger had to call his father to ask what this meant. He remembers his father's reply being something like, "Don't worry; you believe it."[54] In seminary, Coppenger began to use the *Broadman Bible Commentary*, the standard commentary in the denomination. He was troubled by much of what he read: for example, Southern Seminary president and Old Testament scholar Roy Honeycutt's account of the floating axe head in the book of 2 Kings.[55] Here, Honeycutt and coauthor Pierce Matheney Jr. discuss various ways of interpreting the story in the sixth chapter, where the prophet Elisha is said to have made an axe head float. The authors write, "Thus, whether one interprets the miracle stories literally or as cases of combined saga and legend used to glorify the prophet and express the high regard with which he was held in the prophetic circle, the miracle stories should be interpreted for what they are in present form, not what they were in original nucleus."[56] Conservatives often protested any suggestion that some miracle stories might have natural explanations. Moreover, most moderate Southern Baptist Old Testament scholarship assumed that redactors collected and edited Old Testament materials that had been written over a long period of time.

Another Broadman interpretation Coppenger has cited as problematic is the story of the ravens feeding the prophet Elijah in 1 Kings 17. In 1998 Coppenger compared what he remembered finding in the Broadman commentary with the evangelical commentary authored by C. F. Keil and F. Delitzsch. These authors argue that God made the ravens and can have them feed the prophets if He wants. Coppenger comments jokingly, "God can make ravens play the banjo, if he so desires."[57] The problem here is that Coppenger was working from a faulty memory. His preference for taking the miraculous account at face value, which he attributed only to Keil and Delitzsch, was also the interpretation of Honeycutt and Matheney in their Broadman commentary. They wrote: "There is no need to try to rationalize the miracle story. . . . The miraculous element belongs in all these prophetic narratives as testimony to Israel's faith in Yahweh's control over his created order (cf. 19:5–8). He who feeds the young ravens (Job 38:41) can use these unclean, voracious scavengers (Lev. 11:15; Prov. 30:17) to preserve his prophet for the coming crisis."[58] Certainly, anyone could misremember such a story. But the point is that conservatives were quick to pounce on moderate interpretations that even entertained the possibility that parts of Scripture are more mythic than literal.

Still, the fact that Coppenger could turn to evangelical commentaries is of no small significance. He believed that the presence of evangelical publishers and authors gave many conservative rank-and-file Southern Baptists a different influence. "Had there been no other press—no Eerdmans, Zondervan, Baker—I think the [Southern Baptist] people would have had a tougher time finding their voice. . . . We became more cosmopolitan and began to read more broadly." As many began to read Packer, John Stott, Charles Colson, and especially Harold Lindsell's *Battle for the Bible*, they began to be less isolated from this larger evangelical world. They began to move off the SBC plantation, as Coppenger describes it: "How you going to keep 'em down on the farm after they've seen gay Paree?"[59]

In the early 1980s, when Coppenger completed his seminary degree, he still had not identified entirely with the conservative movement. After graduation, he took a pastorate in El Dorado, Arkansas. The church had been led for many years by moderate Don Harbuck, under whom membership had declined from over 900 to 380. Coppenger identified his predecessor along with his own seminary pastor Welton Gaddy as two of the most vociferous crusaders against inerrancy. Both, in Coppenger's view, were ineffectual in evangelism precisely because they were "disrespectful of scripture."[60] Coppenger attended the 1984 Southern Baptist Convention meeting in Kansas City primarily because the trip was in his church's budget. Television preacher Charles Stanley was the conservative candidate for the SBC presidency, but Coppenger voted for one of the moderates. Shortly thereafter someone from the Christian Life Commission contacted him about social issues, assuming that he was a moderate. Then a few years later, Coppenger joined the board of Southern Seminary in Louisville just in time for Prof. Molly Marshall's tenure review. Convinced that her theology was not in accordance with the seminary's Abstract of Principles, Coppenger was among the seven out of over sixty board members present at a key meeting to vote against Marshall's tenure. This was the final step in his transformation from moderate evangelical philosophy professor to conservative Southern Baptist preacher and eventually seminary president. From the pastorate in El Dorado, he became executive director of the State Convention of Baptists in Indiana; then on to the Executive Committee of the SBC for five years, where he was vice president for convention relations and founder of *SBC Life* magazine; and finally to the presidency of Midwestern Baptist Theological Seminary. During his rise to the top echelons of SBC administration, he became a visible member of the Calvinist wing of the denomination and an outspoken critic of women in pulpit ministry.

Other SBC conservatives who have had less contact with evangelicals have nevertheless been in geographic locations or other situations that have exposed them to evangelical influences. Adrian Rogers, like Mohler, lived in south Florida during the 1970s, pastoring a church near NASA headquarters that drew on a much more diverse population than one would have found in the Deep South at that time. In the late 1990s he still believed that Memphis was more southern than south Florida was in the early 1970s. Rogers lists evangelicals such as James Dobson, Gary Bauer, and Charles Colson among those who have solid views of the main problems America faces and the proper roles for Christians within American culture. Like Rogers, James Draper spent the early years of his pastoral ministry outside the culture of the Deep South. As a pastor in Kansas City in the early sixties, he saw the evangelical world beginning to break in on Southern Baptists. Like Land, Mohler, and George, Draper speaks comfortably of Schaeffer as the early voice articulating the view that there was a war going on within American culture. In the 1980s Draper quite naturally used Schaeffer's 1979 film *Whatever Happened to the Human Race?* to mobilize his Euless, Texas, congregation on the abortion issue.[61]

One of the two main architects of the SBC conservative drive to take control of the denomination was Paul Pressler. Like those discussed earlier, he too moved outside the South as a young man, albeit nearly two decades earlier than they. He attended Exeter Academy in New England, then Princeton University. His worldview may have been shaped less by his proximity to northern evangelicals, however, than it was by northern liberals, against whom he reacted strongly. He recalls that while at Exeter, he had to explain to his liberal pastor what Southern Baptists meant by the term "born again." Perhaps the preacher was just humoring the young Texan, but nevertheless the incident points up two very different views of religion in the 1940s. At Princeton in 1950, Pressler helped found a student Baptist fellowship that soon became a church. Student members then organized the first revival the university had experienced in many years. Reflecting on this just two years later, Pressler noted the hostility toward Christianity on the part of many college students, and he exhibited great comfort in using the term "evangelical" to describe he and his fellow Baptist classmates who defied such hostility. By his own reckoning, he and the other Princeton Baptists were presenting an evangelical challenge to the prevailing liberalism of northern elite culture.[62] These experiences outside the South left him convinced that the rest of the United States was not like the South, and he became determined to ensure that the liberal drift of the northern denominations never occurred in the SBC.

Mitigating the thesis being argued here is the experience of Paige Patterson, the other of the two most important individuals of the movement. Of the leading SBC conservatives, he is probably the least influenced by evangelicals. Patterson is more likely to talk about sixteenth-century European Anabaptists when discussing his views of culture and church-and-state matters than he is of Schaeffer or Henry. Patterson also has an admittedly strong Landmarkist streak that militates against alliances with non-Baptists. Still, he has been active in the Evangelical Theological Society and International Council on Biblical Inerrancy, but these memberships in non-Baptist organizations are about as far as he can go toward evangelical ecumenism. Perhaps it could be said that in his area of greatest concern, biblical studies, Patterson has been willing to make limited common cause with non-Baptist evangelicals just as Land and Mohler have done in their areas of concern. The difference is that their focus is much broader and more culturally oriented than Patterson's. Patterson and a few other early leaders in the inerrancy drive within the SBC opened doors that Land, Mohler, and other culture warriors would walk through later.

For nearly all SBC conservatives, inerrancy was and is the central issue of evangelicalism. Coppenger sums up the general conservative position as well as anyone by stating that "Biblical inerrancy is a non-negotiable," but any of them could make this same statement. To balance seminary faculties with inerrantists and noninerrantists is "bunk. It is wrong, wrong, wrong," Coppenger stresses.[63] It was his experience with northern evangelicals that helped him come to this conclusion. What conservatives like Coppenger as well as the moderates they defeated often fail to acknowledge is how different some inerrantists can be from others. When moderates criticized inerrantists, they usually had in mind the most unsophisticated literalists. Moderates were often unaware that within the evangelical world there are well-developed defenses of inerrancy that do not require a wooden, literal hermeneutic. People like J. I. Packer were often unknown to, or at least unacknowledged by, SBC moderates until conservatives forced them to come to grips with the wider world of evangelicalism.[64] Coppenger came into direct contact with this more sophisticated form of inerrancy while at Wheaton and therefore knew that what moderates said about inerrantists was not necessarily true. His experiences with evangelicals legitimized them in his mind and made him suspicious of moderate attacks that seemed so ill informed.

However, Coppenger and other conservatives have been reluctant to acknowledge that inerrancy can mean many different things to many different people—that it may not always have quite the meaning that the most so-phisticated SBC conservatives attribute to it. Moreover, they often play the populist card when discussing this issue. Such is the case when Coppenger reasons that Southern Baptists have determined that inerrancy is what their confession means, a reference to the Peace Committee report of the late 1980s that was adopted by the denomination. The committee also concluded that most Southern Baptists believe the literal account of biblical miracles and that Adam and Eve were real individual people. "So, it is entirely appropriate," Coppenger concludes from this, "for the people who pay the bills . . . to hire people who believe the Bible is true."[65] The problem is that miracle accounts and the existence of a literal Adam and Eve are matters of interpretation, not questions of whether the Bible is true. At a 1987 conference on inerrancy, northern evangelical historian Mark Noll pointed out that early-twentieth-century proponent of inerrancy B. B. Warfield at Princeton was an amillennialist, whereas most inerrantists are premillennial. Warfield also believed that theistic evolution was compatible with the inerrancy of the book of Genesis.[66] In conversation and public pronouncements, conservatives give little indication that some inerrantists could believe such things. Coppenger and others slide easily from the plain term "inerrancy" to these interpretive matters over which inerrantists disagree.

CONCLUSION

What can be made of the neoevangelical influence that has entered into Southern Baptist life via the experiences of the key conservative leaders discussed above? Primarily this: the neoevangelical influence became attractive to Southern Baptist conservatives because of its emphasis on cultural engagement.

For the most part, Southern Baptists did not experience fundamentalism, the realignment of the 1930s and 1940s, or the neoevangelical reengagement of the 1950s. This is because fundamentalism developed to battle modernism, of which there was very little in the South. A few Southern Baptists in the 1920s, such as J. Frank Norris, attempted to import northern fundamentalism into the SBC, but they were unsuccessful largely because there was not enough modernism in the South at the time to cause alarm.[67] Southern Baptists were still comfortable within their culture and had little use for the militancy of fundamentalism and no use for its separatism.

What was it, then, that eventually made neoevangelicalism attractive to the SBC conservatives discussed above and allowed them to succeed in importing that theological/cultural program into the SBC? The reengagement with culture is what most resonated with leaders like Land, Mohler, and the others. As the South ceased to be Zion and became more like the rest of the nation, they found in neoevangelicalism the weapons they needed to engage a secularizing culture that can be hostile to evangelical faith. What is most significant at this point, therefore, is that neoevangelicalism became attractive to Southern Baptist conservatives at precisely the point where it differentiated itself from fundamentalism—that is, at the point of engagement with culture. This was made possible largely as a result of the influence of Francis Schaeffer and Carl Henry. In a sense, therefore, Henry has been responsible for leading a large cohort of fundamentalists from the 1940s and 1950s into neoevangelicalism, and he has also been responsible for leading a large cohort of Southern Baptists into the same stream during the 1970s and 1980s. The difference is that the earlier group had to pass through fundamentalism in order to get to neoevangelicalism, while SBC conservatives skipped the fundamentalist stage and grafted neoevangelicalism into their Southern Baptist identity. On this point, it should be emphasized that of those considered above, only Timothy George was influenced significantly by independent fundamentalism. The others all came from moderate Southern Baptist stock.

SBC conservatives have adopted an attitude of engagement with culture that would have been impossible had they continued to see the South as something resembling a Baptist Zion. Having had experiences outside the South—intellectually, geographically, and culturally—they no longer viewed the South this way. They now think more nationally than regionally, convinced that American culture is hostile and discriminatory toward traditional positions of faith, resembling Babylon more than Zion. Rather than taking on the attitude of fundamentalist separatists, they have taken up the mantle of neoevangelical cultural critics and in some cases culture warriors.

2

"The War of the Worlds"

Southern Baptist Conservatives as Culture Warriors

SBC conservatives perceive the secularization of the public square and the accompanying government hostility to religion to be the greatest cultural concern of our time. There are three distinct ways of articulating this cultural perception: intellectual, informed activist, and populist. The intellectual position tends to come from confessional Calvinists and is marked by a depth of understanding and an appreciation for nuance. The informed activist position is primarily that of Richard Land and those who have worked with him at the Ethics and Religious Liberty Commission (ERLC). Land seeks to utilize his own academic training and understanding of history to fashion a coherent and intellectually compelling approach to politics, but the emphasis remains on what can be done to change American culture. This penchant for activism sometimes requires compromises that cannot be squared with the intellectual position. The populist approach tends to emanate from high-profile preachers such as Adrian Rogers and James Draper. Populists help mobilize the troops behind the kinds of things Land and the ERLC want to do politically in Washington. Because there is a premium on mobilization and because the preachers who articulate the populist positions do not have the depth of academic training that the intellectuals or Land have, this is the least coherent of the three positions. Marked by intellectual and theological inconsistencies and claims about American history and culture that do not stand up to scrutiny, this position opened the door to some of the most extreme charges moderates leveled against the conservative movement in the 1980s when the Southern Baptist controversy was in full swing.

THE INTELLECTUAL VIEW OF AMERICAN CULTURE

Al Mohler may be the most forceful and eloquent on the issue of cultural crisis and therefore represents the intellectual approach quite well. He believes that differing views of American culture played a very significant role in the whole SBC controversy. Along with most of the conservatives, he employs the culture-war terminology of sociologist James Davison Hunter when addressing cultural issues and the differences between conservatives and moderates. Hunter allows that many progressives remain active in religion, but they translate the moral imperatives of their tradition in a way that harmonizes with the tolerant and even relativistic spirit of the modern age. "In other words," writes Hunter, "what all progressivist worldviews share in common is the tendency to resymbolize historic faiths according to the prevailing assumptions of contemporary life."[1] Hunter believes the culture war is fought by about 20 percent of the population on each end of the political/cultural spectrum. While this leaves the majority of people in the middle as noncombatants, their mediating voices are lost in the battle. The middle, Hunter argues, is the first casualty of culture war, as the extremes on both sides define the issues and seek to delegitimize each other.

Hunter's analysis has come in for criticism. Several scholars believe the culture war paradigm explains or defines today's debates very inadequately. While acknowledging the two extremes on either end of the spectrum, these critics argue that the more moderate middle is still where the action is. The extremes simply have not polarized the debate to the extent that moderate voices get lost in the shouting, nor do the extremes inordinately define the debates.[2] Cornell University professor of government Jeremy Rabkin contends: "As historical description, the notion of a culture war is a gross distortion. As a guide to contemporary strategists, it is a needless counsel of despair."[3] Rabkin argues that the culture war paradigm causes conservatives to ignore their victories and exaggerate their defeats. Even if true, this analysis cannot mean that self-professed cultural warriors do not exist. We all know they do, and Southern Baptist conservatives are prime examples. They have bought Hunter's paradigm. The critics serve to remind us that the culture war is not the only thing going on in American politics and religion today. Indeed, it may be misleading to say that America is in a culture war, but it seems hard to deny that such a struggle exists. How else can one understand those who proclaim to be fighting in just such a war? Conservatives make ready reference to culture war when discussing their victory in the SBC controversy. They believe their successful battle with moderate elites in their denomination cannot be understood without reference to Hunter's analysis. This is particularly true of Mohler. When he delineates the differences between the cultural views of SBC moderates and those of conservatives, his preferred term for the former is Hunter's "progressivist."

Mohler's argument regarding the error of the moderate progressivist impulse proceeds as follows: In the three decades after World War II, moderates were clearly right on some issues. The generation of SBC leaders that experienced the war realized that the South was extremely provincial with its own very flawed culture religion. In (Richard) Niebuhrian fashion they recognized the danger of the wrong kind of Christ-culture relationship. Culture religion in the South was symbolized most forcefully in the race issue, and here some moderates took their first stand, and rightly so argue Mohler and other SBC conservatives.[4] In being right on the race issue, however, moderates drew some very bad lessons. Essentially, they bought in to the whole progressivist impulse, not realizing that part of this agenda was the uprooting of religion from its historic public place within American culture. As alluded to previously, in their zeal to vanquish culture religion, moderates became blind to how "antiseptic" the public square was becoming once cultural Christianity was removed. Conservatives arose as a protest movement, and by the mid-1970s the SBC had two very different visions of what American culture should be. Conservatives have a clearer sense of cultural crisis, and this shapes their views on all political issues. Mohler found much that was attractive in the moderates' critique of cultural Christianity, but he eventually concluded that they were in lock step with secular progressivists.[5]

"Abortion was the stick of dynamite that exploded the issue," Mohler said in 1997. "It was the transparent issue that brought clarity at least on one side." How can this be when conservatives had previously rallied around the matter of inerrancy of scripture? Mohler explains that inerrancy was a clearcut issue for many Baptists. Grassroot congregants believed in inerrancy, but many people did not know how to recognize where biblical inerrancy was being denied. When the abortion issue appeared, the division became apparent. If some seminary professors and other moderate elites could be wrong on abortion, that was all the conservatives in the churches needed to know. It really did not matter what the nuances of these issues were, being wrong on abortion, which Mohler believes many of his own Baptist professors were, signaled a systemic problem.[6]

Roe v. *Wade* (1973) came down just before Mohler entered high school and was instantly controversial in south Florida, where he lived. The young man was never tempted by the pro-choice model, however, because as Mohler remembers, "It didn't make any sense to me, not from a Christian perspective." In south Florida, Catholics carried the ball on the issue, and Baptists were not involved at first. Evangelicals began to take to the issue largely as a result of the influence of James Kennedy, the conservative pastor of Coral Ridge Presbyterian Church. When Mohler went off to Samford University, abortion rarely came up in his college classes, but in the fall of 1980, when he arrived at Southern Seminary, it was a hot topic of debate. Mohler recalls that arriving at the seminary was like walking onto a Civil War battlefield and suddenly realizing that people were serious. Southern was a battleground, but there were no conservatives. "All the guns were pointed out." Nevertheless, Mohler fell in love with Southern Seminary and tried to take the most conservative reading of everything he heard there. He remembers that often in conversations that had nothing to do with abortion the issue still came up. Slowly, he became aware of the fact that many of his professors supported abortion rights. "If they're willing to do that, what does that say about the whole system?" he now asks. "I think moderates, to their dying day, are going to underestimate that issue. They just don't get it."[7]

Paige Patterson has said that abortion was by far the key issue that led to the SBC's decision to cease funding for the Baptist Joint Committee (BJC) and to completely reorganize the Christian Life Commission (which will be discussed in more detail in chapter 3). Although the BJC took no official position on the issue, knowing that the executive director, James Dunn, disagreed with conservatives on abortion was enough for right wingers. Pointing also to the Christian Life Commission (CLC) under moderate Foy Valentine, Patterson says that while no one can be sure what might have happened had Valentine not espoused the pro-choice position, a good guess is that other issues could have been negotiated satisfactorily. Like Mohler, Patterson agreed that the fact that the BJC and the CLC would not take a pro-life stand was all conservatives needed to know.[8] This convinced them that they and the moderates had very different perceptions concerning the state of American culture.

It is not that conservatives were intentionally reductionistic, Mohler insists, but the abortion issue signaled to them a larger problem. From their perspective that problem was two-fold. First, the legalization of abortion signaled that something was profoundly wrong with American culture.

Mohler has asked what so many SBC conservatives and evangelicals of other stripes often ask: How could abortion go from being a punishable offense one week in 1973 to being a civil right the next? Indeed, most analysts of the Christian Right mark the *Roe* decision as a major landmark in the eventual political mobilization of conservative people of faith.[9] Second, if the legalization of abortion symbolizes a culture gone wrong, how could some moderate professors and denominational bureaucrats buy into the pro-choice argument? The answer, as Mohler suggests, must have been that they had bought in, or perhaps sold out, to the secular progressivist impulse outlined later by Hunter. In other words, there was a theological problem here, and that perception grew throughout the 1970s as some denominational officials became identified with what conservatives regarded as a pro-choice position. Eventually, the right wing would demand an accounting for why a denomination that was predominantly pro-life at the grassroots should have official spokespersons in the political realm who were pro-choice (which will be further explored in chapter 6).[10] More recently, homosexuality has become a similarly explosive cultural issue, Mohler and other conservatives believe. If an SBC church blesses same-sex unions or ordains openly gay deacons, and the local association or state convention does nothing, that is all conservative Southern Baptists need to know in order to place themselves in an opposing camp.

With these issues as the backdrop, the 1995 annual seminar of the SBC's Christian Life Commission was appropriately entitled "The War of the Worlds: The Struggle for the Nation's Soul." As this title would suggest, the seminar organizer, Richard Land, intended the meeting to be a mobilization effort for conservatives. Mohler's address was entitled "The Struggle over Gender and the Revolt against God." He stated early on that he would not have time to give the entire sermon, but that the manuscript version would be published later. That being the case, he concentrated his remarks on what he called "the homosexualization of America," which probably should have been the title of the address as given that day. Homosexuality for SBC conservatives generally is not just one sin among many. Rather, as Mohler argued, it is an indication that people have been given over to the perversion of the mind of God. Same-sex relationships are a manifestation of the creature shaking his or her fist at the creator and saying, "I will be self-determining." "We cannot over-emphasize the sin of homosexuality. It is biblically impossible to call sin any more sinful than the Bible calls homosexuality." The CLC seminar was just one place where Mohler has taken up this issue. In fact, after becoming president of Southern Seminary and with the backing of the conservative majority on the board of trustees, he added the issues of abortion, homosexuality, and women in ministry to the growing litmus test new faculty would be required to pass. This led to the charge by some moderates that Mohler had an obsessive preoccupation with homosexuality. Mohler mentioned in his CLC address that one former moderate denominational official had even made this charge in a book.[11]

For the conservatives, abortion and homosexuality are only the most visible outward signs of a culture gone bad. "America at the end of the twentieth century," Mohler has argued, "is a society in the midst of a culture-shift. . . . All of this comes as the memory of the Christian worldview becomes ever more remote from modern consciousness."[12] But the problem is even worse than this, for the very notion of objective truth is itself denied by millions of Americans. Here Mohler cites former University of Chicago professor Allen Bloom's heralded book *The Closing of the American Mind.* "There is one thing a professor can be absolutely sure of," wrote Bloom in the 1980s, "almost every student entering the university believes, or says he believes, that truth is relative."[13] This is the postmodern condition, a subject that intellectuals and educated activists among the right wing address quite comfortably. In fact, these more informed SBC conservatives use postmodernism in a way similar to how the populist preachers among the SBC conservatives and in the larger Christian Right use the term "secular humanism"—it becomes the standard indicator of what is wrong with American culture. The difference is that the intellectuals and informed activists understand postmodernism much more thoroughly than many populist preachers understand secular humanism. For many of the latter—as will be illustrated below—secular humanism remains a rather ill-defined bogeyman of culture.

Mohler, by contrast, can articulate the postmodern condition as well as anyone. In one of several articles in which he has discussed the state of American culture, he cited four primary components of postmodernism. First is the deconstruction of truth. Here Mohler laid out both the similarities and differences between the historic biblical view of truth and that of modernity. Both view truth as external to human beings. The difference is that the scientific worldview that emanated from the Enlightenment ruled out revelation in favor of reason and the scientific method as the only sure way to fact. By contrast to this historic search for a fixed and external standard of truth, postmodernism rejects its very existence as held by both biblical conservatives and Enlightenment modernists. Truth is neither universal nor objective. Rather, it is, in Mohler's words, "socially constructed, plural, and inaccessible to universal reason." At this point, Mohler cites Richard Rorty, one of the reigning authorities on postmodern thought, and pits his views against those of evangelical popular theologian Francis Schaeffer, who insisted that among the primary duties of Christians living in a postmodern culture is to contend for the truth.[14]

Second, Mohler outlined briefly the death of metanarrative, or the end to grand and expansive accounts of meaning. Here he cites one of the most prominent of the French deconstruction theorists, Jean-Francois Lyotard, and his definition of postmodernism: "Simplifying to the extreme, I define postmodern as incredulity toward metanarratives." The problem with this view, of course, is that the gospel is the metanarrative of all metanarratives, the overarching story that makes sense of the human condition and its relationship to the creator of the universe. "For Christianity to surrender the claim that the gospel is universally true and objectively established," wrote Mohler, "is to surrender the center of our faith."[15]

Closely related to the death of metanarrative is Mohler's third facet of the postmodern condition, the demise of the text. Quite simply, "If the metanarrative is dead, then the great texts behind the metanarratives must also be dead." Herein lies the basis for deconstructionist literary criticism, where the meaning of a text is not necessarily tied to the intentions of its author but instead can be ascribed to the text by the reader. On this point Mohler cites the other most prominent French deconstructionist, Jacques Derrida, who described this move as the "death of the author," or "death of the text." This approach leads to a radical reinterpretation of the Bible. As Mohler characterizes it: "Texts which are not pleasing to the postmodern mind are rejected as oppressive, patriarchal, heterosexist, homophobic, or deformed by some other political or ideological bias. The authority of the text is denied in the name of liberation, and the most fanciful and ridiculous interpretations are celebrated as 'affirming' and thus 'authentic.'"[16]

Whereas Mohler's first three "Ds" of postmodernism apply to intellectual matters, his final three move from the intellectual to the practical. They are the dominion of therapy, the decline of authority, and the displacement of morality. Citing Philip Reiff's "triumph of the therapeutic," Mohler argued that when truth is denied, therapy, which is designed to maximize feelings of happiness, is all that remains. This even pervades religion when theological systems are designed primarily to enhance the self-esteem of individuals.

These "feel good" theologies jettison all that might be interpreted as negative or offensive, leaving only vague pleasantries. The decline of authority can be seen in the all-encompassing emphasis on liberation—from governmental leaders, teachers, community leaders, parents, and ministers. Finally, displacement of morality brings Dostoyevsky's *The Brothers Karamazov* into historical reality: "If God is dead, everything is permissible."[17]

Whereas Religious Right leaders of the 1980s characterized secular humanism as the overarching enemy, for intellectual and informed activists in the conservative Southern Baptist movement, postmodernism became the real problem. "Postmodernism represents *the* unique challenge facing Christianity in this generation," Mohler insists.[18] The cultural result of the postmodern condition is that America has been thoroughly secularized and is for that reason crumbling at its very foundation. The sense of crisis Southern Baptist conservatives feel is hard to overemphasize. Even the intellectual and informed activists see little ambiguity in American culture. In a sermon delivered at the 1995 Southern Baptist Convention meeting, Mohler laid out his view of the current cultural condition: "We live in a thoroughly secularized culture which is crumbling at the foundations. The great fixed truths of the Christian worldview have been displaced and rejected by an age of rampant relativism, subjectivism, secularism, and even paganism. We are living on the brink of what may be a new dark age. The light of God's revelation is hated and we live amidst a rebellion like that of the Korah in the Old Testament. Everyone does what is right in his own sight."[19] Citing G. K. Chesterton's view that Rome fell because the barbarians assaulted her gates, Mohler said America's condition was worse because the barbarians were within the gates. Southern Baptists for years lived in a "cultural comfort zone," but now they must awaken to the culture of death, humanism, and paganism that have invaded even the Baptist's Zion. Borrowing a quote from an unnamed source, Mohler opined: "World War Two was a generation and a whole civilization ago. . . . The great ideological, moral, political, and cultural battles of the twentieth-century have produced a dangerous culture of post-modern despair, relativism, moral anarchy, and social conflict."[20]

Mohler's sense of cultural crisis is, by his own reckoning, deeper than that of most American conservatives, even deeper than that of most of his allies in the SBC conservative movement. He recognizes that the church is no longer at the center of Western culture as it once was but has become a "moral minority" instead.[21] This pains him deeply, partly because of his own intense personality. As one associate has remarked, "Al's so serious, he sleeps in three-piece pajamas."[22] His sense of cultural crisis is also a product of his confessional Calvinism. Mohler is the most visible leader among the Reformed Protestant evangelicals of the conservative movement. When asked how his thoroughly Reformed perspective makes him different from other SBC conservatives, he replied: "I think my sense of the crisis is deeper than that of other conservatives. I don't think the fixes that most conservatives propose would fix anything. I don't think bringing back in the props of official Christianity is going to get at the darkness at the center of all this."[23]

Mohler has pointed to two models that others often use, neither of which he thinks is appropriate. The first is the Religious Right of the 1980s that evolved into the Christian Right of the 1990s. This movement started at the macro level, attempting to influence the culture from the top down. On the one hand, the Religious Right was successful beyond its leaders' wildest imagination in terms of electing individuals to office and getting conservative appointments to the courts. On the other, however, not much changed fundamentally as a result of the electoral success.

The second example Mohler has cited is one that many informed Calvinists admire. It is the model provided by nineteenth-century Reformed theologian and statesman Abraham Kuyper. Kuyper has had tremendous influence on one large wing of twentieth-century Reformed Protestantism that is sometimes called Neo-Calvinism. An advocate of theological liberalism as a young man, he had an evangelical conversion during his first pastorate and, by the late 1870s, had become the leader of a growing band of ardent Calvinists in the Netherlands. He wrote several books and hundreds of articles outlining his vision for a Reformed Christian worldview that would be broad enough to integrate everything from politics to the arts. His activities were prodigious on both the scholarly and political fronts. He founded the Free University of Amsterdam in 1880, started two newspapers, was elected to parliament as a member of a newly formed antirevolutionary party that is recognized today as the first modern party in Dutch history, led a secession from the state church that resulted in the formation of the independent Reformed Church, and served as prime minister of the Netherlands during the first decade of the twentieth century. Little wonder that his integration of Christian faith and contemporary Western culture has become the reigning paradigm for so many Calvinists. Yet while acknowledging much that is attractive about Kuyper's approach, Mohler believes that the Dutch scholar-politician operated in a completely different cultural context than do American Christians in the late twentieth century. Kuyper lived and worked in the early twentieth century, when the Low Countries were still broadly Christian. His was a basically "intact culture," a term Mohler uses frequently to describe the American South of thirty years ago. That model does not apply to America in the twenty-first century because the culture is now fractured and as a result in crisis. "My concern," Mohler says, "is how do we apply a cultural mandate to a culture in such crisis? I think the answer is that we have to start small rather than large."[24]

It is not at all clear that Kuyper's task was merely to renew public faith in a land still broadly Christian. In fact, one historian recently characterized Kuyper's own perception of his homeland very much as SBC conservatives perceive the United States today. Regarding the Dutchman's visit to America in the 1890s, James Bratt of Calvin College wrote, "[Kuyper] appreciated how Christianity could assume public deference in the States rather than having to struggle for respect as in the Netherlands."[25] Still, given Mohler's belief, correct or not, that America's culture is in much deeper crisis today than that of the Netherlands a century ago, he looks to sixteenth-century reformers for a better model than either the Christian Right or Kuyper. They took nothing for granted as they built a Christian, or at least Protestant, culture from scratch in the midst of great adversity and hostility.[26] This is the task Mohler believes evangelical Christians in America now have before them, and to accomplish it they must concentrate on building localized Genevas, Calvin's sixteenth-century Reformed city, before they can even think about re-Christianizing an entire nation.[27] Mohler's vision for Southern Seminary, therefore, has been to develop pastors who are theologically self-conscious and capable of leading congregations that will have a powerful impact on local communities. He draws an explicit contrast between the role Southern Baptist pastors must play in the twenty-first century versus the role they played in the 1940s and 1950s. At midcentury, Southern Seminary prepared ministers for service in a church culture but not any more. The United States is now a mission field where evangelical leaders must interpret the culture and stand as prophets against it. "If we continue to educate persons as if they are going to minister in Norman Rockwell's America, we have committed a disservice. That America no longer exists, except in some declining pockets throughout the American South—even there it can exist for only a limited duration."[28]

In addition to being different from populist SBC conservatives (discussed below), Mohler also exhibits a slightly different spirit than some of his allies outside the Southern Baptist Convention, especially the neo-conservatives of the larger political world. Their differences are minor and do not hinder a working relationship, but they are instructive nevertheless. Mohler draws a contrast of this sort between himself and public theologian and Roman Catholic priest Fr. Richard John Neuhaus, the founder of both the Institute on Religion and Public Life and the journal *First Things* and author of the widely acclaimed book *The Naked Public Square* (among the more than forty that he has authored, coauthored, or edited).[29] Neuhaus is part of the neoconservative movement in American politics that consists primarily of former 1960s progressives who have moved to a conservative position on cultural and political matters.[30] Mohler attends functions with Neuhaus and counts him as a friend and compatriot. Still, he detects something of the old progressive spirit in Neuhaus and other neoconservatives. As Mohler has remarked about Neuhaus's brand of conservatism, "He really thinks that if you just let him loose in New York and Washington, he'll solve the problems." Mohler, by contrast, calls himself a "paleo-conservative" who thinks much more locally. He traces his politically conservative lineage back to classic sources such as the eighteenth-century political theorist Edmund Burke. From this perspective, change must come slowly, painfully, and locally. At this juncture, Mohler's gradualist, grassroots vision comes once again to the fore. He hopes to remake Southern Seminary into a conservative bastion where pastors will be trained to go into and work with individual communities and congregations. He is much less interested in macro-reform from the top down. Putting certain people in places of power is not the answer, though he stresses that putting the wrong people in power surely will not solve the problems either. The culture is simply too fractured for the sort of easy, top-to-bottom political reforms of the Christian Right to make much of a difference. "If you had told someone that there would be twelve years of Republican presidents with more than half the [Supreme Court] reconstituted and we'd be where we are now, they [the Christian Right] wouldn't have believed you," he says. He contends that his own sense of cultural crisis, and that of those like him, is so deep that SBC moderates and liberals simply cannot understand his type of conservatism.[31] If the Baptist controversy was any indication, he is surely correct in this belief.

Not all intellectuals are as taken with the issue of cultural crisis as is Mohler. Paige Patterson presents a much lower profile. While not disagreeing with much that his fellow seminary president believes, Patterson is more content to focus on theological issues and at times seems to draw more from

Anabaptist beliefs than the "Christ-transforming-culture" approach of the Calvinists, which is understandable given that he is not a conservative of the latter tradition.[32] Timothy George, one of Mohler's Calvinist colleagues, is also an intellectual leader of the Reformed wing of SBC conservatism, but he too has been influenced by the Anabaptists of the sixteenth century. George learned much about them and from their beliefs during his years of Reformation studies at Harvard Divinity School. While he would be unlikely to disagree with much of what Mohler says about American culture, George is at the same time much less likely to talk and write about culture than is Mohler. George likes to stick to theology and church history and often directs conversation to fundamental issues as opposed to analysis of present realities. Where Mohler speaks at length of cultural crisis, cataloguing the demise of the United States issue by issue, George will say, "I find little to celebrate in American culture today," then move on to possible ways that Christians can live within such a society. As a Calvinist, however, George also looks to Kuyper, quoting the Dutch theologian's famous dictum, "There is not one square inch of the entire creation about which Jesus Christ does not cry out, 'This is mine! This belongs to me.'"[33] Still, one can hardly imagine him giving an impassioned address on the "homosexualization of America," as Mohler did at the "War of the Worlds" seminar. Likewise, Patterson's address at that gathering concerned how to be a witness within a fractured culture, not how to fix the culture. His posture seemed more like that of an alien living in a foreign land than like one who planned to reclaim a lost nation.[34]

But even George is not opposed to talking about the possibility that Christians may at some time be forced to break ranks with not only their culture but even the U.S. government. In his scholarly work on Baptist history, he has laid out a historical case for resistance to the state. In concluding an article on seventeenth-century English Baptists and religious liberty, he wrote that the Baptist perspective on the latter "was an important example of a Christian challenge to civil encroachment in matters religious."[35] This civil encroachment, usually characterized as hostility to religion, is precisely what SBC conservatives believe they are resisting, and no one makes the case more forcefully than the informed activist Richard Land.

THE INFORMED ACTIVISTS

The differences between conservatives such as Land and the intellectuals are subtle, and in fact, some in this camp have solid academic credentials and could well be intellectuals except that they have chosen the way of the political activist. It would even be conceivable for one of those classed as an intellectual to switch roles with an informed activist, which was very nearly the case when activist Land was a finalist for the presidency of Southern Seminary. Had he gotten that post, most of the discussion above about Mohler might well have been about Land instead. The primary difference between the activists and the intellectuals is that, for the sake of effectiveness in the political sphere, the activists must mute the ambiguity and tension inherent in many cultural matters and make bold declarations in an effort to clarify the issues. While sometimes rough around the edges and lacking in the sophistication of the more detached views of the intellectuals, the informed activists' positions are usually coherent, even if occasionally populist.

As executive director of the former Christian Life Commission and then the Ethics and Religious Liberty Commission, Land was the unchallenged leader of the informed activists for the entire decade of the nineties. He articulated the conservative positions most forcefully (which will be demonstrated in later chapters). As to perceptions of culture, his is the classic evangelical view that sees the United States as having turned resolutely against traditional faith-based worldviews. This is so obvious to him that he has questioned whether one could be an evangelical Christian and not acknowledge the situation as conservatives perceive it. "I have to ask myself," Land says, "whether they could be evangelical Christians who say [that there is no discrimination against religion in America]." Instead, he believes, anyone who denies that a high level of discrimination exists would almost have to be a mainstream Christian "going with the cultural flow."[36] Land thus implies that moderates who do not see the situation as conservatives do are mainstream liberals too at home in the culture. On more than one occasion Land has compared the situation in postmodern America to that of ancient Rome, where everything was tolerated except the exclusivistic claims of Christians. In his installation address at the CLC in 1989, he declared that the situation in the United States today is "remarkably analogous to the one which confronted our first-century spiritual ancestors. They, too, were immersed in a world dominated by pagan idolatrous philosophies and lifestyles." Land calls American culture "neo-pagan."[37] This descent into paganism has been accompanied by the advance of secularism that has marked the second half of the twentieth century. By the 1960s, America was widely viewed as a secular culture, "aggressively, emphatically secular," in Land's words. Quoting evangelical author Harry Blaimires, Land claimed that by the 1960s there was no coherent and recognizable Christian influence in American cultural life.[38]

Land and other informed activists build a logical program for addressing public policy from this basic position. As such, his views differ very little from Mohler's. For example, if the culture is neopagan with little vestige of its former Christian base, it follows logically that Christians will have to exhibit considerable savvy when in the public square. As Mohler argues, they cannot just attempt to reestablish the props of official Christianity. Land recognizes this and can make the argument in scholarly as well as popular venues. In a 1994 response to Catholic theologian George Weigel, Land advocated the use of natural-law arguments in public, maintaining that this was in the best tradition of historical Protestantism from Martin Luther to Jonathan Edwards to Charles Hodge. Land even wrote that Carl F. H. Henry's chapter "The Rejection of Natural Theology" in his magisterial work of theology *God, Revelation, and Authority* was badly titled because Henry argued only for the "insufficiency of natural theology or natural-law theory by itself." Land defended Weigel's advocacy of natural-law arguments precisely because Americans living in a secularized culture more and more find incomprehensible public positions that emanate primarily from spiritual revelation. Secular elites, however, are likely to be hostile even to natural-law arguments. Land cited as evidence the U.S. Senate hearings on the confirmation of Supreme Court nominees Robert Bork and Clarence Thomas. In both cases, certain elements in the media were suspicious of the nominees' use of natural law apparently because it presupposes a single, created standard of morality. In addition to quibbling with Henry's chapter title, Land also took issue with one of evangelicalism's favorite prophets, Francis Schaeffer, for his having described the United States as a culture with a Christian memory. By contrast, Land once again described the country as pagan.[39]

While there are many forces at work in this cultural hostility to religion, according to Land, government is the chief culprit. Often citing the arguments of scholars such as Neuhaus and Stephen Carter, he argues that religious views are either banished from the public square or trivialized when admitted at all. Borrowing a phrase from Rutherford Institute founder John Whitehead, Land maintains that there has developed in America a system of "religious apartheid," where all perspectives except the religious are allowed in the public square.[40] Public schools in particular have become "religion free zones." He believes this is not only unjust but unwise. In a pluralistic society, Land asks, would it not be better to allow robust religious differences in the schools as a way of preparing students for the kind of world they will face upon graduation?[41]

Government is just the largest and most pervasive of institutions governed by elites who are far more secular than the population at large. At the 1995 Christian Life Commission seminar, Land cited eminent sociologist Peter Berger in making his case against secular elites. Berger, in a response to a study that found India to be the most religious nation on Earth and Sweden to be the most secular, has said that "America is a nation of Indians ruled by an elite of Swedes."[42] Land attributed this condition to an erroneous concept of church-state separation that stipulates religious people should not get involved in politics. Americans have created a situation, in his view, where it is perfectly acceptable for a person to say "I'm an atheist so I believe such and such," but when a person says "I'm a Christian," that disqualifies him or her from the debate because of separation of church and state.[43]

Berger believes that there is, in fact, a cultural elite that would like to see the United States become even more secular. In most places in the world other than Europe, there is "a thin layer of humanistically educated people" that is much more secular than their societies as a whole. (In Europe the population is as secular as the elites.) This has led to conflict in several world societies between societal leaders and much of the rest of the populace. Viewed this way, Berger has argued, the Christian Right is a reactive and populist movement against secular elites lumped together as secular humanists. "Whether 'secular humanism' is the right term or not," Berger suggested in a 1997 *Christian Century* interview, "these people are reacting to an elite culture."[44] Implicit in this analysis is the evidence for both sides of the debate over whether the United States has a naked public square. On the one hand, he acknowledges that the nation is pervasively religious like most world societies. (European culture is the secular exception.) This seems to suggest that America's public square is well dressed in religious garb, as former National Council of Churches general counsel Oliver Thomas argued in a 1997 written debate with scholar Stephen Monsma. Thomas, himself a moderate Baptist and former staff member of the Baptist Joint Committee, articulated a view held by many moderate Southern Baptists by arguing that there is plenty of evidence that the public square is anything but naked. Rather, religion abounds within nearly every sector of society.[45] While Berger might agree with that at one level, the more important point is that elites in America are pursuing a European model of secularization. In church-state matters the federal courts have been moving in a "French direction—moving toward a government that is antiseptically free of religious symbols rather than simply a government that doesn't favor any particular religious group."[46]

Quite naturally, Land identifies Berger's secularization as hostility to religion, and since secularization is fostered by elites, Land often finds himself playing the role of a populist. He is usually careful to point out that when he speaks of elite or official hostility to faith, he is talking about discrimination, not persecution as Christians in ancient times faced or as those in other parts of the world encounter today.[47] On at least one occasion, however, the Ethics and Religious Liberty Commission website fudged the distinction between discrimination in the United States and persecution elsewhere. Barrett Duke of Land's staff at the ERLC offered as sermon material for the SBC's 1997 Religious Liberty Sunday five examples of how bad things are getting for Christians around the world. Along with the denial of jobs to Christians in India, the beating of a young Christian boy by government thugs in Sudan explicitly for the purpose of getting him to renounce Christ, and the kidnapping and murder of a house pastor in China as part of a local campaign to dissuade people from the faith, Duke listed one example of an elementary grade schoolgirl in Denver whose teacher told her not to bring her Bible to class or tell her friends about Jesus.[48] The stark incommensurability of the Denver incident was not lost on *Liberty* magazine editor Clifford Goldstein, who rebuked Duke a few months later by arguing that when Christians in America compare their own "suffering" to that of Christians overseas, they "diminish the seriousness of both."[49] *Liberty* had already carried an article one issue before Goldstein's editorial appeared contrasting persecution of Christians in foreign lands with alleged persecution of Christians in the United States. In it the author wrote, "[A]s the managing editor of a publication that concentrates only on the persecution of Christians in other countries . . . , I must admit that I'm not very impressed by the claims of Christian persecution in America."[50]

Duke's piece may have been out of keeping with Land's stated view, but it shows how easily the perception of a hostile culture can be ratcheted up to claims of outright persecution of common people by secularists in authority. Feelings of persecution are common across America's religious landscape. Legal scholar Douglas Laycock has noted that because there is no majority in the nation on religious issues, virtually all groups at one time or another see themselves as embattled minorities. Evangelicals, Jews, secular humanists, civil libertarians, and the various so-called cults may not actually fear that their worship or way of life will be forbidden, but they are all concerned that they could be regulated to an extent that would make their lives intolerable.[51] Such feelings are even more likely in the climate of political activism where lobby groups such as the Ethics and Religious Liberty Commission do their work. These organizations exist because there are a host of voices that oppose what their sponsoring interest believes. If it were not for such opposition, there would be no need for lobbying efforts. Lobby groups, therefore, are prone to feelings of persecution because they face opposition on a daily basis. All this means that even the most informed activists are less likely than reflective intellectuals to see the merit in the argument of their opponents. That someone like Land often does acknowledge such merit is more surprising than the fact that his arguments are at other times rather populist and oversimplified.

As is the case with Mohler, Land's perception of cultural crisis goes hand in hand with his view that SBC moderates went too far in courting progressivists. Land believes that these progressives ride the cultural flow, while traditionalist conservatives take a prophetic stance against the tide. He has endeavored, therefore, to make the ERLC a conservative voice in the culture war, reversing what had been the trend of the old Christian Life Commission when he took over as executive director in the late 1980s. At the 1995 "War of the Worlds" seminar that he hosted, Land referred to a newspaper article he had read that highlighted the differences between his CLC and that of his forerunners. "I would have been disappointed had they not noticed," he said. The difference was that there would be no more appearances by liberal politicians like Ted Kennedy or George McGovern, nor by Sarah Weddington, who argued the winning side of *Roe* v. *Wade,* or the editor of *Playboy* magazine. All these people had appeared at Christian Life Commission seminars in the 1970s, but this had ended, Land made clear. "This is not your father's Christian Life Commission," he thundered.[52]

When one listens to Southern Baptist conservatives or moderates talk about each other, it is easy to walk away with the feeling that something is missing from the story. This is the case with the conservative attempt to portray moderates as essentially progressivist to the core. Taking the examples of CLC speakers identified by Land, it might appear that moderates had actually schemed to inflame the passions of the conservative Southern Baptist rank and file by inviting the most controversial liberals available to appear at official SBC gatherings. There is more to the story than Land lets on, however. For example, Weddington did argue the *Roe* case in 1973, but when she appeared at the Christian Life Commission's annual seminar in 1980, she was an assistant to president Jimmy Carter, who was, of course, a Southern Baptist. Under the general theme "Women in the Eighties," her lecture addressed the various choices that women have and how such choices present both opportunity and responsibility. In addition to affirming new avenues for women, in good progressivist fashion to be sure, she also said, "One of the good things coming out of the changes of the seventies . . . is the reaffirmation of the value of the role of wife and mother." The three choices she identified for women were: 1) the choice of being a full-time wife and mother, 2) the choice of combining being a mother with paid or volunteer work outside the home, or 3) the choice of emphasizing the professional. If her written address is any indication, she apparently made no mention of the legal choice women have to an abortion.[53]

Land's mention of Kennedy and McGovern was also geared to show that moderates of the pre-Land CLC courted progressivists, but once again there is more to the story. Kennedy and McGovern appeared at the 1976 Christian Life Commission meeting that also featured conservative Republican senators Howard Baker of Tennessee and John Tower of Texas; moderate Republican congressman John Anderson of Illinois, who was a self-professed evangelical; and northern evangelical Baptist Republican senator Mark Hatfield. African American Democratic congresswoman Barbara Jordan also spoke. Jordan and Baker gave Democratic and Republican perspectives on the upcoming elections, Tower spoke on "the conscience of a conservative," Hatfield on civil religion, and Anderson on "Christian Conscience and Political Decisions." Two years later, Baker appeared again along with evangelical favorite Charles Colson, who, ironically, was also on the program in 1995 when Land said there would be no more appearances by the likes of Kennedy and McGovern. Other notables appearing at CLC seminars during the 1970s included Habitat for Humanity founder Millard Fuller, evangelical African American inner-city evangelist Tom Skinner, family values proponent and counselor Charlie Shedd, First Lady Rosalynn Carter, George Gallup Jr., and the liberal theologian Harvey Cox.[54]

In 1997 Land again recalled the appearance of Weddington at the 1980 CLC seminar. He alleged that moderate leader Jimmy Allen had remarked afterward that he had been trying to get Southern Baptists involved in social issues for a long time, and he now had a feeling that as a result of Weddington's appearance, they would mobilize, but on the opposite side of Allen and his fellow moderate leaders.[55] The story may be apocryphal, but it illustrates a point at which the conservatives are probably correct. Weddington's name will forever be linked to *Roe* v. *Wade,* and to the extent that some moderate elites supported that decision or at least opposed a constitutional amendment to remedy it, they were very unrepresentative of grassroots Southern Baptists. Any implication that some moderates were attempting to move denominational agencies toward a pro-choice position was bound to backfire. Support for abortion rights by even a minority of the moderate leadership also illustrates Mohler's contention that, in siding with progressivists on the correct side of the race issue, some moderates drew conclusions that would come back to haunt them. Abortion rights became part and parcel with the progressivist view of civil rights, and moderate leaders like Foy Valentine, the head of the Christian Life Commission in the 1970s, bought into that position. This is another example that abortion became a key to energizing the conservative cause and remains central to their perception of a culture gone wrong. This is the point Land attempts to drive home when he repeatedly mentions the appearance of Weddington at the 1980 CLC meeting.

As executive director of the ERLC, Land has a written forum for his views via the agency's publication, *Light.* In his regular columns he hammers home the need for more Christian influence in politics in much the same way Mohler articulates in Southern Seminary's alumni magazine his views of cultural crisis. In negotiating intellectual terrain that extends from George Weigel to Carl Henry to Francis Schaeffer within a historical context that includes Martin Luther, Jonathan Edwards, and Charles Hodge— with Robert Bork, Clarence Thomas, and Peter Berger thrown in for good measure—Land exhibits an informed approach to cultural issues very similar to that of intellectuals like Mohler. Like them he insists that American culture is pervasively hostile to religious interests. The difference between Mohler's intellectualism and Land's activism is that Land spends the majority of his time and energy trying to change the culture rather than interpret it. This being the case, he projects the sort of optimism and concern at the macrolevel that lobbyists usually possess. As Mohler has said about Neuhaus, Land also seems to believe that if you turn him loose in Washington and give him enough troops, he can change the nation.

What would Land's America look like? On this question he is quite specific, more so than the more cautious Mohler. Land's ideal is "America in 1955 without the racism and without the sexual discrimination against women."[56] To illustrate, Land lists a litany of cultural problems that have emerged since the golden years of the fifties:

> In 1955 we didn't have a higher percentage of our population in jail than any other country in the world. We do now. In 1955 we weren't aborting one out of every three babies. We are now. . . . We didn't have a homosexual rights movement that was trying to make that particular sin a guaranteed constitutional right.
>
> We do now. In fact, homosexuality and lesbianism were considered so perverted that they were not often discussed in polite company. . . . And a woman wasn't being physically beaten every nine seconds by her husband or by her boyfriend in 1955. They are now. A six-year-old American girl did not have a one in three chance of being sexually molested by her sixteenth birthday, and a six-year-old American boy did not have a one in five chance of being sexually molested by his sixteenth birthday in 1955. They do now. One out of every two marriages didn't end in divorce in 1955. And we didn't have significant percentages of our children being reared in single-parent homes in 1955. The year 1955 was not perfect, but it looks better every day compared to what has come since.[57]

While many would agree that American culture has undergone significant decline in many areas since 1955, Land has exempted from consideration two pretty big issues. Racism and sexism made possible the mistreatment of minorities and women with a clear conscience. African Americans could be kept in second-class status because of racism, and women could be abused by husbands because of sexism. Some would even question whether spousal abuse was less prevalent in 1955 than today. It may be that much more of it simply went unreported because most people did not consider it a crime.[58] What at first seems to be an increase in socially destructive behavior sometimes appears on closer examination to be a heightened awareness of such incidents combined with a reinterpretation of what is considered acceptable. In other words, once racism and sexism were exposed and redefined as oppression, what had been considered merely the way things are became an immense social problem. So, while many measures of societal decline have risen since the 1950s, it is also likely that expanded definitions of social pathology make our own society seem much less harmonious and desirable than it did when people kept what is today considered criminal and patho-logical under wraps as a private matter. In some ways, racism and sexism were the blinders that allowed most white middle-class Americans to be-lieve they were living in a good society. Remove those blinders and Ameri-cans come face to face with their sickness. Moreover, the issue of whether the 1950s were better than the 1990s aside, one could take almost any era of American history, remove the two worst social problems, and that era would look better than our own time. These considerations notwithstanding, SBC conservatives are convinced that American culture is in a crisis unlike any-thing ever experienced before, and that crisis has only developed during the last forty years of the twentieth century. The intellectuals articulate this sense of crisis, while informed activists move from discussion of crisis to-ward strategies for political change. A third important approach to culture consists of the populists.

The Populist Preachers

Like all populists, SBC conservative preachers keep things simple. Theirs is the task of rallying the troops behind the denominational policies set by the informed activists in conversation with the intellectuals. This is most often done through sermons but also through pamphlets and, at least in one case, books. James Draper Jr. is president of what for most of its existence was called the Baptist Sunday School Board. In 1998 the agency was renamed the Lifeway Christian Resources of the Southern Baptist Convention. The agency is reportedly the largest publisher of Christian literature in the world. It has its own building that takes up nearly an entire city block in downtown Nashville, and Draper, as chief executive officer of this gigantic enterprise, was quite possibly the highest paid denominational executive of the 1990s. He reached this pinnacle position within the SBC after pastoral stints in Kansas City, San Antonio, and Dallas, among other locations. He was an associate pastor under SBC conservative patriarch W. A. Criswell at First Baptist, Dallas, before taking over as head pastor of First Baptist, Euless, which is located in a Dallas suburb. Draper was the third conservative elected president of the convention and was generally considered to be the most moderate and least ideological of the conservative presidents elected during the controversy. While Paige Patterson and others regularly charged that the SBC was rife with theological liberalism, Draper at one point dur-ing the controversy admitted that there were very few in the denomination who had actually relinquished any fundamental points of doctrine. Rather, the issue was that moderates were soft on inerrancy and therefore susceptible to theological deviation in the future.[59] After his stint as president, Draper left his Euless pastorate to become the head of the Baptist Sunday School Board.

During the 1980s, Draper coauthored with Forrest Watson a book entitled *If the Foundations Be Destroyed.* But using this work to get at Draper's views is a trickier proposition than one might expect since it was written primarily by Watson. Taken in conjunction with Draper's expressed views in other venues, however, the book does seem to be a fairly accurate portrayal of his interpretation of U.S. history and the present state of American culture. While consistent with the intellectual and informed activist views in its broad outlines, the book is problematic in its general oversimplification. In short, *If the Foundations Be Destroyed* makes claims that Mohler and Land would never attempt to defend.[60]

The primary thrust of the book is the standard Christian America interpretation of U.S. history. Draper and Watson contend that, with one exception, the American Founding Fathers were Christian; the exception is an unnamed deist, obviously Thomas Jefferson. The authors also allow that a few of these men were influenced by deism, though not enough to be considered outside the ranks of orthodox Christianity. The fact that there is no mention of sovereignty in the U.S. Constitution, argue the authors, "shows the Christianity of its makers. . . . The men who wrote the Constitution realized that only God was absolutely sovereign." These founders, moreover, intended the United States to be Christian. Draper and Watson acknowledge that there is no mention of the faith in the founding documents but contend that "Christianity was assumed in everything that was undertaken in the founding of our country. The United States was to have no established Church, but it was to be Christian." The subsequent history of the nation has been an arena of God's activity, and this can be detected by the historian who is a committed believer. Draper and Watson admit that their rendition of American history is, of necessity, different from that of a secular, professional historian. "For a historian who does not believe in God," they wrote in one chapter conclusion, "the facts of this chapter will have been put together in a most unscientific manner. But if you accept the fact of a God who controls history, the conclusion is obvious. The providence of God was at work." In the introduction to the following chapter, Draper and Watson lash out at "supposedly Christian historians" who omit reference to the providence of God in their work. The authors call this "anti-Christian history" and charge that to regard history from anything but a God-centered faith is a sin."[61] It is possible that Draper and Watson are referring to evangelical historians Mark Noll, Nathan Hatch, and George Marsden, whose book entitled *The Search for Christian America* appeared the year before *If the Foundations Be Destroyed.* Noll, Hatch, and Marsden argue that historically, the United States cannot be considered a Christian nation in anything other than a demographic sense.[62]

Examples of God's alleged guidance abound in *If the Foundations Be Destroyed.* For example, the authors ask rhetorically why the Spanish were able to establish a large empire in Central and South America before 1600, but mysteriously the eastern coastline of North America was preserved free from colonization until the English arrived. Their answer: "Very simply, God did not allow America's east coast to be settled; in His providence He was keeping it clear for the English Protestants who would come to America to establish the kingdom of God on its shores." Parts of the book are designed to defend not only the English settlers but even the Spanish conquistadors, who come in for such severe attack in some quarters of secular academic life today. Draper and Watson contend that Cortez and his men repeatedly attempted to forge friendships with the natives they encountered, but the natives kept attacking them. Cortez's maneuvers are portrayed as purely defensive, and the slaughter of fifteen thousand Aztecs is attributed to the Spaniard's Native American allies, while he is portrayed as having instructed his own men not to take revenge against the Aztec city of Tenochtitlan. The authors also argue that Montezuma was killed in a riot by his own people and not by the Spanish. "Colonization was on the whole beneficial to the Indians," they surmise because "the Spanish treated them better than the Indians treated one another." Not only was Spanish colonization beneficial, it was also inspired by pure motivations. In one of their frequent populist slaps at elite academic historians, Draper and Watson reject the interpretation that the Spanish were motivated primarily by greed. For the authors, "the most important motive behind Spanish exploration—despite its many failings—was the preaching of the Gospel to the Heathen."[63]

Intellectuals like Mohler and informed activists like Land would never make such claims, either that the United States was founded as a Christian nation by Christians or that one is committing sin by not interpreting American history as being under the meticulous providence of God. Theirs is a much more refined and nuanced view. They believe that there was a moral consensus based on the Judeo-Christian tradition and taken for granted at the time of the country's founding. That consensus has eroded and been attacked to the extent that the nation will not survive if the trend is not reversed.[64] Like Mohler and Land, Draper and Watson also argue that the moral consensus of America has eroded and is now under attack, but they simplify matters into a stark contest between Christians and the con-spiratorial forces of secular humanism in ways that Mohler and Land never would. For Draper and Watson, U.S. history has been not only an arena of God's providence but also a battlefield between His forces and the forces of humanism, and the humanists are winning. As the authors note on the first page of their book, the public schools "are forbidden by the courts to teach the principles upon which America was founded." And later, "The history of the United States has been the story of the steady rise of humanistic statism to power. Today, the control of civil government, public schools, and many churches has fallen into the hands of humanistic men who are fervent, even fanatical enemies of Christ and His church."[65]

For populists like Draper and Watson, the cosmic contest between the forces of God and the forces of secular humanism usually breaks down along conservative-liberal political lines. For this reason, much of their book takes issue with any progressive reform in American history, even the abolition of slavery (which, ironically, was led by evangelicals). Draper and Watson argue that slaves were treated much better than is commonly believed. Their ten-dentious reading of evidence often leads to outright historical errors. For example, the authors characterized as humane a law that forbade masters from freeing their slaves without first assuring the community that the free-person would not be a burden. Misreading the law as an attempt to make provisions for freed slaves, the authors accuse abolitionists of ignoring such magnanimous gestures.[66] It is far more likely, however, that such laws were designed to protect the community, not the freed slaves, and to discourage manumission, not to ensure that freed slaves had adequate provisions.

The most severe charge against the abolitionists is that they caused the Civil War. Earlier in the twentieth century, some academic historians made a similar case, though not in quite the simplistic way that Draper and Watson do in their book. Somehow, the authors arrive at the conclusion that aboli-tionists were primarily Unitarians influenced by German idealistic philoso-pher Georg Wilhelm Friedrich Hegel. Since for Hegel history is a series of clashes between opposing forces, the abolitionists urged armed conflict between North and South, believing that this was the only way to bring about progress. By contrast, in Russia, where there were no Unitarian abolitionists, the government emancipated the country's millions of serfs without a war. "Only America went to war over the issue," the authors charge, "because the American Hegelians believed a war was necessary."[67] There are elements of this line of reasoning that are correct, but there is enough oversimplification to make the interpretation problematic to say the least. Hegel did believe that history is a series of clashes between what he called thesis and antithesis, each clash producing a synthesis that then serves as the new thesis, allowing the march of history to continue when the new thesis meets up with its own antithesis. What is not so clear is whether many Unitarian abolitionists were actually influenced by Hegel. Moreover, Hegel's clash of thesis and antithesis was more within the realm of what he called "Spirit," or ideas, than in actual warfare between opposing armies. He was reluctant to make too facile any correspondence between the clash at the level of Spirit and particular historical events. Later, Marxists influenced by Hegel would indeed advocate armed conflict between the proletarian workers and the bourgeoisie owners, but one is hard pressed to understand on what basis Draper and Watson can attribute such desires to Unitarians in the 1840s and 1850s, which is to say nothing of the evangelical abolitionists who were influenced far more by the Bible than by prevailing academic philosophies coming out of Hegel's Germany. Draper and Watson's belief that abolition was primarily a Unitarian enterprise is a wholly mistaken notion.

The authors' opposition to all forms of progressivism produced a critique of another important nineteenth-century reform, public education. While referring to the "reform fanaticism" of that time period, which often "substitutes for the Gospel," they wrote, "one reform movement which did great damage to America was the public-school movement championed by Horace Mann." Here, they do not merely argue that public schools in the twentieth century have declined along with the rest of the culture, but that the institution itself has been destructive by its very nature. There is a strong implication that the concept of state-supported public education is theologically remiss. Public education, in their view, is an example of the state replacing the churches as the institution that should engage in education. This seems an odd position for an author, Watson, who was a superintendent of a public school system at the time he wrote the book. Following from this indictment of the very nature of public education is the view that public schools have always been hostile to religion. Here, the authors cite evangelical historian Timothy Smith's classic book *Revivalism and Social Reform* as inadvertently proving this.[68] Although they do not elaborate on exactly how Smith's scholarship proves their point, on the page they cite from *Revivalism and Social Reform* this line appears: "Prominent laymen representing several communions had organized the American Sunday School Union in 1830 for the purpose of supplying both rural and urban children with the religious education *forbidden in the public schools*."[69] In this passage, Smith makes no comment as to whether the absence of religious teaching in nineteenth-century public schools is evidence of state hostility to religion or merely a necessity arising from America's Protestant pluralism. Regardless of what Smith intended, however, the reading that Draper and Watson put on the passage is consistent with their view that whenever the state disallows a religious practice, this amounts to hostility.

When asked in 1997 what was the most important church-state issue of our time, Draper listed government suppression of the free exercise of religion. As examples he cited prohibitions against expression of religion in public places—nativity scenes on public property, prayer at graduation ceremonies, and Christmas celebrations in public schools.[70] From the typical church-state separationist perspective, not to mention the view of legal scholars and judges, all three are examples of government support for religion, constituting a low-level establishment that violates the Establishment Clause of the First Amendment. From the SBC conservative populist perspective based on the perception of government hostility to religion, however, these are clear examples that a secular elite with great influence over government is attempting to clear religion from American life, thus creating the proverbial "naked public square." In their book, Draper and Watson merely push this interpretation back into the nineteenth century to argue that things have pretty much always been this way.

If the Foundations Be Destroyed elaborates at greater length and in more populist-historical fashion the standard fare of SBC conservative preachers when it comes to analysis of cultural issues. Preachers with huge congregations and mass followings make similar points regularly. Adrian Rogers is a good example. He has been one of the highest profile preachers in the conservative movement in the SBC; indeed, he was the first to be elected denomination president in the conservative drive to take control of SBC agencies. Rogers is also the only one to serve more than the customary two consecutive year-long terms. Elected in 1979 to kick off the conservative movement, he declined to stand for the perfunctory reelection the following year. He was then reelected later in the 1980s and served two terms at that time.

Rogers has pastored Bellevue Baptist Church for more than twenty-five years. Originally a downtown church in Memphis, it was heralded by the *Christian Century* in 1950 as one of America's "great churches." Since 1989 the church has been in Cordova, Tennessee, east of Memphis. With over twenty-six thousand members, Bellevue's campus comprises 376 acres and a sanctuary that seats seven thousand.[71] The choir loft alone holds more than three hundred people, making it, when full, larger than the average Southern Baptist church. Rogers has been a highly visible and influential Baptist leader for nearly three decades. A booklet published in 1997 to commemorate his twenty-fifth year at Bellevue includes photos of Rogers in the Oval Office with Jimmy and Rosalynn Carter, in the White House shaking hands with Ronald Reagan, aboard Air Force One with George Bush, and at the home of Billy Graham. In addition to proximity to the seat of political power is the shear vastness of Bellevue's outreach. By the reckoning of Bellevue officials themselves, the church's worldwide radio and television audience is potentially 135 million.[72]

Rogers preaching style, facilitated by a remarkably smooth baritone voice, is firm and soothing. He is neither a ranter nor given to hell-fire and brimstone, and he seems to wear a perpetual smile when preaching. He is more like Dwight L. Moody than Billy Sunday. Still, Rogers can be quite direct when dealing with the presumed enemies of the evangelical faith, and a declining culture and liberal government rank near the top of his list of such enemies. "Americans used to live by the word of God and run the government by the Constitution that came out of the word of God," he thundered in a 1993 sermon. "Today we're just kind of making up the rules as we go along."[73] Rogers's views of America are so well rehearsed that he needs barely a prompting to gush forth with a litany of problems. When asked in 1997 about the state of American culture, he replied: "In crisis. . . . We have lost our moral consensus. You can see it in education, the killing of the unborn, the move toward euthanasia, prevalency [*sic*] of teenage pregnancy, breakup of the home, proliferation of sexual perversion, pornographic explosion, the drug culture. I think it's a crisis. I think our society is decadent."[74]

As for the type of discrimination against religion that Richard Land identifies, Rogers believes the issue is more one of ridicule and lack of respect, and he lays a small part of the blame on Christians themselves for not standing firm against the forces of secularism. Nevertheless, while downplaying outright discrimination, the word "hostile" is not at all too strong for Rogers's view of the government's treatment of religion. He sees the state as not only hostile to Christianity but also toward all religion. This is due, in his view, to an overkill in interpretation of the First Amendment. "I think the First Amendment, rightly understood, allows for free expression of our religious values, but I think we've done an extreme overkill to try to keep a few from being offended." When asked if he urges his people to stand within such a culture in an attempt to influence it and mold it, or outside the culture in a more prophetic stance, Rogers responded, "I think we are outside the culture, in the culture, above the culture, and beyond it all at the same time."[75]

Like Draper and Watson, Rogers sees both the decline of the United States and the once-active hand of God moving within American history. In a 1996 booklet, he wrote: "The Lord was instrumental in the founding of our country, and He placed His blessing on us. But now our country has turned away from God, and the blessing of the Lord no longer rests on America." As for the Founding Fathers, "The People who founded our country loved God and relied on His Word and His wisdom." Without actually calling the United States God's chosen nation, Rogers did compare America's situation with that of Old Testament Israel, which turned away from God and was destroyed as a result. "Twentieth-century America offers a startling parallel to Israel in the time of the judges."[76]

His view of secular historians is also consistent with the populist critique of scholarship displayed by Draper and Watson. Rogers labels as revisionists all those who would like to take away "our Christian heritage" by omitting from their work references to God and his providence. For example, while everyone knows that Patrick Henry said "Give me liberty or give me death," the revisionists, according to Rogers, do not want people to know that he also said "It cannot be emphasized too much or repeated too strongly that America was founded not by religionists but by Christians, not upon religions, but upon the Gospel of Jesus Christ."[77] This second quote comes from videos, seminars, and books produced by David Barton, whose organization, WallBuilders, distributes technologically sophisticated slideshows, books, and pamphlets purporting that America's Founding Fathers intended for the country to be Christian and that separation of church and state is a modern revisionist myth. In 1996 he experienced a major embarrassment when a historian, after exhaustive research, concluded that one of the prominent quotes Barton had been attributing to James Madison was bogus. Barton himself then published a list of eleven other quotes he had featured prominently, all of which were now classified by WallBuilders as either questionable or false. The Henry quote used by Rogers was one of those deemed questionable.[78] Other errors in Rogers's booklet may also come from Barton; for example, Rogers cites some lower-court decisions as Supreme Court cases. Throughout his lectures, Barton often mixes the terms "Supreme Court" and "the court" in such a way that the nonexpert cannot tell the difference.[79]

Like Draper and Rogers, Morris Chapman can also be placed among the populist preachers when it comes to statements on American culture. Chapman was pastor of First Baptist, Wichita Falls, Texas, when he was elected president of the SBC in 1990. In 1992 he became the president and chief executive officer of the Executive Committee of the Southern Baptist Convention, which oversees the daily operations of the entire denomination. Chapman epitomizes the evangelistic emphasis that is strong with nearly all conservative Southern Baptist preachers and most moderates as well. He recognizes the need for Christians to hold the line against cultural decay, but he stresses that the ultimate answer is individual conversion. Like Draper, he prefers to keep his message simple. In fact, one of his primary complaints about moderates is their tendency to overintellectualize the faith. "It seems to me like the moderate mindset is to take the Bible and to work towards trying to say something it does not say just in its simplest form," he claims. "I mean it just seems like you can read the Bible and the Bible speaks for itself."[80] He also admits that he simply does not understand the moderate mindset.

In emphasizing simple evangelism as the answer to societal problems, Chapman and other populist preachers are squarely within the tradition of American revivalism, especially as it has existed since Dwight L. Moody's heyday in the late nineteenth century. Moody's premillennial approach stressed saving people from the wreck of culture instead of trying to rescue the culture itself. His famous statement illustrates this view: "I look upon this world as a wrecked vessel. God has given me a lifeboat and said to me, 'Moody, save all you can.'"[81] Chapman recognizes the importance of cultural issues and believes that Christians should do what they can. At the same time, he stresses that the most important issue of our time is the "lostness" of the American people. Only a spiritual awakening, brought about through revival, can remedy this. While advocating that Christians stand with truth against such things as abortion and homosexuality, Chapman also acknowledges that he rarely addresses cultural issues in his own preaching, but when he does it is usually to illustrate a point having to do with salvation or witnessing. While informed activists like Land attempt to change the course of American politics directly and bristle at suggestions of pietistic withdrawal from culture, Chapman sees his role as equipping individual believers to go into society to win souls, not elections. Still, even as he takes a different, more subtle approach to the culture war, Chapman agrees absolutely that there is hostility toward evangelical Christianity in the United States.[82] He presents a reminder that, with Southern Baptists of all stripes, there can be a strong pietistic and evangelistic strain that can lead preachers away from culture-war activity. For this reason intellectuals and activists like Land and Mohler and populist preachers like Rogers must work to keep their right-wing troops mobilized in the face of the tendency to see cultural issues as tangential to the work of the denomination.

REACTIONS TO THE 1996 *FIRST THINGS* SYMPOSIUM

The evangelistic piety of Chapman and the oversimplifications and errors of Draper, Watson, and Rogers show once again the difference between the views of the intellectuals and informed activists on the one hand and the populist preachers on the other. Intellectuals such as Mohler and informed activists like Land recognize the spurious nature of arguments like those propagated by David Barton, but preachers like Rogers find them useful. While the three approaches to American culture that exist within SBC conservatism share in common the view that society has grown hostile and discriminatory toward religion, they vary in the extent to which they are willing to take this analysis. This can be demonstrated by reactions to a symposium that was published in Richard John Neuhaus's journal *First Things* in November 1996.

Entitled "The End of Democracy?" and focusing on judicial usurpation of democratic authority, this special issue featured articles by former federal judge and Supreme Court nominee Robert Bork, law professors Russell Hittinger and Hadley Arkes, political theorist Robert George, and evangelical activist and author Charles Colson. The most controversial statement came from the editors in the introduction. "The question here explored," they wrote, "in full awareness of its far-reaching consequences, is whether we have reached or are reaching the point where conscientious citizens can no longer give moral assent to the existing regime."[83] The statement touched off a furor within the ranks of intellectual conservatism. Two months later, in the correspondence section of the January 1997 issue of the journal, several high-profile conservatives responded, including Bork himself, who wrote in a letter: "While I do not retract a word of my criticism of the judiciary's usurpation of democratic powers, I wish that my remarks had not been preceded by the Editors' suggestion that we may 'have reached or are reaching the point where conscientious citizens can no longer give moral assent to the existing regime.' My criticism of the courts was not intended to support any such proposition. The necessity for reform, even drastic reform, does not call the legitimacy of the entire American 'regime' into question."[84] Neoconservative scholar Gertrude Himmelfarb wrote a similar letter arguing that while judicial usurpation of democracy is a real problem, it in no way makes the U.S. government illegitimate. Even a tentative suggestion of illegitimacy went beyond "a proper mode of political discourse" in Himmelfarb's view. To make her position especially pointed, she resigned her position as a member of the *First Things* Editorial Board. Likewise, Walter Berns of the American Enterprise Institute also resigned.[85]

On an issue as controversial as the *First Things* symposium, differences of opinion among SBC conservatives would be expected. Rogers had not read the articles himself, but after having the above quote from the introduction read to him, he responded, "That's dancing close to the flame." He also pointed out astutely, however, that the quote was a question. "I respond to it by saying that is a good question. I don't have an answer to it."[86]

Four months after its publication, Land recalled the response he had had when he originally read the issue: "Oh my soul, I wish they hadn't said that." His opposition was both substantive and political. Strategically, he feared that the statement would be used in two ways, both disadvantageous to conservatives. First, hostile forces on the left would use the editors' query to portray the right wing as radical and divided; and, second, pietistic evangelicals who often look for any reason to avoid active participation in politics would use the editors' statement as an excuse to withdraw from confrontation with the culture. Land, however, also disagreed substantively with the thrust of the *First Things* symposium, and he had made his case even before the articles appeared in print. Colson had sent him an advanced copy of his symposium essay. In response, Land expressed his reservations and urged Colson to find another way to make his point. The essay went even further in some ways than the editors' introduction in probing the question of whether the United States had reached a point where Christians should consider withdrawing their support. In contrast, Land believes that in America the threshold is very high regarding when Christians can consider resistance to the state. They must first exhaust every other avenue for addressing issues from within the existing system. Unlike the situation for the Confessing Synod of the Lutheran Church in Nazi Germany, to which Colson had alluded, American Christians in Land's view still have plenty of mechanisms through which citizens can address issues such as judicial usurpation of democracy. Land believed in 1997 that the situation was still far from justifying resistance or noncompliance of the kind being contemplated by Colson and the editors of *First Things*. For him, it was almost impossible to contemplate that the last option open to Christians was withdrawal of support from the government.[87]

Like Land, Paige Patterson also rejected the view of the *First Things* editors. Being much less the culture warrior than Land, Mohler, and many other SBC conservatives, Patterson opposed any suggestion that Christians should resist the government by force or withdraw their support. From his perspective, the Bible teaches that Christians are to support the government except where the state expressly violates God's command, and this simply has not happened.[88]

Mohler, by contrast, expressed a positive evaluation of the symposium, though his response was somewhat cautious. He characterized the editors' introduction as "the opening salvo. It is premature, but probably helpful." He stressed that those who made the argument were not fringe people and that there was coming soon a time for just such a consideration. From his perspective, this was an argument that the Religious Right would not have understood in 1979. Now, however, having witnessed the failure of electoral success to translate into conservative cultural change, the position of the *First Things* editors should start to make some sense.[89]

Similar to Mohler was Timothy George's response. Unwilling to say yes or no to the question of whether the United States had reached the point where Christians should withdraw support, he instead advocated an issue-by-issue analysis. Perhaps on some things Christians should and must at least consider civil disobedience. Like Land, he stressed that Americans still have means at their disposal for changing the system, but like Mohler he also agreed that the *First Things* symposium was helpful and appropriate and that Neuhaus and his colleagues had the better argument.[90]

This very limited sampling reveals some interesting groupings that may be significant. The populist preacher Adrian Rogers was not sure what to think about the symposium, owing in large part to the fact that he had not read it before hearing the quote in question during an interview. The intellectuals, Mohler and George, both believed that the question of withdrawal of allegiance to the U.S. government was worthy of consideration in the abstract way that it was presented in the symposium. The informed activist Land was most resistant to the presentation, understandably so. Unlike the detached intellectuals who have the luxury of considering these things in abstract form, Land must go to Washington and lobby for and against particular policies. For him, any question of withdrawing allegiance from the American government is an existential reality affecting the entire enterprise of the agency he oversees. He can scarcely afford to take radical-sounding positions if he hopes to make any headway with Congress in his attempts to amend the U.S. Constitution or help push through some piece of legislation. Still, none of the SBC conservative leaders are radical or sectarian in any social sense. They all have a huge stake in the maintenance of the culture they nevertheless perceive to be hostile to their way of doing religion. At most, some of them are willing to contemplate a day in the distant future when American Christians will have to say "no" to their government, but that day has not arrived.

Even so, the broad outlines of the viewpoints of all three groups are roughly the same. All share a perception that American culture is in decline from a formerly more moral, Judeo-Christian base, and that consequently the culture, and especially the government, have grown hostile to religion. Even though they are far from advocating revolution, Southern Baptist conservatives, unlike their moderate counterparts from the late nineteenth to the mid-twentieth centuries, are very uneasy about the culture in which they live and minister. Such uneasiness usually manifests itself in a range of issues (these will be taken up later). But the transition to evangelical culture warriors could be wrenching for the denomination, as it was for Southern Baptist Theological Seminary in the mid-1990s, when it moved first into mainstream evangelicalism and then into a more conservative position.

3
From *Christianity Today* to *World Magazine*

Southern Baptist Conservatives Take Their Stand in Louisville

The experience of conservative Southern Baptists with the broader evangelical world has been one of mixed success. There is indeed an evangelical constituency with whom they have found a welcome niche. The process of finding that niche, however, was fraught with difficulty and pain largely because SBC conservatives were often unaware of how diverse the evangelical world is. The belief on the part of some conservatives that the answer to the SBC theological drift to the left was an alignment with evangelicalism smashed up against two very important realities. First, when aligning with evangelicalism, one must decide which evangelicals to support. There are many varied groups that fall under the broad term "evangelical." Many are Calvinist, while others are Arminian. There are peace and justice evangelicals, some coming from Anabaptist backgrounds, others not. Some evangelicals are highly doctrinal, while more holiness elements retain a strong sense of revivalism and social conservatism; holiness evangelicals often avoid doctrinal disputes almost entirely. Some evangelicals are highly political, while others believe that personal, individual conversion and piety are far more important than efforts to transform culture through political engagement. Moreover, these variations do not even take into consideration the phenomena of fundamentalism, Pentecostalism, and the charismatic movements, all of which are part of what could be termed "evangelical" in the broadest sense.[1]

The second reality facing SBC conservatives had to do with their own diversity. While the Southern Baptist controversy was in full swing, it was quite easy to retain a working coalition of inerrantists who were united in their belief that a course correction was in order for the denomination. Beginning in the 1990s, there emerged two somewhat distinct visions of what SBC evangelicalism should look like. One was a mainstream version, the other was a more conservative and hard-line approach. While this produced tension in the movement, it by no means resulted in a deep division. It may well be that such diversity within the ranks indicated the maturing of the movement, not its potential demise. Still, the maturing process was not smooth, and nowhere would the effort to make the SBC more self-consciously evangelical be more problematic then at Southern Baptist Theological Seminary in Louisville, Kentucky.

Southern is the oldest and most venerated of the six Southern Baptist seminaries. Founded in 1859 in Greenville, South Carolina, under the leadership of James P. Boyce, the institution moved to Louisville in 1877. From its inception, the seminary has had a confession of faith that all faculty must sign. Called the Abstract of Principles, the confession was authored by Basil Manly Jr., who along with Boyce, John Broadus, and William Williams was one of the founding faculty. Historian H. Leon McBeth has characterized the seminary as having grown alongside the SBC in its early years when the school was essentially a society supported by the denomination. Over time, however, the SBC adopted it through charter changes that allowed the denomination to have authority in matters of funding and selection of trustees. In both its society phase and then as part of the SBC itself, Southern was considered a vital part of the denomination. The seminary's first four presidents—Boyce, John Broadus, William Whitsett, and Edgar Y. Mullins—are considered among the finest denominational statesmen and theologians the SBC has ever produced. Under their leadership Southern Seminary came to be the flagship school of the denomination, producing many of the elite leaders of the SBC, and to this day faculty members sign the same Abstract of Principles that Manly authored in 1859. Moreover, by the early years of the twentieth century, Southern had apparently become the largest seminary in the world, only later eclipsed by Southwestern Seminary in Fort Worth, Texas. Luminaries from the other prominent Protestant seminaries frequented Southern for lectures. When the school celebrated its jubilee anniversary in 1909, for example, professors from Vanderbilt University, Presbyterian Seminary of Louisville, the Divinity School at the University of Chicago, and Newton, Colgate, McMaster, Drew, Princeton, and Crozer Seminaries made presentations. Among those present from these schools were Shailer Mathews and A. H. Strong, two of the most prominent Baptist theologians of the era. From at least this time forward, Southern often had to endure charges that it was too liberal for Southern Baptists, this despite the fact that Mullins sought rather successfully to position the institution on the orthodox side of the fundamentalist-modernist controversy of the teens and twenties. Still, Southwestern Baptist Theological Seminary of Fort Worth was established in 1907 partly because its founder, B. H. Carroll, believed that Southern was too liberal.[2]

From the outset of the Southern Baptist controversy in 1979 and through to the 1990s, Southern passed through three stages. First, it was, as outlined above, a moderate Southern Baptist school generally viewed as the most prestigious and progressive of the six SBC seminaries, a bastion of moderate SBC intellectual sophistication. Second, beginning in the early 1990s, when conservatives became the majority on the Board of Trustees, Southern reached out to the mainstream evangelical world to recruit more conservative faculty members. This was in accordance with what was called the Covenant Renewal document between the seminary's faculty and trustees as well as the 1987 Glorietta Statement, in which the six SBC seminary presidents pledged to balance their faculties by adding additional conservative professors. This new vision was largely under the direction of the seminary's vice president and dean of the faculty, David Dockery. This mainstream, evangelical thrust, however, would be replaced by a much more conservative, even hard line, stance once Al Mohler became president in 1993.[3] Southern Seminary in the mid-1990s, therefore, can serve as a case study in the difficulty Southern Baptist conservatives encountered as they tried to find their evangelical voice. Granted, Southern experienced the worst-case scenario, but its was the most complete and swift transition to self-conscious evangelicalism of any Southern Baptist institution. Southern, therefore, provides the clearest picture of what this change entailed because the competing forces were so visibly and starkly opposed to one another. In addition, the diversity among SBC conservatives that sometimes goes undetected was magnified, making for easier analysis. With the exception of Southeastern Seminary in Wake Forest, North Carolina, the transition to SBC conservatism at the other schools has been much smoother than at Southern, though perhaps for that reason less self-conscious and not as thorough.

BRINGING EVANGELICALS ON BOARD AT SOUTHERN

By 1992 the conservatives held the majority on the Southern Seminary Board of Trustees. Roy Honeycutt was still the moderate president of the institution and was trying his best to work with the conservatives in order to fashion a compromise of some sort that would save the seminary from the sort of turmoil that had taken place at Southeastern a few years earlier. There, the moderate administration and the faculty got so crosswise with the conservatives on the board when they became the majority that the president retired and most of the professors left. Enrollment dropped by nearly half and an accrediting agency put the seminary on probation. Seeking to avoid such turmoil, Honeycutt and the faculty at Southern worked out an agreement in 1991 about how moderates and conservatives would coexist at the same institution. The resulting document was called the Covenant Renewal between Trustees, Faculty, and Administration. Article 4 states that the seminary, in an effort to achieve balance, would seek "conservative evangelical scholars" who would adhere to a very high view of Scripture. The statement on the Bible did not actually contain the word "inerrancy," but it did stipulate that "Scripture is true and reliable in all the matters it addresses, whatever the subject matter. Scripture in its entirety is free from all falsehood, fraud, or deceit." The new hiring policy amounted to affirmative action for evangelicals. This policy was to continue until the trustees, in consultation with the faculty and administration, determined that the seminary had achieved the desired balance.[4]

But what would balance look like, and how would all parties ever agree when it had been achieved? The Covenant Renewal states that the seminary should include views from across "the theological spectrum of our Baptist constituency," but how would moderates and conservatives agree on what the balance of the entire Baptist constituency was? Conservatives believed that the vast majority of Southern Baptists were conservative evangelicals. Paul Pressler routinely made the highly dubious claim that 90 percent of Southern Baptists agreed with the conservatives, at least on the issue of the Bible. For people like Pressler, therefore, a "balanced faculty" would be virtually all conservatives. This is, in fact, precisely what conservatives have sought to achieve, and they have been quite successful in the SBC's six theological seminaries.

The first high-profile conservative evangelical from outside the SBC to join the faculty at Southern was Timothy Weber, who had been at Conservative Baptist Seminary in Denver for more than fifteen years. Weber grew up in an independent evangelical church in California that was fundamentalist and dispensational premillennialist. One of his early memories was receiving a Scofield reference Bible, which was the preferred edition for fundamentalists. After an undergraduate degree at UCLA, Weber did his doctoral studies at the University of Chicago. While there he became a Baptist and joined a church of the Baptist General Conference, a denomination that grew out of Swedish Baptist origins. Having come out of a dispensational premillennialist setting, he became interested in this movement as an object of scholarship, which became the focus of his dissertation and first book. The book made Weber the recognized authority on dispensational premillennialism and launched a fine scholarly career.[5]

In the spring of 1992, while Weber was on the faculty at Denver Seminary, two Southern Seminary professors approached him at a meeting of the Association of Theological Schools. In an attempt to recruit Weber for the Southern faculty, they emphasized the seminary's resources and the fact that going there would give Weber the opportunity to train doctoral students. These preliminary discussions gave way to serious conversations with President Honeycutt and his new faculty dean, David Dockery. Southern needed to hire new professors who could somehow be collegial enough for the faculty and conservative enough for the trustees. Such scholars were almost certainly going to have to be people who had not been involved in the denominational controversy, and Baptist evangelicals from outside the SBC were most likely to fit such a profile. As Weber came to understand, he was being courted as "part of a new evangelical faculty . . . who had not been down and dirty in the Southern Baptist controversy."[6]

As the process formalized, Weber went to Louisville for an interview with a faculty search committee. The big issue for the faculty was not the inerrancy of scripture but the role and status of women in ministry, and this, Weber remembers, was the first question he faced. He told the committee that he fully supported women in ministry, including their ordination. There was an awkward silence, so Weber asked how his view would fit in at Southern. One member responded that all the faculty would probably agree with Weber, but none of the trustees would. When it came time for his interview with the trustees, they were interested primarily in his views of the Bible. Weber told the trustee committee that if allowed to define the term, he would describe himself as an inerrantist. In fact, he said that he had basically the same view of the Bible as Dockery, who had just published a book on biblical inspiration. Only near the end of the interview did someone ask Weber about his views of women in ministry. He gave the same answer he had when interviewing with the faculty search committee. The trustees were stunned, Weber later recalled. They could scarcely believe that someone who held Weber's generally conservative, evangelical beliefs could also support the ordination of women. Nevertheless, he earned unanimous approval from both the faculty search committee and the trustee committee. A recommendation that Southern hire him as a fully tenured chair in the church history department then went to the full Board of Trustees, where only five voted against Weber. (It appears that there were close to forty trustees present at the meeting.)

The trustees actually voted on Weber and four other prospective faculty members, all of whom held views on the ordination of women that were similar to Weber's. The appointment of these pro-women faculty resulted in a resolution by the trustees to the effect that approval of the five faculty members in no way signaled their support for the ordination of women. The vote on the resolution was 23–14.[7] Weber remembers reading later in the statewide Kentucky Baptist newspaper *Western Recorder* that one conservative trustee who had not been on the interview committee had exclaimed during the board meeting, "Why should we be hiring men who are 90 percent correct when there are men in this convention who are 100 percent correct."[8] Looking back, this sort of conservative dissatisfaction was a harbinger of things to come, a bad omen. Perhaps being an inerrantist evangelical would not be enough for the conservative trustees on Southern's board. This may have been the first time that some of them had any inkling that there was theological diversity among northern evangelicals. In hindsight, this incident also presaged that even Dockery's vision of a mainstream evangelical faculty was not going to be conservative enough for the trustees. Later events would seem to confirm this.

Another part of Weber's interview process revealed that trustees were not the only ones who believed that all northern evangelicals were equally conservative. Following the question on women in ministry, Weber recalls that someone on the faculty search committee asked him to describe himself theologically. Weber said that he was "an evangelical, but not a fundamentalist." The interviewer responded by saying that Weber would have to define his terms because "down here [in the South] we cannot tell the difference between an evangelical and a fundamentalist." As Weber remembers this encounter, he muses, "I knew I was not in Denver anymore."[9] Continuing this line of questioning, another committee member said that when he thought of an evangelical, he thought of Jerry Falwell or Bob Jones. Weber explained that where he came from, Falwell and Jones were considered fundamentalists, and evangelicals would never refer to themselves as fundamentalists. Weber recalls getting the distinct impression that Southern Baptist intellectuals were not well informed on these issues, which were very well defined in the North. He recognized that this was not the same kind of evangelical world he had known.[10]

While there were certainly moderate Southern Baptist scholars well acquainted with the evangelical world, Weber's experience shows that there were also many moderates who were not. Whatever moderates thought about evangelicals would be a moot point, however, once conservative Al Mohler became the new president of Southern Seminary. Moreover, his appointment would change things significantly for Weber and other northern evangelicals who had been recruited to the faculty. When Weber interviewed for the position at Southern, he was under the impression that Honeycutt would remain as president for at least five more years, but the president's plans changed rather dramatically as the board became increasingly conservative. Weber was appointed to the faculty in the spring of 1992, but unable to wrap up his duties in Denver until after the fall semester, he did not join the Southern faculty until January 1993. In between Weber's appointment and his arrival, Honeycutt announced his retirement, and Mohler would become president during Weber's first year in Louisville.

President Mohler was on the fast track to change, even faster than some trustees desired. After Honeycutt retired, the board's presidential search committee was made up of conservatives who generally wanted the seminary to move to the right judiciously and gradually. Above all else, they wanted to avoid a tumultuous transition. This being the case, the committee narrowed the list of candidates to three people—Richard Land, Timothy George, and Mohler—and then hired a consulting firm to conduct a personality test on each candidate to determine who might be best qualified to carry out a smooth transition over time. The test showed that Land was least likely to cause controversy, with George next in line. Mohler, the test determined, would be the most likely to move rapidly and, therefore, the most likely to destabilize the seminary and cause problems. The trustee search committee, however, believed that Land would be most likely to want immediate change given his ties with Paige Patterson and Paul Pressler. They thought that since Mohler had served as assistant to President Honeycutt, that relationship would facilitate a smooth transition. This was bolstered by Honeycutt's own support for Mohler. In short, the trustees refused to believe the findings of their own consulting firm. Obviously, even some who supported Mohler's vision would be surprised by how rapidly and radically he moved the seminary to the right.[11]

Observing the way in which Mohler swept the Southern campus by storm, Weber believes that the new president did in three years what should have taken ten, which is consistent with the view of many observers of the Southern situation. In 1996, for example, when *Christianity Today* named Mohler one of the top fifty evangelicals in America under the age of forty, the magazine's editors profiled his arrival at Southern by writing: "[Mohler] took the wheel, and made a strong turn to the right. The speed and velocity of that turn threw some faculty, staff, and students off-balance—a few were thrown overboard. Mohler, foot on the gas, never looked back."[12] The price for such rapid change was turmoil on the faculty. It took less than two years for Weber to realize that he would be unable to function at Southern Seminary under the new conservative president.

Mohler's arrival at Southern would result in something of a shift in hiring strategy. Under Honeycutt, Dockery had been assembling a faculty of what could be called mainstream, *Christianity Today* evangelicals. Mohler would seek professors who were even more conservative, people who could be called *World Magazine* evangelicals. While these two groups have much in common, they also have some rather deep differences and are often somewhat suspicious of each other. As one former Southern faculty member put it, the two different types of evangelicals "really don't have a lot in common. . . . The hardliners would say the centrists are just on their way to becoming liberals; they just haven't gotten there yet. And the centrists would say that the hardliners are on their way to being fundamentalists, or they're already there."[13] Mohler clearly sided with the hardliners and moved to make Southern Seminary a more conservative school than the one that had hired the likes of Weber. It is instructive that the same year that Mohler was hired at Southern, Mark Coppenger, who would soon become president of Midwestern Baptist Theological Seminary, accused *Christianity Today* of "going progressive" while commending *World Magazine* as "an excellent resource for Southern Baptists."[14] Moreover, Mohler wrote (and continues to write) frequent columns for *World Magazine*.

Mohler, on the one hand, disagrees with this assessment of Southern's transition to the right. "I don't think the trustees ever had in mind the sort of moderate evangelicalism that some faculty members envisioned."[15] On the other hand, he allows that there were faculty members and administrators who saw moderate or mainstream evangelicalism as a real possibility, and Dockery seems to have been one. Perhaps it can be said that if Southern appeared to be moving in the direction of moderate evangelicalism, it was because of a lack of a clear vision on the part of the trustees and because of Dockery's policies, not because anyone had officially decided that Southern would be mainstream or moderately evangelical like *Christianity Today*.[16] In other words, what transpired in the interim between the time the conservatives gained the majority on the Southern Board of Trustees and the time Mohler arrived on campus took place somewhat by default. Mohler's task, then, was to institute a more clearly defined vision, and his vision was not that of *Christianity Today*, which he viewed in 1999 as itself a collective of evangelical voices held together in a somewhat ill-defined tension. Mohler opines with a laugh, "You know Carl Henry is my mentor, so you can imagine the *Christianity Today* I like . . . and where I see a golden era." In other words, he prefers the magazine of the 1950s and 1960s, when Henry served as its founding editor. Mohler states emphatically that the evangelicalism to be implemented at Southern was never intended, not by the trustees at least, to be of the moderate variety, which is how he would define that of *Christianity Today*. Southern Seminary's evangelicalism "is concerned that moderate evangelicalism has abdicated too much." If the seminary appeared to be moving toward moderate evangelicalism, as many of the new faculty believed it was, this was happening in the absence of a clearer vision from the top and not the result of a trustee vision that differed intentionally from Mohler's own. The most definitive statement a board of trustees can make about its vision is to hire a president, Mohler believes, and the Southern trustees hired Mohler.[17]

THE CARVER DEBACLE

The event that put Weber and other evangelicals on notice that the SBC was moving to the right of the mainstream was the firing of Diana Garland as dean of the seminary's Carver School of Social Work and the faculty-administration showdown that ensued. But this was hardly the beginning of the tension between Mohler and the holdover moderate faculty at Southern. In 1994 popular professor Molly Marshall had been driven from the seminary for alleged heresy concerning issues of a gender-inclusive understanding of God and universalism. No one is quite sure what the exact charges against Marshall would have been because the administration would not inform her prior to a hearing. Instead of facing such a hopeless situation with no way to prepare an adequate defense, Marshall resigned after having been informed that regardless of the hearing, Mohler and the conservatives on the Board of Trustees were determined to fire her.[18]

Practically on the heels of Marshall's ouster, the Carver School debacle unfolded. Southern was unique in that Carver was the only seminary-based school of social work in the nation that was fully accredited by the Council on Social Work Education. Moreover, founded in 1904, the social work program at Southern was one of the oldest of any kind in the country. In the spring of 1995, Garland needed to fill a faculty vacancy. She wanted to recommend David Sherwood, a northern evangelical from Gordon College in Wenham, Massachusetts. Sherwood met all the publicly stated theological and professional criteria for a position at Southern, and he certainly fit the seminary's emphasis on hiring evangelicals from outside the SBC controversy. Making the issue of hiring difficult, however, was a set of criteria that Mohler had put in place informally. Only the president, the deans, and possibly the Board of Trustees were aware of these new criteria, and the deans had been instructed not to share them with faculty or student search committees. Garland was hopeful that Sherwood could pass the mysterious Mohler test, but she also realized how rigorous the hiring process at Southern was becoming. She wrote in her personal journal, "If I can't get David Sherwood through this process, then there is no one." Both the student and faculty search committees unanimously approved Sherwood, and the candidate's initial interview with President Mohler seemed to go well. The trouble came when Mohler asked Sherwood to submit in writing a detailed theological statement. Among the questions Sherwood was instructed to address were Mohler's new and still unofficial criteria, specifically the issues of abortion, homosexuality, the uniqueness of the gospel in a pluralistic world, the role of women in ministry, and the inspiration of Scripture. After receiving Sherwood's written response, Mohler informed Dean Garland that the candidate was unacceptable based on his view of women in ministry.[19]

This left Garland with a dilemma of not only having to drop Sherwood from the process but also being unable to reveal her reasons, since those reasons had to do with Mohler's criteria, which were not public at that time. Complicating matters was the fact that the School of Social Work's accreditation would be jeopardized if the faculty slot went unfilled for an extended period of time. Garland eventually decided that she had no choice but to go public with the fact that the president had used his own personal standards to deny Sherwood and with her belief that she would be unable to find another candidate who could pass Mohler's rigorous test of conservative evangelical orthodoxy. She made this announcement to students and faculty on March 20, 1995. In a meeting two hours later, Mohler asked for Garland's resignation. She told the president that she would be back in touch, and Mohler told the local newspaper that Garland had resigned. The result of this misunderstanding was that the local press at first reported that Garland had resigned, then the next day, after talking with her, the media reported that she had been fired. Mohler insists that he had understood her to have accepted his demand that she resign during their meeting on March 20, while Garland continues to believe she was fired.[20] Given that there is such a fine line between being asked to resign and being fired, it does seem fair to say that Garland was fired.

The dismissal of Garland as dean grew into a major story among Southern Baptists. It rocked Southern Seminary's faculty and led eventually to the closure of the Carver School of Social Work, a tacit confirmation of Garland's view that the program would be unable to function under the restrictive theological conditions that Mohler and the trustees created. While claiming to have no agenda to eliminate Carver, Mohler had from the beginning of his tenure as president harbored deep concerns about the viability of a school of social work in a theological seminary. The ethic of social work as he understood it "is committed to a worldview and a principle of moral neutrality and non-judgmentalism. When it comes to the church and moral issues, there is no way that I could see that being consonant with the responsibility of the church and the responsibility of a seminary. . . . I believe there are Christians in social work, there are Christian social workers, and there are Christians who support social work. The question was how that could be incorporated here [at Southern]." Even with such doubts, Mohler tried to make the situation work. Prior to the events leading to Garland's termination, there had been a denomination-wide theological education study committee that questioned whether the SBC should continue to fund the Carver program, and Mohler had argued in favor of continuation. For these reasons, at least, Mohler says, "I did not see the issue coming in 1995."[21]

The situation became very significant for Weber and the other evangelicals who had been brought onto the faculty from outside the SBC. Sherwood had been eliminated from consideration precisely because of his views on women in ministry, and his views were identical to Weber's. Garland's dismissal and Sherwood's denied appointment made it clear to Weber that there was no future for him at Southern. He had been brought in as a tenured professor, so he could not be fired for his views on women, but, as he learned, there are other ways to get rid of people the seminary administration did not want around. Mohler had made the women's issue a litmus test for faculty hiring and promotion. That requirement was destined to wipe out two years of recruitment of evangelicals because most of those already hired did not agree with Mohler.[22]

A faculty uproar ensued over Garland's firing and Mohler's handling of it. March 22, 1995, is remembered by those involved as "Black Wednesday." There is a common consensus that the faculty meeting that day was the seminary's darkest day in memory. More than four years later, Mohler himself would say, "There is no doubt; that was the most difficult day I ever experienced, no doubt."[23] On Black Wednesday, Weber decided to take a public stand and in so doing became one of the central figures in the entire drama. The professor later recalled the situation at that explosive meeting just two days after Garland's firing: "I pointed out to [Mohler] that I was elected to the faculty as a full professor in an endowed chair, given tenure. My face was promoted in PR material all over the place. Now, a year and a half later, 'are you telling me that my views on women in ministry, which were perfectly acceptable then and got me all that stuff, are unacceptable today? Could I be hired today?' Mohler answered, 'No!' . . . I pushed him on that. I knew what he would say, but I thought it was very important for everyone else to know that." Weber went home and told his wife, "I'm out of here. It may take one year or it may take ten, but I'm leaving."[24] Weber summarized his views in a statement to the press: "The great middle space occupied by most evangelical seminaries today allows for flex on this issue of women in ministry. Trinity Evangelical, Gordon-Conwell, Bethel and Denver [Seminaries] all have faculties that have agreed to disagree. . . . But the current criteria push Southern Seminary toward the far right. We're not even in the mainstream of evangelical seminaries anymore."[25]

Sherwood himself was from Gordon College, which has been closely associated historically with Gordon-Conwell Seminary. Privately, the former candidate expressed the same views to Mohler that Weber had made publicly. "It seems to me," Sherwood wrote in a letter to the president, "that if the circle of acceptable diversity of biblical interpretation is going to be drawn so narrowly regarding matters of opinion and conscientious difference among Bible-believing Christians that such a statement as mine is unacceptable, then it is likely that the Seminary in all its parts, including the Carver School of church Social Work, is going to have a very difficult time finding and keeping faculty members of competence and integrity." Sherwood told Mohler that he had expected the president "would find my statement to be thoroughly biblical, evangelical, and Baptist" and told Baptist reporters that Mohler's hard-line stance on this issue was "very unusual" among evangelicals.[26]

Weber's views of Mohler's handling of these events were widely shared on the Southern faculty, as evidenced by a resolution in Garland's behalf, which read in part, "[A]s a faculty we do deeply grieve the termination of Dr. Diana Garland as Dean, and offer her and her family our deepest affirmation with regrets over what we believe to be a premature ending of an exemplary tenure as Dean of the Carver School."[27] In a separate report the faculty lambasted the fact "that the President failed clearly to communicate what he understood to be the true parameters of employment at the seminary for a period of two years." Moreover, the faculty found it "unconscionable that he communicated his rejection of both tenured and nontenured faculty in such a callous manner."[28]

Mohler's views are different, of course. From his perspective, Garland's decision to go public was an act of desperation done in hopes that public pressure would force the president to make a different decision. Like the faculty, however, Mohler recognizes Black Wednesday as a defining moment in the seminary's history. "That faculty meeting was officially about the Carver School, but in reality it was about the whole picture. . . . It was apparent then that the transition at Southern Seminary could not be handled in a way that could avoid head-to-head, open, institutional conflict. Hopes for bringing about a more orderly, less traumatic, more strategic, less conflicted transition were then gone because at that moment the faculty was absolutely hardened in its insistence that it would not abide these new policies." Mohler recognized that it was not primarily the old-line moderate faculty who opposed him. Rather, the new conservatives brought in under the Covenant Renewal, Weber among them, took the lead. "I was disappointed at how opposed they were," Mohler recalls of the evangelicals.[29]

Weber and Carey Newman, another new evangelical faculty member, met with the chairman of the Board of Trustees, Rick White, some days later to discuss the Garland matter. They told White that Mohler had to be removed, that the new president was giving evangelicalism a bad name on the campus, even among the evangelicals themselves. Weber advocated bringing in Dockery as president to hold things together. Both Weber and Newman remember White being grieved that two people he trusted and believed in were so upset by what had happened. With tears running down his face, White told them this was not what was suppose to happen.[30]

Within a week of his meeting with Weber and Newman, however, White published an open letter to Kentucky Baptists in the *Western Recorder*. The letter fully supported Mohler's firing of Garland, explaining that she had indeed made public an internal matter between herself and the president. "If you are a layperson who manages a business," White wrote, "you could not allow one of your managers to publicly advocate positions in conflict with yours and to encourage employees to pressure you to change." What especially galled Weber about this statement was that White injected the issues of racism and homosexuality into the conversation. By way of analogy, the chairman pointed out that while women in ministry is not mentioned in the seminary's basic faith statement, the Abstract of Principles, neither are racism or homosexuality, yet he would expect that Mohler would not hire a racist or a homosexual. Then, White continued, "There are those within the secular culture and even a few within our own denomination who do not want Southern Seminary to stand for biblical moral values and conservative theological positions. They have rightly perceived Dr. Mohler as one who opposes their efforts to transform our culture, and have attacked him at every opportunity for his faithful adherence to the values many of us hold sacred."[31]

Weber has called White's argument "a crock of nonsense." White's letter was pure propaganda aimed at making it look as if Mohler were saving the seminary from homosexuals and racists, the scholar argues. He even speculates that the article may have been written, or at least brainstormed, in the seminary's public relations office. Likewise, Newman saw this as the beginning of what would become a consistent linkage between the issues of women in ministry and homosexuality.[32] This letter, coming within a week of White's tearful meeting with Weber and Newman, led Weber to believe that "They [the conservatives had] turned him in four days" and persuaded him that the board had to rally behind Mohler. After Easter break, Weber remembers, the trustees "lowered the boom" with new hiring guidelines and new disciplinary procedures. "It was over," Weber remembers thinking.[33] At that April board meeting the trustees codified Mohler's hiring guidelines, basically stating that Southern would no longer hire or tenure any faculty members who supported women as pastors. At least one Southern student, who like Weber had come to the seminary from northern evangelicalism, echoed the professor and Newman's view that Mohler was moving to the right of the evangelical mainstream. Steve Hills from Abingdon, Illinois, had come to Southern because he liked the new evangelical emphasis. After Garland's firing he was quoted as saying, "There are a lot of us who came in like that and are now discouraged." Like Weber, Hills believed that the evangelical world was large enough to tolerate diversity on issues such as women in ministry.[34] Even so, Mohler had the support of all but a few on the Southern Board of Trustees and could thereby weather the storm. As for Weber, he was through with Southern, though it took him a little more than a year to find another position. In the fall of 1996 he became vice president for academic affairs and dean of the faculty at Northern Baptist Theological Seminary in the Chicago area.

OTHER NORTHERN EVANGELICALS AT SOUTHERN

In addition to Timothy Weber, some of the other northern evangelicals brought to Southern also found that they did not fit well at the institution as it moved to the right. Their experiences also showcase how difficult Southern's transition was. David Sherwood, the person caught in the middle of the Carver School situation, had grown up in the Churches of Christ in Ohio and Indiana before taking a bachelors degree at David Lipscomb University in Nashville, a Church of Christ college. He went on to earn a masters degree in Social Work at Bryn Mawr and then received his doctorate from the University of Texas while on leave from an academic position at Oral Roberts University, where he taught from 1975 to 1985 before joining Gordon College. Virtually all of Sherwood's career as a social work professor had been in a Christian setting. He had developed either social work majors or concentrations at both Oral Roberts and Gordon.[35]

In the early 1970s Sherwood became a member of the North American Association of Christians in Social Work, eventually sat on the board, and finally became editor of the group's journal, *Social Work and Christianity*. In the early 1980s he received a manuscript from Diana Garland, his first contact with her. Later, she too joined the board of the North American Association, and the two became friends as well as colleagues. Garland began to recruit Sherwood for the Carver School long before he would actually agree to come. Arriving on campus as a visiting professor at Carver in the summer of 1990, Sherwood sensed just how polarized the SBC was becoming. He experienced firsthand the level of suspicion that existed at the seminary when students were not sure if he could be trusted. Sherwood believed that being an evangelical with an appointment at Gordon College led some moderate students to wonder if perhaps he had been planted by the conservatives. Concluding that this was not his fight, he turned down Garland about the possibility of ongoing employment at the seminary at that time.

When the dean called Sherwood early in the spring semester of 1995, however, he was willing to listen. His wife, Carol, encouraged him to carefully consider Southern and eventually even went with him to Louisville for the interview process. Explaining his change of attitude toward the seminary in 1995, Sherwood says: "I think God was in it. The Holy Spirit was in it somehow. It seems in retrospect a funny thing to say, but I think that's correct."[36] Sherwood would have agreed with Garland that if he could not get through the process at Southern, there would be no one in the social work field who could. He was conservative theologically and one who avoided conflict. Personally, he exudes an air of calm to such an extent it is almost impossible to imagine him embroiled in controversy.[37] Like Weber, he was coming from outside the SBC conflict and would carry no baggage. He seemed the least likely person to become a central figure in an institutional firestorm.

After Garland called to tell him that Mohler had rejected his candidacy, Sherwood over the course of the next month lived out the very strange experience of, on the one hand, being the reason that Southern was thrown into turmoil while, on the other, having really nothing to do with the situation in Louisville. He even experienced a mild case of "survivors guilt." "It wasn't costing me that much but it was costing a lot of people from Al Mohler on down tremendously. . . . Everyone was paying a huge toll for this." Four years after the event, with voice cracking and tears welling up in his eyes, he recalled experiencing profound sorrow upon hearing that Garland had been fired. "This didn't have to happen. It could have gone a different way, a better way." In reflecting on how things could have gone so wrong in a process he initially believed was being led by God, Sherwood could only muse, "Even good people have mixed motives and make unwise choices. . . . I'm not willing to demonize Al Mohler. . . . I want to believe that people were acting conscientiously as they believed that God was leading them to act, as I believe I was and that Diana was. . . . But I think things could have gone differently at Southern and that it could have been good."[38] Concerning the whole experiment to bring mainstream evangelicals to the seminary, Sherwood's statement has been echoed even by some in the conservative movement; "It could have worked," some of them say.

Clearly, Mohler and some other SBC conservatives were suspicious of the entire social work profession and believed it difficult if not impossible to reconcile its high level of tolerance with evangelical faith. This is especially true on the issue of homosexuality. Sherwood believes that he could have been one of Mohler's strongest allies in combating the secularist elements within the profession. He acknowledges that there are people in social work who say one must be totally gay affirmative in order to do honest, professional work. "I have to oppose them because that is not allowing for religious diversity," he argues. "It is imposing values."[39] Sherwood sees himself as someone who takes a stand against the secularist agenda and is, therefore, much like Al Mohler and other SBC conservatives. Operating within a somewhat hostile professional culture, he insists that Christians have the right to integrate their faith with their work in the same way a feminist or Marxist can. He even differentiated his approach from that of the program at Baylor University, where historically the professional aspects of social work and the religious elements of the university have been kept somewhat separate. Sherwood, by contrast to even Baylor, had always sought greater integration of faith and professional life and believed that Carver was uniquely poised to continue that sort of mission, proving that Christians need not knuckle under to secularist agendas. He acknowledges that at one level SBC conservatives did have something to fear from the social work profession, but he also believes that Carver had staked out a niche in combating its most secular elements and that the attempt to continue that battle was a better and more faithful Christian response than to dissolve the Carver School. Although Mohler and other SBC conservatives were rightly wary, Sherwood believes, they were wrong in believing that the profession could not be harmonized with evangelical faith. Ironically, after a stint at Roberts Wesleyan University, Sherwood landed at Baylor after Garland had also gone there to become dean of a new school of social work and to develop a graduate program in the subject.

Like Sherwood, Janet Furness Spressart also came to the Carver School of Social Work from a northern evangelical background, but she arrived a year before the debacle and stayed a year after the Sherwood-Garland controversy. In fact, she would serve as acting dean of Carver after Garland's dismissal and so has the distinction of being the program's last administrator. Spressart was attractive to Southern because of her impeccable evangelical credentials within the field of social work. She even had fundamentalism in her background, having taken her undergraduate degree from the Philadelphia College of the Bible, where her father had developed the first social work program in a Bible college setting.[40] This served her well when she interviewed for a three-year contract appointment and the associate dean's position in 1994. She believes that Mohler assumed she was more conservative than she was because of her fundamentalist background. Actually, Spressart had been moving away from some of the positions she had grown up with, especially on the issue of women in ministry. She had even switched from the Conservative Baptist denomination to the Evangelical Covenant Church because the latter was more open to women. Oddly, Mohler never asked her about women in ministry when she interviewed one year before Sherwood.

Whatever awareness Spressart had about the growing tension at Southern was overwhelmed by the chance to teach Christian social work. She had served in a variety of professional settings, both Christian and secular, but for many years had harbored a deep desire to teach. The Carver School seemed a perfect fit when Garland recruited her during the 1993–94 school year. Not only was it the right place, but Spressart also believed that she was right for the school. Like Sherwood, she was solidly evangelical with no allegiances in the SBC controversy. She found, however, that when she arrived at Southern she was viewed by some moderates as one of "Al's gals," especially when theologian Molly Marshall squared off with the president and was driven from the seminary. In other words, she was seen as one of those brought in by Mohler and the conservatives to make Southern more explicitly evangelical. She also learned quickly that not everyone had the same view of evangelicalism as herself. When asked in 1999 if she felt hostility from moderates toward her when she arrived at Southern, Spressart responded, "Yes." The odd thing was that she had been moving in a more moderate direction before arriving and was, as would become clear during the Carver turmoil, more like the moderates than she was like conservatives such as Mohler.

Even so, Spressart was comfortable with the term "evangelical," whereas many moderates at Southern were not. Sitting at a table with some of the moderate professors at her first faculty retreat, Spressart made a positive reference to evangelicals. She recalls strong reactions to this. The general thrust of the conversation that ensued was that evangelicalism was destroying the seminary and the careers of some of the closest friends of those sitting around that table. Spressart reflected later, "I felt like I had called them fundamentalists," which, as Weber had learned during his initial faculty interview, is how some moderates perceived evangelicals.[41] Spressart never felt any hostility directed at her personally. Rather, it was a matter of general resistance to evangelicalism as it was perceived by some moderate faculty. The fact that Spressart was self-consciously evangelical put distance between herself and many moderates. Though she lived just down the street from two moderate faculty members, one of them a colleague in the Carver School, it was very difficult to get to know them, she says, because of the pain and grief they were experiencing and the perception, in some cases accurate, that it was the result of evangelicalism as manifested in the SBC conservative movement. Needless to say, Spressart received quite an education about the relationship between Southern Baptists and northern evangelicals before she ever stepped into a classroom for her first semester on the faculty. Having moved to Louisville believing that she could serve the Southern Baptist, evangelical, and ecumenical communities, she would find that relating to all three constituencies at the same time would become almost impossible at Southern.

Spressart was in her second semester at the Carver School when the Sherwood situation and the firing of Garland took place. As associate dean she had been part of the process that had brought in Sherwood for an interview. Like Garland, she was sure that he would come onto the faculty at Southern. "The failure of that process to succeed was astounding," she would say in retrospect. She recalls the meeting where Garland informed the social work faculty that Mohler had rejected Sherwood's candidacy. "I had a physical reaction. . . . It was an enormously traumatic thing for me."[42] She recalls putting her head on the shoulder of another professor-colleague at that meeting. A few weeks later at the Black Wednesday faculty meeting, Spressart was still numb, even though Garland's firing was something she had been expecting once the dean decided to publicly challenge the president.

Spressart believed her days at Southern were also numbered. "I knew on March 22 that my tenure as faculty at Southern Seminary was to be brief, if only because my position was already on record as having supported women in pulpit leadership."[43] When Mohler made it clear at that meeting that Weber would not have been hired had the new policy been in place in 1992, Spressart believed that she had no chance of staying there during the Mohler era. The subsequent Board of Trustees policy change that adopted the president's views seemed to close the door all the more fully. To her surprise, however, Spressart was not only offered another contract but was also named interim dean of the School of Social Work. She agreed to carry out the functions of the office for the duration of the spring 1995 term but would not occupy the office or actually take the title of dean until the following fall. "This was my way of saying that I don't support the administration in the firing of Diana [Garland]."[44] At graduation she declined to sit with the administrators. "I would not walk where the deans walked, and I would not sit where the deans sat." Instead, she sat with the faculty, came forward to read the names of that year's Carver graduates, then returned to her seat. This was her gesture to show opposition to what had transpired that spring. Even while accepting the interim dean post, she knew she would be at Southern only one more year and sensed early that the Carver School would not exist at Southern for much longer. In November 1995 she signed a contract at Roberts Wesleyan College, where she began teaching the following fall. Roberts Wesleyan would also take Sherwood onto its faculty as well as former Carver professor Timothy Johnson, who had left Southern before the debacle. Southern's loss became Roberts Wesleyan's gain as the Free Methodist college in Rochester, New York, assembled its own evangelical social work faculty.

What puzzled Spressart was that she was offered continued, though not tenure-track, employment at Southern, while others who were lifelong Southern Baptists with long tenure at the school were not offered renewed contracts. As she wrote some months later, "[My offer] calls into question why professionals from other schools [within the seminary], colleagues of mine, will not be offered renewed contracts, professionals who have been Southern Baptist all their lives and whose history with Southern Seminary spans many years."[45] David Dockery invited her to remain on the faculty, even after it became apparent that the Carver School of Social Work would close, as head of the Community Ministry Program. Spressart declined and would say later that the situation was a little like asking a surgeon to join a hospital, closing the hospital, and then asking the surgeon to teach first aid. Still, she found it fascinating, indeed incomprehensible, that she was welcome to stay, while genuine, lifelong Southern Baptists were being forced out. "I couldn't understand. It reflects some of my naiveté as to what was going on and the history of Southern Baptists, obviously." She could scarcely believe that Southern Baptists could be so brutal to one another. In looking back four years later at all that had transpired at Southern in 1995, Spressart still believed that she had been called by God to join the faculty of the Carver School of Social Work. That situation needed someone objective to come in and do what needed to be done for the students trying to graduate before the Carver School closed. "It happened to be me," she said. "I believe I was called there. I didn't know why I was called there, but I do now."[46]

MAINSTREAM EVANGELICALS WITHIN THE SBC

The reference to Mohler's "callous" managerial style in the resolution of support for Garland became significant for many of the mainstream evangelicals that Dockery had recruited. At the time of the Carver School debacle, ethics professor David Gushee was already finding it difficult to toe the conservative line on social issues other than abortion and homosexuality. Even after drafting an SBC statement on the killing of abortion doctors in 1994 and playing a role in a racial reconciliation resolution of 1995, he was never quite sure he was fully on the SBC conservative team. His experience at Southern convinced him that he could not be.

Gushee grew up Roman Catholic in Virginia, but in his own words, "It never took." In fact, he actually appreciates the Catholic faith more today than he ever did when he was being reared in it. At the age of sixteen he experienced a conversion in a conservative SBC church and joined shortly thereafter. He attended the College of William and Mary and then Southern Seminary, where he received his masters of divinity degree in 1987. Gushee attended Southern during what he calls the height of the moderate counterattack; the middle to late 1980s represented the moderates' last gasp in Louisville before the conservatives took charge. Moderate ethicist Glenn Stassen was a close mentor, and under his tutelage Gushee fell in love with the study of Christian ethics. Feeling the need to get out of the Southern Baptist environment, Gushee pursued his doctorate at the prestigious and liberal Union Seminary in New York, from which he graduated in 1993. Like many of the conservative leaders discussed earlier, Gushee had left southern culture during his graduate student years and studied outside the Southern Baptist context. He saw theological liberalism up close and found it to be a dry well.

Like the others, Gushee also experienced northern evangelicalism during his graduate years, though it was not the northern neoevangelicalism of Francis Schaeffer and Carl Henry. Rather, he worked three years fulltime at Evangelicals for Social Action (ESA) in Philadelphia. Founded by Ronald Sider, ESA continues to represent a major voice on the evangelical left. While maintaining a full theological orthodoxy, the organization takes on issues of hunger, poverty, racial injustice, and the environment with much the same energy that SBC conservatives exhibit on abortion. Yet Sider and ESA also adhere to what is sometimes referred to as the "seamless garment" human-life ethic that affirms a pro-life stance on issues of abortion, war and peace, and capital punishment. Gushee found that the seamless garment approach dovetailed nicely with the Roman Catholic consistent-life ethic as articulated by Pope John Paul II and Cardinal Joseph Bernardin. In adopting that ethic, Gushee was able to integrate elements from his own Roman Catholic upbringing with his mature thought as a Baptist ethicist.[47]

With the exception of abortion and race, it would be hard to find issues on which ESA agreed with Richard Land and the Ethics and Religious Commission of the SBC. Still, because of his pro-life stance on abortion, basic theological conservatism, and previous training at Southern Seminary, Gushee was an attractive candidate for an ethics position during the years when Dockery was recruiting an evangelical faculty. The dean called Gushee during the spring of 1993, when ethicist Paul Simmons was being forced out at Southern, and Gushee went to Louisville for an interview. Coincidently, the announcement of Mohler's selection as the new seminary president came while Gushee was on campus interviewing, and he recalls the sense of gloom that set in almost immediately among some on the faculty members. He was hired and assumed his duties at Southern in the fall of 1993; thus he had been on the faculty a little less than two years when the Carver School crisis erupted.

Although it was the Carver incident that would convince him that his dream of bringing a new kind of evangelical, ethical vision to the seminary could not be realized, Gushee was troubled first by the treatment of other faculty members. When Molly Marshall was forced out of the School of Theology, Gushee was deeply affected. She had been his theology professor when he was a student and was now a colleague. While not unaware of the theological issues at stake in her contest with Mohler and the conservative Southern trustees, Gushee could never quite bring himself to support the sort of purge that intensified after Mohler arrived on campus. Gushee believes that while theology is important, so are human considerations such as friendship, loyalty, and concern for the careers and dreams of those whom the conservatives were finding theologically unacceptable.[48]

Already experiencing some low-level disillusionment, the firing of Diana Garland and the dismantling of the Carver School sealed Gushee's sense that something had gone wrong with the SBC conservative movement as it was being manifested at Southern. He recalls: "You could feel [the pain] oozing out of the walls, especially after 1995. . . . [There was] a sense that injustices were being done to people in the name of a theological vision and a sense that the boundaries were just constricting tighter and tighter all the time. It seemed as if that process was never going to stop."[49] While the Carver School debacle was at its height in April 1995, Gushee preached a sermon at a meeting of American Baptists entitled "The Tragedy of Christian Lovelessness," in which he testified that he knew firsthand this tragedy.[50] Also during this time Gushee drafted an article that appeared two years later in the Evangelicals for Social Action magazine, *Prism*, which he at one time edited. In that piece Gushee wrote: "I have watched Christians reject one another (Rom. 15:7), judge one another (Rom. 14:10–15), think themselves better than others (Phil. 2:3), speak unkindly and unwholesomely of one another (Gal. 5:22; Eph. 4:29), love only those like themselves (Matt. 4:43–48), and cause one another to stumble (I Cor. 10:23). . . . Finally, I have lived through full-scale internecine Christian 'brawling' (Eph. 4:31), with accompanying slander, ruthlessness, heartlessness, rage, deceit and malice (Rom. 1:29, 31) resulting in the final destruction of Christian community."[51]

Like Weber and some others, Gushee decided to take a stand. During the Black Wednesday faculty meeting, he asked: "Dr. Mohler, imagine this headline in the *Louisville Courier-Journal* tomorrow. 'Mohler Restores Garland as Dean: The Two to Work Out their Difficulties.' Think about what that would say to the community. . . . Here's Christian people working out their difficulties. . . . It would be a great witness to the community and it would be very healing for us." Mohler responded that Gushee's question was frustrating. "The dignity of my office is at stake here," Gushee recalls Mohler saying. "I've already explained why I had to respond to the situation the way I did."[52]

Ironically, when Gushee had joined the faculty in 1993, he, like Spressart, had experienced hostility from some moderate professors who saw him as part of the regime that was in their view wrecking the seminary. Some of this hostility was personal. He recalls one professor in particular whose personality seemed to Gushee to be distorted by anger at everything that was happening. On one occasion, while skipping chapel and checking his mailbox, Gushee encountered this professor who said to him in derision, "I thought you fundamentalists never missed chapel."[53] This experience helped put into perspective some of the rage that had in part driven the SBC conservative movement. He came to believe that while he could not support the conservative movement as manifested at Southern, he could believe that conservatives really did harbor memories of mistreatment at the hands of moderate faculty. When Gushee attended conservative ethics consultations in Nashville, he would hear old war stories: "Back in 1963, when I was a student," various conservatives would say before relating how they had been embarrassed in class by a moderate professor because of their views. Gushee now believed those stories. Similarly, Carey Newman tells of a meeting with conservative trustee Jerry Johnson during the height of the crisis at Southern. Newman said to Johnson, when your side has all the cards and the other side has none, why gloat when you lay one down. Johnson's answer, "Because they did it to us."[54]

Both Weber and Gushee recall their impression that prior to the conservative takeover, Southern Seminary was a bastion of academic elitism and had a sense of status that was in the academics' view largely unfounded. There was "an inflated sense of the supposedly huge academic accomplishments of Southern Seminary," Gushee would say later. This sometimes resulted in an atmosphere where conservative students were put down and embarrassed by their professors. Both Weber and Gushee detected that at times there was an attitude of payback in the conservative movement and that the injustices conservatives felt they had experienced at the hands of moderates were often believable. From Gushee's perspective, moderate hostility toward him began to dissipate once Mohler arrived and it became clear that Gushee, Weber, and the others that Dockery had recruited were not fundamentalists. In fact, when Gushee finally decided to leave Southern a year after the Carver School incident, a moderate professor told him: "We had hope as long as people like you were coming. Now we know it's over."[55]

Having already realized that he was not a perfect fit among conservative social activists like Land and the Ethics and Religious Liberty Commission, Gushee's experiences at Southern convinced him even further that he could not be fully a part of the SBC conservative movement. Reflecting some years later, Gushee wrote of Southern Seminary: "I think it was that alien spirit, that spirit of lovelessness, that most shook me during my days at Southern. I knew that this was simply not 'of God.' It felt as if the Spirit of God had fled the place, and I knew that if the Spirit of God had fled, I did not want to be far behind."[56] In the fall of 1995 he began to look for other positions. When David Dockery became president of Union University, a Baptist college in Jackson, Tennessee, he invited Gushee to come along as a professor on the faculty there, which he did the following year. As a measure of the kind of young talent that Southern was driving off in the mid-1990s, it is worth noting that Gushee's career has flourished significantly in its post-Southern manifestation. He was even listed, along with Mohler, on *Christianity Today's* "Fifty Up-and-Comers" list. In all, six former Southern faculty members ended up at Union, where Dockery continued to assemble the sort of mainstream evangelical faculty he had originally envisioned for Southern.[57]

Gushee's experience at Southern also resulted in his reflection on the way evangelicals engage in cultural warfare. In the same article where he lamented lovelessness among Christians, he also critiqued their political engagement. In doing so, he turned one of the SBC conservatives' favorite theologians against them, writing, "Forty-nine years ago, the father of modern evangelicalism Carl F. H. Henry published his landmark book, *The Uneasy Conscience of Modern Fundamentalism.* In it, Henry lamented the belligerence and lovelessness of the fundamentalism of his day and issued a clarion call for an evangelicalism unwavering in its theological conviction, yet loving and peaceable. On the threshold of the fiftieth anniversary of that work, evangelicals appear to be in need of renewed reflection on Henry's warning." In that article Gushee argued that the same loveless spirit Christians often demonstrate in their relationships with each other is also made manifest in their public political pronouncements. In a critique that surely included the likes of Richard Land and other SBC culture warriors, Gushee charged: "Evangelicals have found a comfortable niche as part of the culture-war-fighting apparatus. . . . We 'blast,' 'target,' 'attack,' and 'assault.' How we love to whip up on homosexuals, pro-choicers, feminists, liberal environmentalists, and anyone associated with Bill Clinton."[58] Even as Gushee's public stance on certain issues has grown more conservative, he still finds un-Christian the way in which evangelicals too often carry out their politics. As he would reflect early in 2000, "Perhaps the key thing that sets me apart from the SBC conservatives is an irenic rather than combative approach to cultural engagement."[59]

Like Gushee, Carey Newman was also an evangelical with Southern Baptist roots who arrived at Southern during Dockery's tenure as dean and around the time Mohler became president. Having grown up in Clearwater, Florida, and taken an undergraduate degree in business at the University of South Florida, Newman earned his masters of divinity at Southwestern Seminary in Fort Worth, Texas, and his doctorate at Baylor under professor

Robert Sloan, who became president of the university in 1995. Along the way, Newman also took time off from doctoral work to achieve a masters of theology degree at the University of Aberdeen, Scotland. After completing his work at Baylor, Newman took a faculty position at Palm Beach Atlantic, a Baptist liberal arts college in Florida. He spent four years there, during which Dockery and Southern provost Larry McSwain began to recruit him to the seminary. Newman was wary and even turned down the overtures initially, but eventually he decided to join the faculty in the fall of 1993.[60]

Newman believes he was attractive to the new Southern for three reasons. First, he had a thoroughly and unimpeachably Baptist record. Even his family ties and especially his wife's family had a long history of service in the SBC. Second, he was achieving academic credentials beyond the Ph.D. degree as a publishing scholar, indeed an up-and-coming biblical scholar of some prominence. Third, he was in serious conversation with the wider evangelical world. He was without reservation an "evangelical Baptist scholar," and that was what Southern was looking for. As was the case with all the others brought on to Southern between 1991 and 1994 or so, Newman had the distinct impression that he was going to be part of the new evangelical faculty that Dockery was assembling.[61]

One of the complicating factors in Newman's going to Southern was that the presidential search was taking place while he was being recruited. Newman knew through the rumor mill who the candidates were and with his wife LeeAnn's input compiled two lists, one made up of those whom he thought he could serve under and another of those whom he thought he could not. Mohler was an in-between selection for Newman. He did not know much about him except for hearing of the candidate's intellectual prowess. When Mohler was named, Newman asked for impressions from people who knew Mohler, then concluded that things would probably be okay with the new president.[62]

When Newman arrived on campus in the fall of 1993, he generally felt welcomed. Unlike Gushee, who sensed some real hostility born of the fact that he was one of the new evangelicals, Newman felt only wariness on the part of the older, moderate holdovers. Aside from some bantering back and forth, he remembers, "I did not find anything out of the ordinary with regard to the faculty's treatment of me." The difference between Gushee's and Newman's early experiences at Southern may be a matter of perception. Both tell of confrontations with the same moderate professor, but Newman interprets the incident as friendly banter, while Gushee believed there was a real attempt to needle him personally. Newman pins the entire responsibility for what went wrong at the seminary squarely on the new president. As he recalled in 1999, his first impressions of Mohler were that he was "cold, distant, insecure, nonexistent—couldn't find him. He didn't show his face. That first fall he was a cipher, just wasn't around." Newman recalls that the new evangelical faculty, those sometimes called the "Covenant faculty" because of the Covenant Renewal terms, all reached out to Mohler and were either rebuffed or just ignored because the new president was essentially asocial. Dockery was in the middle between the faculty and Mohler, and he was able to put a human face on the pronouncements that came from the president's office.[63]

Newman believes that even many of the moderate faculty who had fought to keep the conservatives from coming to power were by 1993 ready to support the new president in the task of building a consensus seminary that would be more evangelical than before. They had fought the good fight, lost, and were ready to move on. Mohler, however, was not interested in a consensus seminary. He wanted total victory and had no desire to reach out to the older constituency. This began to dawn on Newman with the ousting of Molly Marshall and then the Carver School debacle.

Like Mohler and many others involved, Newman did not see the Carver crisis coming. He was in Dockery's office fifteen minutes after the meeting between Mohler and Garland that led to her firing. Dockery, Newman recalls, showed him a resignation letter that Newman thought was Garland's. When he looked more closely, he realized it was actually Dockery's own. "I thought Southern was coming unglued at that moment," Newman recalls. "One dean had been fired and one had resigned." (Dockery did not actually resign at that time.) He thought Mohler's presidency was in deep trouble. Newman recalls the Black Wednesday faculty meeting two days later. Concerning Mohler's announcement that from that time forward all hiring, tenure, and promotion would be based on the president's own criteria that included opposition to women in pulpit ministry, he states: "I can remember the words rolling off his lips and knowing that I was going to the full professor's meeting for tenure and promotion in two weeks. I just saw my career at Southern go up in flames. At least gaining tenure and promotion went up in flames."[64]

Newman believes that all the Covenant faculty felt betrayed at that moment. They had come onto the faculty under one set of guidelines and were now being told the rules were changing. Mohler was declaring that the

Covenant Renewal was dead. Newman grants that an institution has the right, indeed the obligation, to respond to its constituency. For the trustees to have gauged the will of Southern Baptists and to have voted that a particular view of women in ministry was to be a new litmus test for hiring faculty and administrators was fine. What rankles Newman was that Mohler, in his view, was retrofitting seminary policy and rewriting history. Mohler was insisting that opposition to women in senior pastor positions of leadership had always been the new administration's view, and Newman insists that this was not the case. He specifically asked about this during his own interview process back in 1993, which the president-elect attended, and was told that there was no required position on the issue of women in ministry. Even five years after the incident Newman challenges: "Show me a public statement, show me a press release, show me a position paper, show me a memorandum from your [Mohler's] office . . . , show me something scribbled on the back of a bar napkin that indicates that your position on women in ministry was a tenurable question, hiring question, a promotion question, when I was brought on, and I will publicly recant and apologize."[65] Furthermore, Newman argues, if opposition to women in pulpit ministry had always been Mohler's position, then things are even worse than otherwise believed because he brought people onto the faculty knowing they would never be tenured or promoted.

Mohler, however, defends his position by pointing out that back in 1991, when Timothy Weber and Jim Chancellor were hired, the trustees issued the resolution stating essentially that they were not completely satisfied with the two new faculty members' views on women and that their hiring should not be construed as seminary support for those views. Mohler interprets the statement as essentially saying that Weber and Chancellor would be the last two exceptions of hiring pro–women in ministry faculty. "What frustrates me," Mohler said in 1999, "is when people act as if they were surprised in 1995. I believe they have no honest possibility of surprise in 1995 on that issue because we had to deal with it from time to time in faculty searches between 1993 and 1995, and in no case did we do anything other than what we did in 1995." Mohler even claims that David Sherwood was not the first prospective faculty member rejected because of the women in ministry issue; one was even eliminated from consideration in the midst of the final interview process on the basis of the women's issue alone, and this was done with the full knowledge of the academic deans. As for the issue of tenuring faculty who had, in fact, snuck through the process, Mohler emphasizes that tenure at Southern is tantamount to a second hiring. The candidate goes through the entire interview process again. Nontenured people caught in the change were told they would have a chance to make their case during the tenure proceedings.[66]

This brings up an interesting question that Mohler cannot quite answer. Even if one grants that some faculty had been turned away prior to the Carver incident because of their views of women in ministry, there were others who made it through the process. Otherwise, there would be no need for giving them a chance to make their case anew on this issue before the trustees during the tenuring process. Even Mohler admits that what had been an informal administration stance became, as a result of the Carver incident, a formal policy, and the difference between the two is significant. As long as the issue was merely an administration preference, Mohler had every right under Southern's procedures to veto potential candidates; no candidate for the faculty at Southern goes before the trustees without the president's approval. The new trustee policy that resulted from the Carver incident, however, made the women's issue a tenure and promotion question, and that is what alienated the mainstream evangelicals whom Dockery had recruited. Mohler can argue that Weber and Chancellor were to be the last faculty brought on with deficient views, but that is simply not true—consider both Carey Newman and David Gushee. Mohler may want to say that no faculty had been hired since his inauguration with such views, but that is also untrue when one considers Janet Furness Spressart. The fact remains that there were people who were hired under one set of criteria, both before and after Mohler's inauguration, and then told they would be denied tenure according to another set of criteria. This is what shocked the new evangelical faculty and led to such a blistering condemnation of Mohler's actions. The most vocal and animated resistors to the president were the new evangelicals, the Covenant faculty brought on by Dockery.[67] In fact, the battle at Southern in 1995 was largely, almost exclusively, between the new evangelicals and the more conservative Mohler, with the trustees, of course, backing their president. This time it was not a struggle between conservative and moderate Southern Baptists. That battle had already been fought. Rather, this was between mainstream evangelicals and conservative evangelicals.

After a year on sabbatical, Newman began talking to Dockery about a possible buyout of what was left on Newman's original seven-year contract. In the spring of 1996 the parties reached an agreement. Still, Newman taught at Southern for two more years as a research professor before leaving for good in 1998.

Of all those interviewed for this book, only one had any inkling why Al Mohler thought the women's issue should have become a defining one for Southern Seminary in 1995—Mohler himself. He allows that the issue is not theologically definitive in the same way that some others are, and in explaining why it nevertheless became central at the seminary, he sounds like what Newman has called "The Firm." As Newman puts it, "The fundamentalists had interpreted the will of the body, The body had said, 'Change the seminaries.' They had gone through ten, fifteen years of votes, had stacked all the boards, stacked the process so they had everything in place, and now they're going to change." So far, so good, in Newman's view. But "when it came time to change, they did it in such a horrific and sub-Christian way that people who actually believed that change was needed could not sign on to it. This is where the Firm comes in. If you're really part of the Firm, you'll do it and keep your mouth shut."[68] In explaining why Southern made the women's issue so prominent, Mohler can only answer, "Advocating that women serve in the pulpit does not have the same theological value as denying the Trinity, but when you're hiring faculty members, we don't want to hire people simply because they advocate enough, but because they advocate and hold precious as much as we think ought to be requisite for service on this faculty."[69] This statement reveals nothing as to why women in ministry is important except that the seminary trustees and administration have decided it will be so. Mohler has acknowledged that the Bible does not make opposition to women in the pulpit nearly as important as some other issues, yet the Firm has decided to make it central anyway.

CONCLUSION

Certainly, there were many factors that played into the situation at Southern Seminary in the mid-1990s. Some were personal, some were institutional, and others were theological. Those most important for the present analysis have to do with how both conservative and moderate Southern Baptists viewed evangelicals. Much of what went wrong at Southern was related to these basic perceptions.

From Timothy Weber's perspective, the moderates who still dominated Southern when he arrived had little understanding of evangelicals. Certain faculty, Weber remembers, made comments about evangelicals in general that cut him. This is not to say that these faculty were liberals. While there were views at Southern that made Weber personally uncomfortable, he saw very little real theological liberalism. He found that even some on the Southern faculty who thought of themselves as liberals would have been conservatives by the standards of the University of Chicago at the time Weber did his doctoral studies there. "I think I know a liberal when I see one. I didn't find any liberals like [the University of Chicago] at Southern."[70] If there were liberals, Weber says, they were a strange kind, being church people who were Bible centered and believed that one must come to Jesus for salvation.

Although real liberals were hard to find, only a few people at Southern when Weber arrived were comfortable with the evangelical label. Weber believes this was largely because Southern Baptists had never had the sort of experience that fundamentalism in the North went through in order to get to the new evangelicalism that emerged after 1945. Weber recalls a day at Southern when he was teaching about the post–World War II rise of neo-evangelicalism. He put the names of evangelical thinkers, activists, and periodicals on the board only to become aware that his Southern Baptist students had never heard of any of them. Conversely, he knew also that if he had been in a class back at his Denver seminary and had put the names of Southern Baptist luminaries on the board, he would have witnessed a similar response. "There really are two stories here."[71]

But Weber is convinced that the conservatives who desired to make Southern seminary a more evangelical place also failed to fully understand evangelicals. Northern evangelicals who were brought on at Southern and elsewhere were satisfactory to the SBC administration in many respects but defective in others. It was as if these evangelicals all had slight perversions in their theology, such as Weber's own support for women in ministry, or different political views than SBC conservatives held. "Southern Baptist conservatives never quite got the package they were looking for when people like me were brought in," Weber recalls. "After Mohler got there, they stayed away from people like me."[72] David Sherwood's story typified this. He, like Weber, was an acceptable evangelical in every way save one—the ordination of women. The difference between the two professors was that Weber had arrived before Mohler's ascension, while Sherwood was a candidate during Mohler's early tenure. It appears that the initial experience of SBC conservatives with northern evangelicals like Weber and Sherwood failed largely because many conservatives were unaware of the diversity that exists in the northern evangelical world. Mohler understood that diversity and so narrowed the hiring parameters to assure that only those kinds of evangelicals SBC conservatives desired would get onto the faculty.

Analyzing the situation as both a historian of American evangelicalism and as a participant in the Southern Baptist controversy, Weber concluded that northern evangelicals and Southern Baptist conservatives often do not understand each other very well. Southern Baptist evangelicalism is different, primarily in that until recently Southern Baptists had a sense of control over their culture. Now, however, Southern Baptists feel like they are losing their culture. By contrast, northern evangelicals lost theirs a long time ago and have kind of figured out how to live with it. The South, in Weber's view, is still very supportive of evangelical causes, but it does not feel like this to some Southern Baptists. Southern Baptists, therefore, latch on to a certain kind of evangelical in the North and ignore the rest. Likewise, many northern evangelicals themselves fail to fully appreciate the diversity of their own theological heritage.[73]

While there is much to commend itself in Weber's analysis, there is one point on which he is mistaken, even if only slightly. Weber attributes SBC conservatives' lack of understanding to the fact that few of them had spent time outside the South. Actually, some of the most prominent SBC conservatives did live and study outside the South, and they forged their cultural views largely as a result of these nonsouthern experiences. Richard Land, Al Mohler, Timothy George, Mark Coppenger, and Paul Pressler all learned about the wider American culture by leaving the South, even if only temporarily. Still, Weber's basic impulse is correct in that these conservatives learned most of what they know about evangelicals from Carl Henry, Francis Schaeffer, and a few others from the most conservative and Reformed Protestant wing of northern evangelicalism. This being the case, they usually interpret the United States through the Henry-Schaeffer grid, which has its appeal largely because Henry and Schaeffer formed their basic cultural views during the first half of the twentieth century, when America was still in the process of losing its evangelical aura. The Southern Baptist conservative leaders studied here have in similar fashion formulated their cultural stance during the second half of the twentieth century, as the South has seen its evangelical foundation crack and crumble. Little wonder that they are so powerfully attracted to the Henry-Schaeffer critique of America. To them it makes much more sense than older notions of a southern Zion or present-day evangelical acceptance of the reality of living in a hostile culture. This process of becoming self-consciously evangelical with the attendant notions of living in a hostile culture would necessitate a reworking of the Baptist past, especially on the issue of religious liberty. It would be on this bedrock Baptist concern that SBC conservatives would begin to fight a culture war as they moved into the right wing of neoevangelicalism.

4
The Search for a Useable Past

Religious Liberty in a Hostile Culture

Discussions of Baptists and culture often begin with church-state religious liberty issues because Baptists have a record of being at the forefront of the insistence on freedom of worship. This has been their special interest, and in many ways they have succeeded in making a positive mark on American culture.

During the SBC controversy, when charges and countercharges were the order of the day, moderates attempted to portray conservatives as everything from Christian Rightists to Christian Reconstructionists. The gist of the charges was usually that conservatives had walked away from their Baptist heritage on matters of religious liberty and separation of church and state. While conservatives and moderates still stand on opposite sides of many issues when discussing the principles of the Baptist tradition, both sides claim the same turf. In short, both make a plausible claim to the Baptist heritage of religious liberty.

What Southern Baptist Conservatives Are Not

In discussing the conservatives it would be helpful to start with the negative —what they are not. There is a fairly widespread notion that the right wing of the SBC includes constituent members of the Christian Right. This is a plausible charge given that on nearly all the hot-button political issues of the 1980s and 1990s, conservatives did stand on the same side as groups like the Moral Majority and the Christian Coalition. Southern Baptist conservatives are self-professed culture warriors who accept James Davison Hunter's progressive and orthodox categories. In classing themselves on the orthodox side of the culture war, they usually walk in lockstep with the others on the right on a number of very visible cultural issues. It is, therefore, in part true that they are part of the Christian Right, but they also profess different principles on some issues, including matters of church and state.

SBC conservatives themselves characterize their relationship to the Christian Right as tactical and limited as opposed to wholehearted.[1] Moreover, they turn the argument around by pointing out that while many moderate Southern Baptists are on the same side of most church-state issues as the American Civil Liberties Union and other secularist groups, most of these moderates would not accept the notion that they are part of the liberal, secular left as represented by the ACLU. That they do differ from secularists in terms of moral and theological presuppositions shows the weakness of Hunter's culture war model, a weakness that he acknowledges.[2] Both parties in the SBC argue that their alliances with the right and left respectively are issue oriented, and some conservative leaders are on occasion quite critical of the Christian Coalition and other organizations usually lumped together as the Christian Right. Ethics and Religious Liberty Commission executive director Richard Land, for example, calls these groups "neo-establishment majoritarians" on church-state issues and argues that their positions violate Baptist principles.[3] Seminary dean Timothy George has said: "I think it's very important for Christians—evangelical, Bible-believing Christians—to keep significant distance from the politicized religious right. . . . The Republican Party is not the kingdom of God and neither is the Democratic Party." George feels very uneasy about the "cozy alliance" between evangelicalism and the political right. He believes that there are issues where moral convictions will draw evangelicals together with political conservatives, but many other issues of concern for conservatives are prudential in nature, such as the size of the federal budget or whether there should be a tax cut. Those are issues over which Bible-believing Christians can and do disagree. "Whenever we get too much alignment with this party or the other, I think we've sold out some of our spiritual heritage," George said in a 1998 interview. He is a political independent who as a Reformed theologian sees sin in all quarters, so much so that he suggests, only partly in jest, that Christians should vote their consciences and then repent.[4]

Still, there are certain events that give every appearance that SBC conservatives are constituents of the Christian Right and the Republican party apparatus. In March 1998, when several conservative Christian leaders met at Paul Weyrich's headquarters in New York to plan strategy, Land attended with Gary Bauer, James Dobson, and more than twenty other major figures of the Christian Right. *The New York Times* covered the meeting in a front-page article and quoted Land as saying: "The go-along, get-along strategy is dead. No more engagement. We want a wedding ring, we want a ceremony, we want a consummation of the marriage." Land was one of only three individuals at the Weyrich meeting quoted in the *Times* article, and he was quoted in two separate places. In addition to the above statement, he sounded very much like a Republican and Christian Right insider when he said, "It is time for candidates who will not only work with us but for candidates who are us."[5] Those familiar with Land's ability to command an audience will not be surprised that he garnered such notice from the *Times* reporter. But the fact is, he represents the largest Protestant constituency in the United States, and it is news when it appears that a major representative of such a group is contemplating a marriage with the Republican Party. Land does not always walk in lockstep with the Christian Right, but he likes to when he can and as a result sometimes leaves the impression that he is attempting to align the entire denomination with the Republicans.

Moderates were quick to seize on Land's statements. A coordinator for projects in the moderate Cooperative Baptist Fellowship wrote an article criticizing Land's participation in the New York meeting. The author wrote that "the notion of 'a wedding' with a specific political party makes me cringe. I can see Roger Williams, John Leland and George W. Truett doing back flips in their graves." He argued that whether it is SBC conservatives supporting the Republican Party or black Baptists supporting the Democrats, such actions violate historic denominational convictions and also diminish the church's ability to stand as a voice of conscience.[6] Land points out, however, that he is not nearly as partisan as the allegedly backflipping Leland, who presented Thomas Jefferson with a twelve-hundred-pound cheese as an inauguration gift after Jefferson's election as president in 1800. Leland and others of Cheshire, Massachusetts, were so ardently Jeffersonian Republican that they claimed no Federalist cows had contributed milk for the mammoth cheese.[7] Land and other conservatives find themselves under attack for aligning with the right wing of the Republican Party just as moderates at the Baptist Joint Committee (BJC) have to defend themselves for their tacit, issue-oriented alliances with the American Civil Liberties Union and other groups on the left.[8]

A second accusation made against conservatives is that they do not believe in the separation of church and state. The basis for this charge is usually W. A. Criswell's gaffe to Bob Schieffer on the *CBS Evening News* in 1984:

"I believe this notion of the separation of church and state was the figment of some infidel's imagination."[9] Moderates have made much of this statement, one of them claiming that "W. A. Criswell spoke clearly their doctrine when he suggested that separation of church and state is the product of the imagination of an infidel."[10] Whatever the venerable and enigmatic pastor meant by his statement, many conservative leaders reject it outright. Paige Patterson is most direct, saying, "This was not one of Criswell's finer hours."[11] Conservative former SBC president James Draper, still baffled by the remark, said in 1997, "I don't know where Criswell is coming from on that particular statement." If anyone ought to be able to decipher Criswell's remarks, it should be Draper or Patterson. Both served tenures as subordinates of the conservative patriarch, Draper as associate pastor and Patterson as head of the Criswell Bible Institute. Serving with Criswell, however, is no guarantee that one will necessarily agree with him. Draper says that his learning from the minister was mostly negative—how not to run a church—and that once in a head pastorate of his own, he chose a very different style.[12] Indeed, of all the conservatives among SBC leaders, Draper may be the most moderate. His presidency in the early 1980s was the least contentious of any during the controversy as he attempted consciously to bridge the widening divide between the two camps.[13]

Like Draper, fellow former SBC president Adrian Rogers has trouble understanding Criswell, at least on this one issue. While doing his best to put a reasonable spin on Criswell's statement, Rogers nevertheless says that it was "bizarre."[14] Others also have taken a whirl at spin control, interpreting Criswell to have meant only that he rejects the idea that religion must stay out of politics. Mohler and George, for example, are somewhat in sympathy with such a statement largely because they believe the phrase "separation of church and state" to be too stark, implying an impossible division between the moral dimension of Christianity and the affairs of government. George holds out the possibility that Criswell was reacting against the invasion of religious rights by the U.S. Supreme Court. If that was the case, he would agree with Criswell's intention, though not his rhetoric.[15] Conservatives often have a very different view of separation of church and state than do moderates, but Criswell spoke for very few right-wing leaders when he made his comments on national television.

The same can be said for Christian Right spokespersons who offer statements like Criswell's. D. James Kennedy and Pat Robertson, for example, frequently reject the very concept of separation of church and state. In the

1980s, with the Cold War continuing in full force, Robertson liked to say that the founders never intended that there be separation of church and state in America. His evidence was that the words never appear in the U.S. Constitution itself. By contrast, the phrase was in the Soviet Constitution. The clear image Robertson hoped to portray was that separation was a godless concept that had no place in a Christian nation such as the United States.[16] Kennedy also routinely rejected separation of church and state. More recently, Christian Right activist Star Parker and others have attempted to popularize the anti-separationist position. In a fall 1996 speech at a Christian Coalition gathering, Parker launched her remarks by saying, "Anyone who believes in the separation of church and state can leave right now." Criswell's statement dovetailed so nicely with those of Christian Right spokespersons such as Robertson and Kennedy, and later Parker, that moderates were able to issue a one-two punch in response. Conservatives were, first, disbelievers in the concept of separation of church and state and, second, walking in lockstep with the Christian Right. In reality, however, even those conservatives like Mohler and George who have some sympathy with Criswell or Parker are reluctant to actually say similar things publicly for fear of being misunderstood.[17] Even more typical is Patterson's position. When asked for a response to Parker's statement, he said in no uncertain terms, "If I had been in the room when she said that, all she would have seen would have been my back because I would have left the room."[18]

While the charges that SBC conservatives are part of the Christian Right are plausible, they hinge somewhat on how one defines the terms of debate. A broad definition of "Christian Right" would include SBC conservatives, while a narrow definition of "separation of church and state" would exclude them. In other words, if one must take the same positions on church-state issues that SBC moderates take in order to be considered a separationist, SBC conservatives (as will be shown below) do not qualify as such. This does not mean, however, that they take the same position as those who lead Christian Right organizations like the Christian Coalition.

A third and more serious accusation made against conservatives is that they are in a league with Reconstructionists. Christian Reconstructionism, or Theonomy, is a movement emanating from a fringe element within Reformed Calvinism. Reconstructionists argue that the judicial law of the Old Testament is still binding and should eventually be applied in the United States, including capital punishment for a variety of sins like adultery and homosexuality, some of which are not presently even considered illegal activities in much of the country. While there are different views as to how and when such laws should be instituted, the primary spokespersons for Reconstructionism put the time well off in the future, when Americans have become so disillusioned with the breakdown of the present order that they will actually welcome this return to Old Testament law.[19]

In the 1980s, a moderate group called Baptists Committed to the Southern Baptist Convention (BCSBC) issued a document attacking the conservative movement within the SBC. One of the charges read, "[Paul] Pressler has also indicated his endorsement of materials published by the frightening, cultic Reconstructionist Movement."[20] The basis for this charge was a catalog published by Dominion Press of Fort Worth, Texas, a publishing arm of the Reconstructionist movement. Dominion publishes mostly right-wing literature, much of it written by a stable of Reconstructionist authors. In addition, the firm also picks up rights to books by conservative evangelical theologians, such as J. I. Packer, B. B. Warfield, and Francis Schaeffer, who have had no connection to Christian Reconstructionism; Warfield died long before the movement even began, while the only connection one could make for Schaeffer is that both he and some of the Reconstructionists were taught by Reformed theologian Cornelius VanTil. Packer is not even remotely connected to Reconstructionism. Apparently, it is not necessary to be a Reconstructionist in order to be published by Dominion Press. In fact, Dominion sometimes picks up the rights to books that were published previously by other presses and then reissues those books to keep them in print. For example, the press has published at least one book by James Billington, a noted scholar of Russian history and former director of the Library of Congress. Obviously, Dominion publishes many works that are not Reconstructionist.

In the catalog cited by his critics, Pressler's name appeared in a box labeled "Endorsed by Leading Christians" and listed the names of Jerry Falwell, conservative political activist Howard Phillips, D. James Kennedy, and libertarian U.S. congressman Ron Paul.[21] The charge made by BCSBC was, therefore, factually true in the narrowest sense. Pressler had endorsed materials published by the Reconstructionists, but this did not necessarily mean that he endorsed Reconstructionist beliefs.

A second incident seeming to link SBC conservatives with Reconstructionism also concerns Pressler. In 1987 he granted an interview to Gary North, a Reconstructionist author, formerly headquartered in Tyler, Texas, and the estranged son-in-law of Reconstructionist founder Rousas Rushdoony. (The two had a bitter feud some years ago and did not speak to each other for nearly all of the final two decades of Rushdoony's life.) Taken together with Pressler's alleged endorsement of Dominion Press, this appeared to be further evidence that the judge was trafficking in Reconstructionism. In reality, however, North wanted this interview because he was writing a book on the Presbyterian controversy of the early twentieth century, which the liberals won, and was fascinated by the fact that Pressler and his allies had been able to pull off a conservative victory in the SBC. The issue of Reconstructionism never came up during the interview, and North in due time published his book. In it, he referred briefly to the Southern Baptist conservative resurgence, calling it "the most remarkable ecclesiastical reversal of the past three centuries."[22]

Another apparent Reconstructionist link to SBC conservatives concerns the book *If the Foundations be Destroyed,* coauthored by James Draper and Forrest Watson. On a preface page below the words "We gratefully acknowledge the assistance of the following," Rushdoony was listed with two others as an "Adviser/Historian."[23] Chronologically, this was actually the first apparent link between the conservatives and Reconstructionists. After those cited above were added to the list, the BCSBC flier seemed very plausible. But, as with the other pieces of evidence, there was actually less than meets the eye. First, although he is listed as a coauthor, Draper did not actually write much of the book but agreed to allow his name to be used as a coauthor provided that Forrest Watson do most of the research and writing. Watson knew Rushdoony had an extensive library in California with materials relating to America's Christian heritage. Watson and Draper traveled to Rushdoony's headquarters and spent a day doing research. As Draper puts it: "I only met [Rushdoony] one time and was only interested in the technical research he could give in the areas that we talked about. Later on, I found out that his son-in-law is Gary North in Tyler, who's a nut." If Draper believes anything in the book he sort-of coauthored, then his views of American history are very consistent with the Christian America groups in the Christian Right. As for Reconstructionism, however, Draper says, "There are nuts in every bag."[24]

If there is any group in the conservative camp that ought to have an affinity with Reconstructionism, it would be Mohler, George, and the other Calvinists. Making the connection between their strong Reformed Calvinist position and that of the Reconstructionists would be at least as logical as linking Pressler to the movement because he endorsed some books that happened to have been published by Dominion Press. Like most mainstream Calvinists, however, Mohler, George, and the other SBC Conservatives dismiss Christian Reconstructionism as a theological and political error with no basis in either history or biblical hermeneutics. Buttressed by a recent study of sixteenth-century Geneva authored by the eminent Reformation historian Robert Kingdon, Mohler is convinced, along with most historians, that even John Calvin himself did not advocate a Levitical theocracy.[25] For his part, George emphasizes at every opportunity that Theonomy is a church-state heresy from a Baptist perspective because it is coercive.[26]

While Mohler rejects Reconstructionism because of its historical, hermeneutical, and theological flaws from the Reformed perspective, Adrian Rogers argues against the likelihood of an alliance with Reconstructionists from a different theological perspective, premillennialism. Most SBC conservatives are premillennialists, while Reconstruction is postmillennial.[27] Premillennialists believe that the world will get worse, not better, and will be rescued only by the second coming of Christ, who will establish His millennial kingdom after bringing earthly history to a close. This is antithetical to the postmillennial Reconstructionist movement, which teaches that God's kingdom can and will be built on this earth prior to the second coming of Christ. When Reconstructionists use the phrase "eschatology of victory," they are referring to a victory of heavenly values on earth that will occur without the benefit of a supernatural second coming. Rather, Old Testament civil law will become the law of America through the victory of the righteous over the reprobate.[28] Of course, it is possible that a populist form of Reconstructionism could adapt itself to suit the needs of the premillennialists who dominate the ranks of American fundamentalism. Pat Robertson, for example, though usually a premillennialist, seems at times drawn to postmillennial themes. Reconstructionism may be the wave of the future for the Christian Right.[29] The members of BCSBC and other moderates, however, have attempted to establish a link between SBC conservatives and the intellectual leaders of Christian Reconstructionism, and to the extent that Rogers is correct in assessing the conservative movement as being heavily premillennial, such an alliance would seem unlikely, at least at the present.

WHAT SOUTHERN BAPTIST CONSERVATIVES ARE

If Southern Baptist conservative leaders are not full-fledged members of the Christian Right, if they do not believe that separation of church and state was born in the imagination of some infidel, and if they are not Christian Reconstructionists, what are they? The answer, in a word, is accommodationists. Whether accommodation is outside the separationist tradition is a matter of some debate, but most of the church-state quarrels in recent years have broken down along accommodationist-versus-separationist lines, which, of course, means that conservatives and moderates in the SBC are usually on opposite sides of church-state issues. (What exactly "accommodationism" is and how SBC conservatives have adopted it are questions to be taken up in chapter 5.) Is there room within the Baptist tradition of religious liberty and church-state relations to fashion a position, such as accommodation, that is quite different from what moderates profess? It should be said here that, unfortunately, the separationist-accommodationist split often pits the former on the same side of issues as secular humanists, while the latter find themselves alongside ardent conservatives like Pat Robertson, Star Parker, and others in the Christian Right. These alignments make charges like those mentioned earlier all the more likely because activists on both sides of America's so-called culture war often engage in guilt-by-association judgments. So, the moderate charges go, if SBC conservatives are accommodationists and the Christian Right is an accommodationist movement, then SBC conservatives are part of the Christian Right and probably influenced by Christian Reconstructionism. Similarly, SBC conservatives like Richard Land and Al Mohler believe, erroneously, that James Dunn, James Wood Jr., and others in the separationist camp believe in a civic philosophy that divorces religion from the body politic, thus creating the proverbial "naked pubic square." This has never been the stated moderate position, but by using the term "strict separation," SBC conservatives can taint moderates as inadvertent promoters of secularism just as moderates often lump conservatives together with theocrats.[30] Nuance, once again, is the first casualty of culture war.

Given the overheated climate of the late 1980s and the clear differences between moderates and conservatives on cultural issues, it is not surprising that such erroneous charges materialized. In reality, conservatives vigorously reject the notion that they have sold their Baptist birthright for a mess of Reconstructionist or even Christian Right pottage. Rather, they claim as their own virtually the same heritage of religious liberty as do moderates. Moreover, there is virtual unanimity among conservatives on the principle of religious liberty. The differences between them and moderates are primarily over Establishment Clause issues. Even here, conservatives bristle at the suggestion that they have walked away from the principle of separation of church and state. Rather, they have joined a vigorous and viable debate over what separation means and what it should mean. Some conservatives would like to continue using the term but find it problematic as presently used in public debate. It is accurate, therefore, to say that SBC conservatives do not support separation of church and state in the same way that their moderate forerunners did, but it is much less certain that this necessarily means that conservatives have simply jettisoned the Baptist tradition, because that tradition itself is being contested in ways unimaginable just a generation ago. Conservatives are in the process of reworking the Baptist emphasis on religious liberty to make it applicable to current cultural exigencies (as will be shown in later chapters). To get there, though, one must consider what conservatives actually claim as the Baptist tradition with regard to both religious liberty and the separation of church and state.

Of all the conservative leaders, Paige Patterson may have been the most important during the controversy. He did his doctoral work at New Orleans Baptist Theological Seminary with William Mueller, who studied with perhaps the twentieth century's greatest Protestant theologian, Karl Barth. Ironically, therefore, it could be said that Patterson is Barth's intellectual grandson. As offspring often do, Patterson rebelled against his own mentor's generation, the moderate Mueller, and the neo-orthodox influence that came down from Barth. On church-state issues, however, Patterson claims to be much closer to the old moderate position than people usually assume.

Patterson says that those who believe they are opponents of his church-state views have mostly "bought a pig in a poke." They assumed something that simply is not true. Patterson goes so far as to characterize his views on church-state matters as fairly consistent with the Christian Life Commission (the former name of the Ethics and Religious Liberty Commission) prior to the appointment of conservative Richard Land as head of that agency. The only difference he sees is that, gradually, he changed his perspective on exactly what is or should be meant by the phrase "separation of church and state." As he sees it, the church-state rule of thumb by the 1980s had become that the church should not speak to the state, or at least that conservative churches should not. The reason conservatives became tagged as anti-separationists, Patterson believes, was that they failed to make clear that they were rejecting only a particular view of church-state separation. Criswell's infamous statement is the prime example. In Patterson's view, Criswell may have overstated his case because he was reacting to the condescending view secular elites often take of Protestant conservatives and fundamentalists. This view seems to say, as Patterson characterizes it, "All you conservative preachers need to shut up and go back and do church . . . [because] you don't have anything to say to the general public."[31] As evidence of this, Patterson registers his impression that whenever conservatives backed a resolution on abortion at a Southern Baptist Convention meeting, they were told they were somehow breaching the wall of separation between church and state. By such a definition, Patterson points out, the great separationist Roger Williams was in violation of separation, for he was driven from Massachusetts Bay Colony in large part because he made unpopular pronouncements on political questions. Given this perception, real or imagined, Criswell's extreme statement is understandable even if problematic and unrepresentative of the actual views of conservatives.

While there were certainly activists and analysts in the United States who held the view that Christians should not get directly involved in the political process, this has not been the view of the archenemy of SBC conservatives, James Dunn, who headed the Baptist Joint Committee in Washington during the 1980s and 1990s. The fact that conservatives so detest Dunn seems to prove the dictum that people from the same tradition who have differences are usually more antagonistic toward each other than those on opposite sides of an issue who have little in common. Indeed, there are a whole host of current cultural issues that Dunn and conservatives could stand together on, but they nevertheless talk as if western society itself will disintegrate if the other side gains the upper hand. This may be an example of another dictum that comes to us from sociology, which holds that while people with general political disagreements soften their views toward each other when they actually meet face to face and discuss things, those with religious disagreements actually harden in their views as a result of conversation.

Dunn likes to say that the problem with Christian Right activists is not that they are wrongly involved, but that they are involved wrongly. In other words, conservatives should be involved, they just should not be conservatives. Taken at face value, such a position affirms the right of SBC conservatives to join the political process, which would refute Patterson's view that conservatives are actually being told to go home and do church. But, there is often a gap between what is said and what is heard when moderates and conservatives talk at or about one another, and this problem has been exacerbated by Dunn's own tendency to convey two contradictory messages at the same time. Specifically, in the very same speeches where he affirms the right of conservative evangelicals to be involved politically, he also refers to Christian Right activists as extremists, thus engaging in what James Davison Hunter calls "delegitimation," which is a standard technique of culture warriors on both sides.[32] On at least one occasion in 1997, Dunn called Beverley LaHaye's organization, Concerned Women of American, "Disturbed Women of America."[33] This sort of rhetoric can only convey a message of illegitimacy that Patterson and others came to view as characteristic of separation of church and state as espoused by moderates and liberals. In their finer moments, conservatives carefully define or redefine what they mean by this phrase, but the less sophisticated and less guarded members of the conservative movement often shoot from the hip, such as Criswell did in 1984, and thereby give the impression that they reject outright the whole notion of separation of church and state.

For his purposes, Patterson is unwilling to jettison "separation of church and state," bad interpretations notwithstanding. Some, however, find the phrase so problematic that they have stopped using it publicly. Mohler falls into this camp. While he cherishes the Baptist tradition of religious liberty, he is at the same time a staunch critic of the way SBC moderates have interpreted separation of church and state. Uncomfortable with the phrase, Mohler calls himself a constitutional "strict constructionist" dedicated to original intent. He further divides those who believe in original intent into two camps: antiquarians, who want to go back to the type of culture that existed at America's founding, and contemporary strict constructionists, who recognize how different the United States is today but nevertheless believe the principles of the founders should still apply in constitutional matters.

Mohler avers that religious liberty is genuinely part of the Baptist heritage. Although not alone in this, Baptists cherish religious liberty as a distinctive precept of their faith, and not for cultural reasons alone, he argues. Rather, it is rooted in theology, and Baptists have constituted a decisive influence at some critical moments in American history. But, Mohler continues, moderates made a creed out of the amorphous idea of religious liberty, taking it out of all proportion to where it belongs in the whole Baptist system and insisting that there is only one way to view all issues. There has been little disagreement on purely religious liberty matters, but where establishment is debated, Mohler believes it unfortunate at best that moderates outlined one approach and have insisted that it alone represents the Baptist way.[34]

Like nearly all the conservatives, then, Mohler believes that in matters related to the separation of church and state, as distinct from religious liberty, moderates have been profoundly in error. He believes that they have accepted a separationist position that emanates from progressivism and that this stance contributes to the secularization of American culture, which is the primary cultural concern of all SBC conservatives. Mohler thus can say: "I'm very sympathetic to [anti-separationist statements like Criswell's], but I would be very reluctant to throw them out in the public square where I wouldn't be understood. . . . I think the phrase 'separation of church and state' is a very unfortunate statement." Still, though, while this may sound un-Baptist to some, Mohler can also sound downright separationist when he defines more closely what he opposes in the way of church-state partnership: "I do not believe that any of the states have any right to establish a state church. I do not believe it is the government's role to take on the priestly function. I do not believe the church should serve the government nor the government serve the church. But, on issues of morality, it is ridiculous to believe you can disestablish Christian morality without fundamentally undoing the American experiment."[35]

This is a nuanced position, not given to reductionist sound bites that often emanate from both conservative and moderate camps. The key issue is a distinction Mohler is making between the American state and American culture. The state cannot endorse or promote religion, but American culture is built on a moral foundation. What happens, Mohler wants to know, when the secularity of the state appears to be undermining that foundation? Mohler is a separationist who pulls up short whenever he believes separation contributes to the stripping away of the moral bedrock of Western culture, rooted in the teachings of the Old and New Testaments. This can be a very elastic line that can stretch this way and that, making one's approach to Establishment Clause issues very difficult. It is much simpler to take the more consistent separationist position, but conservatives believe the risk of doing so is too great. Moreover, convinced as they are that the real danger in the United States is violation of religious liberty emanating from secular hostility, they are willing to err on the side of occasionally supporting relatively low levels of government endorsement of religion. The position here is similar to that of evangelical historian George Marsden in another context. He argues that state universities should allow for expressly religious points of view in the scholarly work carried on by their professors. Marsden acknowledges the inequity of the nineteenth century, when state-supported universities were expressly Protestant, but he states that given the pervasive secular nature of state universities today, there is virtually no risk that religious viewpoints will come to dominate as they did then. Rather, the real threat is discrimination against religion within higher education.[36] Likewise, SBC conservatives believe there is virtually no threat of an establishment of a state religion in present-day America, so their efforts are aimed at eliminating what they believe is hostility toward religion fostered by the state.

What Marsden has found in one sphere of American culture SBC conservatives have writ large, arguing that all of America is as secular and hostile to religious points of view as universities (Marsden does not believe this).[37] This being the case, we should err on the side of a bit of government endorsement here and there rather than on the side that lends itself to the banishment of religion from public forums. As Mohler likes to say, the moderates rightly recognized the danger of culture religion, but in stripping that away, they were rendering the public square antiseptic as far as religion was concerned. "We are now seeing the debris left when there is an attempt to separate the Christian moral heritage from the society and still try to keep some kind of democratic experiment." In sum, Mohler believes that the Establishment Clause has been misused in such a way that religious liberty is under threat. Appropriation of the Baptist principle of religious liberty, therefore, means that at times one may have to take the ironic position of being opposed to the separation of church and state as presently held by the courts. Still, however, early-twentieth-century Baptist theologian E. Y. Mullins was, in Mohler's view, basically right, even if a bit individualistic. God created human beings in such a way that "we should acknowledge the freedom for each to follow his or her own conscience as religion dictates." This is what Baptists in Colonial America stood for against Erastian systems of state supremacy that dictated the preferred religion and merely tolerated everyone else. The First Amendment, Mohler argues, was meant to preclude Erastianism, but there can never be an absolute separation of church and state.[38]

George has views very similar to those of his former student and Calvinist compatriot Mohler. A scholar of historical theology specializing in the Reformation, George came to appreciate parts of several church-state belief systems from the sixteenth century. Luther's Two Kingdoms view recognizes the importance and God-ordained nature of both church and state while holding that the two should not be confused. Calvin stressed the Christian's responsibility for bringing all of culture under the auspices of righteousness. The Anabaptists stressed the autonomy and integrity of the church. George has integrated parts of all of these into a Baptist system that holds religious liberty as non-negotiable while eschewing withdrawal from the world—a kind of "Christ Transforming Culture" view, to use one of H. Richard Niebuhr's classic types, tempered by an Anabaptist bias.[39] The bottom line is religious liberty, however, and not necessarily the separation of church and state. George draws a distinction between the American experiment, which has utilized separation, and the Baptist view of religious liberty. The first is contingent on circumstances. The United States utilizes separation as the means to accomplish religious liberty. George does not believe that Baptists must be committed to the means, only to the end goal. We often speak of religious liberty and the separation of church and state as the same term, he argues, when in reality they are not. This does not mean that George opposes the separation of church and state but rather that he is willing to contemplate the possibility of other ways of achieving religious liberty. He holds England out as an example where religious liberty has been achieved without separation. Conversely, Nazi Germany or the Soviet Union are examples of separation of church and state being mandated without there being religious liberty. For George, the point is to place the discussion of religious liberty in a Christian context and to stop viewing the American experiment as somehow theologically necessary. "I don't find the American experiment spelled out explicitly in scripture," he says. A Christian needs to stand back and ask what his or her responsibility is under God in the present situation. Given the church-state landscape today, George believes that nonpreferential accommodation is the best option for accomplishing full religious liberty.[40]

Of all the SBC conservatives, Richard Land is the most visible on cultural issues. With a doctorate in Baptist history from Oxford University and a career in academic work, Land was well poised to take the helm of the Christian Life Commission and then transform it into the Ethics and Religious Liberty Commission. With his depth of background and on-going involvement in religious-liberty matters, he, like Mohler, is better prepared than most other conservative leaders to discuss the nuanced differences between his own position and that of the moderates, but the stated principles he employs are virtually the same as those held by moderates. Put most simply, like most Baptists in history, Land vigorously affirms religious liberty for all people and rejects the state sponsorship of any one religion.

Land grew up in Houston in the late fifties and early sixties and witnessed the unconscionable establishment of Protestantism that existed at that time. He remembers wondering what his few Jewish classmates must have experienced when the school day began with the Lord's Prayer. "Christ was not their Lord," Land remembers thinking. For this reason he agreed with his own Baptist pastor in supporting the Supreme Court decisions that ended state-mandated prayer in schools. Land also credits the shaping of his views to John F. Kennedy's famous visit to Houston during the 1960 presidential campaign. Kennedy went there specifically to speak to pastors in an effort to allay fears that a Catholic president would seek to merge church and state. The candidate assured Southern Baptists that if elected, his Catholicism would not unduly influence his presidency. Land remembers thinking at the time that this was a good answer, but he would be appalled today if a Catholic or Southern Baptist president made such a statement.[41] For conservatives, this event is indicative of where they believe separation of church and state was taking the nation. It had become illegitimate for a public figure to admit that his or her views were shaped or even influenced by religion.

Land's upbringing in staunchly Baptist Texas seems to have shaped him in two ways. On the one hand, he learned from his own pastor and other denominational leaders that Baptists believed in religious liberty and separation of church and state, and on the other, he saw wholesale violations of these principles all around him. When he went to England for doctoral work, his misgivings about established religion were confirmed. While a student at Oxford, he pastored a Baptist church and had to "deprogram" his young people, who were required to take religion classes in their public schools. As Land puts it, "[Establishment] always results in government distorted and government diluted religion." Little wonder that with these life experiences, Land fashions himself a defender of religious liberty and an opponent of establishment. It would seem that his training might well have prepared him for a career as an SBC moderate dedicated to separationist principles. This was not the case, though, largely because he perceived himself to be much more conservative theologically than typical moderate elites; so conservative, in fact, that upon completion of his doctorate at Oxford in the 1970s, he accepted a position at Criswell College. His beliefs and affiliation with Criswell put him on the far right of the SBC, where he was comfortable theologically and where he would remain poised for leadership once conservatives took control of the denomination. Land also admits that being Southern Baptist was so much a part of his identity that he could never be anything else; he could no more leave the SBC than renounce his American citizenship.[42] Such statements could make him look like an opportunist who could have gone whichever way the denomination went, but he actually bided his time on the SBC's right-wing fringe with Criswell until the conservatives won. In taking the position at Criswell, he virtually ensured that he would never teach at a moderate SBC institution, and moderates at that time controlled all six of the SBC seminaries. Land claims that he was even told by a dean at Southwestern Baptist Theological Seminary that he was too conservative to be hired there. As good fortune would have it, Land was able to stick to his conservative views and still end up in a major leadership position within the SBC. Once conservatives had solidified control of the denomination, he emerged as the most visible Southern Baptist employee in the United States in the areas of church-state relations and religion and politics.

Like other SBC conservatives, Land speaks forthrightly in favor of religious liberty. Parting company with some political conservatives, Land argues that religious liberty is not a matter to be left to state and local governments. The federal government must assure that every American enjoys full First Amendment rights whether they are Jews in Alabama or Baptists in Utah.[43] He believes, however, that what he calls strict separation of church and state is unwise and even un-Baptist. "Regarding the establishment clause and the free-exercise clause," he has written, "these two clauses certainly cannot be totally separate, but there is a comma between them, one of the more important commas in American history. As a Baptist I would argue from the free-church tradition that we do not want any entanglement of the institution of the state with the institution of the church. However, we must accommodate, acknowledge, accept, and understand the right of individual believers to the full 'free exercise' of their religious convictions."[44]

The only difference between this statement and what one usually hears from Baptist separationists is Land's "however." It is necessitated by the conservative view that in separating the institutions of church and state, American society has actually allowed discrimination against religious views. When Land and other conservatives speak of separation, they nearly always qualify it. "We believe in separation of church and state, *but* not James Dunn's interpretation of it."[45] So, Land continues, "if we are going to require our children to be on public-school property for most of their waking hours, for most of the months of their formative years, then they must be free to exercise the religious convictions that they bring with them from home and from church."[46] Few separationists would disagree with this general statement, but what this means for Land is that his self-expressed passion for religious liberty compels him to support the "right" of children to have prayer in their classrooms.

At this point, the conservative articulation of principles becomes rather incoherent, for Land also writes: "What we want is maximum acceptance, maximum acknowledgment, maximum accommodation, because our duties and responsibilities to God as we understand them are far too important to allow any mere secular government to impose upon them. What we demand is religious liberty, not mere toleration."[47] In the span of a few pages of a written essay for a symposium, Land has stated, on the one hand, his support for institutional separation of church and state and, on the other, his desire for maximum acceptance, acknowledgment, and accommodation of religious views by that very same government. It is unclear how a "mere secular government" that is separated institutionally from religion could maximally accept, acknowledge, and accommodate religion, or why Land would want the state to do this. How can such a desire be consistent with institutional separation?

A hint appears in Land's stated position of nonpreferentialism and equality. These are the principles accommodationists have developed against the "no aid" view of separationists. Nonpreferentialism means that government can aid religion in general and religious groups in particular so long as no group is excluded from the benefits. The corresponding principle is equality, which holds that when the government supports various activities, charitable efforts for example, religious organizations that carry out these activities cannot be excluded summarily. This extends even to monetary aid, as was demonstrated in the case *Rosenberger* v. *University of Virginia*, in which the Supreme Court ruled that if the university funded student publications generally, it could not refuse to fund explicitly religious publications.[48] For Land and many others, this is a simple matter of fairness. Religion cannot be singled out for a benefit, but neither can religious groups be denied a benefit merely because they are religious. Accommodationists such as Land make sense of this by pointing out that the alternative to nonpreferentialism and equality is government discrimination against religion. There is no such thing as neutrality in these matters. If the government fails to accept, acknowledge, and accommodate religion, then it is engaging in hostility to it *ipso facto*. This is the zero-sum game where neutrality means failure to accept, acknowledge, and accommodate, which is the secular position. If government adopts such supposed neutrality, it actually establishes secularism, which always refuses to accept, acknowledge, or accommodate religious influences in public affairs.

Many Christians, Land believes, are so disgusted by what they perceive as pervasive discrimination against religion that they are willing to adopt almost any alternative. Land envisions his role as helping Baptists see that some solutions would be just as bad as the problem. How he does this on a case-by-case basis will be discussed later, but at the level of principle, Land is attempting to maintain the Baptist insistence on religious liberty while rethinking and adjusting what has been the Baptist position on separation of church and state. Though not ready to jettison separation, he knows his views on this aspect of church-state relations are different enough from previous considerations that he needs to use a different term, hence his use of "accommodation" to encapsulate his principles. He believes that he is taking a middle position between "strict separation" and "neo-establishment majoritarianism," and he is convinced that this is where most Southern Baptists are too. Land accuses the Christian Coalition, Congressman Ernest Istook, and those who supported his proposed Religious Freedom Amendment in its original form in 1997, and others generally viewed as part of the Christian Right as holding the majoritarian view. This perspective holds simply that since the United States is majority Christian, it is acceptable for the nation's institutions to reflect the Christian faith. Land rejects this as a matter of principle because of the strong religious liberty views outlined above. Land says that he does not believe America can get the church-state issue right without the input of Baptists; that is, without the Baptist leaven, the nation is more prone to the extremes of secularization and majoritarianism.

Overall, then, Land's principles look something like this: Baptists should insist on the religious liberty rights of all people, but they should also resist all governmental policies that in any way discriminate against religion by favoring secularism. He reasons that Baptist forebears would never have supported a church-state system that favored secularism, and since that is what strict separation does, one cannot be consistent with the Baptist tradition and be a "strict separationist."

When Land and other conservatives use the term "strict separationist" to describe moderates, doing so becomes a rhetorical ploy that is itself part of their critique. In 1985 constitutional scholar Carl Esbeck wrote an article outlining what he believed were the five basic approaches then in use on church-state issues. Three of those approaches were separationist—strict separationist, pluralistic separationist, and institutional separationist. Esbeck's strict separationists were for the most part secularists who believe religion to be a wholly private matter that should have no influence in public affairs. Pluralistic separationists, by contrast, recognize that in a pluralistic culture all groups must be permitted a place within the debate. They support the prophetic witness to the state that strict separationists do not. Pluralistic separationists believe that the best way for government to ensure that religious groups have a voice in the public square is to be neutral not only among religions but also between religion and irreligion.[49] Esbeck put the traditional Baptist view in the category of pluralistic separation, but Land and the conservatives collapse the strict and pluralistic categories in order to class moderates in the same camp with strict separationists as represented by secular organizations such as the American Civil Liberties Union. The result is that Land's three views—strict separation, accommodation, and majoritarian—take the place of Esbeck's five. This, then, supports Land's position that the separationist position held by James Dunn and the BJC helps promote secularism. This ploy can come back on conservatives, however, in that Esbeck classes nonpreferentialists as one of his two groups that exist outside the separationist fold. This militates against the conservative desire to espouse nonpreferentialism without wholly rejecting separation. On this score, historian Robert Linder has used Esbeck's categories to ask, "Shall the Accommodationists Win?" Linder interprets the nonpreferentialist principle as the heart of accommodationism and, like Esbeck, argues that it is clearly outside the three separationist traditions. Going further, Dunn classes the SBC conservative position with the Christian Right majoritarians that Land explicitly rejects. Then, having thus lumped them together, Dunn delegitimizes the whole group by calling them extremists.[50]

Patterson, Mohler, George, and Land can be grouped among the ideological or intellectual leaders on the conservative side of the SBC debate. Moving to the more popular level, one encounters preachers whose views are far less developed and nuanced but who nevertheless wield tremendous influence, perhaps more than that of the intellectuals. By his own admission, James Draper Jr. likes to keep things simple. Ironically, Draper is the only one of the SBC conservatives who has authored or coauthored an entire book on the issues discussed here. As noted above, however, he had little to do with its actual writing. In some respects Draper and coauthor Watson were in over their heads when they address issues such as nineteenth-century abolitionism and the Civil War. They often display a lack of sophistication that makes their argument easy to dismiss. In one area, however, they have actually hit on a very important issue having to do with Baptist history and what can be made of it.

The Search for a Useable Past

Draper and Watson's book, *If the Foundations Be Destroyed*, makes at least one rather sophisticated argument that surprisingly other conservatives have been slow to pick up. The authors state that while eighteenth-century Baptists were in the forefront of the battle for separation of church and state, some of the most prominent among them were not separationists in the sense that today's moderates are. This historiographical move is in response to the moderate charge that conservatives "have given up on Baptist ideas."[51] Instead of giving up on the Baptist tradition, Watson, Draper, and other conservatives are attempting to reinterpret it in light of the issues they believe are most important for our own time. Isaac Backus serves as the primary example showing that some Baptists touted religious liberty only within the parameters of a generally Christian culture. He apparently supported a test oath in the Massachusetts Constitution that required state office holders to be Christians. "No man may take a seat in our legislature till he solemnly declares 'I believe the Christian religion and have a firm persuasion of its truth,'" Watson and Draper quote Backus as saying. The authors then provide this commentary on Backus's position: "Here again, we see that Backus approved of the state supporting the Christian faith generally." This "doctrinaire Baptist" believed that church and state "both have a duty to uphold the Christian religion generally." As a summary statement prefacing this discussion of Backus, the authors wrote, "The Baptist position was separation of Church and State, not separation of *Christianity or the Bible and the State*." They even applaud Backus's support for government licensing of Bible translations to prevent heretical versions, but the authors say that Backus went too far when he and the Massachusetts Baptists of his day favored paying missionaries with state money.[52]

All the above lead Watson and Draper to the conclusion that separation of church and state in Backus's day meant only that the state could not favor one denomination over another.[53] As with their treatment of abolitionism and the Civil War, here again one finds an oversimplified analysis that could have been taken out of a David Barton seminar. In Barton's presentations, any statement uttered by a Founding Father that is positive toward religion is used to show that they were all Christians and that they all intended the United States to be Christian. He makes little distinction between a statement supporting the basic moral program of Christianity, something even the unorthodox Jefferson could say, and one that would actually affirm the historic tenets of the Christian faith that make it unique, such as the incarnation, death, and resurrection of Christ. Moreover, Barton allows for little variation in the way founders used the term "Christian nation." Did they mean America was demographically Christian, a notion that is hardly controversial; legally Christian, a notion that is hard to support given that no founding document declares the nation such; or actually redeemed by the blood of Jesus Christ, a notion that evangelical theologians would find repugnant?[54] While Draper and Watson share with Barton a similar historical outlook, Draper rejects the view that Christianity should be the state-favored religion in America.[55]

Like Barton, Watson and Draper are amateurs who have stumbled into an important historical question, and like him their methodology tends to incorporate source mining, the technique of scouring the record and culling out only that evidence that fits one's argument. But they have used good sources. For their analysis of Backus, they do not rely on Barton or any other of the popular Christian Right authors. Rather, they cite the eminent historian of American religion, William McLoughlin, formerly of Brown University and a well-recognized authority on eighteenth-century New England Baptists. McLoughlin edited a collection of Backus pamphlets that seems to show that Backus supported the test-oath provision of the Massachusetts state constitution and probably voted in favor of the petition requesting that the U.S. Congress establish a bureau to license publication of Bibles.[56] Draper and Watson are in error when they assert that Backus supported state aid for missionaries—he was no longer living when New England Baptists voted in favor of this provision—but the point they make is correct. Backus did not reflect the views of twentieth-century separationists who argue against all forms of government support for religion.

John Leland did, however, and here is where the confusion arises. As McLoughlin writes, "Though Backus' views on church and state are often equated with those of Leland, it is clear that the two had distinctly different positions on many aspects of this question."[57] Leland's views were much closer to those of Thomas Jefferson and James Madison than to the pietists of New England, probably due to his long stay in Virginia from 1776 to 1791. At any rate, when he returned to New England and spent the rest of his life fighting for separation of church and state as he perceived it, he was viewed as eccentric by Baptist leaders for both his theological and his social views. Leland combined rationalism and pietism to form a powerful individualism.[58] Although recent research gives more weight to the piety, Leland's individualism is without question. As one student of Leland has written, "Whether decrying religious tyranny or making pronouncements upon tariff laws, he did so from the conviction that nothing should come between God and the individual."[59] Influenced by the rationalism of the Enlightenment and the pietism of New England Puritanism, Leland became a Jeffersonian individualist who supported his views with religious reasons. This made Leland wary of virtually all religious organizations except local congregations, and even these were in no way essential to the Christian life. He opposed missionary societies for fear that they would come between the individual and God, and he found ordinances such as the Lord's Supper to be of little value.[60] Little wonder, then, that he opposed the concept of a Christian nation; he scarcely conceived of a Christian church, let alone a nation. McLoughlin believed that a clear indication of the differences between Backus and Leland "can be seen in the fact that while most of Backus's friends who lived into the age of [Andrew] Jackson became theocratic Whigs, Leland, who actually lived through Jackson's presidency, was an ardent anticlerical Jacksonian Democrat."[61]

The similarity or dissimilarity between Backus and Leland has become a contested historiographical question among Southern Baptists. At stake is whether the conservative shift away from separation and toward accommodation can be reconciled with Baptist history. This is not a new question, however. In the late 1950s, almost a decade before McLoughlin's seminal work, historian Edwin Gaustad argued for a Backus-Leland tradition. Gaustad was writing when the influence of the consensus historians was still pervasive within the history profession. Consensus historians, like scholars from most eras, tended to read the dominant themes of their own time back into history. The 1950s have been known as the consensus years in American life, so quite naturally historians tended to find commonalities among Americans in other eras as well. Gaustad read mid-twentieth-century Southern Baptist consensus back into history to find a church-state tradition broad enough to include both Backus and Leland, yet still somewhat diverse within agreed-upon parameters. His analysis was by no means simplistic. He recognized complexity when he wrote that Leland's views made sense from the point of view of Jeffersonian democracy. Backus, by contrast, had more in common with the Puritan founders of New England. As Gaustad wrote, "I would suggest that Backus genuinely believed that the eighteenth century Baptists stood in the true line of descent from early seventeenth century separating Puritanism."[62] Gaustad was not arguing that Backus was a Puritan theocrat, rather Backus believed that the separatists had started a process in the seventeenth century that was in need of completion in the eighteenth. John Robinson's seventeenth-century separation from the corrupt Church of England for the purpose of forming autonomous congregations should lead naturally to the separation of the church from the state. Still, for all the diversity and complexity that Backus and Leland exhibited, it is instructive that Gaustad found a single Baptist tradition on church-state separation.

Nearly thirty years later, Gaustad wrote again of "some fine distinctions" Baptists and others have always had concerning religious liberty. This time he sums up Backus thus: "Not the thoroughgoing Jeffersonian that Leland was, not the zealous purist regarding church and its ministry that Roger Williams was, Isaac Backus fought for liberty within limits—limits essentially of a Protestant province. It is a distinction, and it does make a difference." He continues from this, arguing that just as Baptists had diversity of views on separation of church and state, so did the nation as a whole. Moreover, Gaustad writes, "Those divisions did not go away in the nineteenth century, nor have they gone away in the twentieth." Curiously, when Gaustad brings the church-state debate up to 1987, the publication year for the article, his appreciation for Baptist diversity on church-state issues seems to dissipate, if not disappear altogether. He couched the contemporary debate in such a way as to suggest that James Dunn and the Baptist Joint Committee's position was the only legitimate one, writing: "A final contest of our own time and place is that between the Baptist Joint Committee and . . . , and . . . ? Well, at times I am sure it must seem like the whole world. Let me suggest that it is, at least, a contest between this Committee on the one hand, and on the other those who would forget or distort history—twenty centuries of Christian history and nearly four centuries of Baptist history." The fine distinctions in the Baptist tradition (or perhaps traditions), which would seem to allow for differing interpretations, disappear in the conclusion to Gaustad's 1987 article. He states that the contemporary contest is between the BJC and those who would distort history, implying that there is only one way to interpret the Baptist heritage, no fine distinctions allowed. He continues, "We forget that Jefferson and Madison, together with Backus and Leland, saw religious liberty as the 'First Liberty,' the one from which other liberties ultimately depend."[63] Again, Gaustad seems to be taking back what he had argued earlier in this article—that there were fine distinctions among Baptists on church-state issues. Whereas earlier he highlights the differences between Backus's religious liberty within Protestant limits on the one hand and Leland's full-blown Jeffersonian individualism on the other, he now groups Jefferson, Madison, Backus, Leland, and even Roger Williams together with the BJC against everyone else. To be fair, it must be remembered that Gaustad wrote this article during the SBC controversy, when otherwise reputable moderates were peddling the erroneous charges that conservatives were in league with Christian Reconstructionists and other theocratic types. He may well have believed that SBC conservatives were outside either the Leland or Backus traditions. The possibility that the conservatives may fit quite well with Backus but not Leland evidently never crossed his mind.

Rich traditions develop over time and almost always contain tension within them whenever their tenets are applied in a given historical context. Southern Baptist moderates point to Roger Williams and John Leland and arrive at a conception of separation of church and state that is indistinguishable from that of Jefferson and Madison except for its source. They often throw Backus into this mix even while acknowledging that he was somewhat different. When they argue that this is the Baptist tradition, they are correct in one sense, for this perspective developed from Baptist sources and prevailed among Southern Baptist elites for much of the twentieth century. But it is a product of the consensus years of mid-twentieth-century America and fails to appreciate the full diversity that existed in Baptist history on the issue of separation of church and state.

An example of this reluctance to accept diversity in the Baptist tradition of church-state separation can be found in a 1989 masters thesis at Southeastern Baptist Theological Seminary. The author of this work argues for the similarity between Backus and Leland and attempts to refute McLoughlin, a rather ambitious project for a brief thesis based largely on sources collected, edited, and published by McLoughlin himself. In it the author quotes Leland, "The notion of a Christian commonwealth should be exploded for ever." On the next page he seeks to refute McLoughlin's position that

Backus actually retained much of the Puritan view of Christian common-wealth. To this end, Backus is quoted, "the religion of Jesus . . . will never be restored to its primitive purity, simplicity, and glory until religious estab-lishments are so brought down as To Be No More." The author then con-cludes, "Thus, Leland and Backus did agree that religious establishments (including the Christian commonwealth) should be done away with." The error here is that the author simply equates the established church, which the Backus quote condemns, with the Christian commonwealth, which the Leland quote condemns. Then, some pages later, he concludes that "Backus and Leland maintained that the best relationship for the church and the state was for them to be completely separated, the *Christian commonwealth exploded forever* [emphasis mine]." This time the author removed the paren-theses around "Christian commonwealth," giving the impression that Backus and Leland both wanted to explode that concept. Only Leland, however, actually made such a statement. Backus, by contrast, desired only an end to the established church; he seems to have been quite comfortable with the existence of a generally Christian and even Protestant country. Ironically, even the author of the thesis acknowledges that one of the differences be-tween Backus and Leland was that "Backus's arguments also tended to be more closely related to the New England Puritanism than did those of Leland."[64]

Unlike the author of this thesis, McLoughlin did not equate "established church" with "Christian commonwealth." Rather, he acknowledged that Backus believed there should be no specifically established church but at the same time argued that Backus believed society and government should reflect broadly the general teachings of the Christian faith. This seems to be what Backus actually believed and it does carry within it a remnant of the Puritan view of Christian Commonwealth, even though Backus's views on an established church differed from those of the Puritans. Understood this way, the Backus view is very much like the principles SBC conservatives articulate, and Richard Land says explicitly that he favors the Backus tradi-tion.[65]

It should be emphasized that the masters thesis cited above is not repre-sentative of moderate scholarship at its best. Rather, it is a work done by a graduate student that perhaps symbolizes the last gasp of moderate control over the seminary where its author earned his degree. Moderate historiog-raphy on this issue does reflect, however, a consensus view of Baptist history that is a product of twentieth-century Baptist life prior to 1979, when the

SBC controversy began in earnest.[66] During this period, division and strife were problems to be overcome in order to maintain the unity and peace of the denomination. Moderates, therefore, tended to argue that Baptists fought for religious liberty as a matter of theological principle and that they applied this equally and consistently to all people regardless of their particular faith. For evidence they pointed to Williams and John Clark allowing Jews and Quakers into Rhode Island and to Leland's famous statement, "Government has no more to do with the religious opinions of men, than it has with the principles of mathematics."[67] This is a hallowed feature of the Baptist tradition, one that many Baptists rightly cherish, but there is more to the story. In between Williams's Rhode Island and Leland's Jeffersonian individualism was the slow evolutionary development of Backus and the New England Baptists, whose pleas for religious toleration were sometimes based on pragmatic, self-interested concern for their own denomination. Backus did not argue for a principled religious liberty for all dissenters until after 1773, and throughout his life he took for granted certain church-state arrangements that twentieth-century separationists oppose and thought were remedied a generation ago in the *Everson* case of 1947. Now many of these issues are once again unresolved, much to the consternation of those favoring the "wall of separation" articulated first by Williams and then by Jefferson. Backus's own position on church and state was never as consistent as theirs. In fact, he drew very little from either Williams or Jefferson, a development that seems at first anomalous given that Backus was a Baptist who supported Jefferson politically. In reality, however, Backus developed his church-state views before he had ever heard of the Virginian (or Madison), and he knew that Williams had little claim to being a Baptist, having been one for only about four months. Backus's position was always more pragmatic and fluid, and as McLoughlin wrote long ago, throughout most of American history, the pragmatic middle-ground approach of Backus prevailed.[68]

It is not unusual for moderate Southern Baptist church historians and ethicists to acknowledge the tensions that existed in the Baptist tradition of religious liberty and separation of church and state. It is rare, however, for moderates to entertain the notion that their heritage might be broad and diverse enough to encompass a position different from Baptist separationism. But even this position had boundaries that most took for granted, and for much of the twentieth century those parameters, especially in the South, were not very different from the ones that existed in the days of Isaac

Backus. Scholar C. C. Goen has pointed out that in the early part of the twentieth century, the Baptist conception of religious liberty was confined largely to the Protestant consensus. "At the turn of the century," Goen writes, "Baptists were more concerned about religious liberty than the specifics of church-state separation, and they defined that liberty within the operating assumptions of the Protestant consensus." Most early-twentieth-century Baptists never thought to question devotional exercises in schools, Sunday laws, or prohibition while sharing with other Protestants a deep suspicion of Roman Catholicism. One should not be surprised to learn that the Baptist General Convention of Texas (BGCT) passed a resolution in 1912 calling on the Board of Public Education to disallow teachings that were religiously unorthodox or that attacked the Bible as the inspired word of God. In 1921 the BGCT approved a program through which public-school children could be released from classes to attend religious instruction (released time) and approved the use of the Bible in schools so long as not utilized for sectarian teachings.[69] Moderate Southern Baptist separationists of the late twentieth century oppose some or all of these practices; conservatives support them.

In Texas during the 1920s, "nonsectarian" still meant "generally Protestant." BGCT messengers (delegates) evidently had no problem with generally Protestant instruction in public schools. The United States, in their view, was still generally Protestant. As long as no one group was getting an edge in publicly funded institutions, all denominations were getting a fair deal. This and other evidence has convinced conservatives that what they call "strict separation" is merely a twentieth-century development within Baptist history. While moderates point to the twentieth-century "preacher" George Truett as one of the great Southern Baptist champions of religious liberty and separation of church and state, conservatives point out that even he preached graduation sermons at state universities, taking for granted the cultural establishment of Protestant Christianity. Conservatives believe that "strict separation" was, therefore, a post-Truett phenomenon in Southern Baptist life.[70]

The situation has changed. The United States is no longer a broadly Protestant country, and moderates can argue that the application of truly Baptist principles to the new cultural context should result in a separationist stance in church-state concerns. It seems implausible, however, for moderates to acknowledge the differences between Backus and Leland while allowing for no such diversity among true Baptists today. Backus "would never have agreed with Jefferson that the United States, or any one of them, was not a Christian country," McLoughlin has written, and that is the point that conservatives like Draper and Watson want to make. Backus was a champion of religious liberty, but for him and most of his fellow New England Baptists, this meant almost exclusively an end to compulsory taxation to support religion. There should still be a "sweet harmony" between church and state as opposed to the high wall preferred by Williams, Jefferson, Leland, and the U.S. Supreme Court of 1947.[71] One may want to argue that Backus's position is no longer viable given the pluralism and diversity rampant in late-twentieth-century America. The Protestant Christian limits that were de facto and taken for granted in Backus's time could exist today only if imposed. This would be a way of saying that SBC conservatives attempt to appropriate a part of the Baptist tradition that will not work anymore, but that is different from saying that conservatives "have given up on Baptist ideas" or forgotten their history.[72] Moreover, it seems equally disingenuous to line up quotes by Backus, Leland, and Supreme Court Justice Hugo Black's *Everson* opinion, identify Black as "a former Baptist Sunday School teacher," and then argue that all either did or would have supported the interpretation of the Establish Clause found in *Everson*.[73]

Gaustad, like many moderates in the late 1980s, may have believed that the conservatives had forgotten much more history than they actually have, but conservatives have their historians too, and they are much more sophisticated than amateurs like Draper and Watson. Timothy George, for example, has done scholarly work on seventeenth-century Baptist origins as they relate to religious liberty. He argues that the Baptists made a—perhaps *the*— seminal contribution to religious liberty in the West. Their position was in between Anabaptist pacifism, with its rejection of the state as outside the ordination of God, and the Calvinist tradition of a magisterial reformation. George would find agreement among most Baptist historians when he writes that while Baptists were in some respects part of the Calvinist-Puritan-Separatist tradition, their view of religious toleration was a "radical departure from this tradition." He identifies seven lines of argument in early English Baptist literature, among which are the necessity for keeping the two kingdoms of church and state distinguished from each other, the inviolability of conscience, and the noncoercive character of faith—all elements that moderate historians also recognize in early Baptist history. Moreover, George writes about seventeenth-century Baptists who advocated only limited toleration in order to control the number of Catholics in England,

"They clearly are exceptions to the larger Baptist consensus which continued to advocate unrestricted religious liberty."[74] For George, unrestricted religious liberty has been the Baptist battle cry in matters of church and state and should continue to be. He and other conservatives speak frequently and passionately against coercion in matters of faith, which they consider a violation of religious liberty. They remain unconvinced, however, that separation of church and state as construed by twentieth-century moderates is required of Baptists. Instead of the "no aid" position outlined by the Supreme Court in the *Everson* case of 1947, George advocates "no coercion" and "non-preferentialism." He and other conservatives do not worry too much about the establishment of religion because they believe it is a very remote threat.

While agreeing substantially with the moderate interpretation of the seventeenth-century Baptist view of religious liberty, conservatives are now figuring out that the eighteenth-century Backus was quite different from Williams, Leland, and Jefferson on the question of separation of church and state. The single Backus-Leland tradition identified by Gaustad in the late 1950s is looking more and more like two traditions, just as the Southern Baptist tradition of the twentieth century is clearly bifurcated. This should not obscure the similarities between the two men, however, for in their time they were on the same side of the church-state debates. It was just that Leland was further toward the separationist side than Backus. Arrayed against these two Baptist forefathers were all those who wanted to continue tax-supported churches. The extent to which Backus and Leland do sound similar is owed to the fact that the paramount church-state issues of their time were religious liberty for dissenters and the disestablishment of churches. Today the issues are different, so conservatives who prefer Backus are squared off against moderates who lean toward Williams and Leland. In an age such as ours, where religious liberty and disestablishment are accepted and defended by almost everyone, the relatively smaller differences get all the attention because they are virtually the only ones that exist. SBC moderates and conservatives (as will be shown) both stand against the fringe views of Christian Reconstructionists, against direct government funding of churches and church schools, against any type of compulsory religious activity, and many other things. In essence, they argue for very nearly the same principles, though with one clear exception. They mean different things when they say the words "separation of church and state," and some in the conservative camp have become reluctant to use that term anymore because to them it carries a secular connotation.

All church-state advocates must reckon with the two distinct features of church-state separation—free exercise and nonestablishment. Baptists have historically thought of themselves as holding these two elements in balance, but that balance is precarious and is itself contingent. A nation can disestablish religion without protecting religious liberty—the Soviet Union proved this. It is less certain that a nation can do the opposite—protect religious liberty without disestablishing religion—though Timothy George wants to argue that England has succeeded in this. While conservatives do not support the establishment of religion in any direct sense, they do believe that they can, like Backus, defend religious liberty while advocating that the state accommodate religion in several discretionary ways.[75] Northern Baptist historian William H. Brackney probably had independent Baptists in mind when he wrote, "Unaware of their basically liberal heritage in matters pertaining to religious liberty, many modern Baptists are not as concerned about freedom as with their task to create a cultural Christianity."[76] He might just as well have been talking about SBC conservatives. They believe that being a good Baptist does not necessarily mean that one must oppose all government support for the cultural influence of Christianity. Rather, being Baptist means merely that one should oppose all efforts to coerce faith or intentionally use the state to favor one faith over another. If the Baptist Joint Committee is representative, moderates argue that any level of government support for religion will likely result in discrimination against minority faiths. Conservatives and moderates share the Baptist goal of full religious liberty, but they differ substantially over how the Baptist tradition should be applied to Establishment Clause issues.[77] Moderates focus on the state and attempt to head off any aid that might accrue to religion. Conservatives focus on the effects of government policies and ask only whether anyone is being coerced. Theirs is a less rigorous test for the establishment of religion. If no one is coerced, nothing is being established. Moderates, however, are more vigilant against the possibility that the state might further the cause of religion even when few if any would be directly affected by such action.

The two groups also differ vigorously over whether the type of separation usually associated with moderates prior to the conservative takeover of the SBC is the best means for attaining the religious liberty both sides advocate. Moderates believe that it is, while conservatives argue that accommodation is now necessary in order to achieve religious liberty because "strict separation" has become hostile to the faith. As historian Bill Leonard has noted, this is an example of Baptists responding to their traditions in different and sometimes contradictory ways.[78] What has recently become more clear is that those traditions themselves are not quite as static or homogenous as once thought. While espousing the same goal or principle—religious liberty—SBC conservatives advocate a different way of attaining it than did their moderate predecessors. The key to the differences between the two groups is the conservative perception of the current cultural situation in the United States. These cultural perceptions shape SBC conservatives' positions on all the hot-button issues of our time—church-state, abortion, the role of women, and race.

5
Using a Useable Past

Church–State Positions

Both moderates and conservatives in the SBC attempt to look to a rather remote Baptist past for clearly defined advice about modern church-state issues. Both sides come away convinced that their Baptist forebears would agree with them. While there is some historical merit in looking to past traditions for clues and principles, few exercises could be more futile than trying to enlist the forefathers behind today's causes, but even historians do this. As Edwin Gaustad has written: "Historians of the twentieth century put questions to the seventeenth century that the colonists themselves might not have been able to answer, often because the questions would seem pointless or obscure or absurd. In that earlier day, it was a 'self-evident' truth that church and state must labor side by side for their mutual benefit and for the sake of all those placed in their care."[1]

Examples of this abound. One student of religion, Joe Coker, believes that Isaac Backus's views on church and state are consistent with the accommodationist position of today's evangelicals, which is exactly what James Draper and Forrest Watson argue in *If the Foundations Be Destroyed.* This is debatable, and it is always problematic to enlist colonial Americans in support of present-day positions, but this view is merely an echo of William McLoughlin, who has made reference to the similarity between Backus and the neoevangelicals of the 1960s who supported the general concept of separation of church and state while disagreeing vigorously with the prayer-in-schools decisions. If one insists on matching eighteenth-century thinkers and activists with those in the twentieth century, Backus and modern-day evangelicals go together about as well as John Leland, Thomas Jefferson, James Madison, and modern-day separationists, some of whom are evangelicals themselves. For most of American history, the views of Leland,

Madison, and Jefferson have been held by a minority, and those of Roger Williams by even fewer, "[b]ut," McLoughlin writes, "Backus probably represents most adequately the evangelical view of Separationism—the 'sweet harmony' of a Christian nation—that has predominated."[2] McLoughlin believed, therefore, that while Madison and Jefferson (and I would add Leland) would have supported twentieth-century separationism as exemplified in the Supreme Court's prayer decisions, Backus would not.[3] This is plausible but inconclusive.

BAPTIST ACCOMMODATIONISM

Acknowledging these differences, Richard Land has adopted the term "accommodation" instead of "separation" because it more accurately reflects his position and that of the Ethics and Religious Liberty Commission (ERLC) he heads. Like other conservative leaders, he insists that his views are consistent with Baptist tradition, and, like McLoughlin, he argues that Backus did not support the Leland-Jefferson-Madison approach.[4]

While accommodationists come in different stripes, this position holds basically that government should take a friendly stance toward religion, accommodating it wherever possible. One opponent of this, Ira Lupu of George Washington University Law School, has defined accommodation as "actions taken by the state or its agents that (1) respond affirmatively to religion-based claims for exceptional treatment . . . and (2) are not required by the Free Exercise Clause or any other provision of the Constitution."[5] Defined this way, accommodation sometimes requires that government do something positive to enhance the exercise of religion beyond merely staying out of the way. Challenges to this approach, therefore, are based on the view that positive state action toward religion violates the Establishment Clause of the First Amendment. In other words, accommodationism is an Establishment Clause issue.

Accommodationist scholar Michael McConnell, however, defines accommodation as "government laws or policies that have the purpose and effect of removing a burden on, or facilitating the exercise of a person's or an institution's religion." McConnell stresses that, for him, it "does not include government action that acknowledges or expresses the prevailing religious sentiments of the community, such as the display of religious symbols on public property or the delivery of a prayer at public ceremonial events."[6] Many popular accommodationists do want these officially sponsored activities, however, including some SBC conservatives. They eschew strict neutrality between religion and irreligion and urge the state to instead engage in policies that may at times aid all religions equally. Rather than the "no aid" to religion position of separationists, the battle cry of accommodationists is "no discrimination" against religion and no preference for one faith over another. Accommodationists are willing to permit far more government support for religion under the Establishment Clause than are separationists, even to the point of supporting government funds for religious institutions so long as this is done on a nonpreferential basis. Generally, separationists want only as much accommodation as is required under the Free Exercise Clause.[7]

If there is one Supreme Court case that best illustrates the accommodationist position, including its accompanying "equal treatment," or nonpreferentialist, principle, it is *Rosenberger* v. *University of Virginia* (1995). The facts of this case are as follows: The University of Virginia, ironically one of Jefferson's prized achievements, had a policy of subventing the printing costs for student publications. But, claiming separation of church and state, the university refused to fund a Christian newspaper whose purpose was to share the faith and proselytize. The student group that published the newspaper sued and won the case in the Supreme Court. Michael McConnell argued the students' cause on the basis of the neutrality principle. In short, their argument was that to refuse funding for the publication purely on the basis of its religious nature was far from being neutral; rather it was discrimination on the basis of religion. By contrast, true neutrality would entail funding the newspaper, which was merely a reasonable accommodation of religion, not an establishment thereof.[8] Of course, no-aid separationists argued that defraying the printing costs of an explicitly sectarian publication was government funding of religion, the very kind of establishment the court has rejected time after time for the past half century.

The accommodationist-separationist split runs right through the popular and scholarly communities and even through the Supreme Court itself. It seems clear that over the past fifteen years, accommodationists have had the upper hand, and to this extent SBC conservatives have been riding a wave. As Lupu has written, "The constitutional era in which separation is the dominant theme appears to be over."[9] That era lasted from the Everson Bus Case of 1947 until sometime in the 1980s, when the justices began to appropriate accommodationist principles. Land, however, sees three groups in the national debate, and he positions himself and the SBC Ethics and Religious

Liberty Commission between what he calls the "neo-establishment majoritarians" in the Christian Right and the "strict separationists" like SBC moderate James Dunn, formerly of the Baptist Joint Committee (BJC), whom Land views as being to his left. As activists are so often inclined to do, Land claims the vital center between what he views as the extremes.

By "neo-establishment majoritarian," Land is referring to those who believe that since the majority of people in the United States are Christians, their faith should be preferred (established) by the state. Many in this camp make their argument on local issues. There is nothing wrong, they say, when Christian symbols are displayed on local public property or Christian prayers said in local public schools because the majority of people in the community are Christian. It is just natural that the community should be able to reflect its collective values in public life. This view is sometimes stated in baldly democratic terms: Christians are the majority, and in America the majority rules. Land has rejected this view outright, saying unequivocally that matters of religious liberty should not be subject to majority deliberation or left to states and local communities. Like the vast majority of those involved in religious-liberty issues, he has been a vigorous critic of the Supreme Court's *Smith* decision (1990), and he blasted the striking down of the Religious Freedom Restoration Act in *Boerne* v. *Flores* (1997), calling it "the worst religious liberty decision in the last 50 years."[10]

In *Smith*, the Supreme Court ruled against Native Americans in Oregon who had lost their jobs for using peyote in their religious rituals and afterward denied unemployment benefits because they had been fired for violating the state's drug laws. The plaintiffs argued that the state's denial of benefits was a violation of their free exercise of religion. In the past the court had often used a "compelling interest" test in deciding when to allow religious exemptions from otherwise generally applicable laws: Only when the state had a "compelling interest" in enforcing such laws would it be allowed to do so. Otherwise, exceptions should be made and exemptions granted for religious exercise. One might call this free-exercise accommodation, which is different from the type of Establishment Clause accommodation defined by Lupu and utilized in the *Rosenberger* case.

Had the court in *Smith* used the compelling-interest test and found that the magnitude of today's drug problem gives the State of Oregon a compelling reason for enforcing its drug laws even against the religious practices of Native Americans, few people would have disagreed. But instead, the court reached beyond what many thought necessary and junked the compelling-interest test altogether. Justice Antonin Scalia, usually a favorite of conservatives like Land, wrote the majority opinion in which he argued basically that if a law was not intended to discriminate against religious practice, it was constitutional even if its application did, in fact, militate against free exercise. Those adversely affected by such a law should seek redress in the political process in order to have their legislatures change such laws.[11]

Soon after the *Smith* decision, the U.S. Congress passed and Pres. Bill Clinton signed the Religious Freedom Restoration Act, which reinstated the compelling interest test by law. RFRA, as the law came to be called, was used by a Roman Catholic parish near San Antonio, Texas, to challenge a city ruling that the church could not expand its building. The city of Boerne cited the church's status as a historical landmark. The church countered that the city needed to show a compelling interest for restricting expansion. On appeal, the city challenged the constitutionality of RFRA, and in *Boerne* v. *Flores* (1997), the Supreme Court struck down most of the law, at least as it applies to states. The justices reasoned here that Congress had overstepped its bounds by usurping the authority of the states, though one wonders if they were determined to find some way to overturn a law that so boldly reversed a Supreme Court decision.[12]

While Land was a staunch religious liberty advocate on the *Smith* and *Boerne* decisions, he positions himself as a moderate on church-state separation. Having rejected the neomajoritarians to his right, he turns his heaviest artillery against the "strict separationists" to his left. When he uses the term "strict separationist" to describe the likes of Dunn and the Baptist Joint Committee, Land makes no distinction between Christian separationists, on the one hand, and those who work from a secular perspective and believe religion should have no voice in the public square, on the other. This is possible because both types of separationists so often stand on the same side of church-state issues, especially Establishment Clause issues. A secularist who wants as little religion as possible cluttering up public life and a believer who views religion to be too sacred for government sponsorship will both oppose government funding of explicitly religious activities. Thus, the BJC often stands with the ACLU on church-state issues, which makes it easy for SBC conservatives to argue that there is something amiss.

So Land stakes out this middle position between neo–establishment majoritarians, whom he believes are often insensitive to the religious liberty concerns of minorities, and strict separationists, whom he believes are too often oblivious to the secularizing tendencies of modern culture.

SBC ACCOMMODATION IN ACTION

In the late 1990s there were at least three issues that illustrated the accommodationism of SBC conservatives. In each case one can see how conservatives have filtered Baptist principles through their perception of cultural crisis to arrive at a position different from what moderate Southern Baptists who supported the BJC would have preferred. The first is the perennial issue of religion and education, which has two parts: religious exercises in public schools and public funding for religious schools. As to prayer and Bible reading in public schools, the position of many moderates, as reflected by the BJC and the pre-1982 SBC resolutions affirming separation of church and state, is simply that the school, as an arm of the state, has no business mandating, organizing, promoting, or encouraging prayer or other devotional exercises. Doing so constitutes an establishment of religion that is by its very nature coercive for dissenting students and demeaning to prayer.

Of course, the issue of prayer in schools has been hotly contested since the early 1960s, when the Supreme Court ruled in *Engel* v. *Vitale* (1962) and *Abington* v. *Schemp* (1963) that organized prayer and Bible reading in public-school classrooms constituted a violation of the First Amendment's Establishment Clause. Congressional attempts to circumvent these rulings have been legion and need not be rehearsed here. Suffice it to say that many—perhaps most for all we know—rank-and-file Southern Baptists have been troubled by these decisions, and some of the congressmen who have supported legislation or constitutional amendments to reverse them have been Southern Baptists. What has changed recently is that SBC conservatives, like many other conservative evangelicals, have tried to transform prayer in schools from an Establishment Clause to a Free Exercise Clause issue. Seen this way, prayer in schools is not about the state establishing religion but about the right of school children to exercise their faith freely in their classrooms.

Some conservatives agree that the prayer judgments, as originally decided, were correct. What happened, then, to turn conservatives in favor of organized prayer in classrooms? Quite simply, they became convinced that the Court's rulings were being used to secularize the public schools and to discriminate against religious students. All of the conservatives I have interviewed reject any notion that the state should be used as a tool of evangelism or to expressly promote religion. This would violate the SBC's confession of faith, which contains the dictum, "The church should not resort to the civil power to carry on its work."[13] Critics who cite the prayer-in-schools issue to show that conservatives want the state to promote religion miss the gist of the conservative argument. Conservatives do not view this issue as an establishment problem. Rather, for them it is a matter of religious liberty versus government discrimination; some even see the issue as a matter of free speech. Paige Patterson, for example, says that whatever prayer is, it is at least speech, and the government should not, therefore, restrict it in any way. In arguing this line, he is in good company. The Supreme Court has increasingly shifted the debate in some Establishment cases over to the Free Speech Clause of the First Amendment. This was the case in *Rosenberger*, where the Court said that once the University of Virginia opened a forum for speech, it could not then discriminate on the basis of the religious content of speech.[14] Critics of this approach point out that this relegates religion to the same level as everything else, making the religion clauses of the First Amendment superfluous. From Patterson's perspective, however, the courts should never have gotten involved in the issue of prayer in schools. For him, it is an example of government regulation of something over which government should have no power—a form of speech.[15] Going even further toward the view that prayer in schools is a free-exercise or free-speech right instead of an Establishment Clause issue, Adrian Rogers says, "I do believe with all my heart in the right of a freeborn American to pray anytime, any place, any where, OUT LOUD—I mean silent prayer, don't tell me that, you can do that in a Russian concentration camp—and with anybody he or she pleases."[16]

The belief that prayer in schools is really a matter of religious free exercise and not establishment of religion is born out in the SBC resolutions that conservatives have been able to pass since they began to take control of the denomination. SBC resolutions are, as stated elsewhere, nonbinding. Technically, they represent only the will of the messengers to the annual meeting at which they are passed. Moreover, prior to the conservative takeover, and perhaps still, the vast majority of messengers were employed by either the SBC or by SBC churches. Thus, messengers, as one would expect, represent the elites of the denomination.[17] Still, resolutions are often symbolic, especially when the SBC passes the same type over the span of a number of years. Prior to the 1980s, the moderate-led SBC passed several resolutions that supported the prayer decisions of the early 1960s. A 1969 resolution stated that the prayer and Bible reading decisions of 1962 and 1963 "did not restrain the free exercise of personal religion but restrained public officials from using their public office for promotion of religious experience."[18] Two years later, the resolution "On Voluntary Prayer" concerned itself primarily with the potential threat to voluntary prayer, not when the courts forbid prayer in schools, but when there is government intrusion in the area of religious exercise. In other words, organized classroom prayer in schools is a threat to authentic voluntary prayer. This resolution reaffirmed one of 1964 that came on the heels of the Supreme Court prayer decisions. That resolution explicitly opposed the adoption of constitutional amendments then being proposed as a way around the prayer decisions.[19]

Clearly, the drafters of these resolutions viewed organized prayer in schools as a form of "governmental intrusion" forbidden by the Establishment Clause of the First Amendment. There was, however, heated debate over the 1964 resolution, as messengers had to reject a proposed change that affirmed the right of public schools to "engage voluntarily on a non-sectarian basis in prayer, bible reading, and other devotional exercise as may be desired by them and their constituents."[20] There was probably never a consensus among grassroots Southern Baptists that the Supreme Court prayer decisions were correct.[21] Still, even as late as 1980, the second year in which conservatives won the SBC presidency, the convention passed a resolution entitled "On Voluntary Prayer in Public Schools," which opposed attempts "either by law or other means to circumvent the Supreme Court's decisions forbidding government authored or sponsored religious exercises in public schools." The resolution also pointed out that these decisions had never forbade voluntary prayer, and it affirmed "the right to have voluntary prayer in public schools."[22] During the period of moderate control, the clear emphasis of resolutions on prayer in schools was support for the Supreme Court's decisions, which were viewed as attempts to eliminate the establishment of religion.

In 1982, as conservatives continued to win SBC presidential races and therefore more influence in the denomination, the tone of the resolutions on prayer in public schools changed abruptly. As the Southern Baptist Convention met that year, there was before Congress a proposed constitutional amendment put forward by the administration of Pres. Ronald Reagan. It read: "Nothing in this Constitution shall be construed to prohibit individual or group prayer in public schools or other public institutions. No person shall be required by the United States or by any state to participate in prayer." Messengers to the convention meeting that year passed a resolution supporting the amendment. Critics believed that the amendment's support of "group" prayer was meant to do exactly what the SBC's 1980 resolution decried—that is, "circumvent the Supreme Court's decisions forbidding government authored or sponsored religious exercises in public schools." James Dunn of the BJC later told Bill Moyers that the 1982 resolution supporting the amendment was authored in the White House by a Republican operative.[23] In addition to supporting the Reagan amendment, the SBC resolution of 1982 also alleged that "[f]or 170 years following the writing of the First Amendment, the right of prayer in public schools was a time-honored exercise and a cherished privilege."[24] The "170 years" stood for the time period between the adoption of the First Amendment and the prayer decisions of the early sixties. The clear implication, therefore, was either that those decisions were in error or were being misinterpreted, which was a complete reversal of what had been claimed in the SBC resolutions from 1964 through 1980.

When it finally came to the floor of the U.S. Senate in 1984, the Reagan amendment failed by eleven votes to achieve the required two-thirds majority, but it still stands as a historical marker for the SBC. From the resolution of 1982 onward, SBC resolutions have affirmed the right of students to pray in schools. Sometimes, such as in 1986, these have sought only to "decry interpretations of Supreme Court rulings which deny the right of voluntary prayer and Bible reading in the public schools."[25] At other times, such as in 1992, the denomination went much further. That year's resolution charged that the prayer decisions "have been greatly misunderstood and grossly misapplied by some public schools boards, administrators, and teachers to mean that the United States Constitution prohibits voluntary prayer and Bible-reading in America's public schools." It also portrayed the issue of prayer in schools as a free-exercise right, not an establishment problem, saying, "The free exercise rights of students are not forfeited at the doors of America's schools." The 1992 resolution was even entitled "On Free Exercise of Religion in Public Schools." Moreover, it solidified the shift in the SBC from its separationist leaders, now all ousted from power, to Land's accommodationism. The resolution read in part, "The Supreme Court has indicated by recent decisions that the 'strict separationist' doctrine which has dominated church-state philosophy and constitutional law for several decades may be giving way to an 'accommodationist' doctrine of religious expression in the public school."[26]

The shift from support for the prayer decisions of the early sixties, which were based on the belief that government should not foster religious exercises in public schools, to a primary concern for the free exercise of students, even to the extent of advocating group prayer in the classroom, is a clear example of how perception always stands between principle and position. The Baptist principle that government should not discriminate against people on account of their religion is filtered through the conservative perception that secularization of culture and discrimination against religion are the most important issues of our time, resulting in the position that students should have the right to pray in their school classrooms in whatever manner they choose so long as no one is required to participate. Shaped by their perception, conservatives have taken what the courts, scholars, and separationist advocates have always considered an Establishment Clause issue and turned it into a right protected by the Free Exercise Clause. Moderates who agreed with the Court looked at a school and saw an arm of the state that should not be in the business of promoting religion. Conservatives look at the same school and see an arm of the state that is suppressing students' free-exercise right to have prayer in their classrooms. One conservative Alabama pastor argued in rather bald terms that even if support for prayer amendments reversed the historic Baptist position on separation of church and state, it was necessary because of the threat of humanism.[27] More articulate and thoughtful SBC conservatives are not quite so bold. Rather, they argue that the issue for Baptists has always been religious liberty first, separation of church and state second, so if prayer in schools is a religious-liberty issue, Baptists are being consistent with their past to argue in favor of it. Rogers, for example, suggests that the state, through compulsory education laws, has placed students in a situation where they cannot freely exercise religious faith because they have to be in the classroom most of the day yet cannot have prayer while there.[28]

There should be no doubt that the SBC resolutions since 1982 are part of a monumental shift in the church-state position of the denomination. More than anyone else, Land has been the influential force in moving the SBC in its new direction. He has written, "I am firmly committed to the maximum accommodation of students' First Amendment rights under the Free Exercise Clause while remaining careful not to allow teachers and school officials to sponsor or impose any religion upon students in violation of the First Amendment's Establishment Clause." If there is to be organized classroom prayer, how can this proceed without it being sponsored or imposed? How could SBC conservatives support school prayer without violating their own stated principle that government should not promote religion? At this point, Land is nothing if not consistent when he says plainly that if there is to be classroom prayer, it must be student led, open to all faiths, and required of no one. Translated, it cannot be led by an employee of the state (teacher) because that would be establishment; cannot exclude any faith because that would be discrimination; and cannot be required because that would be coercion. The official position of the Ethics and Religious Liberty Commission under Land's leadership is that the state should not promote or advance religion but should not discriminate against it either. Accommodation is intended to end discrimination. As Land likes to say, Baptists and Buddhists, Mormons and Methodists, and even adherents of the earth goddess Gaea will all have their day to lead the class in prayer. Land calls this accommodation of the students' free exercise of religion.[29]

Separationists point out, however, that this will result in a majoritarianism not much different from that advocated by the Christian Coalition that Land criticizes as neoestablishment. Even if minority faiths have an equal right to lead the prayers, the number of prayers will end up being proportional to the religious makeup of the classroom. This might have been marginally better for Land's Jewish high school friends in that they occasionally would have had the right to lead classroom prayers just like the Baptists and Methodists. But for every day a Jewish student would lead prayer, she would have to endure twenty to thirty Christian prayers as the others in the class took their turns. There would be true equality only in schools where there is an even distribution of religious faith, but in most areas of the country, the exercise of classroom prayer would be so pervasively Protestant and Roman Catholic that the schools would take on a distinctly Christian tenor.[30] No one on either side of the separationist-accommodationist divide believes government should ensure equal representation of religion in the private sector. In public, state-supported facilities, however, separationists are wary of policies that give advantage to the majority faith because this gives every appearance of state preference for that particular view and places individuals from minority faiths in a coercive situation. Such problems notwithstanding, conservatives perceive the current "religious apartheid" as being worse than any scenario a separationist could envision should organized prayer in schools become a reality. Land characterizes the lack of prayer in schools as "anti-majoritarianism" and "dictatorship of the minority."[31]

The issue of vouchers for private religious schools is but a variation on the story of Southern Baptists and prayer in schools—a kind of same song, second verse—for once again conservatives have taken the SBC from one side to the other with the topic of religion and education. This issue is complicated somewhat by the history of Roman Catholic education in the United States. In the nineteenth century, Roman Catholics were often frustrated either by the distinctly Protestant tenor of the nation's public schools or by their secular character wherever religious exercises were discontinued. Moreover, they were mystified by the charge that they were somehow un-American for criticizing public schools for whatever reason. Some Catholic leaders, following a directive from the Vatican, advocated that the church should develop more parochial schools to educate Catholic children. Hand in hand with this effort came lobbying for government funds to support Roman Catholic schools. The argument was either that since Protestants had the public schools, it was only fair that Catholics also get government funding for theirs, or that it was discriminatory for the state to fund secular schools but not religious ones. This argument was based on the fact that Catholics were paying taxes for the secular public schools but required by their faith to send their children elsewhere at their own expense. Bernard McQuaid, bishop of Rochester, stressed three basic points for this nineteenth-century argument: 1) the need for religion in education; 2) the priority of parents over the state in education; and 3) the right of Catholics to their fair share of public funds for education.[32] There arose in response a Protestant hue and cry against any government funding of private religious schools, the vast majority of which were Roman Catholic. Some scholars even believe that Catholic attempts to gain state funding for parochial schools is what made Protestants into strict separationists on church-state issues.[33]

Beginning in the late 1940s, one of the leading organizations opposing tax monies for parochial education was called Protestants and Other Americans United for the Separation of Church and State (POAU). Even the name indicated the organization's resistance to Roman Catholicism. (Today, it is known merely as Americans United for Separation of Church and State.) During the 1950s and 1960s, articles by POAU officials appeared regularly in Southern Baptist state newspapers, seeking to refute the logic of the Catholic argument in favor of tax funds for parochial education. Even in the fifties, the Catholic rallying cry was "choice," as various church officials argued that parishioners should have the choice of sending their children to whatever school they desired and still receive a tax subsidy for doing so. Several leaders advocated a form of vouchers or government certificates that parents could redeem at the school of their choice, whether it be Catholic or public.

In the late 1950s, POAU articles appeared in the *Texas Baptist Standard* refuting these arguments. POAU executive director Glenn Archer called such reasoning "Jesuitical causistry [*sic*]" because however the tax money arrives at the parish school, the result is the same; the state is funding religion and thus violating the First Amendment.[34] Associate director of the POAU C. Stanley Lowell wrote: "It is being demanded by the largest religious denomination in our country that the tax-payers, ourselves among them, shall be required to pay for its program of sectarian indoctrination. This is the very thing that Madison called the ultimate form of tyranny, and it is now being seriously proposed among us." Lowell called this "the battle of the century" and even charged that the First Amendment could not be put into the U.S. Constitution today because the Roman Catholic Church would block it.[35] In addition to such articles, SBC newspaper editors also lauded the efforts of the POAU, and the organization held regional meetings in prominent Baptist churches. Moreover, as late as the mid-1950s, ardent Baptist separationists such as Joseph Martin Dawson, the founding director of the Baptist Joint Committee, referred to those who were soft on separation as having "failed to become thoroughly Americanized."[36] Clearly, many of the elites who ran the SBC quite naturally and logically connected the historic Baptist witness in favor of religious liberty with the First Amendment to the U.S. Constitution, the idea of being a good American, and the Protestant disdain for Catholic arguments that challenged the educational monopoly of the public schools. Being opposed to government funds for private education was often articulated as nearly an article of faith for Southern Baptists. Ironically, it was easier to articulate this position than live by it, for even while opposing all efforts by Roman Catholics to gain funds for their schools, Southern Baptists began to accept indirect government funds for Baptist hospitals and colleges during the 1960s.[37]

Times changed, however. Many Protestants, including Baptists, began to promote private education at the elementary and secondary levels during the 1980s in much the same way as Catholics had. In his study of Alabama Baptists, Wayne Flynt calls the waning support for public schools "[o]ne of the most dramatic shifts in the ethical agenda of Alabama Baptists. . . . Baptist support for public schools eroded rapidly after 1980."[38] He attributed this erosion to racial integration of public schools, the prayer decisions, and charges that public-school textbooks promoted New Age religion, evolutionary science, and alternative lifestyles. Where Catholics formerly detected a pervasive Protestant bias in public schools, many evangelicals today believe those schools are pervasively secular and humanistic. This is just one part of the larger perception that American culture itself is secular and hostile to religion. In short, many evangelicals have joined Roman Catholics in arguing that the public schools are not, and indeed cannot, be neutral; someone's presuppositions always stand behind the educational philosophy. The most extreme voices claim that schools are governed by secular humanism. The logical upshot is that if this philosophy is funded by the state, then it is discriminatory to exclude other philosophies, including religion, from funding. In other words, religious schools are being discriminated against precisely because they are religious. Once again, as with prayer in schools, an Establishment Clause issue is transformed into a Free Exercise Clause concern. SBC conservatives do not carry the argument quite that far because the next logical step is a call for direct government funding of religious education. Still, many of them do support the kind of indirect funding via vouchers that Southern Baptists considered anathema a generation ago.

This shift in the SBC position can be seen once again in convention resolutions. In 1970, moderate leaders drafted a resolution on public and private education that was clearly in line with the historic separationist stance of the denomination. The statement criticized the efforts in more than forty states to garner public funds for parochial education as contributing to an erosion of religious freedom. It cited Pres. Richard Nixon's appointment of a panel to investigate the financial problems of private schools and protested that the board was made up primarily of those committed to parochial education without enough "representation of persons committed unalterably to keeping public money in public channels." The resolution also stated that the American public school system has historically had the support of Southern Baptists, while charging that some "private church-related schools are being formed simply as a strategy to avoid racial integration." The statement resolved that the Southern Baptist Convention "Vigorously oppose every effort to open channels for tax money to support private church-related elementary and secondary schools."[39]

In 1996, with conservatives in control, the denomination's messengers passed a resolution entitled "On Parental Choice on Education." The very title of this statement reflected how the issue had shifted from "parochiaid," which denoted tax monies for Roman Catholic schools, to the idea that all parents should be able to choose whether their children attend private or public schools and receive some form of tax support for whichever choice they make. By the 1990s, the preferred form of tax support for private education was vouchers that could be used to defray the cost of tuition at private schools, including those that are religious. The 1996 SBC resolution, however, carefully avoided the word "vouchers," indicating that the issue of tax monies for private education was perhaps still too controversial for Southern Baptists. Instead, it used more-vague language. The second and third "Whereas" statements cited respectively the collection of tax funds by the government to foster education and the belief that education was primarily the responsibility of parents. This was followed by a statement that parents, as "the principle educators of their children, require the freedom and ability to elect the educational process best suited for their family needs." The statement then resolved: 1) that the messengers "recognize and affirm the God-given right of parents to direct the education of their children"; 2) that the SBC "affirms and encourages the thousands of excellent Southern Baptist public, private, and home-oriented educators"; and 3) "that we encourage our legislators, at all levels of government throughout our nation, to develop the means and methods of returning educational and funding choices to parents."[40] This last statement, of course, was a veiled reference to vouchers. The return of educational funding choices, if indeed such choices ever existed in the first place, meant allowing parents to use their tax monies for public or private education.

Although the 1996 resolution still had to tip-toe around the actual mention of vouchers, Land made it clear in other venues that he believed they were neither unconstitutional nor a violation of the historical principle of religious liberty. He argued, in fact, that Baptists already utilize something very much like vouchers in higher education. He has asked why it is constitutional for an eighteen-year-old freshman at Baylor University to accept government grant money to pay for tuition while it is considered unconstitutional and un-Baptist for an eighteen-year-old senior in high school to receive a tuition voucher for religious secondary education. While vigorously opposing direct government grants to religious schools, he argued that vouchers constitute government aid to parents, not aid to the religious institutions themselves.[41]

As with prayer in schools, Land has attempted whenever possible to emphasize that the voucher question can be interpreted as a free exercise concern and not a matter of establishment of religion. A lawsuit in 1996 gave him and the Ethics and Religious Liberty Commission just that opportunity. The city of Milwaukee, Wisconsin, initiated a pilot voucher program in 1990 that originally excluded religious schools. After it was amended to include them, People for the American Way, a secular separationist organization, challenged the program as a violation of the separation of church and state, specifically as a violation of the Establishment Clause of the First Amendment. When the case went to the Wisconsin Supreme Court, Land's Christian Life Commission (CLC), as it was still being called, joined in a legal brief arguing that to exclude religious schools would be a violation of the free exercise of religion. This was similar to the winning argument in the *Rosenberger* case: once government decides to fund a certain activity, it cannot discriminate against religious organizations that engage in that activity. Land hammered home this view when he wrote: "This case is not about vouchers. It is about religious freedom and government discrimination against religion." This, of course, was a clear overstatement because the case actually was about the constitutionality of vouchers, but Land was attempting to keep the issue in the free exercise, and not the establishment, vein. To that end he continued: "This case does not say that the government must or should offer vouchers to parents who choose alternative schools for their children. It does say that if the government chooses to offer such vouchers, it must not and can not discriminate against religious schools as opposed to other private schools."[42] Here is the *Rosenberger* argument and its open-forum doctrine that the Supreme Court has adopted in other cases. This doctrine holds that in the area of speech, once a public entity opens a forum, it cannot then discriminate on the basis of the content of the speech that takes place within that forum. So, in this case, once the government decides to fund private education, it cannot discriminate against religious schools. There is a limit to such funding, however (as will be seen in the discussion of the Istook amendment below), which is that Land will not support direct government funding of religious institutions. When it comes to vouchers, however, he argues that government funds should go to the parents of the child and not directly to the religious schools. The parents then make the decision as to where the money goes.[43]

In addition to the perennial issue of religion and education, the specific controversy in the late 1990s surrounding Judge Roy Moore of Etowah County, Alabama, serves as a second example of how Baptist principles are filtered through the conservative perception of the cultural situation. A state appeals court judge ordered Judge Moore to remove the Ten Commandments from the wall of his courtroom and to stop opening his sessions with prayer. Moore refused. As of 1997, Land agreed with the appeals court and opposed Moore because the judge made clear that he posted the Commandments and solicited the prayers to promote Christianity. Land believed that if the judge had ministers deliver the prayer on a rotating basis so that no faith would be excluded, or if the judge continued to pray but allowed those of other faiths to recuse themselves until the prayer time was completed, the practice would be acceptable. As already mentioned, Land, as a matter of Baptist principle, opposed government promotion of the Christian faith and, therefore, opposed Judge Moore's practice of using his courtroom as a platform for his own faith.

Other SBC conservatives who were less attuned to the nuances of church-state jurisprudence than Land, saw nothing wrong with Judge Moore's prayer and the Ten Commandments in his courtroom. Both Rogers and Draper, for example, found it hypocritical that the Supreme Court has the commandments on its wall but Judge Moore could not have them on his. Draper saw the attempt by the government to stop the judge from expressing his faith as one more example of government suppression of religion.[44] Timothy George was unwilling as of 1998 to make a judgment on Moore's action. He recognized that Land opposed the judge and generally respected Land's evaluation of such matters. George, however, knew Moore personally and had preached in his church. Respecting him as a committed Christian, family man, and fellow Alabamian just down the road from his own home in Birmingham, George was reluctant to say whether he believed the judge was right or wrong. For George, the bottom-line question was whether or not anyone was being coerced by Judge Moore's actions. If so, George would be opposed. But if the situation were not coercive, he even suggested that Moore's actions might be acceptable as long as a Mormon judge in Utah and a Muslim judge in New York were afforded the same right to exercise their faiths in their courtrooms. Clearly, SBC conservatives prefer a vibrant, wide-open marketplace of religious ideas, even on public property, because for them the alternative is the proverbial naked public square.

Land answered the arguments of Draper and Rogers by pointing out that there is a difference between the Supreme Court's display and Moore's. The former has several images in addition to the Ten Commandments, all of which pay respect to various influences that have shaped Western law. Judge Moore, by his own admission, had placed only the Ten Commandments on the wall of his courtroom because he wanted to honor God, and as Land stressed again, government should not prefer one faith over another. This is an important but rather fine distinction that both Rogers and Draper missed, as did Fob James, the governor of Alabama at the time. After hearing Land expound on his perception of cultural crisis at a conference on religion and politics, the nominally Episcopalian governor felt inspired to proclaim that he would call out the Alabama National Guard if necessary to protect Judge Moore's right to keep the Commandments on the wall and to pray in court.[45] It appeared that Land's perception, when appropriated by Governor James, completely filtered out the principle of nonestablishment, but the similarities between the governor's position on the Moore situation and SBC conservatives' view of prayer in schools should not go unnoticed. In both situations the perception of cultural crisis led to the view that free exercise is the only consideration. The difference between Judge Moore and prayer in schools, at least as Land saw it, was that the latter situation dealt with the free exercise of students in a government-sponsored institution, while in the former case, Judge Moore was the government-sponsored institution. When he promotes the faith, the state is promoting the faith. This distinction between religious exercise by private citizens on public property versus religious exercise by public officials is one the Supreme Court has wrangled with, generally giving much wider latitude, as one would expect, for private citizens.[46]

The third issue that highlighted SBC conservative accommodationism in the 1990s was the push in the U.S. Congress for a religion amendment to the U.S. Constitution. When the 104th Congress convened in 1995 with Republican majorities in both houses, three such amendments appeared. This was in keeping with soon-to-be House speaker Newt Gingrich's call for an amendment that would restore prayer and Bible reading in schools. Senators Jesse Helms (R-N.C.), Robert Byrd (D-W.Va.), and Strom Thurmond (R-S.C.), Southern Baptists all, as was Gingrich (R-Ga.), along with Rep. Bill Emerson (R-Mo.) offered proposals that focused specifically on prayer in schools. Others, however, began to envision a broader approach that would tie prayer in schools to religious expression in other public venues and to tuition vouchers. Rep. Ernest Istook (R-Okla.) emerged as the leader of this broader approach.[47] His own religious odyssey seems a fitting commentary on the church-state climate of the time. A graduate of Baylor University, a bastion of moderate Southern Baptist separationism if ever there was one, Istook later converted to Mormonism, a denomination that is decidedly accommodationist on most church-state matters.

Istook convened a meeting of several representatives from organizations concerned about discrimination against religion in public places. The group included Jay Sekulow of the American Center for Law and Justice, Forrest Montgomery of the National Association of Evangelicals, Steve McFarland of the Christian Legal Society, Lou Sheldon of the Traditional Values Coalition, Michael Whitehead of the SBC Christian Life Commission, and John Whitehead of the Rutherford Institute. Other individuals in attendance at this brainstorming session included William Murray, son of the infamous atheist Madelyn Murray O'Hair; David Barton; and former Republican congressman William Danforth. From this meeting emerged a consensus that the proposed amendment should focus on the broad issue of religious equality, meaning that religious speech should be treated equally with nonreligious. Istook then solicited the help of church-state scholar Michael McConnell, then of the University of Chicago, who became the principle drafter of the first of the three sections of the proposed amendment. As discussed earlier, McConnell's own definition of accommodationism does not include support for official religious expression of the public's majority views on religion. Nevertheless, the sections of the Istook amendment not authored by McConnell moved well beyond the scholar's views. A series of public hearings followed in settings across the country where a variety of interest group representatives could have their say. At the first such hearing, Istook himself summed up the rationale for his proposed amendment in language that revealed the perception of hostility to religion held by SBC conservatives and many other evangelicals in the United States, which has resulted in the turning of an issue formerly thought to be a matter of establishment into one of free exercise. "[D]espite the freedoms enshrined in our Constitution, millions of Americans today believe their freedom of religion, and of religious expression, is endangered."[48] Istook's amendment would go through several permutations, including a name change. Before reaching the floor of the House of Representatives, it would be called the Religious Freedom amendment.

The reaction to this proposal on the part of SBC conservatives, especially Land, was interesting to say the least. In 1995 the convention passed a resolution calling on Congress to adopt a constitutional amendment "to protect the freedom of private persons, including students in public schools, to engage in voluntary prayer and other religious expression in circumstances in which expression of a nonreligious character would be permitted; and to prohibit the denial of benefits or other discrimination against persons on account of the religious character of their speech or status; and to permit government accommodation of public or ceremonial acknowledgments of religious heritage, beliefs and traditions of its people." This portion of the resolution appeared to be a request for something very much like the Istook amendment, but the resolution also called on the CLC to advocate a form of religious freedom that would "prevent government from composing, compelling or subsidizing prayer or religious expression by any person."[49]

Land's position on the Istook amendment evolved from vigorous opposition to firm support precisely because the measure itself originally seemed to allow the government to compose prayers and directly fund religion. As of April 1997, the amendment, in his view, was a classic neo–establishment majoritarian piece of work. It included phrases like "the right to pray or acknowledge religious belief . . . shall not be infringed," but it did not say specifically whose right. This left open the possibility that government agents themselves could lead public prayers or even compose them. The only thing government could not do would be require people to participate. In Land's view, this violated the Baptist principle espoused by conservatives and articulated in the SBC confession of faith that admonishes the church not to rely on the state to do its work.[50] Moreover, the amendment also stipulated that government could not "discriminate against or deny a benefit on account of religion." While at first glance this appears to be exactly the sort of equal treatment principle conservatives wanted, and what they had called for in their 1995 resolution, Land maintained that without the qualifier "any person" after the word "against," the amendment would allow or even require direct government grants to religious schools and perhaps even churches. "[W]e're back to parochiaid," quipped Land in April 1997. The amendment was, in his words, "awful and appalling. [It] denies everything we believe as Baptists."[51] Actually, the Istook amendment was about three words from being supportable by the SBC's accommodationist conservatives.

While staunchly opposing the Istook proposal, Land also argued that some kind of amendment was needed to remedy the appalling state of discrimination against religion that existed in the United States. Again, he was acting consistently with the 1995 resolution's call for a constitutional amendment. So, he continued to apply pressure on Istook and his supporters. Partly as a result of this, the proposed amendment was revised in early May. The originally objectionable passage now read: "To secure the people's right to acknowledge God according to the dictates of conscience: The people's right to pray and to recognize their religious beliefs, heritage or traditions on public property, including schools, shall not be infringed. The government shall not require any person to join in prayer or other religious activity, initiate or designate school prayers, discriminate against religion, or deny equal access to a benefit on account of religion."[52]

Separationists continued to find many things wrong with the Istook amendment, not the least of which was that the changes were not all that significant. An adjustment even Land emphasized in early 1997 but did not get was the provision relating to public prayer. At that time he charged: "The Istook Language says that the government cannot 'initiate or compose school prayers.' Thus, outside of the school arena, the government *can* initiate and compose prayers and the only thing the Istook language would keep government from doing is to 'compel joining in prayer.'" As the final version of the amendment read, this was still the case. The astute observer will also notice that Land's concern over direct government aid to religious institutions was not remedied. As he wrote while still opposing the amendment, "[W]hen the notion that 'government shall not . . . deny a benefit on account of religion' is used without the qualifier 'any person' it *guarantees* that the government will be giving direct government aid to parochial and religious schools (i.e., parochiad [*sic*])."[53] The placement of "any person" in the revised amendment simply did not do what Land argued was needed. There would appear to be the need for "any person" after the word "deny" as well. For many separationists, these changes were all moot because, in their view, there was no need for another constitutional amendment dealing with church-state issues; the First Amendment was enough. James Dunn summed up this position in down-home language when he likened the changes to "putting lipstick on a pig."[54]

In early August, three months after Land and the ERLC had signed on as supporters of the revised Istook amendment, Al Mohler said that he believed the amendment had been moving in the right direction, away from state-mandated religious expression. Remaining somewhat skeptical because of the amendment's many permutations, he could still say: "I do think that the First Amendment has been so badly distorted by the courts . . . that religious freedom is now so much under attack that the one thing you cannot do is exercise your First Amendment rights to religious expression. If an amendment is necessary to bring that back into balance, then I'm going to support the amendment." In this context, he added, "I want no state-initiated or state-mandated religious expression, period."[55]

Given that Land, the ERLC, and other conservatives have consistently advocated a constitutional amendment, it is hardly surprising that they eventually found their way clear to support Istook even as they failed to get all the changes they desired. This is especially understandable in light of rumors that Land was under pressure from the board of trustees of the ERLC to find a way to support the measure.[56] What is puzzling, however, is that the former opposition to the amendment was not just over wording but over philosophy as well. In a summary analysis issued before the changes were made, Land and ERLC legal counsel Will Dodson characterized their objection, writing, "The Christian Life Commission [the former name of the ERLC] has pushed consistently for an amendment which would bar government discrimination against any person on account of religious belief, expression, or exercise." Contrasting this position with that of Istook, they wrote, "Istook's amendment would replace one form of government discrimination (i.e., preference for the secular or nonreligious) with another (i.e., preference for the religious views of the majority)."[57] In other words, the difference between Istook and the ERLC was not just over word choice, rather the fundamental church-state philosophies of the two camps were at odds. Istook and his supporters wanted government acknowledgement and support for religion, while Land and other SBC conservatives argued that they only wanted government to stop discriminating against religion. It is highly unlikely that the rewording of Istook's amendment constituted a fundamental shift in his and his supporters' philosophy, one that Land had decried as a state "preference for the religious views of the majority."

As late as April 1997, these philosophical differences drove Land to speak with great force against Istook and his supporters, drawing a stark contrast between their views and the proper views of Baptists. A month later he, the ERLC, and SBC conservatives who take their cues from Land had become Istook's allies. Because of their perception that government discrimination against religion and the secularization of culture are the paramount church-state issues of our time, SBC conservatives joined in an alliance with "neo–establishment majoritarians," as Land called the likes of Istook, the Christian Coalition, and James Dobson. This coalition threatened to undermine the conservative claim that Baptist principles animated their church-state views, and it once again fueled the moderate charge that the SBC was in lockstep with the Christian Right. Eventually, the Istook amendment gained a majority vote in the U.S. House of Representatives but not the two-thirds majority needed for passage.

As with prayer in public schools, the Istook amendment was another example of strong Baptist principle being filtered through a perception of cultural crisis and hostility to Christianity to produce a position that was quite different from what moderate SBC leaders traditionally had supported. The Judge Moore situation, however, pitted moderates and some conservatives, Land at least, on the same side, while other conservatives such as Draper interpreted even this as a free-exercise issue. This was an example of the informed activist Land recognizing the difference between private religious speech on public property and religious speech by a public government official. The distinction, however, was sometimes lost on the more populist advocates within the SBC conservative ranks.

CONCLUSION

What one is left with is a situation where moderates and conservatives are primarily at odds over their respective perceptions of culture, and these perceptions are then played out in the context of church-state issues. Moderates believe that threats to religious free exercise are at the margins of culture, primarily among minority faiths. Activists like Dunn and scholars like James Wood Jr. speak forcefully for the rights of such minorities. A major part of this plea for free exercise is the corresponding attention to Establishment Clause issues. In the view of the separationists, even low levels of establishment of the majority faith curtail the rights of minorities. In the view of the conservatives, though, the moderates have been paying too much attention to Establishment Clause concerns. Conservatives, by contrast, became convinced that a decadent culture was being stripped clean of religion with the help of a secularizing state hostile to faith. Whatever concern conservatives have for minority faiths is no different from the concern they have for their own free exercise of religion. They have rated low the danger of establishment because they are so convinced that free exercise is the paramount, indeed the only, issue of our time. In differentiating the conservative accommodationist position from that of separationists like Dunn or Wood, Land puts the situation like this: they are mostly concerned about government violation of the Establishment Clause of the First Amendment, while conservatives are mostly concerned about government violation of the Free Exercise Clause.[58] Patterson concurs, having written in 1991, "In recent years so much effort has been expended in the interpretation and enforcement of the 'Establishment Clause' that the 'free exercise' clause has gone begging."[59]

Had Patterson applied that interpretation only through 1981 instead of 1991, he would have had a significant ally in legal scholar Ira Lupu, who wrote in 1992 that from the *Everson* case of 1947 until the early 1980s, a "strong Establishment Clause, weak Free Exercise Clause" jurisprudence prevailed in constitutional law. This is exactly what Land, Patterson, and the other conservatives believed had happened, and they decried its development. According to Lupu's analysis, however, the problem in more recent years was not that the Establishment Clause had been too strong, as SBC conservatives believed, but that the Free Exercise Clause had become so weak. By Lupu's way of reckoning, conservatives were rightly concerned about this weakness of the Free Exercise Clause. But in the 1990s, they were wrong to argue that the Establishment Clause was too strong. Rather, Lupu argued, there has been since the early 1980s a tendency toward a "Weak Establishment Clause [*and*] weak Free Exercise Clause" jurisprudence, with the infamous *Smith* decision of 1990 especially putting the Free Exercise Clause in peril.[60] The Supreme Court was out of balance from *Everson* to the 1980s. The best way to remedy the imbalance would have been to strengthen the Free Exercise Clause so that it would have become equal to the Establishment Clause. Instead, in the view of Lupu and others, the Court remedied the imbalance by weakening the Establishment Clause to put it on par with the Free Exercise Clause, then weakening the Free Exercise Clause even more in *Smith*. The SBC conservatives of the 1990s wanted to see the Free Exercise Clause strengthened, but they were relatively unconcerned about the Establishment Clause. Lupu and others saw a need for keeping both strong.

Where one comes down in this balance between establishment and free exercise is determined by one's perception of the cultural situation. SBC conservatives such as Mohler could agree with moderates that in the 1950s established religion in the form of cultural Christianity was an issue of great importance. Later, however, the sense of cultural crisis began to go so deep among conservatives that the civil religion of the 1950s seemed a quaint memory. Clearly, they would rather be faced with the challenges of the fifties than those that exist today. Recall Land's stated ideal for the culture being an America of 1955 minus the racism and sexism.[61]

This delicate Baptist balancing act has been interpreted by moderate Baptist historian Walter Shurden. He has argued that in church-state matters, Baptists have usually been "Matthew 22 people." Matthew 22:15–22 contains the story of the Pharisees who asked Jesus whether it was lawful to pay a tax to Caesar. Jesus' famous reply was, "Render to Caesar the things that are Caesar's; and to God the things that are God's."[62] Shurden's view of

Baptists is that they have most often legitimized but limited the state, as the Matthew passage seems to teach. Only occasionally have Baptists had to be Revelation 13 people. In that apocalyptic chapter the state has become a beast against which believers must take their stand.[63] While Shurden's interpretation is compelling when applied to most of Southern Baptist history, it appears that many conservative Southern Baptists began in the 1980s to lean increasingly toward Revelation 13. They saw American culture as something akin to the beast from which Christians must be protected. Establishment of religion was a threat so remote that they scarcely considered it. Instead, nearly all church-state issues were viewed as free-exercise concerns. Often lurking beneath this perception was a belief that there can be no such thing as government neutrality, a view shared by many evangelicals outside the SBC. As this line of reasoning goes, government will always promote some kind of worldview, and in the situation of the 1990s, the government was promoting secularism over Christianity and using the guise of strict separation to do it.

There is one more point worth noting here related to the moderate charge that conservatives have forfeited their independence and become captive to the Christian Right. The flip-side of this is the conservative charge that moderates are strict separationists and therefore in lockstep with the secular left. On church-state issues moderates do ally themselves often with the ACLU and other secular organizations that are separationist. And, conservatives, as shown above, often find themselves in alliance with the neo–establishment majoritarians of the Christian Right. This is again related to culture, specifically the culture war.

Southern Baptist conservatives see themselves as culture warriors, and as mentioned earlier, in culture war the first casualty is the nuanced middle voices. For this reason Land's attempt to steer SBC conservatives down the middle between neo–establishment majoritarians on his right and strict separationists on his left while attempting to be a culture warrior himself has been self-defeating. This is what happened with the Istook amendment. Land was forced to choose a side, and he quite naturally chose the side with cultural perceptions like his own. He may find that maintaining the middle will be possible only in the abstract, that when real issues arise, he will always have to choose. There just is no middle ground when the question is, do you support an amendment to the Constitution? While scholars can debate the nuances of the issue, those who believe they are engaged in a battle for the soul of the nation feel compelled to do something. By contrast to church-state issues, SBC conservatives do not even attempt to take a moderate position on abortion; there has been no attempt to find the middle course. They have proudly taken the lead on the conservative side of the abortion battle and call upon others to join them. It appears, then, that while conservatives willingly tack to the right on issues like abortion, they will also be pushed to the right on issues related to church and state even though their principles suggest a more moderate point of view. In culture war, perception is everything. No matter what one's principles are, individuals and groups who declare themselves combatants will align with others whose perceptions match their own.

6
No One Has Been Shot Yet

Southern Baptists and the Abortion Controversy

In 1994 James Davison Hunter published *Before the Shooting Begins: Searching for Democracy in America's Culture War*. This was a follow-up, companion volume to his much-debated *Culture Wars*. In the introduction he reiterates his basic culture-war argument and ties it specifically to the intractable positions the opposing sides take on key public issues. Hunter writes: "I focus here on one controversy in particular—the one surrounding abortion—as a window into the relationship between democratic practice and the culture war as a whole. . . . Abortion remains the knottiest moral and political dilemma of the larger culture war, contested now for more than two decades with little hope of a satisfying resolution."[1]

During the Southern Baptist controversy, abortion was a far more important issue than many believed. Conservatives kept saying publicly that the primary issue animating their movement was theology, particularly the inerrancy of scripture, while moderates claimed that the conservative movement was solely about political control of the denomination. The right-wing movement was not just theological, however, and it was not just about denominational control. In many ways it was a response to culture and, therefore, could not avoid the central cultural issue of our time. While the moderates whom conservatives sought to unseat within the denomination were by no means pervasively pro-choice, there was a small cadre of elites who did espouse that position. Some in this group operated from what has come to be known as a Rawlsian liberal position that allowed them to argue fervently for the right to an abortion without claiming to actually favor abortion itself. It was at these moderates that conservatives took aim. What emerged was a struggle between two competing views of how religion and politics relate to each other. This battle mirrors a larger part of America's culture war between two competing political, and perhaps moral, visions.

In 1971 John Rawls published his widely discussed book, *A Theory of Justice*. After several years of debate and criticism, he then wrote *Political Liberalism*. These two works established Rawls as the most important political theorist of our time and spawned a major philosophical debate between liberals and communitarians that continues to the present.

For Rawls, in order for a law to be just, it must not rely on metaphysical constructs or language that are not accessible to all people and widely shared in a society. In his words, any limitation on individual freedom "must be supported by ordinary observation and modes of thought . . . which are generally recognized as correct," as opposed to deep personal convictions based on revelation or faith.[2] The latter stem from what Rawls calls a comprehensive doctrine, one that aspires to explain all of life. Whether religious or secular, Rawls believes that comprehensive doctrines are not proper sources from which to make public policy. By contrast, a political conception, as Rawls calls it, is much narrower and more proper for political decision making. This distinction is sometimes discussed as the difference between the substantive and procedural. In a pluralistic society we can never agree on substantive, comprehensive worldviews, Rawlsian liberals believe, but we can perhaps agree on procedures that are fair and just.[3]

In tandem with his emphasis on public reason and accessibility, Rawls also believes that liberal justice requires that individuals "go behind a veil of ignorance" when choosing principles of justice on which to build public policy, which means they should act as if they do not know how a particular position will affect them or whether or not it is consistent with their own most deeply held beliefs. This ensures that their position is in accordance with public justice and not private advantage.[4] The obvious result of this form of political liberalism is maximum individual freedom because only widely held, publicly accessible reasons justify restricting what people can do. In fact, so much emphasis is placed on the individual's right to chart his or her own autonomous course that deliberations over what constitutes a good society must be held in abeyance. There is, in effect, little room for a communitarian approach to what constitutes the good, as individuals are left free to settle this question for themselves.[5]

A small handful of moderate intellectuals in key positions of the Southern Baptist Convention and its related institutions adopted this Rawlsian approach to political issues, specifically abortion. SBC conservatives seem not to have detected the basis of the moderate pro-choice position, but it may have made little difference if they had, given that most rank-and-file Southern Baptists would not have understood the nuances anyway. It is not even clear that all the moderates who espoused what I will argue is a Rawlsian position were aware that they were appropriating his political theory of justice, but at least one did cite Rawls by name. The most significant aspect of all this is not who if anyone was utilizing Rawls or whether this was an appropriate theory for Southern Baptists. Rather, what is most important to note is that the Southern Baptist debate over abortion mirrored the larger liberal-communitarian debate, that the moderates were out of step with the vast majority of grassroots Southern Baptists, and that their argument in favor of the pro-choice position, therefore, played directly into the hands of the conservatives who were attempting to unseat them from positions of power within the denomination. In short, moderates could not have chosen a better strategy for putting themselves on the defensive had they actually set out to do so.

But this is just part of the story—the part that made the SBC conservatives' position easier. The greater part is identifying how the conservatives have made the pro-life position on abortion a high-profile item for the denomination.

SOUTHERN POLITICAL CHANGE AS A BACKDROP FOR THE ABORTION CONTROVERSY IN THE SBC

The Southern Baptist battle over abortion and the more fundamental culture war it represented took place against the backdrop of southern political change that saw the region move from being solidly Democratic to a competitive region where Republicans clearly have the upper hand among white voters. This political transformation has been a complex phenomenon that has included economic, demographic, and racial factors. It has also included moral concerns that have been translated into political issues. On these, the New Religious Right has been largely responsible for mobilizing conservative white southerners. As Oran Smith writes in his book *The Rise of Baptist Republicanism*, "The success of the New Right replaced overt racial appeals with moralistic social issues that energized conservative voters for the GOP, and also energized fundamentalist Baptists (Jerry Falwell and Bob Jones), then Pentecostal Baptists (Pat Robertson), and finally Southern Baptists."[6] Political scientist James Guth's research during the 1980s showed that the new Religious Right was making serious inroads into the Southern Baptist Convention and that conservatives in the denomination were becoming more active politically as a result.[7] On a broader scale, Republicans won the South by focusing on issues that were highly symbolic of ideological conservatism—big government, gun control, national defense, welfare fraud, anti-communism, and even the Pledge of Allegiance. Smith argued that there has been a parallel in the SBC as conservative leaders used highly symbolic issues like liberalism in the seminaries to win the voters to their side as well as highly symbolic political issues like abortion, prayer in schools, and the Equal Rights Amendment.[8] Of these, abortion has clearly had the most staying power. It has been and remains central to the conservatives' belief that they are engaged in a contest to save American culture.

When moderates in the 1980s charged repeatedly that conservatives were selling out to the Republican Party, they were consistently misreading the situation. Conservatives engaged in political action on an issue-by-issue basis, just as moderates had before them, but they were interested in a different set of issues, or at least different solutions to some of the same cultural problems. SBC conservative elites had indeed become Republican almost to a person, but this was primarily because of their belief that they were engaged in a culture war and that the GOP stands on the correct side of the cultural issues. Of these issues, abortion loomed largest, and nearly everything else became subordinate. To be wrong on that issue was to be wrong on virtually everything.

Still, while SBC conservatives make the case that they have not wedded the denomination to the right wing of the Republican Party, that image does exist in many quarters, and not just among SBC moderates. Well-known evangelical activist Tony Campolo, for example, said in 1997: "In theory, Southern Baptist theology is on target. It is in the practice where the denomination falls down. . . . I'm not sure where the Southern Baptist ideology ends and the Republican Party begins."[9] Campolo's criticism can probably be accounted for by his own concern for issues of social justice. Research by Guth and others shows that conservative activists in the SBC, as one would expect, pay much less attention to issues such as poverty, environmental concerns, and civil rights than do moderate or liberal activists in the denomination.[10] The result is that SBC conservative elites tend to find common ground with Republicans in the most visible social debate of our time. Campolo or Jim Wallis of *Sojourners* magazine, by contrast, are consistent with the Democratic Party on many concerns but differ even on the highly contentious issue of abortion. This leaves them less open to the accusation of marrying their theology to a political party than is the case for SBC conservatives. Still, many charge that Campolo and Wallis are the flip-side, mirror image of the Christian Right, the "evangelical left" as they are often called. Campolo's close association with Pres. Bill Clinton helped foster this image.

SOUTHERN BAPTIST MODERATE ELITES AND THE ABORTION ISSUE

In 1973, after the U.S. Supreme Court decided *Roe* v. *Wade*, SBC fundamentalist patriarch W. A. Criswell said, "I have always felt that it was only after a child was born and had life separate from its mother that it became an individual person, and it has always, therefore, seemed to me that what is best for the mother and for the future should be allowed."[11] While this statement could be touted as clear evidence for a pro-choice ideology in SBC history, it is more likely evidence of how little Southern Baptists had thought about abortion before the *Roe* decision.[12] Once they began to think through the implications, it did not take long for Southern Baptist conservatives to develop a strong pro-life position. Shortly after Criswell's statement, the SBC right wing began efforts to pass an anti-abortion resolution. Having secured control of the denomination in the 1980s, they began to maneuver to make the pro-life position the dominant and mandatory principle in all SBC agencies and seminaries. Indeed, in 1986 a reporter quoted Paige Patterson as saying, "We want an open, pro-life position in all of our institutions and agencies, dealing with both abortion and euthanasia." Patterson was reported to have said that such a pro-life position would be mandatory for all seminary faculty, members of the Christian Life Commission, authors of all literature published by the Sunday School Board, and employees of all denominational hospitals and other agencies.[13] He later denied having said that a particular position on social issues would be mandatory, arguing strenuously that he was merely articulating his hopes for the denomination, not a new set of organizational requirements.[14] Clearly, however, in between Criswell's statement and Patterson's—whatever he actually said—something profound had happened. Specifically, the SBC had gone from a denomination with a moderate official position on abortion and room for a variety of views to one in which virtually all leaders favored the outlawing of abortion in all cases except where the mother's life is in danger.

As discussed earlier, the abortion issue played significantly in the development of the cultural perceptions conservatives came to hold. By 1998, Richard Land could trumpet that the SBC had become the most pro-life denomination in America, even more so than the Roman Catholic Church when it comes to the person in the pew.[15] Few would contest this statement.

While it is hard to know just how the average Southern Baptist felt about the abortion issue during the consciousness-raising years of the 1970s, it is safe to say that the denomination was never firmly pro-choice at either the grassroots or elite levels. In 1970 a Baptist organization called VIEWpoll surveyed Baptist leaders. When asked, "Would you favor or oppose a law which would permit a woman to go to a doctor to end pregnancy at any time during the first three months?" 79.8 percent of the pastors and 75.9 percent of Sunday School teachers said they would oppose such a law. Only 19.6 percent of the teachers and 12.7 percent of the pastors said they would favor such a law. The remainder had no opinion. By way of comparison, Gallop determined that 50 percent of the American people opposed legalized abortion while 40 percent favored it.[16] A 1985 survey of Southern Baptist pastors and lay people by sociologist Nancy Ammerman resulted in the following breakdown: 11 percent believed abortion should be illegal without exception; 29 percent that abortion should be permissible only to save the life of the mother; 50 percent included rape and incest along with the life of the mother as acceptable reasons for legal abortions; and only 10 percent believed that abortion should be a matter of personal choice.[17]

Another set of statistics has been provided by the American National Elections Survey, conducted by the University of Michigan's Center for Political Studies. This study showed the pro-choice position among Southern Baptist "regular attenders" to have grown from 8 percent in 1984, roughly equivalent to Ammerman's 1985 percentage for pastors and lay people, to 20 percent in 1992. It is difficult to account for the fact that the pro-choice element was on the rise during the years when conservatives were taking control of the denomination. It should be remembered, however, that many "regular attending" Southern Baptists pay little attention to what takes place at the national level of the denomination. Even while the pro-choice segment of the SBC was growing, the 20 percent of Southern Baptist "regular attenders" supporting choice was significantly lower than the American population at large, of which 43 percent was pro-choice. Moreover, that same survey concluded that 70 percent of Southern Baptist "regular attenders" favored restrictions on abortion (excepting only for rape, incest, and to save the life of the mother), which was down from 84 percent in 1972 but up from 63 percent in 1980, roughly when the SBC conservative movement began. By contrast, only 47 percent of all Americans favored such restrictions in 1992.[18]

It appears that from shortly after the *Roe* decision to the present, Southern Baptists as a group have been much more willing to restrict abortions than the American population at large. Most of the debate within the denomination over the past quarter-century has been over what the nature of the restrictions should be. This broad, moderately pro-life position, however, should not be taken to mean that there has been a consensus sufficient to satisfy both conservatives and moderates. At the elite level the denomination has been very polarized. This is because the moderate party has included not just moderate pro-lifers but also moderate pro-choice individuals who have been the lightning rods for criticism from conservatives who have taken a hard-line pro-life stand.

Among the moderates, Foy Valentine and the Christian Life Commission he headed came under withering criticism once conservatives began to mobilize. Typical of the Valentine position was a 1981 CLC pamphlet that asked "how should we put into law whatever moral conclusions Christians may reach on abortion?" The author, presumably Valentine, answered with three bulleted points: First, the pamphlet rejected the view that abortion is a religious issue "into which the state has no right to intrude." Rather, the pamphlet admonished, "The Christian concern for the value of the defenseless fetus . . . should prevent advocating the removal of all legal protection surrounding the fetus' right to live." Second, "At the same time it is questionable that Christian love and justice would be served by extremely restrictive laws which do not give conscientious people with proper medical advice the opportunity to choose when they are faced with very grave moral dilemmas related to abortion." Third, "The present legal situation in this country, for all practical purposes, permits the casual use of abortion as a means of birth control, a situation that is socially irresponsible and morally indefensible. Christians may properly work to change this situation without moving to the other extreme and insisting that the whole nation be required to accept the Roman Catholic dogma related to abortion as the law of the land."[19]

It is hard to determine exactly the position of this pamphlet. Clearly, it opposed unregulated abortion on demand, but it also rejected the Roman Catholic position that calls for outright, across-the-board legal sanctions, which would be identical to the position held by SBC conservatives today. Overall, the pamphlet seems to typify the position that while abortion is problematic morally, it is so deeply personal that some leeway should be reserved for difficult choices. It would seem best to characterize Valentine and the CLC as moderately pro-choice. By the mid-1980s, Valentine was grouping Roman Catholics and the Religious Right together as the chief proponents of the pro-life position and charging, correctly, that SBC conservatives had joined these two groups. In a 1985 interview he made several references to both the Roman Catholic Church and the new Religious Right before closing with this statement: "While I am still not eager to help Jerry Falwell get his political choices elected to public office nor am I willing to shape public policy to the demands of the Roman Catholic bishops, I am nevertheless convinced that the issue deserves the careful attention which is being given to it by the Christian Life Commission of the Southern Baptist Convention."[20]

While Valentine's reference to the Roman Catholic Church was in one sense an attempt to clarify his own position, it was also a rhetorical device that played on vestiges of southern anti-Catholicism. Throughout this 1985 interview is the strong implication that Roman Catholic bishops were attempting to foist a particular theological position onto the rest of "pluralistic America." Still, Valentine's own position was only moderately pro-choice in that he repeatedly emphasized the grave moral nature of abortion, rejected the notion that it was a purely private and individual matter, and pointed out that, increasingly, Americans were not comfortable with the abortion-on-demand status quo. At the same time, though, he held that abortion should be left to the decision of the mother in cases of rape, incest, gross deformity of the fetus, and, most importantly in the view of conservatives, when there is clear danger to the mother's physical health or mental well being.[21] From the conservative point of view, this reference to the mother's mental well being was very much like a purely pro-choice position. The moderate tone that Valentine and the CLC exuded was characterized by Paige Patterson as a "lack of energy" on the abortion issue.[22] Adequate energy (as will be shown below) would have meant a call for the elimination of all abortions except those to save the life of the mother.

Valentine's position seems typical of many moderate elites in the 1970s and 1980s. In a 1986 address to the Texas Christian Life Commission, Baylor University ethics professor Dan McGee spoke of several important issues that should be considered when thinking through the abortion dilemma. Church-state concerns loomed large in his address. He asked, how should abortion be regulated in a pluralistic society? He identified two poles of thinking based on the theocratic claims of the medieval church and Calvin's Geneva at one end and the Anabaptist view of the Radical Reformation at the other. The former attempts to translate God's law specifically into human law. The latter sees church and state as having different functions. According to McGee: "The [second] view, more often identified with the Anabaptists and the radical Reformation, separates the function of church and state and limits the purpose of law to enforcing only broadly held convictions while leaving plenty of latitude wherever possible for minority perspectives. This is a tradition that focuses on the radical demands of the Christian faith and therefore recognizes the impossibility of trying to implement those demands in the godless public. This position is also instructed by history and by remembering the importance of religious freedom. There is the perennial danger of setting the precedent of enforcing our view of God's will through the state and someday being victimized by the state as a moral minority."[23]

Without actually saying that abortion rights are religious-liberty rights, McGee tied the two together in such a way that one could reasonably conclude that the Anabaptist and Baptist tradition of religious liberty was a kind of libertarian doctrine that shied away from legislating morality. This view was common among many moderate spokespersons. Cecil Sherman, one of the primary leaders of the moderate defense against the conservative movement, held this view. In 1983 he said that he had never counseled anyone to have an abortion, never intended to, and was opposed to abortion. "But I am also unwilling to make my abortion position to be the law of the land." Why? Because of the principle of voluntarism. "It is a Baptist idea," he wrote, "and just because most of the people in this country are living like pagans[,] [that] does not give us the right to abandon our first premise and force those pagans to be moral. All religion and all religious rule ought to be voluntary." Making the relationship between the Baptist tradition and the pro-choice position all the tighter was the fact that Sherman wrote this in an article entitled "The Idea of Being Baptist" in a section entitled "I Believe in Voluntary Participation."[24] This was his own personal confession of Baptist faith in which he used abortion as an example of the voluntary principle. Thus, even if Baptists believed that abortion was immoral, they should not necessarily attempt to have it outlawed by the state, especially since the United States is a pluralistic, and even godless, society that should not be expected to reflect the laws of God.

Even more overt in this vein were the arguments of James E. Wood Jr. Wood was the founder of Baylor University's J. M. Dawson Institute of Church-State Studies and, for eight years during the 1970s, served as executive director of the Baptist Joint Committee (BJC). He was consistently and explicitly pro-choice, and he tied his abortion position tightly to both the First Amendment and to Baptist history. Shortly after *Roe,* the BJC voted to oppose the Buckley-Hatfield constitutional amendment and all other similar amendments intended to overturn the effects of the Court's abortion decisions. The BJC took such action, as Wood wrote in early 1974, "out of concern that in our pluralistic society the state should not embody into law one particular religious or moral viewpoint on which differing views are held by substantial sections of the religious and nonreligious communities. The action of the Committee came also out of its long tradition for upholding liberty of conscience and the separation of church and state."[25] For Wood, liberty of conscience and separation of church and state required one to affirm the pro-choice position that would leave the very personal decision of abortion to individuals.

Some years later, in written testimony concerning a Pennsylvania law restricting state funding for abortion, Wood developed his views more fully, arguing that certain restrictions on access to abortion were a violation of Baptist tradition. He writes: "I believe that this statute violates the free exercise clause of the First Amendment as we understand it in the Baptist faith. To be consistent with the freedom of conscience protected by the free exercise clause, public policy decision should neither condone nor espouse abortion and should take no position on the nature of the fetus. The selective funding of abortion and childbirth by Pennsylvania's Medicaid program is a powerful disincentive to poor women to make a conscientious decision to terminate a pregnancy and an equally substantial impediment to carrying out such a decision."[26]

Acknowledging that Baptists differ on the question of the personhood of the fetus, Wood nevertheless ventures his own view: "My own belief is that person begins upon birth. During pregnancy there is a fetus, upon delivery or birth, the fetus becomes a person." The irony here is that this was precisely the position Criswell had articulated in 1973. One would be hard pressed to find two Southern Baptists more unlike each other than Wood and Criswell. Wood continues, moreover: "I believe the government is acting as an arbitrator of the morals of the people of this country when it says that public funds are available for a vast panoply of medical services including child delivery services, yet withholds funding for abortion. It is discriminatory, punitive, and morally offensive for the government to withhold a necessary medical service and impose a stigma on a poor woman who out of conscience decides that she must have an abortion." He concludes that the First Amendment not only protects a woman's right to choose, but mandates state funding of abortions as well. "Fundng both abortion and childbirth," he writes, "is the only position compatible with the First Amendment because it allows for the absolutist's moral stance against abortion as well as a different point of view. This would preserve the neutrality which is necessary if the religious freedom of poor women is to be protected."[27]

Valentine, McGee, Sherman, and Wood all shared the view that Baptist tradition led to the pro-choice position. Joining them as perhaps the most ardent proponent of this view among Southern Baptists was Southern Baptist Theological Seminary ethics professor Paul Simmons. Simmons's articulation of the argument that abortion was a religious-liberty issue came as little surprise when it appeared in 1990. In the 1970s and 1980s, he had often taken the lead on this issue. In 1976 he told a Christian Life Commission conference that since *Roe* v. *Wade,* the theater of discussion of abortion had shifted from the courts and halls of legislatures to churches and other private venues. He urged Christians to take a pastoral approach to abortion that focused on caring and liberty of conscience instead of rights, legality, and due process of law. Like McGee a decade later, Simmons addressed liberty of conscience and "freedom of responsible choice which are basic ingredients in the meaning of person." Simmons also criticized those who made absolutist moral and legal pronouncements on the issue. "The great temptation," he was quoted as saying, "is to do the greater wrong—act as the moralistic external judge—ascribing rightness or wrongness to decisions and actions past and present. The mote-hunters are alive and doing well but leaving behind a veritable path strewn with guilt-ridden clients who made the mistake of seeking counsel from well-meaning, but misdirected moralists."[28]

It is worth noting that Simmons was the leading pro-choice advocate on the Southern Seminary faculty when Al Mohler was a student there. As mentioned elsewhere, Mohler's recollection is that the progressives set the tone of debate on this issue, even dominated it, and that abortion came up in discussions that otherwise had nothing to do with the issue. All the guns were pointed out, Mohler remembers, because the conservative position was just not viable among the faculty on campus.[29] Corroborating his perception that moderate professors at Southern Seminary had their guns pointed outward is a 1980 lecture Simmons delivered to the Symposium on the Theology of Pro-Choice in the Abortion Decision, which was sponsored by Religious Leaders for a Free Choice and the Religious Coalition on Abortion Rights. The lecture was entitled "A Theological Response to Fundamentalism on the Abortion Issue." By the time Simmons wrote this paper, the debate had shifted back into politics, dashing his 1976 hope that *Roe* had moved abortion to the private realm where it could be dealt with pastorally instead of politically.

Simmons opens his 1980 address with these words: "A new and frightening factor has been added to the politics of abortion, 1980. This is the powerful movement of fundamentalists into the anti-abortion cause. What is frightening about this development is the way religious fervor has been combined with reactionary political movements. The result is a type of neo-Fascism that threatens the very foundations of American life." After placing the stakes so high, Simmons uses the bulk of his paper to refute the biblical and natural-law arguments of the Religious Right. In so doing, he takes their arguments seriously and deals with them carefully and fairly, a noted change in tone from the lecture's introduction. He argues that neither the Bible nor natural law support the idea that the personhood of the fetus is equal to that of the mother. He notes that while surrounding cultures had strong prohibitions against abortion, the ancient Hebrews apparently had none. This seems to indicate that the issue was left to the private choice of a woman and her family—that she and they, as created in the image of God, were to exercise a "god-like decision." "Like the creator," Simmons argues, "she reflects upon what is good for the creation of which she is agent."[30] Simmons emphasizes throughout his address that the decision to have an abortion is deeply moral, not just personal, and that it should never be made casually. Moreover, he favors some legal protection for fetal life, especially after viability.

Turning to a key component of Baptist identity, Simmons also cites briefly 1 Peter 2:9 and the cherished Baptist principle of the priesthood of believers. "The person is one with direct access to God and the ability and responsibility to know and do His will. No other person may arrogate to themselves the right to stand between the person and God. Religious imperialism and moralistic authoritarianism are contradictory to this Biblical principle." Then, tying this Baptist principle to the woman's right to choose, he writes, "The woman has priestly powers—in her own conscientious obedience to the Creator-Redeemer; she bears his image in making her decision."[31]

Simmons concludes that since fundamentalists could not convince people on the basis of scripture and natural law, they were now turning to human law in an attempt to force their interpretation on others. This is what he believed was so ominous about the pro-life movement that at the time was calling for a constitutional amendment to outlaw abortion. "The very Bible to which they claim such devotion," he emphasizes, "refutes their position at every significant point. That helps to explain [the fundamentalist movement] resorting to heavy-handed tactics." Pro-choice activists need to redouble their political efforts to protect the precious right of a woman to choose against the pro-life forces that had politicized the issue. Simmons predicts that the fundamentalist political movement would eventually be discredited just as McCarthyism had been. "It will be exposed for what it is," he closes. "A house built upon the shifting sands of deception of the truth, a power-crazed authoritarianism, a win-at-any-cost ethic and a total disregard for personal values or religious freedom, has the seeds of its own destruction already sown."[32] For good measure, he also adds a reference to the Salem witch trials.

It is important to note that Simmons was not just arguing that the abortion decision should be left to the woman as a matter of private conscience. Rather, he was saying that the Bible supports the pro-choice stance.[33] In a 1983 article in a Southern Baptist publication, he writes: "Because the biblical stress on personhood plainly lies with those who are responsible directly to God, and because of the New Testament emphasis on the priesthood of every believer, the primary responsibility seemingly falls directly upon the woman. . . . The silence in the Bible regarding elective abortion seems also to indicate this [private choice] was the Hebrew attitude."[34] In the memory of at least one of his students during the 1980s, this biblical argument was central in his ethics lectures at Southern Seminary.[35]

In a 1990 article in the *Journal of Church and State*, Simmons provides the moderates' most articulate defense of abortion as a religious-liberty right. In this article he also cites John Rawls and eludes to the theorist's conception of justice as being consistent with what Simmons understands to be the Baptist position. In short, his conception of religious liberty is supported by

Rawlsian liberalism. Responding primarily to what he detected as the theological underpinning of the Missouri abortion statute upheld in the Supreme Court case *Webster* v. *Reproductive Health Services* (1989), Simmons argues that the "anti-choice" movement, as he calls it, relied in this instance on an argument that the fetus is a person from the time of conception. The language of the Missouri law makes it clear that the statute does indeed rest on this assumption, and Simmons states that such a notion fails the Rawlsian test of public reason. There are, writes Simmons, only two grounds on which a conceptus could be considered a person. One is religious. The Roman Catholic Church promulgated this belief in 1869, and it has been standard church teaching ever since. The second is the symbiotic bonding of the woman and her potential child, whereby the family begins to anticipate full personhood even while the fetus is in its earliest developing stage. The problem with the first understanding of the conceptus as a person is that it is a theological tenet decreed by the Roman Catholic Church but held by many Protestants as well. Founded in theology, the conceptus-as-person view is ineligible as a basis for secular law because it is not derived from publicly accessible and broadly held notions of justice. The problem with this second basis for the conceptus-as-person view is that it is highly subjective and, therefore, also not fit as a basis for law.[36]

As interpreted by Simmons and many others, Rawlsian liberalism usually results in individual rights trumping all competing claims. Under such a rubric, *Roe* v. *Wade* becomes a stroke of genius, for it neither coerces a woman to have an abortion in violation of her own belief that the fetus is a person, nor does it restrict a woman's choice for an abortion based on someone else's theological belief that the fetus is a person. It is, the argument goes, procedurally fair while leaving to the individual the substantive question as to whether abortions are proper. As Simmons writes: "It belongs to the woman to decide based upon her religious beliefs. . . . Without ever saying so, *Roe* v. *Wade* was an exercise in protecting religious liberty." Simmons does not oppose all restrictions on abortion, however, because "[i]t violates no groups religious teachings nor any premise of logic to provide legal protections for a viable fetus." His primary target here is the belief explicit in the Missouri statute that a fetus has personhood from the time of conception. This is a purely theological view that, according to Simmons's argument, is neither widely held nor in accordance with plain logic. If taken literally as the basis of law, Simmons asks rhetorically, would the conceptus-as-person provision of the Missouri statute mean that when a pregnant

woman is imprisoned, two people are actually jailed, one of them an inno-
cent fetus? Or would social security benefits be due nine months earlier than
originally thought, or foodstamps made available for an unborn child?[37] For
Simmons, as a matter logic, common sense, and the separation of church
and state, the law should steer clear of defining the conceptus, and by extension the fetus, as a person.

Simmons concluded this 1990 argument in much the same way he had
opened his 1980 lecture, by referencing the dangerous forces of the Christian
Right. "There are disturbing signs that the atmosphere of support for First
Amendment rights is seriously eroding," he warns. "New alliances have
emerged that threaten the guarantees at the heart of religious liberty." This
new alliance consisted primarily of Protestant fundamentalists in the Christian Right and traditional Roman Catholics. Simmons cites Richard John
Neuhaus specifically. Since his 1984 book *The Naked Public Square*, Neuhaus
had been leading an effort to think publicly about how religion might be
allowed to shape public policy. This is precisely what Rawlsian liberals oppose. Instead, people should set their private views aside and draw on a common stock of public reason when arguing political matters. Simmons describes Neuhaus's efforts as an attempt "to impose sectarian opinion upon all
Americans," a statement that reveals the liberal penchant for equating the
religious, the private, and the sectarian. For many Rawlsian liberals these
terms are nearly synonymous with one another, and the extension of this
view is that private, religious, sectarian views are not the proper foundation
for public policy. As Simmons perceives, "Puritan theocrats are very much
alive in the New Christian Right. . . . It is not by accident that those in the
religious coalition working to ban abortion are those most hostile to religious liberty." In his final paragraph, he takes aim squarely at SBC conservatives when he writes, "Even many Southern Baptists—traditional champions of religious liberty—have joined that crusade."[38]

Apparently, not many other moderate elites were, like Simmons, self-
consciously Rawlsian, for I have found no other overt references to Rawls's
philosophy. It seems quite possible, however, that Rawls's views may have
been the unacknowledged underlying foundation for moderate positions on
the abortion issue. How else can one explain this odd marriage of the historic Baptist principle of religious liberty to an issue having to do with the
life and death of a fetus/unborn child. A few influential moderate elites appropriated the notion wrought from political liberalism that religion should
not influence law. In doing so, they were at cross-purposes with each other,

and Simmons's position in particular was problematic as a matter of logical consistency. On the one hand, prior to his 1990 article on the *Webster* case, Simmons had argued that the pro-choice position was biblical and Baptist. If this were so, what would prevent a Roman Catholic from arguing that since the Baptist position was pro-choice, and since that position had been codified into law, there has been an establishment of the Baptist position? Moreover, based on Simmons's biblical position that the ancient Hebrews had been pro-choice, a secularist could argue that there has been an establishment of Old Testament beliefs. Compounding this logical inconsistency was Valentine, Simmons, and other moderates who were saying that the Roman Catholic pro-life stance should not be made law because the First Amendment forbade that kind of establishment of a religious moral position.

Moderates got around this inconsistency by arguing in essence that the pro-choice position was not really a position—it was procedural, not substantive. They viewed the results of *Roe* as merely the absence of laws outlawing abortion thereby resulting in government neutrality on the issue. This was Wood's explicit view. For him, the state was neither condoning nor condemning abortions even if it funded them. Rather, it was leaving the question to individuals to decide. Simmons's Rawlsian argument, however, belied such notions of neutrality by presenting a firm case based on public reason accessible to all in a pluralistic society. From this perspective, it was not the difference between a position (pro-life) and a nonposition (pro-choice), but between a legitimate public position (pro-choice) and an illegitimate private one (pro-life). Simmons's earlier biblical argument, taken together with his 1990 Rawlsian treatise, showed clearly that the pro-choice view was not merely negative, not merely the absence of a position, and not merely neutrality. Rather, the pro-choice position could be supported by biblical teaching, Baptist history, and public reason—take your pick. The last of these trumped all others, rendering the other two superfluous. In other words, if a position passed the test of Rawlsian liberalism, it did not matter whether it was coincidently consistent with any particular religious view, for that would be incidental. Only if the position rested solely or primarily on a religious, private, or sectarian foundation would it be illegitimate. This view is precisely Rawlsian. A policy is acceptable if religious views just happen to coincide with public justice, but religious views should not be the source of public policy.

As moderate elites like Valentine, Wood, McGee, Simmons, and others attempted to convince fellow Southern Baptists that the pro-choice position furthered the Baptist ideals of neutrality and religious liberty, conservatives were beginning to adopt the belief held by many evangelicals, traditional Roman Catholics, and even communitarian political theorists that holds there is no such thing as public neutrality, Rawlsian or otherwise—someone's worldview always gets reflected in law. While this position contains its own logical tension, SBC conservatives may not have noticed that Simmons's argument unwittingly supported their point. The pro-choice view was indeed a position that had a particular foundation, in this case Rawlsian liberalism if not Baptist history and biblical teaching. Conservatives did recognize, intuitively at least, that what moderates called neutrality was actually the legitimation of a pro-choice stance that was anything but neutral. Still, during the 1970s at least, it was difficult to rally Southern Baptists against the pro-choice position of a few moderate elites because that was not the view that dominated the denomination. As a review of SBC resolutions shows, the denomination was equivocal, and that did not satisfy conservatives.

SBC ABORTION RESOLUTIONS DURING THE ERA OF MODERATE LEADERSHIP

James Wood at the BJC and Foy Valentine at the CLC had higher profiles and more political clout outside the denomination than virtually any of the Southern Baptist officials of the 1970s. By the mid-1980s, Sherman had emerged as the leader of the moderate side of the SBC controversy. Meanwhile, McGee and Simmons, as professors at the largest Baptist university and the most prestigious Southern Baptist seminary respectively, seemed to represent the denomination's most erudite thought on the abortion issue. Not surprisingly, the more moderate view of Valentine prevailed in Southern Baptist Convention resolutions throughout the 1970s. The views of Wood, McGee, and Simmons, which tied abortion rights to religious liberty, were consistently ignored in official denominational statements.

In 1971 the denomination for the first time issued a resolution on abortion. SBC Resolution No. 4 that year called for laws that "state a high view of the sanctity of human life, including fetal life, in order to protect those who cannot protect themselves." The resolution rejected the unregulated pro-choice position. After this nod to the sanctity of life, it dismissed the pro-life stance that allows for abortion only when the mother's life is endangered. Instead, the statement ultimately concluded that Southern Baptists should work for legislation that would allow for abortion in a variety of circumstances including where there was "likelihood of damage to the emotional, mental, and physical health of the mother."[39] Thus, what the resolution seemed to give with one hand, a strong statement on the sanctity of fetal life, it took back with the other, allowing for abortion where a woman's mental or emotional health might be impaired by a pregnancy.

However some moderates would like to characterize the 1971 resolution, it was clearly a rather pro-choice statement consistent with the *Roe* decision that would come two years later, and some from the most liberal and conservative ends of the Southern Baptist spectrum viewed the resolution this way. Looking back some years later, Wood said that the statement showed that even denominations that do not condone abortion can still support the *Roe* decision. Similarly, conservatives have viewed this resolution as "a strong call for the liberalizing and legalizing of abortion in this country."[40] Timothy George would point out that the language of the 1971 resolution was similar to that of one passed eight years earlier by the Unitarian-Universalist Association. Specifically, George was referring to the clause that allowed for abortion in cases where there was "carefully ascertained evidence of the likelihood of damage to the emotional, mental, as well as physical health of the mother."[41] The irony that America's most liberal and one of its most conservative denominations were together on this would eventually come to outrage SBC conservatives and provide them with their strongest evidence that moderate leaders in the denomination were out of touch with grassroots Southern Baptists on some of the most important issues of our time.

By 1976, three years after *Roe* v. *Wade* had begun to raise the consciousness of virtually all Americans on the subject, the SBC issued another ambiguous resolution, but this time the serious difficulty and moral gravity of abortion were delineated more forcefully. The "Whereas" section of the resolution stated that "The practice of abortion for selfish non-therapeutic reasons wantonly destroys fetal life, dulls our society's moral sensitivity, and leads to the cheapening of all human life." The declaration then resolved: 1) that the SBC "reaffirm the biblical sacredness and dignity of all human life, including fetal life"; 2) that Southern Baptists, as well as all citizens, should "work to change those attitudes and conditions which encourage many people to turn to abortion as a means of birth control"; and 3) that Southern Baptists "reject any indiscriminate attitude toward abortion, as contrary to the biblical view." Still, however, while these three "resolves" leaned heavily in a pro-life direction, the fourth and final clause stated "that we also affirm our conviction about the limited role of government in dealing with matters relating to abortion, and support the right of expectant mothers to the full range of medical services and personal counseling for the preservation of life and health."[42] So once again, the moderate leadership of the SBC had shepherded through the resolutions process a moderate statement on abortion that in its "limited government" clause seemed to be either pro-choice or at least opposed to a constitutional amendment outlawing abortion.[43] Clearly, the SBC bureaucrats recognized that there was division in the denomination and crafted another compromise resolution. In this, as in 1971, the pro-lifers got the bulk of the document, but the pro-choice moderates got their own clause that could be interpreted as consistent with the *Roe* decision. This was just one of the many compromises that would begin to unravel in the late 1970s.

The following year, the resolutions committee, instead of writing yet another pronouncement on abortion, reissued the 1976 statement with an introductory gloss aimed at eliminating any question as to what it had intended. This introduction read, "Resolved that this Convention reaffirm the strong stand against abortion adopted by the 1976 convention, and, in view of some confusion in interpreting part of this resolution we confirm our strong opposition to abortion on demand and all governmental policies and actions which permit this."[44] It seems curious that the 1976 "strong stand against abortion" resulted in such "confusion in interpreting part of this resolution." If the stand was so strong, why the confusion? Evidently, there was uncertainty, so the 1977 introduction attempted to clarify the SBC position by putting that convention on record as opposing "abortion on demand." That was what the 1976 resolution now meant. The 1978 convention merely reaffirmed the 1977 resolution, and the 1979 messengers reaffirmed what had been done by the conventions of 1976 and 1978 (but curiously did not mention 1977). In retrospect, it appears that pro-life forces were gaining momentum as each successive resolution or new interpretation emphasized more strongly that abortion was undesirable. Still, however, the denomination left the door open for choice in a fairly wide array of cases having to do with the mental and emotional welfare as well as the life of the mother.

In 1979 there was an attempt to eliminate the ambiguity of the denomination's position. Conservatives tried to amend that year's proposed resolution to make it reflect a thoroughgoing pro-life position: "Be it further Resolved," the amendment read, "that we call upon our spiritual brothers and sisters to work on all levels of government, as individual citizens, to bring about passage of legislation and/or Constitutional Amendment which would protect the personhood of all human life at all stages of development whether born or unborn, and ensure every conceived human being of his inalienable right to life and liberty."[45] "Personhood" was now attached to the fetus, which would have fundamentally changed the nature of SBC abortion resolutions. This would have required a rejection of the "limited government" clause of 1976, but the 1979 amendment was defeated. This conservative attempt to eliminate the pro-choice portion of the abortion resolution, however, set the stage for the dramatic shift that would come the following year.

THE CONSERVATIVES TAKE CHARGE OF THE ABORTION ISSUE

While defeated on the abortion issue at the 1979 convention meeting, SBC conservatives won the presidency in a victory that started their takeover of the denomination. This shift to the right in the SBC was part of a shift to the right for the whole country, as indicated by Ronald Reagan's election to the U.S. presidency the following year. Riding this wave, SBC conservatives in 1980 were able to accomplish on the abortion issue what had eluded them before. They pushed through a clearly pro-life, anti-abortion resolution that eliminated all ambiguity. The resolution stated, "Our national laws permit a policy commonly referred to as 'abortion on demand.'" Therefore, be it resolved, "That we abhor the use of tax money or public, tax-supported medical facilities for selfish, non-therapeutic abortion, and . . . That we favor appropriate legislation and/or a constitutional amendment prohibiting abortion except to save the life of the mother."[46] Gone was any notion of the "limited role of government in dealing with matters relating to abortion" or the "right of expectant mothers to the full range of medical services," both of which were affirmed in 1976 and apparently reaffirmed from 1977 through 1979. The SBC was now on record as supporting legal sanctions against all abortions except those to save the life of the mother. This stand continues to the present to be the position of SBC agencies and of subsequent convention meetings. In at least one year, 1989, conservatives even beat back an effort to include rape and incest as exceptions to their hard-line position. Mark Coppenger, who served as chairman of the Committee on Resolutions that year, summed up the conservative position well when he said,

"[W]e do not want to victimize the child in the womb because evil things have happened to bring that child into the womb."[47] Contrary to the wishes of Wood, Simmons, and even Criswell (at least in 1973), the fetus was now granted full status as a person with rights equivalent to those of the mother. It is worth noting that the 1980 resolution was the first victory for the conservatives on any political or cultural issue, and it came before they had taken over even one trustee board within the denomination. They had charged for some time that the views of the moderates were out of sync with the vast majority of Southern Baptists. The ease with which the conservatives were able to pass the 1980 resolution suggests that they may have been correct.

In a 1986 article in the Christian Life Commission's publication *Light,* the policy change of 1980 on abortion was characterized as the basic position of previous convention resolutions with "a couple of new wrinkles." The article, written by a moderate CLC employee, saw a general continuity in the history of SBC abortion resolutions and concluded that Southern Baptists had never been very far apart on the issue.[48] One could hardly think of a more grotesque misreading of the situation. The 1980 shift was a sea change of major proportions, representing radical discontinuity with the past.

The 1980 resolution can be interpreted as an announcement to the American body politic that the conservatives were in control of the SBC. This did not go unnoticed in the press or the burgeoning pro-life movement. Reporter James Franklin of the *Boston Globe* called the 1980 resolution "a shock wave from a major earthquake within the nation's largest Protestant denomination."[49] He reasoned that the SBC statement laid to rest any notion that abortion was only a Roman Catholic issue. Rep. John Ashbrook of Ohio had the resolution read into the *Congressional Record* after prefacing it with these remarks: "Once again, the absurdity of the pro-abortion [*sic*] movement as a Catholic bishop's plot is revealed. The influence of Catholic bishops at a Southern Baptist convention is generally agreed to be minimal."[50] Likewise, physician Carolyn Gerster, at that time president of the National Right to Life Committee, interpreted the statement as a harbinger of Protestant support for the pro-life cause. Indeed, here was an instance where Southern Baptists were prepared to lead the wider evangelical world. Floyd Robertson, legislative representative of the National Association of Evangelicals (NAE), said that his group was opposed to abortion except in cases of rape or incest or where the mother's life was in danger. This was only a slightly softer stance than the SBC, but the NAE had not yet taken a position on a constitutional amendment. In the wake of the Baptists' move, however, Robertson said that it was likely his organization would now back a human-life amendment despite the group's strong stand for separation of church and state. "The moral issue in the case of abortion . . . far overrides the consideration of separation of church and state," the *Boston* Globe quoted him as saying.[51] Apparently, if a denomination as solidly separationist as the SBC could support a human-life amendment, this would liberate the NAE to act likewise without appearing to retreat from its historic stand in favor of separation of church and state.

Of course, SBC conservatives, especially those who were politically active in the infant Religious Right, were ebullient about the 1980 resolution. Southern Baptist Ed McAteer was one of the founders of the Religious Roundtable, an organization that helped mobilize evangelicals for conservative political causes. He announced exuberantly, "I'm planning to personally send a letter to every congressman and senator to tell them we [Southern Baptists] are against abortion." SBC conservative activist Paul Pressler saw the resolution as an indication that the denomination was "back in the people's hands," having been liberated from the clutches of moderate elites who were out of touch with the thinking of rank-and-file Southern Baptists. SBC moderates, especially James Wood, also interpreted the resolution as a radical change, but unlike Pressler, of course, Wood opposed it. Recognizing that the statement "cannot be ignored," he nevertheless characterized the 1980 convention meeting as being dominated "by the extreme, far right groups that are very militant and strident."[52] Most moderates in 1980 believed the conservative movement was an aberrant blip that would be corrected in the years to come.

Since SBC resolutions are nonbinding and actually represent only the consensus of a particular year's convention meeting, the 1980 resolution was more like a beginning than an end. The battle between moderates and conservatives over the abortion issue would continue, the primary change being that the moderates were now on the defensive. We know now that during the twentieth century moderates never came back from their 1979 defeat in the SBC presidential election, but for several years SBC agencies did not have to follow the lead of the 1980 convention because agency heads could say that the resolution was merely a one-year statement. So it was that in 1981 Foy Valentine of the CLC issued the pamphlet that continued the moderate, ambivalent position that had characterized the 1970s. Moreover, Wood was out of the BJC and back at Baylor, a university with fairly broad academic freedom. This meant, of course, that he was at liberty to continue to espouse his own pro-choice position rooted in his interpretation of the First Amendment, which he often did in his graduate seminars during the 1980s as well as in his writings.

That moderates such as Wood and Valentine could defy the 1980 resolution with impunity frustrated conservatives, who began to strengthen their own drive to make the SBC into America's leading pro-life denomination. Such frustration was especially acute in the case of Valentine, who was on the denominational payroll.[53] In 1986, conservatives formed an organization called Southern Baptists for Life (SBL). Following the development of this denomination-wide organization, the first local chapter was created at First Baptist Church, Dallas by Richard Land and an associate. SBL began to circulate pamphlets at SBC convention meetings, promote films such as *The Silent Scream*, hold workshops, and supply pastors with sermon material in hopes of developing a Sanctity of Human Life Sunday that would be widely observed across the denomination. Some conservative Southern Baptist pastors had already been using Francis Schaeffer's film *Whatever Happened to the Human Race?* which attempted to depict the horrors of abortion and its moral implications for American culture. The CLC responded with a new set of resources as Sanctity of Human Life Sunday became a reality.[54] The event is now a regular annual feature in many SBC churches.

While conservatives continued to mobilize their ranks for the pro-life cause, they also sought to oust from power those moderates who stood in their way. Valentine retired from the CLC in March 1987 and was first replaced by Larry Baker, a former dean and professor of ethics at Midwestern Baptist Theological Seminary in Kansas City. Baker was the compromise choice of the Christian Life Commission Board of Trustees, which was divided between conservatives and moderates, but he quickly proved to be unacceptable once the conservatives gained the majority. While Baker headed the CLC, the agency moved to address abortion more visibly and forcefully, something conservatives had demanded. The commission hosted a conference on abortion and then devoted the November–December 1987 edition of *Light* to the subject in preparation for the 1988 Sanctity of Human Life Sunday. In it Baker wrote a "Reflections" column decrying the frequency of abortions in the United States and the casual attitude society takes toward the practice. In a longer column that had apparently been his address at the CLC conference, he outlined six things he believed Southern Baptists should do about abortion. The column and address were pro-life in every way, save the one that was most important to conservatives: Baker never called for a legal remedy. Asking rhetorically, "What can we do?" he answered: "We can raise the consciousness of our society about the dignity, value and uniqueness of the unborn. We can attack the full range of conditions that nourishes the practice of abortion. We can teach the biblical sex ethic and call people to the practice of it."[55] Missing from his list was advocacy for a constitutional amendment or some other legal prohibition against abortion. Thus, Baker was perpetuating the moderate position of condemning abortion while not seeking to outlaw all abortions except those necessary to save the life of the mother, which had been the official position of the conservatives as articulated in convention resolutions since 1980.

As his articles indicated, he deplored abortion on demand, but he also believed there should be exceptions to abortion prohibitions that included rape, incest, and perhaps even fetal deformity. Baker was a solid moderate, therefore he would not last long at the CLC. In addition to being too soft on abortion, he also supported ordination of women and opposed capital punishment. As one trustee put it: "For the first time in 20 years we're being listened to. However, we want an anti-abortion activist—a dynamic activist who can stir the hearts of people and I don't think Larry Baker's the activist type." Looking toward the next CLC board meeting, this trustee predicted, "If he [remains] director, I wouldn't be surprised to see a move to remove him this time."[56] Baker spared the trustees the decision of having to fire him by resigning and taking a pastorate in Louisiana in early summer of 1988. He was replaced on the commission by Land, who would prove to be the dynamic anti-abortion activist for whom the conservative trustees had longed.[57]

This still left conservatives with the problem of the Baptist Joint Committee. Although Wood was gone, and despite the fact that the BJC had never taken an official position on abortion, Land wanted the agency to go on record as repudiating Wood's personal position that the right to an abortion was protected by the Free Exercise Clause of the First Amendment. Wood's successor, James Dunn, was reluctant to repudiate a position that the BJC as an agency had never actually espoused. The problem for conservatives was that the SBC was only one of several Baptist groups that supported the committee and thus they could never gain a majority on its board of trustees. In other words, SBC conservatives could not control Dunn or the BJC the way they could the Christian Life Commission, even though the denomination was funding the BJC to the tune of almost four hundred thousand dollars per year. Eventually, they just defunded the BJC and re-organized the CLC to takeover BJC tasks.

The length of time necessary for this process to succeed is evidence of how deeply committed to the BJC Southern Baptist moderates were, but the determination displayed by the conservatives is also testimony to how central they believed the abortion issue is within American culture. The first attempt to defund the committee came at the 1984 SBC meeting, but not until 1991 was the process complete. The key event was the February 1990 reduction in funding from $391,796 to $50,000. The vast majority of state Baptist newspapers (at least thirteen that I have counted) editorialized against the cutback with titles such as "BJCPA Action Is Step in the Wrong Direction," "You Wouldn't Have Believed It," "Executive Committee [of SBC] Consistently Inconsistent in Treatment of BJCPA," and "A Tragic Mistake."[58] These editorials highlight the disconnect between what was going on at SBC headquarters from what was happening at the state level. While the denomination's national machinery was firmly in the hands of the conservatives by 1990, most of the state conventions were still under moderate control. The BJC itself responded the following year with bylaw changes that decreased the number of Southern Baptist seats on the BJC. Then in 1991, at the Atlanta SBC meeting, messengers finalized a merger between the newly created Public Affairs Committee of the SBC and the Christian Life Commission, the latter of which was now under the leadership of Land. This was combined with the final phase of defunding. From 1991, the CLC would maintain a consistent presence in Washington and in 1997 changed its name to the Ethics and Religious Liberty Commission to reflect its new role as the religio-political lobby arm of the denomination. Of course, the BJC continues its own activities and is supported by Baptists outside the SBC as well as many state Baptist conventions affiliated with the SBC and by other Southern Baptist churches and institutions that simply route their money directly to the agency instead of through the SBC's cooperative program as they did before 1991.[59]

Abortion was by no means the only issue that led to the withdrawal of funding from the BJC, but some conservative leaders believe it was the most important factor. Paige Patterson would recollect years later that the abortion issue was the key reason conservatives decided to reorganize the CLC.[60] SBC conservatives simply were not going to send the denomination's money to an organization that refused to take the conservative position on abortion and on church-state issues in general.

While these events unfolded, the CLC continued to raise the stakes in the abortion debate even while attempting to address a range of other ethical issues at the same time. In 1989 its board balked at giving the annual distinguished service award to a medical missionary until they were assured that his views were thoroughly pro-life on abortion. Once assured by Land that the recipient "believes life begins at conception and that abortion on demand is abhorrent," they proceeded with the award.[61] The next year, the CLC trustees voted narrowly, 12–11, to request that Director Land refrain from inviting speakers to CLC functions who were pro-choice, even if they were to speak on issues unrelated to abortion. The occasion of this vote was the scheduled appearance of moderate ethics professor Glen Stassen of Southern Seminary. His topic was domestic violence and peacemaking, not abortion, but many conservative trustees were troubled by his 1977 signing of an abortion-rights petition. Land was less than enthusiastic about this decision, saying: "It says we're extremely concerned about abortion, but it also makes it more difficult to be in ongoing communication with as many Southern Baptists as possible. There are people who have things to say to us who won't meet this requirement."[62]

This was one of the few times Land would be outflanked to his right on the issue of abortion. The degree to which abortion loomed large for him can be seen in his initial response to the Religious Freedom Restoration Act of 1991. Nearly every religious and secular group in America with any kind of interest in religious liberty supported RFRA. In fact, it was one of the few times after 1988 that Dunn and the BJC were on the same side of an issue as Land and the CLC or Ethics and Religious Liberty Commission. Even in this instance, however, although Land supported the bill in principle, he tried to pressure Dunn to issue a statement saying that abortion was not a religious-liberty right. Given Wood's earlier position and the fact that he had been the executive director of the BJC for most of the 1970s, conservatives believed they needed reassurance from Dunn that the BJC was not going to try to tie religious-liberty and abortion rights together. To this end, Land wrote a letter to Dunn asking the BJC executive director whether abortion was considered a First Amendment right. He asked the BJC to "state for the record whether abortion is a practice which should prevail as a free exercise of religion claim." Perhaps to tweak Dunn further, Land also asked the BJC to send letters to congressional leaders saying "government has a compelling interest in protecting pre-born life, which should override claims of a religious right to abortion." Such a statement would have tied the compelling-interest test of RFRA to the abortion issue, protecting potential anti-abortion laws from First Amendment challenges. Land's effort was another attempt to get the BJC to take a position against abortion, something the agency would not do. Moreover, he requested that Dunn make a commitment to Southern Baptists that the BJC "will never advocate, especially in the courts or in Congress, the view that abortion claims should prevail as religious liberty claims," which, of course, would be a clear repudiation of Wood's position. Turning to the other religion clause of the First Amendment, Land also asked for a BJC statement, in writing, as to whether the agency considered legislation restricting abortion an infringement of the Establishment Clause. In all of this, Land quoted past claims made by Wood.[63]

In response to Land's letter, Dunn said that the BJC "does not support abortion as a free exercise right, or address the issue of abortion in any fashion." He elaborated: "As everyone knows, or should know quite well, the BJCPA [the old acronym for BJC] since I have been here has never addressed abortion as a free exercise right, nor have we addressed the issue of abortion in any fashion. [Land's] story makes a leap of generalization that completely misses the truth." Dunn then referenced a quote Land had been using against him: "My 1983 quote simply acknowledges that abortion, like all serious moral and ethical decisions, has religious dimensions. Who can deny that?" Dunn's 1983 statement was: "The complex issue of abortion is reduced to the simple cry of 'infanticide' by Mr. Reagan, who would redress 'a great national wrong' in the name of civil religion, making it virtually impossible for mothers to make their own decisions in this very private, very religious matter." Dunn's reference to abortion as a "private and religious" issue would anticipate Simmons's more explicitly Rawlsian position of 1990 that grouped the private, religious, and sectarian together as inappropriate bases for legislation. After Dunn had clarified his 1983 statement, Land responded: "If James Dunn now is willing to make such a renunciation (abortion as protected by the free exercise clause) to the Congress of the United States, we are delighted and relieved. . . . I'm sorry that Dunn feels his statements have been misconstrued. I can assure him that many Southern Baptists don't [believe Dunn's views have been misunderstood]."[64] At one point during this dispute, Land charged that the BJC, by not taking a position against abortion, was in fact advancing the cause of abortion rights. The BJC responded with a letter threatening a defamation suit.[65] While the Land-Dunn dispute proceeded, the SBC passed a resolution calling for a remedy to the *Smith* decision that would "not advance abortion rights."[66]

Eventually, the CLC under Land supported the Religious Freedom Restoration Act. How concerned Land actually was about such a law being used as protection for abortion rights is subject to debate, but clearly the conservatives were in the process of making opposition to abortion a litmus test for denominational employment and funding. Patterson's 1986 hope (or demand) that he wanted an open pro-life position in all denominational agencies was indeed coming to pass. Land was just following through on that objective, and it should be noted that his exchange with Dunn over the RFRA came while the BJC was still being funded by the denomination. Many moderates believed that the right wing had some hidden agenda for which they were using the abortion issue. The conservative answer to this remains Al Mohler's response: "I think moderates, to their dying day, are going to underestimate that issue. They just don't get it."[67]

The conservative position on abortion has been tightly bound to their views of American culture as a whole. Along with homosexuality, they believe abortion is the most egregious violation of biblical morality in society today. As stated in a conservative document from 1994, "We believe that abortion on demand is the leading, but not the only, example of a broader national moral and social crisis of disrespect for human life." This statement listed abortion as "the single gravest failure of American democracy in our generation."[68] Much of the time, conservatives feel little need to spell out why they oppose abortion so vigorously. It almost goes without saying, they believe, that any sincere evangelical believer should oppose the taking of unborn life.

Still, abortion is not just a political issue for conservatives, it is also deeply theological. Timothy George has developed a theological articulation of the conservative pro-life position rooted in the doctrine of God, the Incarnation, and the mission of the church. Since God freely chose to invest his image and glory in human life, George argues, any attack on human life, especially in its embryonic form, "is nothing less than an attack on the Creator of life itself." Second, fundamental to the Incarnation is the unity of body and soul. "The eternal word, *Logos,* could not have become flesh, *sarx,* if this unity were not the distinctive reality of human beings." Any notion that fetal life lacks personhood is obviously beside the point if the fetus as an embryonic body already possesses such a soul, and if there is a unity of body and soul at that early point, as George believes, then even the embryonic body must possess a soul. Third, on the mission of the church, George addresses the moderate argument that Baptist conceptions such as soul competency, the priesthood of believers, and religious liberty all lead to privatized choice on the abortion issue. "To reduce the decision of abortion to the level of privatized morality is to equate Christianity with a kind of modern individualism which in its flight from community and responsibility is the very antithesis of the biblical metaphor of the church as the body of Christ."[69] In this reference to privatized morality, George hits upon Simmons's Rawlsian argument. Whether he recognized this was unclear, as he did not mention Rawls. Many conservatives, however, often rejected the type of private/public distinction that is the hallmark of modern liberal theory. It may well be that, just as many moderates are Rawlsian liberals without being aware that they are, many conservatives often seek to refute Rawlsian liberalism without explicitly citing Rawls.

In his theological articulation, George hones in on Simmons's argument that the Bible does not explicitly prohibit abortion. He points out that neither does the Bible explicitly prohibit uxoricide, the killing of one's spouse, or infanticide, the killing of a post-born child. Recognizing that Simmons might point out that these are already covered by general prohibitions against killing, George references Michael Gorman and others who have attempted to show that the Bible's silence on abortion may well reflect an assumed continuation of a pro-life norm that Christians inherited from Judaism. This is a compelling argument, George believes, considering that so many other early church writings, such as the *Didache,* the *Epistle of Barnabas,* the *Apocalypse of Peter,* and later church fathers like Tertullian, Cyprian, Chrysostom, Jerome, and Augustine all condemn abortion. As the second-century Christian apologist Athenagoras wrote to Emperor Marcus Aurelius: "How can we kill a man when we are those who say that all who use abortifacients are homicides and will account to God for their abortions as for the killing of men? For the Fetus in the womb is not an animal, and it is God's providence that he exists."[70] Using this evidence from the early church, Gorman and other evangelicals argue that when the issue actually arose during the early Christian era, the response of the church was apparently opposition to abortion. George's argument, as outlined here from a 1994 article, attempts to refute Simmons's 1980 claim that pro-life evangelicals were reverting to law because they had no scriptural case to make.

Beyond theological arguments, from time to time in various venues, conservatives attempt to personalize the issue, telling how and why abortion became so important for them. Land did this in 1998 on the very first broadcast of his daily radio program *For Faith and Family.* This program, his cohost emphasized, was aired just a few weeks after the twenty-fifth anniversary of *Roe* v. *Wade*. Land told how the abortion issue became real for him when he was in high school in the 1960s. For a science project on the development of the human body, a classmate had brought to school a twelve-to-fourteen-week-old human fetus in a jar. Her father was a doctor and had somehow procured the fetus for the project. Land remembers being profoundly disturbed. He took his objection to his teacher, who sent him to the principal, who asked Land, "Well, Richard, are you Catholic?" Land says that in addition to clarifying how and why he came to his position on abortion, this experience illustrates that in the 1960s, and for some time thereafter, the abortion issue was the domain of Roman Catholics. He is very proud that it is now the domain of Southern Baptists and virtually all evangelicals as well.[71]

Conservatives have had to be cautious, however. Throughout the 1980s and into the 1990s, moderates accused them of delivering the SBC into the hands of radicals in the Religious Right. This was especially problematic following the killing of abortion doctors in the early 1990s and can be a problem every time another abortion provider is attacked. Land once again took the lead, convening a symposium in 1994 to draft a document entitled "The Nashville Statement of Conscience: Why the Killing of Abortion Doctors Is Wrong." This statement is now a standard part of the ERLC's Human Life Kit. Its authors include Land; Mark Coppenger; Al Mohler; ethics professors David Gushee, who was at that time at Southern Baptist Theological Seminary; Daniel Heimbach of Southeastern Baptist Theological Seminary; and former ethics consultant to the CLC C. Ben Mitchell, who was at the time a doctoral candidate at Vanderbilt.

In a move that was deeply symbolic, the pro-life Gushee had replaced Simmons in the ethics department at Southern Seminary in the fall of 1993. Before he could even get his things unpacked in Louisville, Land called and asked Gushee to come to Nashville to talk. Even though his views on capital punishment, the environment, and peace and justice concerns were not in line with most SBC conservatives, it was clear from the beginning that Land and the CLC liked Gushee's stand on abortion. The statement on the killing of abortion doctors became a prime opportunity for Land to pull the young ethicist into the SBC conservative orbit. In response not only to the killings but also to the increasing defense of the murders made by some radical anti-abortionists, Land asked Gushee to draft a statement outlining why violence against abortion clinics and providers was morally indefensible. All the participants then met in Nashville and honed Gushee's draft line by line, developing what Mohler would call "the first Baptist encyclical."[72]

In the document, the authors articulate a Christian concept of resistance to the state first fashioned by sixteenth-century Reformed Calvinists and reiterated in many historical contexts since. This view stresses that it is never justifiable for private citizens to take up arms on their own. Land likes to point to America in the 1770s, where revolutionaries first declared independence and then set up a resistance government that authorized revolutionary violence. He makes clear that individuals who take it upon themselves to kill abortion doctors, even if they believe they are thereby defending unborn babies, are outside the bounds of biblical morality and the Protestant revolutionary tradition.[73] The statement's authors make clear, however, that revolution of any kind is not what is required presently because the U.S. government has not lost its legitimacy. "We deny that our nation is nearing or has reached such a crisis. Our goal must be reform, not revolution." The Nashville Statement of Conscience rejects not only the right of private citizens to engage in violence as revolutionary lone rangers but also repudiates the notion that individuals can act as private executioners of abortion doctors (so-called murderers) or as defenders of unborn human life. Execution, like revolution, can only be carried out by legitimate authority, while defense of the unborn is a practical impossibility given that the killing of individual abortion doctors does not actually stop abortions from taking place.[74]

While rejecting all arguments used to support the murder of abortion doctors, the Nashville Statement affirms the classic right of civil disobedience as the morally justifiable method of drawing attention to unjust laws. Using the nineteenth-century example of resistance to slavery as an analogy, the authors draw a distinction between, on the one hand, those who engaged in the underground railroad in nonviolent defiance of the fugitive slave laws and, on the other hand, John Brown and his supporters who attempted to foment insurrectionary violence. The latter action "was the advocacy and exercise of lethal force by private citizens and is beyond the prerogative of individuals, Christian or non-Christian." While denouncing violence, the authors of the Nashville Statement, and SBC conservative leaders in general, are somewhat ambivalent about groups like Operation Rescue that engage in radical protest. While affirming the moral legitimacy of civil disobedience, they also state that such a course of action is not "morally obligatory for Christians." Rather, civil disobedience "is ultimately a matter of individual conscience before God."[75] As Paige Patterson puts it, he has not marched with Operation Rescue and has no plans to do so.[76] SBC conservative leaders lend their moral support to those who take the issue to the streets, but their own actions are more likely to come in the halls of Congress and through media statements intended to sway public opinion.

The pro-life stance articulated first in the resolution of 1980 and now a standard requirement for SBC agency employees and trustees has finally worked its way into the denomination's confession of faith, at least indirectly. When the convention meeting of 1998 amended the Baptist Faith and Message Statement, adding a section on the family, most of the ensuing debate focused on the call for a wife to "submit graciously to the servant leadership of her husband" and to serve as his "helper." Overlooked in the furor over equality within marriage and women's rights in general was the final clause of the statement, which read in part, "Children, from the moment of conception, are a blessing and heritage from the Lord."[77] As Land saw it, this put the confession on record as stating that "Children are children from the moment of conception."[78] He speculated that the general public missed the profound nature of this phrase because the abortion issue has become so uncontentious among Southern Baptists. The SBC is, as he notes with great satisfaction, the most pro-life denomination in the United States, which is a real change from the position stated by W. A. Criswell in 1973.

WHAT SEPARATES CONSERVATIVES AND MODERATES

When discussing the significance of the fact that moderates did not take a strong stand against abortion during the 1970s, Timothy George uses as an analogy a story from the life of Swiss theologian Karl Barth. In 1914, when Barth saw the signatures of his former professors on a manifesto supporting Kaiser Wilhelm's war policy, he was so profoundly disturbed that he began a complete reevaluation of the liberal theology those professors had taught him. Their ethical lapse suggested to Barth that perhaps their views had been built on a faulty theological foundation.[79] Likewise, as Al Mohler has said about his and many other Southern Baptists' reaction to the abortion issue: If moderates could be wrong on abortion, that was all conservative people needed to know.[80] Putting the case even stronger, George has argued, *"The failure of the Southern Baptist Convention to make a timely and prophetic response to the holocaust of abortion on demand reflects the loss of theological vision resulting in the malign neglect and distorted understanding of the most basic doc-*

trinal affirmation we profess to believe." He attributes this failure to a larger systemic problem within the denomination, "the erosion of doctrinal substance and the failure to think through theologically the great issues of our time."[81] This failure was a far greater problem, in his view, than having a few theological liberals in the denominational seminaries.

It seems difficult to argue, however, that moderates such as James Wood, Foy Valentine, Dan McGee, and Paul Simmons failed to think through the abortion issue. Their positions were deep and reflective, and all of them were trained as scholars. The rift was actually much deeper than even George acknowledged, which is saying a lot given that conservatives have consistently sought to highlight the great differences between themselves and moderate elites. The real distinction is that moderate elites, like those covered here, had a conception of culture that was informed by Rawlsian political liberalism. Even as Simmons, for example, laid out his explicitly biblical argument for the pro-choice position, Rawlsian liberalism seemed to serve as a background set of precommitments. This is quite different from the charge usually made by conservatives that moderates are theological liberals. Even an evangelical can find a place within political liberalism without compromising the specific tenets of theology usually attendant to orthodoxy. It takes only two things: 1) an attitude that in a pluralistic culture one should not in any way impose by law a moral position that cannot be justified apart from one's religion; and 2) one should defer the question of what constitutes a good society in favor of individual freedom. The fact that Simmons and other moderates proceeded beyond this argument to the view that their position really could be justified on the basis of Baptist history and biblical teaching was acceptable within political liberalism only because their position could also be justified apart from their religious persuasion. The confluence of the religious argument with the argument from political liberalism was mere coincidence. They could go behind the veil—that is, disregard their religion—and come to the same conclusion, and they believed that in a pluralistic society, justice demanded that they do this.

In addition to citing moderate elites for their alleged failure to think through the abortion debate, George also indicts the entire denomination for following the moderate lead in adopting the resolutions of the 1970s, particularly 1971. But this too becomes understandable in light of one of the major critiques of Rawlsian political liberalism. Reformed Christian philosopher Nicholas Wolterstorff has argued that the problem with Rawlsian liberalism is that it asks too much of common people who are not intellectuals. It is likely to be very difficult for them to find secular reasons for positions they hold on religious grounds. Moreover, he asks whether it is even equitable to challenge believers to set aside their comprehensive doctrines when they enter the public square. For many, this looks suspiciously like denying one's most fundamental beliefs.[82] Unlike the moderate leaders who could understand the nuances of the situation and thereby reconcile their own opposition to abortion on demand with their support for *Roe* v. *Wade,* the common Baptists were asked to trust their leaders that this was the best way. Such trust was an early casualty of the Southern Baptist controversy, as the 1980 resolution indicated. Once weakened, many grassroots Southern Baptists could be persuaded easily that their moderate leaders really were not like the majority of congregants. Moderates for their part were operating on Rawlsian assumptions that the common folk could not even understand, let alone appropriate in any helpful way.

By contrast to the political liberalism of moderates and their appreciation for the difficulty of living in a pluralistic society, conservatives are so sure that American culture has been informed deeply by the Judeo-Christian tradition that to enact laws consistent with that tradition is to bolster the society, not deform it. Conversely, they believe that to engage in public-policy debates without reference to the nation's Judeo-Christian heritage or to pretend that such a heritage does not matter, which seems to be the upshot of Rawlsian liberalism, is perverse. There is no need to translate religious language into neutral terms or to go behind the veil, as political liberalism demands, because the language of biblical morality is the historic language of the culture, the protestations of some liberal elites notwithstanding. Here we find that Hunter's division of orthodox and progressive breaks down, as he himself acknowledges that it does at some points. As to the origins of morality, both moderates and conservatives are for the most part orthodox according to Hunter's schema. Key leaders in both groups believe that morality comes from God as mediated through the Judeo-Christian tradition. Morality has as its origin a fixed, external, and transcendent standard. If the culture wars are always fought between Hunter's orthodox and progressives, the latter believing that humans create their own morality, then conservative and moderate Southern Baptists would be on the same side. But they are opposed to one another on the issue of abortion because the moderates are to a large extent Rawlsian liberals willing to go behind the veil, which in the case of abortion means to act as if it does not matter that they are orthodox. Conservatives, by contrast, often sound as if they believe that the United States is one big community that has already decided collectively what its values are. Individuals are members of this community, come under its authority, and are, therefore, not autonomous.

The irony is that some of the most vocal moderates are products of communities that are almost impossible to maintain on the basis of highly individualistic political liberalism. This was highlighted at a 1997 conference at Baylor University when James Dunn lectured from his church-state separationist perspective. During the dialogue at the end of the conference, Notre Dame philosopher David Solomon, himself a former Texas Baptist, characterized Dunn's address as the most radical defense of political liberalism delivered at the conference, though the one with the thinnest foundation. Solomon noted that the kind of society Dunn was articulating, where individual rights trump all other considerations, would be highly unlikely to produce the kind of passionate, public-spirited community advocate that Dunn was himself.[83] While Solomon is no Southern Baptist conservative, his point is often echoed when conservatives argue that Southern Baptist stalwarts, even those who lived as late as the first half of the twentieth century, did not grow up in a culture where individual rights precluded communitarian values. Conservatives do not actually use this liberal-communitarian language, but they do seem instinctively to have picked up on this contemporary debate and intuit, sometimes correctly, sometimes not, that some moderates appropriate a language and disposition that reflects political liberalism over and against the more communitarian values that made for an intact southern culture as recently as the 1950s and 1960s. This seems especially to be the case on a subject like abortion.

In another respect, however, the moderate-conservative fight over abortion, as on many other issues, is consistent with Hunter's analysis of the culture wars. Both sides seek to delegitimize the other. On abortion, the moderates are especially adept at charging that conservatives are theocratic extremists, as Simmons and others repeatedly claimed. In such an atmosphere, dialogue is impossible, so neither side comes to understand the other very well.

All this is not to say that moderates have sold their Christian and Baptist birthright to political liberalism. Rather, they believe that biblical justice and Rawlsian justice both demand that they acknowledge the limitations a pluralistic culture places on believers. They can say genuinely and consistently that they oppose abortion and support *Roe* v. *Wade*. That is a limitation conservatives are unwilling to accept and a consistency they could never acknowledge.

7
Graciously Submissive

Southern Baptist Conservatives and Women

"Southern Baptists have basically followed their host culture in their teachings and attitudes about women. . . . This leads one to conclude that as society grants further rights to women in the future, Southern Baptists will possibly follow." So wrote Baptist Church historian H. Leon McBeth in a 1977 article.[1] Southern Baptist conservatives would set out in the 1980s to render false both parts of McBeth's statement. By the end of the century they had succeeded.

The issue of women in ministry was central to the unhappy experience Southern Seminary had with evangelicals. Tim Weber, David Sherwood, David Gushee, Carey Newman, Jim Chancelor, and others were acceptable to Southern president Al Mohler and the seminary trustees in every way save one—their views on the ordination of women. They all had very high views of scripture and were orthodox on all the major historical points of Christian doctrine; Sherwood apparently even passed Mohler's five-point test of Calvinist orthodoxy. Yet all were from what could be called the mainstream of evangelicalism, where there is diversity on the issue of women in ministry. As both Weber and Sherwood tried to get Mohler to understand, there is room for conversation and disagreement among evangelicals on this issue. In other words, one's views on women in ministry are not central to one's identity as an evangelical.

The firing of Diana Garland as dean and the closure of the Carver School of Social Work show the extent to which certain views of women and Christian ministry were becoming central to the Southern Baptist conservative theology. The Carver debacle was SBC conservatism's public declaration that this issue was nonnegotiable. Unlike the broader evangelical world that had nurtured and formed Weber and Sherwood, the Southern

Baptist conservative subculture has placed its prohibition against ordained women pastors at the center of its theological-cultural program. This was merely one aspect of an overall theology of gender that carves out separate roles for men and women, both in churches and in families.

The SBC story of gender becoming central to a movement because of the cultural forces that movement wishes to oppose is not without historical precedent. Historian Betty DeBerg has argued that early fundamentalism's anxiety about the modern world was caused largely by the shift in gender roles that took place during the early twentieth century and by the concomitant desire of fundamentalists to resist that shift.[2] Likewise, Southern Baptists in the late twentieth century have also been uncomfortable with changing gender roles. They have concluded that attempts to accept and encourage the ordination of women constitute a sellout to secular progressive culture. Sociologist Mark Chaves argues that denominations often construct gender policies as a way of signaling their position within the culture. Writing in 1997, he argues, "A denomination's policy allowing (or prohibiting) women's ordination is better understood as a symbolic display of support for gender equality (or of resistance to gender equality) than as a policy either motivated by or intended to regulate the everyday reality of women inside the organization."[3] This is especially true with Southern Baptists, who hold to the concept of the autonomy of local churches. Even as the new leadership of the SBC makes every effort to stand against the ordination of women, it is left to local congregations to decide for themselves what roles women will fill. The conservative effort to resist the cultural forces favoring gender equality is part of a broader attempt to be faithful to scripture as conservatives understand it, but this issue also offers them a very visible platform to oppose the prevailing trends of society. These countercultural efforts culminated in 1998 with the addition of the "submission statement" to the standard confession of faith of the Southern Baptist Convention, but the struggle over the place of women in both the home and the churches began long before. What would become a full-blown battle against the egalitarian forces of American culture started first as a debate between conservatives and moderates within the SBC.

Moderates and Women

In the 1970s and 1980s, some moderate Southern Baptists were moving in a decidedly progressive direction with regard to women in ministry. This was especially the case in the elite intellectual circles of the denomination. Southern Seminary was probably the most progressive institution in the SBC on that issue, matched perhaps by Southeastern Seminary. When Tim Weber interviewed for a faculty position at Southern in 1992, his support for the ordination of women was practically a requirement for his getting the vote of the faculty, even though his position was a sore spot for conservative trustees. Even at Southern, however, the atmosphere was far from egalitarian. As a study of the twenty-six women who earned doctoral degrees at that seminary between 1982 and 1992 reveals, some reported that they were sexually harassed, treated differently in the classroom, and taught by a faculty that was nearly all male and quite ignorant of issues of gender. In short, for all of its progressivism, Southern was still part of a network of culturally traditional moderates who controlled the denomination before conservatives came to power.[4] As one female doctoral student put it: "I think there was general support for [women in ministry] in the abstract. In that regard some professors were very supportive. I think it was more a question of ignorance where some professors would call us men or keep talking about men in ministry, assuming a male model. One professor used an image of not putting accents [on Hebrew words] was like a woman going around naked. And I thought being the only woman there made me feel self-conscious."[5]

Another woman among the Southern doctoral students reported that after a professor gave her one of the two highest grades in her class, he requested, "Please don't tell the boys what you made," the implication being that "the boys" would not take kindly to a woman out-theologizing them. Still, while the professors did little to actually further feminist theology, they at least supported the presence of these women over and against the outright hostility that some male students expressed. Some of those professors who supported the women, however, were very much in the dark about how certain statements and behaviors affected their female students. As one of the women said: "It's almost a comical thing, sardonically comical, to know of genuinely good-intentioned men who could behave in such demeaning ways toward women. . . . [T]he men, I think in many ways thought that some of the things they were saying and doing were, you know, in my best interest. And they were just clueless. They didn't get it." According to many of the women who studied there, Southern was a "chilly climate" for them even during the progressive years of the 1980s.[6]

Still, a chilly climate that results from ignorance and insensitivity is quite different from the sort of active opposition to women in pastoral ministry that the conservatives were able to bring to Southern Seminary in the 1990s. Even as early as 1973, Southern Seminary students passed a resolution affirming openness to women in virtually all forms of ministry. Shortly thereafter, Southern's president, Duke McCall, wrote: "Most Baptists have long since explained the admonitions to women to keep silent in the church as being rooted in a local situation. It has not been understood by most Baptists as a universal prohibition against female speech in church."[7] The same women who at least gave some credit for whatever feeble attempts at sensitivity their old-line moderate professors proffered were also unified in their dismay and even grief over what happened when the conservatives took control of Southern Seminary. In fact, comments about Southern being chilly toward women and issues of gender dissipate quickly when these women talk about the seminary under conservative leadership. Southern in the period "BF" (before fundamentalism), as some call it, was "a marvelous place for me to grow and be stretched and become and clarify a sense of vocation and get launched into the future. I had wonderful teachers and wonderful friends. And, you know, probably the seven most significant years of my life."[8] As the interviewers of these seminary women put it, the Southern these women remembered was both a chilly climate and Camelot, the place that once was that they want to remember fondly. Summing up the Southern experience for women could very well be summing up the whole moderate project of gender inclusiveness. The authors of this study write, "Southern Seminary was not perfect, any more than Camelot, but it was a place where we as women came to construct an initial understanding of ourselves as women in ministry."[9]

Some of these same women believed by the mid-1990s that the new moderate Baptist institutions like the Cooperative Baptist Fellowship (CBF) had yet to escape fully from the male-dominated mentality of the old, moderate Southern Baptist Convention. One claimed: "[Y]ou look at the Cooperative Baptist Fellowship offices, and it's a man in every single position in their office. It's a man in every one. There are no women. None. So I feel like, you know, you're lying to us still. You're perpetuating the same old shit that the fundamentalists did." Another put it this way: "The CBF . . . patriarchy all over again. They wear better ties."[10] Actually, the CBF, by the late 1990s, had women in several positions and in 1999 even had a woman moderator, Sarah Francis Anders. There was also an effort to balance genders in its various meetings and convocations. Still, perceptions of patriarchy die hard.

Southern Baptist moderates are sometimes either in denial about their own exclusionary past or simply oblivious to it. One former female doctoral student at Southern tells of hearing a moderate pastor in her area using a baseball metaphor. He claimed that before 1979, when the conservatives began to take over the game, anyone could get a bat, go up to the plate, and take a turn at hitting. This woman said she was sitting next to an African American man who had grown up Southern Baptist. He poked her and asked, "Sister, did you ever get up to bat?" She answered, "No, did you?"[11]

Such a sentiment is born out statistically. During the days of moderate control of the denomination, enrollment in Southern Baptist seminaries dropped from 17.1 percent in 1950 to around 10 percent by the 1970s. By contrast, the national trend in seminaries, at least in liberal or mainline schools, was an increase in their proportion of female students, so that by 1975 one-third of the students at Harvard Divinity School were women. The SBC decline seemed to some close observers of Southern Baptist trends to be changing by the mid-1970s. Historian H. Leon McBeth wrote in 1977 that the new factor in the Southern Baptist debate over the role of women in ministry was the presence of a cadre of female teachers and scholars. Moreover, while overall percentages of women had declined from the 1950s to the 1970s, the enrollment of women in the seminaries' schools of theology was rising. "One may no longer assume that women seminarians are preparing for the traditionally 'feminine' church jobs. Many of them are preparing and planning to be ministers."[12]

Even so, as late as 1974 there were believed to be only eight women ordained as Southern Baptist preachers. Some moderate leaders predicted that this trickle of female ordination was about to become a stream, and indeed the number was probably up to two hundred ordained SBC women by the early 1980s.[13] Representing a twenty-fold increase in less than a decade, the increasing trend placed Southern Baptists on the same trajectory as the mainline, liberal denominations, which conservatives believe have sold out to the prevailing norms of a progressivist culture. Little wonder, then, that reversing this trend became important for them.

Traditional southern sexism notwithstanding, many moderates had by the 1980s developed biblical and theological arguments for the full participation of women in ministry, including ordained roles. One might say that while the record of SBC moderates' support for full participation of women in churches has been checkered at best, by the 1980s there was movement toward equality. The seminary training of women in theology meant that moderate voices for inclusiveness would be increasingly female as more and more women took doctorates. Jann Aldredge Clanton provided what could be taken as the standard moderate or progressive argument on the issue of women in her address at the 1988 annual meeting of the Southern Baptist Historical Society. At the time, Clanton was serving as minister to family life at St. Johns United Methodist Church in Waco, Texas. She was, nevertheless, a long-time Baptist who was trained in Southern Baptist institutions and was a member of Seventh and James Baptist Church, Waco, even as she served on the ministerial staff at St. Johns.

Clanton argues from both the Old and New Testaments, as well as from Baptist history. Citing Genesis 1:27–28, she claims that the creation stories, properly interpreted, show that both male and female bear the image of God equally. In Genesis 2, the word for "helper fit," which refers to God's creation of woman as an assistant suitable for man, is used throughout the Old Testament sixteen times but never as a subordinate helper. As for Genesis 2:21–23, which conservatives use to indicate woman's biological derivation from man, Clanton cites eminent Old Testament scholar Walter Bruggemann, who has argued that when properly interpreted in light of its ancient linguistic context, the passage supports the mutual relationship of men and women. Moreover, Clanton points out that the subordination of women based on the order of creation, another favorite conservative argument, would lead logically to the superiority of plants and animals over men since they were created first.[14]

Continuing her Old Testament exegesis, Clanton writes that many passages on the subordination of women are descriptive or predictive in nature, not prescriptive. Such is the case for Genesis 3:16–19, which describes what will happen to women as a result of sin. Women will bear children in pain and have their husbands rule over them. But these are a result of sin and not, Clanton maintains, God's divine intention for all time. Other passages of the Old Testament similarly describe a patriarchal society but not God's perfect intention. Within the context of this patriarchy, where women are clearly treated as inferior, God uses women to challenge the sinful norm. "In Israelite culture," Clanton explains, "women had no rights of inheritance if there were male heirs (Num. 27:1–11), women received harsher sentences for adultery than men (Num. 5:11–31), and a father or husband could nullify a woman's religious vows (Num. 30:3–15)." In the midst of such an oppressive society, however, God repeatedly chose to use women as highly significant leaders. Clanton lists Miriam, whose song proclaims Israel's deliverance from Egypt; Micah 6:4 lists her as coequal with Moses and Aaron. Deborah served as prophet and judge, exercising society's highest authority. Huldah was chosen over Jeremiah as the most reliable prophet. These examples and others lead Clanton to conclude that "[a]lthough the Old Testament describes a culture oppressive to women, it shows God working to restore women to full personhood in God's image."[15]

Turning to the New Testament, Clanton reminds her audience that the Baptist Faith and Message Statement, the SBC's confession of faith, says (prior to its revision in 2000), "The criterion by which the Bible is to be interpreted is Jesus Christ." She then shows the ways in which Jesus was truly innovative in his dealings with women. He accepted their testimony, even though Jewish oral tradition held that the testimony of one hundred women was not equal to that of one man. He violated a societal taboo by speaking and traveling with women openly, clearly calling them as part of his larger band of disciples. While some conservatives use as an argument against ordination the fact that Jesus called no women to be part of the select twelve, Clanton replies that Jesus also called no Gentiles. Clearly, no one would suggest that only Jewish males can be ordained. Clanton concludes her brief discussion of Jesus by saying, "By His teachings and actions, Christ leads us to affirm the equality of men and women in every sphere of life, including the ordained ministry. Jesus' followers who founded the church gave less freedom to women than did Jesus." Even these followers in the early church, however, gave women more voice than did the Greco-Roman world of their day, and more than Baptist churches of our own time, Clanton stresses.[16]

Turning from Jesus to Paul, Clanton attempts to show that one simply cannot take a few of his statements as blanket and timeless prohibitions against women speaking in church without forcing the apostle to appear inconsistent and incoherent. If women cannot ever speak or prophesy, then why does Paul say they should cover their heads when they do? She also argues, along with other moderate and progressive Baptist scholars, that the grammatical construction of 1 Corinthians 14:34–36 suggests that Paul was quoting from a letter he had received from the men at Corinth. This is known as a diatribe stylistic device in which the biblical author quotes his opponents' position first, then refutes it. Read this way, the passage has the men of Corinth writing, "the women should keep silent in the churches. For they are not permitted to speak." Paul then replies indignantly, "Did the word of God originate with you, or are you [men] the only ones it has reached?" Baptist New Testament scholar Charles Talbert believes the passage can even be read with Paul exclaiming an indignant "What! Did the word of God originate with you or are you the only ones it has reached?" the obvious answer being that the word is not the domain of the men at Corinth. Another example of this diatribe style is 1 Corinthians 6:12, where the Apostle Paul quotes his libertine opponents, "All things are lawful for me," then responds with his own view, "but not all things are helpful." Clanton may have been relying on Talbert's scholarship, a brief version of which had just been published the year before her address.[17]

Clanton also points to several other passages where Paul seems to affirm women in ministry. Again, Talbert has argued that the striking difference between the words of 1 Corinthians 14:34 ("women should keep silent in the church") with other Pauline verses lends to the view that the former passage was a diatribe.[18] Clanton cites Romans 16:3, where Paul refers to both Priscilla and Aquila as "fellow workers in Christ Jesus." In Philippians 4:2–3, the same word used for "fellow worker or co-worker" is applied to Euodia, Syntyche, and other women. Scholar Paul Jewett believed that the apostle Paul was referring to these women as apostles like himself. The apostle also commended the deacon Phoebe in Romans 16:1–2, while 1 Timothy 3:11, interpreted contextually, likewise seems to give instruction for the behavior of women deacons.[19]

Addressing the 1984 SBC resolution against the ordination of women, Clanton argues that the statement took 1 Timothy 2:11–15 out of context. It supported the barring of women from ordained ministry partly on the basis of the view that they bore greater responsibility for the fall into sin, Eve having been first deceived, and of woman being second in the order of human creation. In Clanton's view, this was an example of selective literalism in that Southern Baptists do not take as timeless the command just two verses earlier forbidding women to wear braided hair, jewelry, and fine clothes (1 Timothy 2:9) nor do they emphasize a later verse that says women will be saved through bearing children (2:15). Again, Talbert's scholarship, among others to be sure, sets the foundation for the moderate, or progressive, position. He argues that the likely historical context of the pastoral epistles is one where the author is instructing churches in how to combat the early Christian heresy of gnosticism. Second Timothy 3:6 seems to suggest that those spreading gnosticism had gotten to a group of "weak women," who were then responsible for the further spread of that heresy. As defense against this, the author of the three pastoral epistles (1 and 2 Timothy and Titus) lays down a line of succession from God to Paul, then from Paul to

Titus and Timothy, then to faithful men who will further spread the orthodox faith. Those most easily swayed, in this historical situation the "weak
women," could not be entrusted with the spread or defense of the faith.
Talbert concludes that the intent of 1 Timothy 2:11–12 is, "When women are
the source of heresy, they are not to be allowed to teach."[20] From Clanton's
perspective, the greatest weight should be given to Paul's statement in Galatians 3:28. This is so, she argues, because here Paul is writing in a doctrinal
setting as opposed to addressing a particular historical context, and he states
explicitly that in Christ "there is neither male nor female."[21]

Finally, Clanton argues that Baptist history supports the ordination of
women as pastors and deacons. Here she cites seventeenth-century English
Baptist founders John Smyth and Thomas Helwys, both of whom recognized men and women as deacons. Likewise, America's Separate Baptists,
viewed by many as the forerunners of the SBC, regularly ordained male
and female deacons. There were also several well-known female preachers
among the Separate Baptists, a few of whom were ordained. Clanton concludes her address with an allusion to the Civil Rights movement by stating,
"As in the issue of equality of the races, Southern Baptists have failed to take
a prophetic stand on the equality of men and women."[22] The bulk of her
argument, however, is not based on an analogy from the Civil Rights movement or any secular progressive ideology but on biblical exegesis and her
reading of Baptist history. Conservatives argue that she is wrong on both
counts.

THE CONSERVATIVE REBUTTAL

Dorothy Patterson was invited to the 1988 Southern Baptist Historical Association meeting to give the counterpoint response to Clanton's argument,
and both papers were published together in the SBC journal *Baptist History
and Heritage*. In one sense, Patterson's theological preparation would seem
to make her a likely candidate for the role of pioneer progressive. She went
through New Orleans Baptist Theological Seminary in the mid-1960s with
her husband, Paige, taking identical courses all the way through with but
one exception. While there, she was the only woman in the seminary's
school of theology. She remembers having good rapport with her professors
but also recalls being patronized and in at least one case experiencing outright hostility to her presence. In this respect her experience was a precursor
to that of the female doctoral students at Southern in the 1980s, even worse

perhaps. One professor of biblical languages refused to put Patterson in a translation group with men in the class. Working alone, she was nevertheless required to translate the same amount of text as the multimember groups. She made A's on the exams but still received a B in the course; the professor claimed that her class participation was deficient. Patterson says, "That was the only professor in my academic career that I thought resented me because I was a woman." As for being patronized, Patterson tells of her preaching course. When she completed her sermon to the class, the professor's only comment was, "Well, Mrs. Patterson, that was a little bit WMUish," a reference to the SBC's Women's Missionary Union.[23] These experiences might well have set Patterson on a course to be a progressive rebel against the status quo. Instead, she has emerged on the conservative side as the SBC's leading theologian of women and the family, a position made possible both by the conservative takeover of the denomination and her own eventual doctoral work and dissertation on a theology of the family. In the 1980s, however, she was the dissenter against moderate hegemony when she squared off against Clanton.

The Southern Baptist Historical Society has always been the domain of moderate SBC academics, so Patterson was in hostile territory at that 1988 meeting. Indeed, one of the questions asked of Patterson following her lecture was whether her appearance at the meeting violated the biblical principle against women teaching men. In response she apologized and said that she did not intend to teach men but was merely "sharing what she found in Scripture."[24] With little chance of endearing herself to her audience, Patterson began her address by throwing caution to the wind. One paragraph into her introduction she told conferees: "Having researched many published historical papers on male and female feminists, this writer is amazed at the lack of careful documentation concerning women throughout history who allegedly engaged successfully in teaching/ruling positions in local churches. One wonders if some have employed jesuitical casuistry or historical hanky-panky in order to create a female Mt. Everest out of an anthill to prove a point." In the corresponding endnote of the published version of this address, she cites historians Donald and Lucille Dayton as the culprits, singling out a *Christianity Today* article they wrote in 1975 entitled "Women as Preachers: Evangelical Precedents." Patterson writes in her endnote, "[T]here is not a single documentation for the bold assertion that 'Denominations in the National Association of Evangelicals have by and large ordained women earlier, in larger numbers, and more consistently than those in the National Council of Churches.'"[25] Patterson overstates her case, for the Daytons' article shows that evangelical denominations like the Free Will Baptists, Wesleyan Church, Free Methodists, Church of God (Anderson, Indiana), the Church of the Nazarene, the Pilgrim Holiness Church, and a number of Pentecostal assemblies all had women preachers in the late nineteenth and early twentieth centuries, long before most mainline denominations began the practice.[26]

The central point of Patterson's argument comes from 1 Timothy 2:8–15 and 1 Corinthians 14:33–35. As Clanton's attention to these verses reveals, these are the problematic passages for moderates and, along with Ephesians 5, the crux of the conservative position. Patterson warns against the impulse of some conservatives to jump to the conclusion that biblical teaching precludes women from positions of leadership in the church. She terms this overwrought response the "neither shall ye touch it lest ye die syndrome."[27] In her view, these passages admonish women to receive instruction quietly while forbidding them to teach or exercise authority over men. The latter prohibition looms large throughout Patterson's address. She allows that women can do or be anything in churches so long as they do not exercise authority over males. This, in her view, makes the question of ordination moot, however, because the ordained ministry requires the wielding of authority.

"Frequently feminists disregard the directive of I Timothy 2:11 by a process of deculturation," Patterson argues. "This process of hermeneutical gymnastics does not, however, erase the meaning of the text." The meaning for Patterson is that the prohibition against women teaching or exercising authority over men is tied to the order of creation and to the fact that Eve was the first deceived (1 Timothy 2:13–14). To make these verses timeless and apply them literally is not a case of "selective literalism," as Clanton alleges in her address when she says that Baptists do not adhere to Paul's teaching about braided hair and fine clothing. Rather, Patterson counters, Paul's admonition against braided hair and jewelry is merely a way of highlighting the underlying principle that women should adorn themselves in modesty. When he moves from appearance to action, that same principle carries over to women taking their instruction quietly and willingly refusing to teach or exercise authority over men. This is something women should do on their own as a result of their desire to follow biblical principle, but it should not be imposed on them by men. "Biblical submission is forever a self-imposed discipline. Men are not directed by Scripture to force or require submission."[28]

Patterson considers analogies to slavery in the writings of the apostle Paul unconvincing. Even if Paul admonished slaves to obedience, at most this would be an acknowledgment of how Christian slaves should comport themselves while in a bad situation. There is no biblical admonition to continue slavery. "However," retorts Patterson, "the opposite is true concerning the subordination of women since the Scriptures declare that women are to be submissive because of the order of creation." Here Patterson cites 1 Corinthians 11:2–16 as well as 1 Timothy 2:11–13. In these passages, Paul teaches that women should not teach men, and since teaching and exercising authority over men are activities inherent in pastoral ministry, this settles the question of the ordination of women. They should not be ordained because they are forbidden to carry out functions necessary to pastoral ministry. Moreover, in the 1 Corinthians passage, the apostle places marriage in the same context of submission that he does orderly worship. Therefore, concludes Patterson, "to dismiss the role relationships in the church as simply cultural would dismiss the analogous role relationship in marriage as also merely cultural. Thus, the theological matrix for this order in worship is the order of creation."[29]

Moving to 1 Corinthians 14:33–35, Patterson denies the argument of Clanton, Talbert, and other moderate and progressive scholars who believe that Paul is merely quoting from an erroneous prohibition against women speaking in the church. Rather, Patterson believes that the apostle is tying this prohibition to the Torah. "[I]n verse 34 the use of the article in conjunction with 'law' implies more than mere custom but rather a connection to the commands of the Torah." But Patterson still has to make allowances regarding the admonition that women keep silent in the church. As Clanton points out, conservatives do not take this literally, for their women do speak in church, and Patterson acknowledges this. "Obviously, the silence mandated for women in I Corinthians 14 does not exclude their vocal participation in worship services since both praying and prophesying are permitted (I Cor. 11:15) with certain restrictions, specifically that the women not take charge of the worship service within the teaching/ruling function."[30]

Patterson concludes her address by rehearsing a familiar refrain of conservatives. "To repeat, the real issue at hand is not ordination itself but the authority of the Bible."[31] This is questionable, however. As historian Leon

McBeth summed up at the Southern Baptist Historical Society meeting the year before Clanton and Patterson presented their views, Southern Baptists have had equally competent and dedicated Bible scholars on both sides of the issue. "So it is not a question of whether one believes the Bible, but of how we understand the Bible."[32] Both Clanton and Patterson ground their arguments in the authority of Scripture. The real issue is one of interpretation, each arguing that the other's exegesis is faulty. Patterson concedes, "Without doubt women did have a variety of positions of service, influence, and even leadership and teaching in the early church." She maintains, however, that "the functions they assumed were done with modesty and order (I Cor. 11:2–16; 14:40), and they did not teach or exercise authority over men (I Tim. 2:11–15; I Cor. 14:33–35)."[33]

The Clanton-Patterson debate stayed on a high plane for the most part. During the discussion period, however, Clanton got in one dig by saying that she thought it was sad to see a woman with Patterson's gifts using her talents to deny other women the right to use their gifts. Patterson replied that she was willing to sacrifice whatever career she might have pursued on her own because Scripture required it. Then, in a refrain Patterson has espoused often during her career as a conservative spokesperson, she said, "And I can truthfully say that the most exciting thing I've done as a woman is be the wife of Paige Patterson and mother of Carmen and Armour." Continuing, she stressed that her assignment from God for the home was more important than any amount of success she might have had doing something else. Further challenges came from the moderate-dominated audience. One participant asked Patterson how she justified having a doctorate of ministry (this was prior to her attaining the PhD). She responded that her husband wanted her to get the degree and that it was done through an extension program allowing her to take classes without being gone from her home while her children were there. To laughter, another conference participant took the floor microphone and made reference to Patterson's hat. He said, "I commend you for covering your head before you so eloquently spoke to us this morning," a clear reference to Paul's admonition that women should cover their heads while speaking in church. Patterson replied that God may have given her a passion for hats because she does have an independent spirit. "[P]erhaps it is a way of saying that I do accept the authority of my husband in our home." To the charge that she had exercised teaching authority over the men present at the meeting, she responded, "My apologies to all the gentlemen here if you thought that was my purpose."[34]

Moderates got the last word at that meeting. The moderator of the discussion closed the proceedings with these words: "I'm sure we have not settled all the issues, nor the questions, nor the problems. But I'm also sure that God will continue to call whomsoever he will and that the churches in their wisdom will ordain whom they see fit."[35] This was perhaps the last time moderates would have the upper hand on the issue of women in ministry. By 1988 the tide had already turned, and conservatives were well on their way to consolidating their hold on the denominational machinery. The result was that for the question of women in the Southern Baptist context, 1998 would look quite different from 1988.

THE SUBMISSION STATEMENT OF 1998

The resolution of 1984, with its emphasis on women as second in creation and first in the Fall, was the first major breakthrough for conservatives on the issue of women in ministry. The process of making the conservative view of the roles of women dominant in the denomination would culminate with the submission statement of 1998. Because this declaration became part of the denomination's official confession of faith, it carries far more weight than a mere resolution.

Written and adopted in 1925, the Baptist Faith and Message (BFM) was updated and revised in 1963. Both its inception and revision came in response to cultural or denominational crises. In 1925 the issue was evolution. With the fundamentalist-modernist controversy still perking along in northern denominations, creedal fundamentalists in the SBC were clamoring for an official statement that would put Southern Baptists on record as anti-evolution. The right wing, led by J. Frank Norris and C. P. Stealy, met opposition in the form of denominational statesman and preeminent Southern Baptist theologian E. Y. Mullins. Mullins and his allies were able to steal the fundamentalists' thunder by adopting the idea of a confession, but they were also able to produce a moderate statement that contained no mention of evolution. This did not mollify the fundamentalists. In fact, the very next year they were able to push through a resolution on evolution. Still, resolutions come and go and usually get little attention after their passage. By contrast, the 1925 statement remained the denomination's confession of faith. It was a suitable compromise that satisfied most Southern Baptists and was typical of how the denomination headed off controversy during its years under moderate leadership.[36]

The Baptist Faith and Message was revised in 1963, again in response to denominational controversy having to do with the origins of the earth and ancient natural history. Ralph Elliott, a professor at Midwestern Baptist Theological Seminary, wrote a commentary on the Book of Genesis. Utilizing the tools of modern biblical criticism, he questioned the literal factuality of the Creation story, even laying open the possibility that Adam and Eve were representations of humankind and not individual human beings. After a tortuous process of investigation, administrators relieved Elliott of his seminary post. Concurrent with this controversy, the denomination updated its confession of faith. In the 1990s, Elliott wrote his own account of the controversy and argued that this was the beginning of the conservative movement that would result twenty years later in the successful right-wing effort to take control of the denomination. He was especially critical of the moderate strategy of resolving disagreements by making concessions to conservatives and engaging in "doublespeak" to keep rank-and-file Southern Baptists from an awareness of what was being taught in the seminaries. Elliott believed that moderates' inability and unwillingness to stand on principle and to fight for what they believed emboldened conservatives and alienated grassroots support for moderate elites once their true beliefs were made known.[37]

The addition of the 1998 submission statement, therefore, was only the second revision of the Baptist Faith and Message and only the third time the denomination had moved to outline its beliefs officially. Still, the submission statement, which would become an amendment to the confession, came swiftly and naturally. The process began at the 1997 convention meeting in Dallas. There, a relatively unknown convention messenger from Maryland made a motion that Tom Elliff, the SBC president, appoint a committee to consider adding a statement on the family to the BFM.[38] The motion passed, and some months later Elliff appointed a committee headed by Anthony Jordan, a pastor and denominational official from Oklahoma. The committee met for the first time in April 1998. Jordan had instructed members to do preliminary study and to bring resources to the meeting that might help in fashioning a statement. The plan was to devote a long day to the task and to leave that very first meeting with a drafted statement.[39]

On the day of the meeting, the committee was divided into three groups, each with a specific challenge. One group worked on the overarching introduction to the statement and the basic definition of biblical marriage, a second focused on the relationship of husbands to wives, and a third considered parents and children. Given strict word-count limitations, each group was to construct its portion of the overall statement and cite all scriptural references pertaining to its specific issue. By the end of the day, the committee had a working draft that was later revised slightly before being submitted to messengers at the SBC meeting in June.[40]

The committee was aware that the relationship between men and women was a touchy cultural issue likely to be subject to misinterpretation and even opposition. For this reason, in two separate places the statement emphasized that men and women are created in the image of God and are equal before Him. The drafters also recognized that the word "submission" carried many negative connotations, but the committee nevertheless decided that there was no getting around that term because of its prominence in key biblical texts, particularly Ephesians 5:23–31. To clarify that submission did not mean that men could demand subservience, members inserted the adverb "graciously" to convey the idea that women should voluntarily take it upon themselves to submit to their husbands. On the other side of the submission-headship issue, the committee inserted the adjective "servant" to modify "leadership" in order to convey the type of example modeled by Christ. When completed, therefore, the key passage of the statement, which would become so controversial, read: "A wife is to submit herself graciously to the servant leadership of her husband even as the church willingly submits to the headship of Christ. She, being in the image of God as is her husband and thus equal to him, has the God-given responsibility to respect her husband and to serve as his helper in managing the household and nurturing the next generation."[41] This was based on Ephesians, where the analogy is that the husband heads the wife as Christ heads, or leads, the church.

The committee anticipated resistance on the floor of the convention meeting, especially concerning the concept of the wife being a "helper" for her husband. Dorothy Patterson argued for keeping the word because she believed that it was the proper biblical term, and her view prevailed. On the floor of the convention, however, the main attack came on the issue of submission, not over the word "helper." When drafting the statement in April, the committee had decided against using the concept of mutual submission. Patterson explained the reasons. Even though Christ in one sense submitted Himself to the church, even suffered and died for it, His service was in no way equal to or the same as the church's deference to His leadership. Mutual submission, Patterson believed, carries the connotation of just such an equal partnership or sameness. The committee wanted to be clear that while husbands and wives in one sense submit to each other, the husband is the leader. When the statement was being debated on the floor at the June SBC meeting, a messenger made a motion that the submission passage be amended to read, "both husband and wife are to submit graciously to each other."[42] Patterson was called forward to address this proposed alteration. She explained that the phrase "mutual submission" was misleading because it implied that husband and wife submitted in the same way, rather than the view that women submit to the Christlike leadership of their husbands. The motion was defeated.[43]

The attempt to revise the statement in favor of mutual submission was another clear indication that Southern Baptist moderates and conservatives have two different views as to how men and women relate to one another both in the church and within families. The mutual submission that moderates stress is a form of egalitarianism. It is based on the belief that the sexes stand equal before God in such a way that both men and women can carry out social, ecclesiastical, and familial tasks without reference to gender roles or restrictions. The only restriction is biological—men cannot bear children. Moderates believe that egalitarianism faithfully represents the core teachings of Scripture.

Patterson and other conservatives, by contrast, argue for a "complementarian" position. The word "complement," or some variation thereof, appears three times in the official two-page commentary, written by Dorothy Patterson, that accompanied the submission statement.[44] She argues that while the types of submission exercised by spouses complement each other, they are not the same and are not equal in the way that moderates stress. Patterson and the committee that drafted the submission statement were afraid that if the term "mutual submission" were used in the document itself, it would have carried the connotation of egalitarianism. They believe in a mutuality or reciprocity of submission as long as it is clear that such mutuality consists of two different types of deference, not one.[45] Richard Land, who was also on the drafting committee, has emphasized that the statement does not rule out mutual submission. From his perspective, the idea that a husband is to love his wife as Christ loved the church "means that he will always, always put his wife's needs above his own needs—always. And, the wife is to put herself under the authority of her own husband."[46] The rejection of "mutual submission," especially when it was motioned from the convention floor, indicates that conservatives want to steer clear of the moderate view, which is an egalitarian understanding of mutuality, rather than the headship-servant reciprocity that conservatives prefer. Put another way, it could be said that conservatives believe in two different types of submission that are mutually reinforcing, while moderates believe in one type of submission exercised mutually within marriage.

Inserting "mutual submission" probably would have helped diffuse much of the opposition to the statement, but in the view of conservatives, it also would have been a concession to the progressive norms of popular culture. In the marriage section of the statement's commentary, the committee warned that in sexual relationships, believers must be careful not to "fall prey to an accommodation to the spirit of the age." This concern goes well beyond the practice of sexual relations, however. It could actually be applied more broadly to the whole concept of marriage and the relationship of wives to husbands. In fact, the conclusion to the commentary stressed again the danger of selling out to culture. "Doctrine and practice, whether in the home or the church," it reads, "are not to be determined according to modern cultural, sociological, and ecclesiastical trends or according to personal emotional whims; rather, Scripture is to be the final authority in all matters of faith and conduct."[47] In short, conservatives believe that egalitarianism is an unbiblical sellout to the spirit of secular progressivism. They are absolutely sure that the Bible's teaching on husband-wife relationships require headship from the husband and submission from the wife. Patterson says that the intention of the submission statement is not to say "this is what you have to do to be a Southern Baptist," but merely "to put on the table what the Bible says."[48] She believes that it is easy to get away from biblical guidelines because of the pressures and hubris of our age. Conservatives, therefore, wanted to bring the denomination back to what they believe are the simple teachings of the text of scripture on this issue.

The outcry against the submission statement came from many quarters. It received wide coverage in the secular press, appearing above the fold on the front page of *The New York Times,* where religious journalist-scholar Gustav Niebuhr pointed out that the statement was one of the most conservative of public declarations on marital roles. He contrasted it with a four-year-old statement by the American Roman Catholic bishops that characterized marital relationships as "mutual submission."[49] Both secular and religious commentators weighed in with criticism. Al Mohler, who had done so much in 1995 to focus attention on the issue of women, was again brought into the forefront of a controversy. While he had not been on the committee that drafted and proposed the submission statement, his wife,

Mary, had. Nevertheless, when CNN's Larry King wanted to discuss and even debate the issue, Mohler was the man who ended up on the live television program in a roundtable discussion that included Patricia Ireland, Jerry Falwell, and Robert Schuller. Ireland, of the National Organization of Women, tied the issue of biblical submission to the issue of slavery, arguing that if one is to retain the idea from Scripture that wives must submit to husbands, why not the accompanying notion that slaves should submit to their masters? After all, she pointed out, that issue also appears in the Ephesians passage from which the submission statement was largely drawn. Mohler responded that the admonition to slaves is that as Christians they are to comport themselves in a particular way. This does not mean that there must always be slavery or that the Bible condones the practice. King asked, "You don't condemn those who ran away, do you?" Another panelist interjected, "Or Harriet Tubman who ran the underground railroad?" Mohler responded, "I want to look at this text seriously and it says submit to the master, and I really don't see any loophole there, as much as our popular culture would want to see one."[50] Like Mohler, Land and other conservatives also pointed out that the big difference between slavery and wifely submission in marriage is that Scripture clearly teaches that marriage is an institution created and ordained by God. The Bible does not say the same of slavery. The Pauline admonition in Ephesians that slaves submit is moot, therefore, because slavery no longer exists, but the admonition for wives to submit is still operative because marriage continues to be part of God's plan for human relationships.[51]

Secular progressives like Ireland were by no means the only ones to attempt to bring slavery into the discussion. Evangelical historian and columnist Diana Butler Bass also raises the issue. In a column that appeared in several newspapers, she argues that early Christians actually challenged pagan norms of domination by asserting a newfound freedom in Christ. Women and slaves were converting to the Christian faith in higher numbers than nonslave males, often disobeying authorities in order to be baptized. This led to the charges that Christianity was a religion of women and slaves and that it undermined social order. The Ephesians passage was Paul's response to a chaotic situation that Christians were exacerbating. "Ephesians 5 is not timeless morality," Bass writes. "Rather, it reflects particular problems faced by early Christians in the cultural context of ancient Rome." What struck Bass as odd is that all Christians today recognize that Paul's admonition to slaves was contextual. "But when it comes to women," she charges, "conservative Christians have drawn the line." In other words, they miss the cultural context of early Rome and enshrine wifely submission as biblical when it was actually cultural. "The 'biblical' family—now enshrined by Southern Baptists—is not biblical at all," Bass emphasizes. "Pagans practiced male headship; early Christians rejected it. They experienced a God who lifts the oppressed."[52]

Bass bases her analysis on a widely held interpretation of the Ephesians 5 passage. Evangelical New Testament scholar Judy Gundry-Volf of Fuller Theological Seminary was cited in *The New York Times* as saying that the dominant view of the passage is that it was written in response to the charges that early Christians were upsetting the patriarchal social order. This interpretation acknowledges that Ephesians 5 represents a retreat from the even more egalitarian views of Jesus, but the passage also constitutes a revision of Greco-Roman household codes. Put another way, the passage presented a softer, gentler version of pagan patriarchy but was not merely an accommodation to that system. Rather, it was an attempt to reform and, indeed, Christianize the social order of the time. It was an attempt to infuse pagan patriarchy with Christian love, thus transforming it into what some scholars have called "love patriarchalism."[53]

Another popular author to weigh in on the SBC submission statement was Gary Wills, a Roman Catholic historian and social commentator who writes for major news magazines in between turning out scores of books on American political, religious, and social history. An astute observer of religion, and one who recognizes and decries secular bias against it, Wills, like Bass, declares that the submission statement more accurately reflected pagan rather than Christian attitudes toward women. He references classical philosophers Aristotle and Plato, showing that they both taught that women were subservient, indeed inferior, to men. While not totally disengaged from this view, Wills argues, early Christianity showed a new, more egalitarian spirit, which is captured in brief in Galatians 3:28, "[There is] neither male nor female, for you are all one in Christ Jesus."[54]

Wills offers an interpretation of the Ephesians 5 passage from biblical scholar Markus Barth, who argued that it is taken from ancient hymn language concerning Jewish wedding ceremonies. In Jewish marriage the groom pays for the bride. In this passage, the price of Christ's bride is the sacrifice of his own life. Verse 25 reads in part, "Husbands love your wives just as Christ loved the church *and gave himself up for her.*" "The parallel in marriage," Wills offers, "would suggest greater sacrifice on the husband's part rather than greater power." He then points to Barth's handling of verse 28, which says that the husbands should love their wives "as their own bodies." Many interpret this to mean that the wife is as dear to the husband as his own body is, but Barth disagreed. Rather than the husband cherishing his wife as he would his own body, he is to cherish her because she is his own body; the two have become one flesh just as Christ and his church are one. Verse 23 reads in part, "Christ is the head of the church, *His body.*" In verse 28, therefore, "'[H]is own body' is the wife herself." Read this way, the two (husband and wife) are one, so the whole idea of one dominating the other or one submitting to the other is moot. This interpretation clashed head on with Dorothy Patterson's assertion that Christ and the church are two different entities that submit to each other in different ways and, therefore, the husband and wife also submit differently. Barth, by contrast, eliminated the distinction between Christ and the church; the church is Christ's body. Likewise goes the distinction between husband and wife; they are one flesh. All of this is complex interpretation, which is part of Wills's larger point. "It is a pity," he concludes, "to see such a rich theological passage reduced by modern anti-feminists to a kind of biblical 'Taming of the Shrew.'"[55]

Wills was not only reflecting some of the cutting-edge theological and hermeneutical work on the Ephesians passage, he was also staying attuned to his own Roman Catholic faith. Not long ago it would hardly have been news that Southern Baptists disagreed with the Roman Catholic Church on a major social or theological issue. Currently, however, SBC conservatives usually find themselves standing with Catholics on the same side of the major cultural battles of our time. On the issue of husbands and wives, the SBC even has the Roman Catholic Church outflanked on the right. Pope John Paul II, in his papal letter entitled *Mulieris Dignitatem* (*On the Dignity of Women*), states that the portion of the Ephesians passage instructing wives to submit to husbands must be understood in light of verse 21's admonition that husbands and wives must submit to each other. Utilizing the same interpretation that many evangelicals and most moderate Southern Baptists use, the pontiff argues that verse 21 introduces and serves as the controlling statement for the entire passage. The primary point of the entire passage, therefore, is one of "mutual subjection out of reverence for Christ."[56] Special subjection of wives was part of the old custom of ancient culture, the pope continues, but Paul was issuing a new way, "an innovation of the gospel."[57] Following the pope's lead, in 1994 the American Catholic Bishops issued their own document recognizing marriage as "a partnership of a man and a woman, equal in dignity and value" and marked by "mutual submission—not dominance by either partner."[58]

The morning after the *Larry King Live* segment, Al Mohler appeared with former Southern Seminary professor Molly Marshall on the CBS News program *Saturday Morning*. Marshall referred to the submission statement as a "retrenchment of patriarchy" and a misinterpretation of Scripture, which teaches mutual submission. Mohler responded that the issue was clearly scriptural and that "[t]hose who have a problem with this statement have a problem with the Apostle Paul and with scripture." Marshall would have none of that line of argument and attempted to seize the scriptural high ground by pointing out that Ephesians 5:21 calls for mutual submission. That verse, she argued, was cited but not exegeted in the SBC statement. The statement, therefore, failed to take a high-enough view of Scripture.[59]

Like Marshall, some moderate former Southern Baptists who have become alienated from the SBC used the submission statement as a venue for explaining the fundamental differences between Southern Baptist conservatives and what the most progressive of moderates like to refer to as "real Baptists," which means themselves. Stan Hastey, executive director of the Alliance of Baptists, writes in the alliance's newspaper, *Baptists Today*, that his first reaction to the submission statement was "So what?" and "Who cares anymore?" After all, the statement came just a year after the announced Southern Baptist boycott of Disney for its policy of covering live-in partners, both heterosexual and homosexual, in its health insurance coverage. Hastey decided, nevertheless, that the issue was important because of what it represented. The real issue was authority. "Here's the low-down dirty on fundamentalism," he offers. "Despite its indefensible insistence that the Bible is an inerrant document, fundamentalism doesn't take the Bible seriously. In the fundamentalist system, what one purports to believe about the Bible is deemed more important than believing what the Bible actually says. The flap over Ephesians 5 is but the latest example."[60] Hastey continues by arguing that SBC conservatives have made the modern notion of inerrancy their ultimate spiritual authority.

Hastey then cites the prologue to the Baptist Faith and Message Statement, which says that confessions are merely guides and have no authority over conscience. Moreover, the prologue states, Christian faith is rooted and grounded in Jesus Christ. For Hastey, this means that Christ "is the Word behind the words of the Bible. . . . He directly refuted ancient scriptures, thereby demonstrating that not even the Bible can contain or constrain the very Word of God who was in the beginning with God and without whom nothing was made that was made." Hastey then quotes at length theologian J. William Angell from the *Mercer Dictionary of the Bible:* "Thus the revealed Word, found supremely in Jesus Christ, became the written Word in the Bible, both in human form; and the purposes of God are made complete when the revealed Word, constantly rediscovered in the written Word, is proclaimed, heard, and faithfully received by every believer in every generation." The point Hastey wants to drive home is that, for moderate or progressive Baptists like himself, inspiration is a dynamic process that includes the written text, the living Christ, and the faithful present-day reader. By contrast, he charges in his conclusion: "It's well past time progressive Baptists stopped being cowed by fundamentalists' claims about the Bible. The truth is, those claims are nothing short of idolatrous, as are all declarations that men are to rule over women."[61]

Hastey and the Alliance of Baptists represent the most progressive wing of moderate Southern Baptists who opposed the conservative movement. While many moderates for years after 1979 attempted to show that they were not guilty of the charges brought by conservatives, Alliance Baptists often met the conservatives head on and simply acknowledged that there were actually two different views of the Bible at work. Hastey's argument reflects this in his attempt to refute the whole conservative hermeneutic. Stated most simply, he is arguing that conservatives have a defective view of inspiration and interpretation of the Bible.

While Hastey and the Alliance of Baptists chose to refute directly the SBC submission statement, the other less-progressive moderate organization, the Cooperative Baptist Fellowship (CBF), decided against issuing a counterresolution. Meeting just two weeks after the SBC convention, the CBF declined to issue its own statement on marriage. This was due partly to a CBF bylaw against issuing resolutions on social issues, which grew out of the SBC controversy, during which such statements became politicized, exacerbating the hostility between moderates and conservatives. Even without a resolution, it was quite clear where the CBF stood on the issues of wifely submission and women in ministry. The organization has been something of a refuge for the egalitarian position as it has been pushed out of the SBC. CBF coordinator Daniel Vestal told reporters: "As I understand the scripture, marriage is a companionship between husband and wife, not a hierarchy. It requires mutual submission and sacrifice. It calls for shared responsibility and respect, not the exercise of authority and control." With regard to women in ministry, Vestal said that he believes "[God is] calling and gifting of all people for ministry at all levels."[62] While not an official CBF statement, it was clear that Vestal spoke for many in the organization.

While one might have expected the CBF to issue a direct challenge to the submission statement, it was actually left to the state Baptist conventions to take that approach. In its November 1998 meeting, the Baptist General Convention of Texas (BGCT) passed a resolution emphasizing mutual submission of husbands and wives. The declaration read in part that both men and women are to "submit to one another as a witness to the world of the transforming power of servant leadership." The following year messengers at the BGCT voted to reaffirm the 1963 edition of the Baptist Faith and Message Statement, thus rejecting the revised SBC confession that included the submission amendment.[63] The Texas convention is controlled by moderates, who have insisted that the state organization need not walk in lockstep with the SBC. At the same 1998 meeting where messengers passed the equality statement, the BGCT also adopted a revised funding scheme that would allow churches more options in directing their denominational monies. Essentially, this made it even easier for BGCT churches to support the CBF and non-SBC seminaries while remaining in good standing with the state convention. Conservatives in the state, charging that this was a direct slap at SBC conservative leaders in Nashville, organized their own fledgling state convention with the intention of moving in concert with the national organization. Thus was set in place a possible scenario for schism. If SBC leaders in Nashville decide at some point to recognize exclusively the new conservative state convention in Texas, churches in the BGCT may well be faced with a decision over whether to remain Southern Baptists or become merely Texas Baptists. From the other side, the BGCT could conceivably accept churches from outside the state, thus becoming an interstate denomination itself. Even without an influx of non-Texas congregations, it would be by itself one of the ten largest denominations in the United States, but that is presuming that all its churches remained in the BGCT in the event of a split with the SBC. It seems likely that many churches presently comfortable with being in both conventions might choose the SBC over the BGCT if forced to make a decision. Still, the Texas convention has the potential to do what neither the CBF nor the Alliance of Baptists has been able to accomplish, and that is to become a major, independent Baptist denomination in the South. If that happens, the status of women within marriage and the question of their roles in ministry will be key issues in the split.

Opposition to the SBC submission statement should not be taken to mean that conservatives have few allies. In fact, there is a large wing of evangelicals nationwide, including some of the most visible constituent groups, who are delighted that SBC conservatives chose to take the lead on this issue. More than fifty leaders representing a wide array of conservative evangelical organizations signed a paper affirming the SBC submission statement. The effort was spearheaded by Dennis Rainey, who founded FamilyLife, a marriage and family organization that is part of Campus Crusade for Christ. In the face of widespread and very visible opposition to the submission statement, Rainey wanted to document the fact that many evangelical groups are in full agreement with Southern Baptist conservatives. During a press conference at the July 1998 Christian Booksellers Association Convention in Dallas, Rainey was quoted as saying, "I knew that the vast majority of Bible-believing Christians would not only agree with their statement but embrace it unashamedly as the timeless truth of scripture." Among those signing Rainey's statement were evangelical author, activist, and intellectual spokesperson Charles Colson, Promise Keepers founder Bill McCartney, President of the National Religious BroadcastersBrandt Gustavson, and Arkansas governor Mike Huckabee, himself a Southern Baptist.[64]

Focus on the Family founder and Religious Right activist James Dobson supported the submission statement in part by being present as keynote speaker at the SBC's Salt Lake City convention, where the statement was adopted. He was quoted as giving his full support. Such a high-profile presence of a non-Baptist shows the degree to which SBC conservatives have elevated social-cultural issues like the role of women. The theology of Dobson's own Church of the Nazarene is in some ways clearly at odds with Southern Baptist theology, especially on matters such as baptism and the eternal security of believers. Ironically, therefore, while Dobson stands with SBC conservatives on most social-cultural issues and supports the submission-statement revision to the Baptist Faith and Message, the Nazarene Church's Arminian theology is in direct opposition to another article of that same SBC confession, the article that touts the Calvinist belief in the eternal security of the believer, or what Baptists refer to popularly as "once saved, always saved."[65] There is strong precedent for bringing in non-Baptists as keynote speakers, however, as long as they line up culturally with

SBC conservatives. Previously, conservative activist and former Iran-Contra figure Oliver North and Pres. George Bush have been among non-Baptists who have appeared at SBC conventions under conservative auspices.

From other evangelical quarters, in *World Magazine* longtime evangelical journalist Edward E. Plowman heralded the submission statement, Paige Patterson's election as SBC president, and the appearance of Dobson as evidence that the SBC had been rescued from its slide into liberalism and placed in the "conservative evangelical mainstream."[66] Considering the distinction suggested earlier between the evangelicalism of mainstream *Christianity Today* and the more conservative *World Magazine*, Plowman's choice of words was apt. Indeed, *Christianity Today* merely reported on the submission statement in a one-page article covering Patterson's election.[67]

There is an important parallel between the issue of submission within marriage and the role of women in ministry, and it again highlights an important aspect of both Southern Baptist life and of wider evangelicalism. The mainstream of the evangelical world has demonstrated a willingness to live with tension on the issue of women in ministry. Southern Baptist Theological Seminary, however, shifted to the right of this position by making opposition to ordained women in ministry a requirement for faculty positions. Likewise, mainstream evangelicalism has representatives of both the "complementarian" and the egalitarian views of spousal submission. Both the complementarian Council on Biblical Manhood and Womanhood and the more egalitarian organization, Christians for Biblical Equality, can receive a hearing in *Christianity Today*. But in the SBC, conservatives want no such tolerance of differing views. Indeed, when they revised the Baptist Faith and Message again in 2000, they included a statement that only men should serve as head pastors of churches. This was so uncontroversial that when all the revisions of the proposed new confession were debated on the floor of the convention meeting that year, the women's issue was never even mentioned; rather, the primary debate was on views of the Bible as expressed in the 1963 Baptist Faith and Message and in the one being proposed in 2000. The question, then, is why have SBC conservatives sought to codify their opposition to the egalitarianism that is so well represented in the larger evangelical world? In a denomination of nearly sixteen million people, why not agree to let individuals and congregations decide for themselves what approach they believe is most biblical? In one sense, that is exactly what is going to happen anyway since there is as yet no way to enforce the Baptist Faith and Message on individuals or congregations. Southern Baptists remain congregational, and each church decides democratically whether to ordain women deacons and pastors. As of 2000, no church has ever been refused seats at an SBC meeting because of its position on women, and only on the issue of ordination of gay deacons and gay marriage have messengers been refused seats, an incident involving only two churches in North Carolina. This did, however, lead to a bylaw change stating that churches that accept the gay lifestyle as legitimate cannot send messengers to SBC meetings. Whether the same will happen eventually with the ordination of women is an open question.

The reason that conservatives will not accept diversity and tension in denominational institutions and statements is that they believe these are ultimately matters of biblical authority, and, as shown above, Stan Hastey of the progressive Alliance of Baptists agrees. Conservatives and moderates often read the Bible differently. Conservatives believe that on issues like women's rights, Scripture is more perspicuous and less culturally influenced than many moderates are willing to contemplate. Thus, Dorothy Patterson, Al Mohler, and many others can say what conservatives have said for twenty years on a variety of issues: Those who disagree with them, really, deep down, have a problem with the Bible itself. "These aren't my words," Patterson says with regard to the submission statement. "This isn't my idea. . . . But this is what I understand the scriptures to say."[68]

Morris Chapman, the head of the SBC Executive Committee, could scarcely fathom how passages of scripture like Ephesians 5 could be honestly interpreted any way other than the way conservatives understand them. In the context of a discussion over the submission statement, Chapman said, "It seems to me like the moderate mindset is to take the Bible and to work toward trying to get it to say something it does not say just in its simplest form." In contrast to this approach, Chapman believes that one can just read the Bible and let it speak for itself.[69] Likewise, in response to the Baptist General Convention of Texas's decision to reaffirm the 1963 Baptist Faith and Message Statement, Richard Land was quoted in a *Christianity Today* news article as saying: "I find it curious that the BGCT, while affirming the inerrancy and full authority of Scripture, would question the Baptist Faith and Message's article on the family . . . which is little more than a paraphrase of the Apostle Paul's teaching. As for me and my house, we are going to stick with the Apostle Paul." In response to this kind of coupling of inerrancy and submission of women, Wheaton College New Testament professor Gary Burge was quoted in the same article as saying: "This is an inappropriate use of the notion of inerrancy. The place of women in the Bible is an interpretive, hermeneutical question. It is not an inerrancy question. There are countless evangelicals who embrace inerrancy and an egalitarian view of women."[70]

There are, indeed, many examples of people with solid evangelical credentials who believe quite differently from Southern Baptist conservatives. In 1989, Christians for Biblical Equality (CBE) issued a statement that was different from the SBC declaration at almost every turn. Its "Biblical Truths" section ran to roughly 450 words (the SBC statement was about 270), and it was followed by an "Application" section that was another 450. The CBE statement contained over sixty references to scripture, whereas the SBC document had roughly forty. There are several key points of contact with the submission statement: (1) On the use of the term "helper" for women, the CBE document argues that the same Hebrew term was used frequently in the Old Testament to refer to God. "Consequently the word conveys no implication whatsoever of female subordination or inferiority." (2) There is a direct refutation of the view of the Edenic fall that had formed the basis of the 1984 Southern Baptist resolution on women; "The Bible teaches that man and woman were co-participants in the Fall: Adam was no less culpable than Eve." Conversely, the CBE document states, "The Bible teaches that the rulership of Adam over Eve resulted from the fall and was therefore not a part of the original created order." And (3) on the issue of women in ministry, the document reads in part: "The bible teaches that both women and men are called to develop their spiritual gifts and to use them as stewards of the grace of God. Both men and women are divinely gifted and empowered to minister to the whole Body of Christ, under His authority. . . . The Bible teaches that, in the New Testament economy, women as well as men exercise the prophetic, priestly and royal functions." The "Application" section of the CBE document amplifies and further defines the role of women in ministry by listing among the services women can provide in the church such things as pastoral care, teaching, preaching, and worship. The list was not intended to be exhaustive but rather representative of the full participation of women in all church offices. As such, the document stresses, the church will honor God as the source of spiritual gifts and will also fulfill "God's mandate of stewardship without the appalling loss to God's Kingdom that results when half of the church's members are excluded from positions of responsibility." Finally, on the issue of submission itself, the "Biblical Truths" section of the document could not have been clearer. "The Bible teaches that husbands and wives are heirs together of the grace of life and that they are bound together in a relationship of mutual submission and responsibility."[71]

More than 160 evangelical leaders, scholars, authors, and preachers endorsed CBE's "Men, Women, and Biblical Equality." Included were eminent biblical scholar F. F. Bruce, activists Anthony Campolo and Ronald Sider, theologians and scholars such as Gabriel Fackre, Vernon Grounds, Roberta Hestenes, Richard Lovelace, David Allen Hubbard, Richard Mouw, Nicholas Wolterstorff, Mary Stewart Van Leeuwen, and Timothy Weber, who loomed so large in the story of Southern Seminary in the 1990s. Even Bill Hybels, pastor of one of the largest evangelical congregations in the United States and virtual founder of the seeker-church approach to evangelism, lent his name to the document. Authors of the statement were Gilbert Bilezikian, Stanley N. Gundry, Catherine Clark Kroeger, W. Ward Gasque, Gretchen Gaebelein Hull, Jo Anne Lyon, and Roger Nicole.[72] Without claiming to represent all evangelicals by any means, the statement demonstrated that a large swath of the evangelical mainstream accepted the egalitarian position and was therefore in direct opposition to the official position of America's largest evangelical denomination.

Countering the CBE is the Council on Biblical Manhood and Womanhood, which represents the complementarian position and has its own set of evangelical supporters. Both Dorothy and Paige Patterson have served on the council's board of reference, and in 2000, Southern Seminary professor Bruce Ware was the organization's president.[73] The existence of Christians for Biblical Equality and the Council on Biblical Manhood and Womanhood shows clearly that the evangelical world is divided on issues of gender relations.

This being so, then what motivated SBC conservatives to take an official position on an issue over which evangelicals disagree? Clearly, such action was not necessary to remain firmly in the evangelical camp, nor was it necessary just because conservatives believe that the complementarian position is biblical. If there is such diversity of interpretation on the issue of women, why include a submission statement in the basic confession of faith, especially when there is no precedent for this? No confession in the history of English-speaking Baptist life has ever before included a statement on the proper role of women in marriage.[74]

THE WOMEN'S ISSUE AS CULTURAL RESISTANCE

The answer to the question "why a submission statement" is that SBC conservatives want whenever possible to strike a countercultural posture. When Mohler appeared on *Larry King Live,* the first question King asked was why this statement needed to be issued at this time. Mohler responded: "No one really thought it needed to be said until recently. It is a major event for a denomination to change its basic confession of faith, and in adding this statement, Southern Baptists are responding to what we see as a real crisis in the culture over the family."[75] The following morning on CBS News, he reiterated the same point, stressing that while the belief in wifely submission had been around for two thousand years, now was the time it needed to be restated with such force.[76] Likewise, Richard Land, when asked a similar question, hardly hesitates before saying: "This is not issued in a vacuum. This is issued in a situation where people are trying to define homosexuals as a family, lesbians as a family, people living [together] out of wedlock as a family. . . . We reject this." At the suggestion that perhaps the cultural time is right for such a statement, Land corrects the term "cultural time." A more accurate term, he insists, is "cultural crisis." He then outlines this cultural crisis statistically, comparing 1998 to 1963, when the Baptist Faith and Message Statement was last revised. Then, 83 percent of the American children were being reared in intact homes. Thirty-five years later, fewer than half are. Land reiterates his view, clearly informed by his study of Baptist history, that confessions of faith are written or revised during times of crisis.[77]

Other conservatives agree. Dorothy Patterson admits that originally she had thought of wifely submission as merely a biblical issue, but having heard Land's historical interpretation, she clearly embraces it as her own. Even before the submission statement had been approved by the Salt Lake City convention, Patterson was quoted as saying, "I'm very pleased at this time, when the family is under such an assault and attack from every quarter, that Southern Baptists have decided to go back to their biblical roots, determine what God says about the family, and include that in their statement to the world."[78] Chapman argues that while the denomination was not seeking to be confrontational, "nevertheless [in] striving to be true to the definition of the family as we understand the Bible, [we] created quite a controversy. Fortunately, it is giving us an opportunity to frame the debate."[79] Framing the cultural debates of our time is what SBC conservatives want most. They want to be at the forefront of the culture war, resisting secular forces at every turn. Southern Baptist conservatives insist that wifely submission, as outlined in their statement, is what the vast majority of Southern Baptists have always believed. They also acknowledge, however, that the time was ripe for addition of this doctrine to their basic confession of faith as a statement of resistance to a secular culture.

Mohler's experience highlights how the issue of women can be one of biblical authority and cultural resistance at the same time. Having gone through Southern Seminary's masters of divinity program when the school was still quite progressive, at least for a Southern Baptist institution, Mohler had come to accept the legitimacy of women in ministry even in ordained roles. He accepted the same logic employed in favor of the Civil Rights movement. This was a common argument among SBC moderate elites who were on the cutting edge of Christian responses to social issues in the 1960s and 1970s. Essentially, the argument ran like this: A wooden hermeneutic had proven disastrous for nineteenth-century Southern Baptists who used the Bible to support slavery and for twentieth-century Baptists who used it to support segregation. It would be equally disastrous to use biblical texts to argue for the subjugation of women within churches and the necessity of submission of women to men within the family. While Mohler was a doctoral student and administrative assistant to the seminary president, he bought into this progressive line of argument and became something of a defender of the full rights of women within congregations. When the Southern Baptist Convention messengers adopted the 1984 resolution that opposed the ordination of women, claiming that they were second in Creation but first in the Fall, Mohler was filled with a sense of righteous indignation, so much so that he helped lead a student protest that resulted in the placement of an advertisement in the *Louisville Courier Journal* opposing the SBC resolution.[80]

This was about the time that Carl F. H. Henry visited Southern and began to mentor Mohler into the conservative wing of neoevangelicalism. As the two walked across the campus together, Henry asked Mohler where he had ever gotten the idea that women should be ordained preachers; what biblical justification did he have for such a position? Mohler recalls that it was as if Henry had stuck a dagger in his heart. Having come to respect Henry as the greatest evangelical theologian of the twentieth century, Mohler was sent reeling as a result of this challenge. Henry's confrontation sent the student on an intense reevaluation of his position on women in ministry, and he soon emerged on the other side of the debate, convinced that his old position, and by extension the position of many moderates, had actually been a product of cultural forces that could not be supported by the Bible. It was one example, he believed, where moderates had learned a good lesson from the Civil Rights movement but then applied it in the wrong place. Contrary to American culture, Mohler came to believe, the Bible really did support fundamental differences between men and women that resulted in certain prescribed and proscribed roles for each gender.[81] In short, women cannot simply decide for themselves what their call is because they are already excluded from ordained ministry by the word of God. As conservative patriarch W. A. Criswell put it in an interview with journalist Bill Moyers, if a woman believes she is called by God to preach, "she is mistaken; God never called her." Patterson attributed the belief of a woman claiming to be called to ministry as "her own personal ambition or longing for recognition."[82]

Of course, Mohler's reversal on this issue is baffling to many moderates, including the women who were in doctoral studies at Southern the same time he was. One such student has asked rhetorically: "Al Mohler, what are you thinking? You received the same education the rest of us did. You were exposed to the same ideas and same issues. What in the world happened to cause you to go in the direction you've gone?" Another said: "It grieves me to think I went to school with [Al Mohler]. And I think, 'Where in the hell were you? And how did you get out of this institution with that mindset and ideology?"[83] The clear answer to that question is that he was brought upright by a bolt from the world of neoevangelicalism in the person of Carl Henry. But beyond this is the broader issue of American culture. A major part of the neoevangelical heritage that conservatives grafted into the SBC historical tree is a certain stance in opposition to culture. While they do not mindlessly attempt to move in opposition to the forces of American culture, conservatives are more inclined to oppose those currents than to ride along with them. If it seems even remotely biblical to oppose culture, SBC conservatives stand ready.

Mohler and like-minded Baptists are surely not the first evangelicals to reverse the trend toward greater acceptance of women in ministry. Many early-twentieth-century fundamentalists did as well, but not without first going through a period of ambivalence. In the 1920s, Moody Bible Institute, the flagship fundamentalist school in Chicago, felt compelled to respond to charges that it was being inconsistent in its insistence on biblical literalism while training women for public Bible teaching. The editor of the *Moody*

Bible Institute Magazine acknowledged that passages of Scripture apparently forbidding women teachers were confusing. "We cannot speak for Fundamentalists, nor even for Bible Institutes as such," he wrote, "but for ourselves we repeat that we take Paul's words literally, but we are not clear as to the application of them under all conditions and in every case."[84]

Similar to Mohler's situation was that of William Bell Riley, one of the leading early fundamentalists, who also experienced a reversal on the issue of women in ministry. As late as 1928 Riley wrote that "it will be forever a debatable question as to whether this choice of a profession by women can be Biblically defended."[85] Riley's Northwestern Bible School in Minneapolis trained women pastors and traveling evangelists who preached in churches throughout the Midwest, some of them as ordained ministers. By 1930, however, the school's leaders were speaking against women in public ministry, and by 1935 Riley was pointing out that there were no women preachers mentioned in the Bible. Riley's own reversal was typical of fundamentalism between the wars, when the more open position of Moody Bible Institute gave way to a hardened position against female preachers. Various scholars attribute this reversal to the cultural antimodernism of fundamentalists, their determination to read scripture literally, and the movement's institutionalization and specialization, which relegated women to a lower-rung status.[86] The first two attributes could be said of SBC conservatives as well. Their determination to resist the prevailing secular trends of American culture has combined with their own resolve to read scripture as strictly as possible to produce a position on women with which there is little room to maneuver and virtually no appreciation for the spectrum of views that exists in the larger evangelical world.

INSTITUTIONALIZING THE CONSERVATIVE VIEW

When Southern Seminary made opposition to the ordination of women a prerequisite for faculty appointment, it set the pattern for other SBC seminaries. Midwestern followed suit by placing in its questionnaire for prospective faculty three questions related to women. As of 1999, the questionnaire asked first, "Do you believe it is appropriate for women to serve as pastors?" This question was preceded by two brief paragraphs pointing out that virtually all Southern Baptist churches call men to be pastors, that the North American Mission Board (formerly the SBC's Home Mission Board) and the International Mission Board (formerly the Foreign Mission Board) both support only male pastors, and that some state conventions and local associations have excluded churches that call women pastors.[87]

The second and third questions concerning women were grouped together: "How do you assess women's ordination? Please give your interpretation of I Timothy 2:11–14? [sic]" These were preceded by a longer paragraph citing the 1984 SBC Resolution on the Ordination of Women, quoting the sentence that reads, "We encourage the service of women in all aspects of church life and work other than pastoral functions and leadership roles entailing ordination." While acknowledging that the North American Mission Board supports ordained women as chaplains, this section of the Midwestern questionnaire also stresses that "the basic [Southern Baptist] Convention stance is one of resistance to the notion of women's ordination, including ordination to the church's deacon body."[88]

The gist of the faculty questionnaire could not have been clearer. Anyone who believed in ordaining women, even as deacons, need not apply. As would be expected, this was in accordance with changes in the degree program that took place after conservatives took over and Mark Coppenger became president of Midwestern Seminary. While women can still enroll in the masters of divinity program, they cannot take Preaching Lab or the course entitled Pastoral Leadership. Instead, women M.Div. students take a course called Biblical Teaching Lab and another called Principles of Leadership.[89] While there are few women in the program at Midwestern (ten for the 1999–2000 school year), it is difficult to claim that the conservative takeover of the seminary is the cause of the low numbers. Even in the late 1980s, before conservatives took control, women M.Div. graduates were in the single digits.[90] A new program called WISDOM, Women in Seminary Developing Our Ministries, is burgeoning, however. It is designed for wives of seminarians and leads to a "Diploma of Ministering Wife." In addition to basic courses such as How to Study the Bible, Understanding the Old Testament, and Exploring the New Testament, the program also has courses designed for the kinds of tasks SBC conservatives believe are appropriate for pastor's wives, which include Ministering Wife, Home Life, Deaf Interpretation, Piano, and Computer Basics.[91]

Southeastern Baptist Theological Seminary developed a special women's studies program headed by Dorothy Patterson, whose husband, Paige, is president of the seminary. Female students take many of the same courses as men and have the same language requirements. But they take a core of interdisciplinary courses specially designed for women. In terms of students, the backbone of the program consists of women who are or will be pastor's wives, but Patterson also hopes to develop a small cadre of female theologians who can go into the marketplace of ideas and make the case for the complementarian position. As for preaching, students take two courses that are intended to address the special way that women communicate with women, the assumption being that graduates of the program will engage in public speaking to other women. Patterson believes that communicating with women requires different emphases and techniques. Eschewing the word "preaching" for this type of communication, Patterson says, "We're trying to move away from language that would be deceptive or would be a stumbling block to someone."[92]

At Southern Seminary the masters of divinity track is exactly the same for women and men, but women can elect to opt out of the preaching courses. The number of women students in the School of Theology at Southern is about equal to what it was when Mohler arrived as president in 1993, which represents a rebound from the female (and African American) exodus that followed the conservative takeover of the Board of Trustees. The more interesting and perhaps significant issue at Southern and the other SBC seminaries has to do with women faculty. Dorothy Patterson and some others draw the line at women teaching men, which is exactly what seminary professors do in large part. Moreover, Southern has intentionally adopted the pastoral model for its professors over the more academic-scholar model that had existed when moderates were in control. Mohler would like to see every position in the School of Theology as tantamount to a pastor's position. "In a school that trains pastors, that has that as its central purpose, we should be very serious about modeling the role and function of the pastor even in our instructional faculty." There was no hard and fast policy as of 1999. The issue is not as fully defined as Mohler expects that it will be in the future largely because Southern has not had to face the prospect of a woman professor in a tenure-track position in the School of Theology. None have applied for open positions and there are no female theology, church history, or biblical studies professors left from the moderate era; there is one woman teaching pastoral care and counseling. "We want to think that through as rigorously, as biblically, as possible," Mohler has said. "It has not presented itself as an issue, which is to say we have not had qualified women apply or be considered for those positions."[93]

Samford University's Beeson Divinity School, where Timothy George is dean, differs substantially with the seminaries that are actually under the direct auspices of the SBC. At Beeson, women take the same course of study as do men. George recalls getting a phone call one time from an upset Alabama pastor who asked, "You don't let women take preaching, do you?" To which George replied, "No, we make them take preaching." The interdenominational nature of Beeson requires that the seminary have some latitude on the issue of women in ministry. In other words, it reflects the diversity on this issue that is present in the wider evangelical world. George explains that the faculty and students at Beeson have agreed to disagree while recognizing that many of the churches the seminary serves do not accept women in ministry. "We respect those views," he says.[94]

As of 1999, Southern, Southeastern, and Midwestern were all well along in settling the issue of women in ministry and in defining what is required of faculty on this issue. The other seminaries were still working this out, and the submission statement was playing a role. At Southwestern Seminary in Fort Worth, for example, the president and trustees issued a directive saying that faculty there would be expected to sign on to the statement because it was now officially part of the SBC confession of faith.[95] This dictum, of course, puts Texas Baptist professors at Southwestern in an ironic position given that their state convention has rejected the submission statement while their place of employment is requiring them to affirm it. Of course, the state convention has no authority or power to impose its position on those seminary professors; their place of employment does.

Clearly, the seminaries and their presidents and boards of trustees believe this is a biblical issue, but it is just as clear that they believe they must take a stand against culture. Thought of in this way, then, the issue of women, like that of abortion, gets framed in the context of political liberalism and its emphasis on the autonomy of individuals and the supremacy of their rights. Liberalism says that men and women as individuals should be free to chart their own courses. Conservatives are wary of the prevailing views of secular culture and are therefore inclined to oppose them whenever possible. Moreover, they are certain that moderates have bought into the progressivist paradigm of political liberalism that holds as its starting place the autonomous individual and her right to chart her own course. Mohler's own transition on the issue of women in ministry is especially instructive here. While it was not possible biblically to oppose secular progressivism on the issue of race (to be shown in the next chapter), it was possible to do so on the issue of women.

This resistance to culture sometimes takes forms much more strident than the changing of seminary curricula and rules for faculty, which is not surprising given the SBC conservative acceptance of the culture-war model for understanding the United States in the late twentieth century. Former Midwestern Baptist Theological Seminary president Mark Coppenger has taken an unequivocal stand on the issue of women. For a brief period in 1996, he came close to eclipsing Mohler as the SBC's leading culture warrior on this subject. Preaching in a seminary chapel service, he called women pastors "an affront to home and family" and "one of the raging, raging heresies and confusions of the day." Directing his comments at those who support women in ministry, he said: "It is astonishing to me how people who should know better just roll over and buy this kind of stuff. I beg you, don't touch it with a stick." He then identified two types of people who "buy" in: The first are "experience based Christians," specifically charismatics. He made reference to television preacher Kenneth Copeland and his wife, whom Coppenger referred to as "Mrs. Copeland." "[O]nce you base it on experience and not the word," he charged, "anything goes." Then, turning to the cultural element, he said that the second ideology susceptible to the raging heresy of women in ministry was "culture-based religion." "Let's just open the paper and see how we're supposed to be in this century." At this point, he broadened the issue to include other supposed capitulations to culture, specifically homosexuality. Using an effeminate voice to mock gays, he said, "Well, I just have my gay lover and we're just having a bonding and an affirmation."[96]

Coppenger even addressed the very difficult passage of scripture found in 1 Timothy 2. The passage, Coppenger emphasized, requires women to "learn in quietness and full submission." The author of the epistle then writes that women will be saved through childbirth. While admitting that this was puzzling indeed, Coppenger interpreted it to mean that there were women whom Paul was addressing who "were repudiating childbearing, motherhood, this kind of thing." Paul's response, therefore, was, according to Coppenger's paraphrase: "You women have a problem. I tell you what—you go home and raise a family and you may just see God." "By the way," he continued, "that doesn't sound so culturally different, does it? If you want to make it culturally bound, hey, bind it to our culture. We can play the culture any time you want. That's in the culture. And it is a threat to the family."[97] While these words are somewhat obscure, he seems to be saying that modern culture also suffers from women who are defying their God-ordained role of childbearing and homemaking.

Coppenger's outburst shows that there is sometimes a fine line between a carefully reasoned theological position and inflammatory culture-war rhetoric, but these public statements are very consistent with what he says privately in settings where the passions would be expected to subside. In a 1998 interview, he said, "Secular feminism is a galloping, huge thing in America, and I think a lot of our people have gotten a snoot full of it, and it has let them be callous toward scripture." When asked what he would have to say to an avowed inerrantist like Tim Weber who nevertheless supports the ordination of women, Coppenger responded, "Okay, you're an inerrantist, but you're a confused one." Then, bringing the biblical issue back around to views of culture, he remarked: "This is a big part of the culture war. It is the perversion of the understanding of women in society."[98]

Clearly, for conservatives, the women's issue is both theological and cultural, and in Coppenger's case, it may also be complicated by his own difficulties in controlling his anger. In August 1999 the *Baptist Standard* reported that Coppenger had confessed to a "misappropriation of anger" following an investigation by a trustee committee at Midwestern Seminary. Trustees required Coppenger to follow specific steps in dealing with what was termed a "chronic problem with anger." The examples provided in the report dealt mainly with interpersonal relationships with subordinates at the seminary, bringing to light the facts that two of the four "dream team" administrators he brought on had resigned and that Coppenger had gone through five secretaries in four years as president of the school. Little more than a month later, the board fired Coppenger as president.[99] His chapel sermon, especially his use of an effeminate voice to mock gays, may stem as much from anger at what he perceives as cultural attacks on the faith as from a reasoned response to those pressures, but this hardly explains the women's issue in the larger denomination.

In addition to this strident opposition to culture, Paige Patterson sometimes seems to enjoy tweaking the prevailing views of the secular media. What else could he have been doing when in 1997 he quipped to a newspaper reporter who had asked about his views of women, "I think everybody should own at least one."[100]

On the subject of women in church life, there is long precedent for the Southern Baptist impulse to resist the forces of secular progressivism. In 1885, for the first time in its then forty-year history, the issue of women as messengers (delegates) to the Southern Baptist Convention was debated when two women among Arkansas's delegation tried to register for the national meeting. Two days of debate ensued despite the fact that the SBC constitution did not forbid female messengers. The two eventually withdrew, and the constitution was shortly thereafter amended to exclude women. This could be seen as acquiescence to a culture that denied women the right to vote in secular affairs. As historian Leon McBeth argues, however, this was also an example of the desire of SBC men to resist in every way possible the pressure of the nineteenth-century women's rights movement. "This was the voice of Southern Baptists against the entire feminist movement," McBeth has argued. (In reality, it was the voice of Southern Baptist men, since women had no power in the denomination, as this example shows.) "Other opinions from the 1885 Convention show that Baptists were seriously concerned not to appear to endorse any part of the women's movement of the time."[101]

The difference between 1885 and 1998 was that in the earlier period the denomination was supporting the prevailing trends of culture against a minority women's rights movement that was viewed as radically countercultural. By the 1990s, that radical counterculture strain had become the dominant social position. SBC conservatives in the late twentieth century were therefore resisting the prevailing trends of the larger culture by denying women full equality within their churches and insisting that they submit to the authority of their husbands within the family. Full equality of opportunity for women in all spheres had become the culturally orthodox position, and SBC conservatives continue to resist this and even attempt to reverse it.

Conclusion

It is tempting to conclude that the gender issue has become the central focus for SBC conservatives. Such a position would be very close to what Betty DeBerg concludes about early fundamentalists in her study *Ungodly Women: Gender and the First Wave of American Fundamentalism*. Where others missed the importance of gender to that first fundamentalist movement, DeBerg sees it as central. In her conclusion she takes issue with the view that gender issues were added to fundamentalist concerns by the new Religious Right activists of the 1970s and 1980s. Rather, she concludes, late-twentieth-century fundamentalists and evangelicals who emphasize the dangers of feminism, abortion, and the disintegration of the traditional family are actually proving themselves to be good heirs to the early-twentieth-century fundamentalist tradition. "Regarding matters of gender, perhaps especially so, late twentieth-century evangelicalism is truly the heir of its own past."[102]

In their opposition to abortion and in their opposition to ordained women ministers, SBC conservatives further prove their adopted neoevangelical heritage, albeit there are many neoevangelicals who do not share the conservative view of women. Still, it is hardly contested that neoevangelicals, while differentiating themselves from fundamentalists in many ways, are still heirs of the fundamentalist movement. SBC conservatives have intentionally adopted for themselves the neoevangelical identity and then, true to the most conservative wing of that heritage, have set out to make opposition to ordained women a high-priority issue, nearly as important as abortion. From the convention resolution of 1984 to Southern Seminary's hiring criteria of 1995 through the submission statement of 1998, the gender issue has moved to center stage in the SBC conservative drama. This is not merely a matter of biblical authority, as SBC conservatives would like everyone to believe. What historian Margaret Bendroth has written about evangelicals applies equally well to SBC conservatives within evangelicalism. "Although many fundamentalists and evangelicals frame the issue [of women] as one of biblical authority, the continuing debate is clearly rooted in recent history."[103] For Southern Baptists, that recent history has been an experience of cultural change that must be met head on with conservative countercultural positions based on traditional, some would say outdated, readings of Scripture. With appearances on CNN and other news programs, Southern Baptist conservatives have relished their opportunity to stand against the larger culture on the nature of women's roles. This is their best issue. The culture is divided on abortion and church-state concerns, making it less clear which side is countercultural. On race, conservatives are on the same side as the majority. On women, though, the culture has clearly decided in favor of egalitarianism, which provides SBC conservatives an opportunity to do what they do best—oppose the cultural mainstream in the name of biblical authority and conservative evangelicalism.

8
Conservatives Can Be Progressive Too

Southern Baptist Conservatives and Race

It would be hard to overemphasize the importance of race in Southern Baptist history. The denomination was founded in large part because of a controversy over slavery. Leon McBeth includes three reasons that southerners formed the SBC, but then adds, "[S]lavery was the final and most decisive factor which led Southern Baptists to form their own convention."[1] Prior to the formation of national Baptist denominations, Baptists in the United States were organized in what is called the society system. Beyond local associations and state conventions, the only national bodies were missions societies that met occasionally to coordinate national or international efforts. These home- and foreign-mission associations, while the forerunners of Baptist denominations, usually existed for a single purpose. In other words, they were not broad-based organizations with multiple programs and departments.

As slavery became a sectional issue in the 1820s through 1840s, antislavery sentiment among Baptists and other evangelicals in the South disappeared. In its place there developed an elaborate biblical defense of the peculiar institution. One of those who wrote such a defense was South Carolina Baptist stalwart Richard Furman. Furman, like several other southern churchmen, based his argument primarily in scripture. At the same time that southern Baptists came to support and defend the practice, many northern Baptists and other evangelicals began to agitate for abolition, believing that slavery was a heinous sin most offensive to God. The two leading national Baptist societies of the time were the Home Mission Society and the Triennial Convention. Both attempted to follow a policy of neutrality, believing that the slave question was not relevant to their work in home and foreign missions. Two events in 1844 thwarted this effort, though, and led to the schism between northern and southern Baptists. First, Georgia Baptists, unconvinced by the neutrality assurances of northerners, nominated a slaveowner for appointment by the Home Mission Society in an effort to test the neutrality statements. The Board of the Home Mission Society restated its neutrality and then refused to act on the appointment of the slaveholder, apparently believing that this test case was an attempt to inject the slave question into the missions enterprise.

Second, the Baptist State Convention of Alabama wrote an inquiry to the Board of the Triennial Convention asking whether churches or the board had the authority to appoint missionaries. Additionally, the "Alabama Resolutions," as they have been called, asked hypothetically whether a slaveholder could be appointed to mission work. The board responded that it was the body authorized to appoint missionaries and added, "[O]ne thing is certain; we can never be a party to any arrangement which would imply approbation of slavery."[2] They immediately faced a dilemma, for some northerners wanted a stronger antislavery statement, while southern Baptists were ready to bolt if the original decision stood. Had the Board of the Triennial Convention backed off, it is possible that northern Baptists would have split among themselves.

Some southern Baptist newspapers advocated immediate withdrawal from the Triennial Convention, while others urged caution. Virginia Baptists called for a meeting of southern Baptists to discuss the issue, and in 1845 at Augusta, Georgia, delegates met. Influenced by William Johnson of South Carolina, they went far beyond a mere discussion of the issue at hand and instead voted to form the Southern Baptist Convention. Johnson had arrived in Augusta with a written constitution for the new body, so adamant was he in favor of a separate denomination. As outlined in his constitution, both home and foreign mission boards and other agencies as well would be under the auspices of one organization. Johnson's was the convention model as opposed to the society plan. With the formation of the SBC, southern Baptists became Southern Baptists. While delegates to the Augusta meeting issued a disclaimer saying that the new organization had in no way been formed for the defense of slavery, slavery had, in fact, played the primary role in the creation of the SBC.

One scholar has called the proslavery racism that gave birth to the SBC the denomination's original sin. He argued that the controversy of the 1980s was part of God's judgment on a denomination that for most of its history engaged in racism, sexism, and a sense of denominational superiority.[3]

Whatever the merits of this particular argument, the Southern Baptist Convention, like most southern institutions, reflected, manifested, and in many instances led the racism of the region as a whole. Nowhere was this more prevalent than during the Civil Rights era of the 1960s, when most of the leaders of the opposition to desegregation were Southern Baptists. For just one example of a fairly typical Southern Baptist attitude, one can turn to Douglas Hudgins, pastor of one of the South's most prominent churches in the 1950s and 1960s, First Baptist, Jackson, Mississippi. Hudgins used the moderate theology of E. Y. Mullins, with its emphasis on individualism and soul competency, to argue that the Christian faith had nothing to do with a corporate, societal problem like segregation. He, therefore, refused to speak up for African Americans and, in more ways than he could have known, helped inspire a whole generation of Southern Baptists to rest comfortably in their belief that segregation was natural and that the Civil Rights movement was a perversion of the gospel.[4]

Along with Hudgins, SBC conservative patriarch W. A. Criswell also represented the denomination's mainstream when he said in an address to a South Carolina evangelism conference in 1956 that he favored both religious and racial segregation. He called African Americans who desired integration "infidels, dying from the neck up."[5] (By 1970 he had repudiated this view.) Such statements were barely controversial in the 1950s and 1960s, and Hudgins and Criswell were merely the most visible representatives of the prevailing racism of the denomination. Their views were then reflected in the work of southern legislators, many of whom were Southern Baptists, as the whole region resisted the Civil Rights movement and even at times defied U.S. Supreme Court rulings and congressional statute.

Still, there was always a minority of progressive moderate Southern Baptists who supported full civil rights for African Americans and attempted to move the denomination away from its racist tradition. Many of these activists remained on the margins of the SBC power structure as part of David Stricklin's "genealogy of dissent." They were marginalized in large part precisely because they were too progressive to move into the mainstream of SBC life, but they also cared little about the denominational power structure, choosing instead to take a prophetic stance against the elites of the SBC.[6] Occasionally, one of the dissenters would find a place in the denominational power structure, usually as the executive director of the SBC's Christian Life Commission. Through the influence of those who got inside the denomination, the SBC actually passed a resolution in 1954 supporting the Supreme Court's *Brown* v. *Board of Education* (1954) decision that ruled de jure segregation unconstitutional and called for the integration of public schools "with all due speed." The irony of this resolution was that so many of those who resisted the results of *Brown* were Southern Baptists. Of course, SBC resolutions represent only the will of the few thousand messengers who happen to be present at a particular yearly convention meeting and can be guided through the adoption process by skillful denominational politicians. While most of the time these statements probably do represent the majority opinion of the denomination as a whole, 1954 was clearly not one of those times. As one historian writes succinctly, "The near-unanimous approval of the commission's resolution at the 1954 convention was not an accurate measure of Southern Baptist feeling about desegregation."[7]

Present SBC conservative leaders give high marks to progressives like Foy Valentine of the CLC who risked their careers and sometimes their bodily well being to be out in front on the race issue. For the conservatives, race is the one topic where the progressives were right. Naturally, therefore, conservatives have attempted to continue, and even accelerate, the trajectory toward racial inclusiveness that began slowly in the 1970s and 1980s. It seems fair to say that under moderate leadership, this course was well established so that when Richard Land became executive director of the CLC, overt racism was no longer acceptable in the denomination. The question for conservatives then was not whether they would revert to such racism, but whether the race issue would become a priority for them. Specifically, the question was whether they could actually take a strong stance on the same side as progressives, both Southern Baptist and secular progressives. On other issues, conservatives have been countercultural, and this is where they are most comfortable. On race, they have had to join the cultural flow in order to achieve the sort of progress they claim to value. There is a good bit of evidence that suggests conservatives are willing to be progressive and in the cultural mainstream on this one topic, but the story is still somewhat mixed and filled with irony.

THE RACIAL RECONCILIATION RESOLUTION OF 1995

Richard Land became executive director of the Southern Baptist Christian Life Commission committed to doing something on the race issue. It even appears that he made the freedom to move forward on this a condition of his appointment.[8] While there is no evidence of widespread opposition to

Land's desire, there were still vestiges of racism in the denomination and even in Land's organization. In 1988 Curtis Caine Sr. of the CLC was quoted widely as saying during a commission meeting that Martin Luther King Jr. was a fraud and that apartheid in South Africa "doesn't exist anymore and was beneficial when it did, because it meant separate development."[9] Such vestiges of segregation thought notwithstanding, it can probably be said that the days have long passed when there was any surviving power structure in the SBC that countenanced this sort of open racism—Caine spoke out of turn as a loose cannon. As ethicist David Gushee has put it, while there were surviving racist elements in the denomination, the center of gravity had shifted. The question was no longer whether the official position of the denomination was going to be racist, but rather what the SBC was going to do, or not do, on the issue.[10] Land was determined to do something.

Among African Americans, pastor Gary Frost of Youngstown, Ohio, was a pivotal figure. He became aware of a resolution that the director of missions for the state of New York and another individual from Washington, D.C., had written in 1994, a measure that had fizzled. After becoming second vice president of the SBC, Frost took a copy of that resolution to Land, and the two began to discuss developing a race resolution. Land then pulled together a panel of sixteen individuals—eight white, eight black. His aim was to draft a resolution that would be submitted to the SBC convention during the denomination's sesquicentennial celebration in 1995. On May 22 the sixteen members met for a race relations conference in Nashville and spent a day working over a draft that Frost had taken to Land. When completed, the group sent their version to the resolutions committee, which is charged with bringing prospective resolutions to the floor of the convention meeting in June.[11]

The occasion of the denomination's one hundred fiftieth anniversary was important to many SBC leaders precisely because of the role that slavery had played in the formation of the denomination. Land was quoted as saying, "Many of us feel it would be unseemly and terribly wrong to celebrate our sesquicentennial without addressing forthrightly the more unsavory aspects of our past."[12] Moreover, 1995 also marked the fifth year in which conservatives had been in complete control and the fifth consecutive SBC convention meeting where there would be no challenge in the presidential election. In light of this, there were those who recognized that the denomination still had a huge problem in the area of race relations. In some urban areas, SBC home missions were meeting resistance from African Americans because of the perception that the denomination was still racist. This was Frost's concern.[13] Another who was deeply troubled about this perception was the conservative SBC president, Jim Henry from Orlando, Florida. This issue was personal for him, and that, combined with the influence of African American Southern Baptists like Frost, resulted in the momentum needed to push the resolution through the process very smoothly.[14]

The SBC resolution on race was also part of a trend in which many groups apologized for past sins. As *Los Angeles Times* writer John Dart pointed out in a widely circulated article, among these were German Christians in Holland apologizing for their complicity in the Holocaust, Lutherans for Luther's anti-Semitism, New Zealanders for their sins against the Maoris, American Christians for massacres of Native Americans, and Pope John Paul's 1992 acknowledgment of error in the condemnation of Galileo and his apology for the Roman Catholic Church's complicity in the African slave trade and exploitation of Latin America.[15] Dart and others pointed to a book by a Los Angeles Baptist from New Zealand, John Dawson, as inspiring the wave of regrets. Dawson headed up an organization called International Reconciliation Coalition, and his book, entitled *Healing America's Wounds,* has been called a "virtual textbook for the reconciliation phenomenon." He believed that repentance may help open people to evangelistic efforts by disassociating the faith from injustice.[16]

One of the issues the SBC drafting committee had to consider was whether it was theologically acceptable for one generation to repent for another's sins. Members eventually agreed that they could acknowledge sins of the past, recognize their effects, and repent of their own participation in racism. As the white and black Southern Baptist leaders sat together hammering out the resolution, "something remarkable happened," Frost later recalled, "I'll call it spiritual."[17] It truly was a remarkable meeting. As evidence, Frost mentioned that Emmanuel McCall, although having been deeply involved in Southern Baptist life for many years, had never even met some of the key leaders of the conservative movement. As he sat across the table from these white conservatives, they became real people to him, and he to them. Some representatives shed tears as this happened. One was Eugene Gibson, who wept and said that he had always hoped he would see this day. He could scarcely believe that Mohler, Patterson, and the others of the white power structure of the SBC were actually addressing this issue and admitting that the denomination's history had been bound up in the sins of slavery, segregation, and racism. "We were the sons of slaves and the sons of slave owners sitting down together," Gibson was quoted as saying.[18] Expressing his shock at the dedication white conservatives showed on this, Gibson said that the white members of the commission were the ones who insisted on an apology and plea for repentance in the resolution. They presented an apology while the black leaders listened and critiqued. Likewise, even five years after crafting the resolution, McCall remembers marveling that white SBC leaders, who would be considered "far right" in political matters, were taking the lead in the area of racial reconciliation. As Frost put it: "Blacks weren't involved in making the resolution. They were involved in hearing it, receiving it, and making sure that it really dealt with the issues." White participant Gushee concurs, "we were the ones doing the apologizing."[19] By the end of the day, there was a consensus that together they had really dealt with the issues involved. Frost and others believed that racial reconciliation had to be addressed before the sesquicentennial celebration could begin, and there was a great sense of accomplishment among those who had participated on the committee. Four years later Gushee called it "the best experience I've ever had in the Southern Baptist Convention."[20]

On the floor of the convention meeting the following month, the adoption process went almost as smoothly. Again, SBC president Jim Henry received high marks for his leadership, this time from Emmanuel McCall. Henry prepared the messengers by emphasizing the importance of what they were about to undertake and how their actions and deliberations would be perceived by the outside world. He mentioned the effect this action would have on perceptions of SBC missionaries around the world. "I don't think we could have been better prepared for the action to be taken," remembered McCall five years later. "There was also gentleness in his manner, in the way that he presided and a thoroughness." McCall spoke of seeing whites and blacks joining hands for prayer in a highly emotional experience.[21]

There was an objection from a messenger who claimed the resolution was inappropriate because Africans were not the only ones enslaved in the United States. This was rejected out of hand with the observation that the issue was racism toward African Americans, not slavery per se.[22] Another messenger decried the resolution for its bringing "discredit to those great men who founded this great convention. We must understand that they didn't start slavery. They were born into this context." After brief debate, a woman from Mississippi was given the floor and made an impassioned plea that the time for discussion had passed; it was now time to act. The vote was then called, and the resolution passed with support that exceeded 95 percent. Frost was called to the podium, where he stood next to Henry as the two prayed. Then, addressing the convention, he said: "On behalf of my black brothers and sisters, we accept your apology. And we extend to you our forgiveness in the name of our Lord and Savior Jesus Christ."[23] Frost recalled later that he was in no position to accept the apology on behalf of all black people. Instead, he accepted it on behalf of those African American Christians who were committed to the reconciliation process. He based his comments on Ephesians 4, making the point that "we" do not forgive because the offender deserves forgiveness, but because "we" have been forgiven by Christ.[24]

The resolution itself ran to one and a half pages in the published *Annual of the Southern Baptist Convention*. It contains ten "whereas" paragraphs and eight "resolved" statements. The third paragraph acknowledges that "Our relationship to African Americans has been hindered from the beginning by the role that slavery played in the formation of the Southern Baptist Convention." The following paragraph recognizes that many Southern Baptist forebears defended the right to own slaves and participated in the inhumane nature of slavery. The next "whereas" cites the failure of Southern Baptists to support, and their actual opposition to, civil rights for African Americans. Paragraph eight deals with the exclusion of African Americans from Southern Baptist churches, a practice that had been common even into the 1970s.[25]

The most significant "resolved" sections include recognition that "we continue to reap a bitter harvest" from "acts of evil such as slavery." Perhaps the most significant "resolved," and the one that elicited the greatest response from media, is the apology, which reads: "Be it further RESOLVED, that we apologize to all African Americans for condoning and/or perpetuating individual and systemic racism in our lifetime; and we genuinely repent of racism of which we have been guilty, whether consciously (Psalm 19:13) or unconsciously (Leviticus 4:27)." This carefully worded section addresses the need for an apology and plea for forgiveness without the theologically problematic notion of repenting for the sins of others. The next paragraph continues the theme of forgiveness, saying, "we ask forgiveness from our African American brothers and sisters, acknowledging that our own healing is at stake."[26]

The media response to this racial reconciliation resolution was not quite what it would be three years later, when Southern Baptists called on women to submit to their husbands, but there was widespread response nevertheless.

Perhaps it can be said that Southern Baptists are more newsworthy when they clash with the culture, as they did on the women's submission statement, than when they do something that the larger culture applauds. The most interesting responses came in editorials in the week following the convention meeting. Moreover, among these, the most significant were written by African American journalists, some of whom saw significance in the fact that the resolution made the connection between past sins and present realities. While congratulating Southern Baptists, columnist Deborah Mathis pointed to the resolution's argument that "the racism which yet plagues our culture today is inextricably tied to the past." For her, this raised the issue of affirmative action to right past wrongs. In her view the resolution "refutes the current popular argument that some people today are using the past as an excuse for their conditions, while others are unfairly held accountable for the sins of their fathers. Which, mind you, is a favorite premise for turning inside out affirmative action, school-desegregation programs, and other implements of equality."[27]

In a column entitled "Late Regrets about Slavery," Les Payne of *New York Newsday* writes: "The largest white Protestant group in America has finally gotten around to repenting for its key support of slavery, some 132 years after the Emancipation Proclamation. Next century, perhaps, the Southern Baptist Convention might consider denouncing the 'curse of Ham' or even supporting the 14th Amendment. One should not expect miracles." Payne goes on to recount not only the SBC's support of slavery but also its resistance to civil rights desegregation. King ignored Southern Baptists in his famous "Letter from a Birmingham Jail" because they were beyond hope at that time, Payne reminds us. "Now," writes Payne, "with its leadership becoming more right-wing conservative than ever, the Convention decides to come out four-square against slavery." Like Mathis, Payne also cites as the most significant aspect of the resolution, the Southern Baptist acknowledgment that the racism of the present is tied to the past. "In this, the white southerners seem to be running ahead of the north. Here [in the north] white Baptists along with second-generation Europeans in all levels of power, grapple with issues such as affirmative action and Afrocentrism with little apparent knowledge and no feeling whatsoever for America's three-century-long experience with slavery and its bitter aftermath."[28]

Paul Delaney, chairman of the Department of Journalism at the University of Alabama, wrote a column for the *Birmingham News*. He argues that having passed a commendable resolution, Southern Baptists would have to deal with a number of troubles: strong anti-black feelings among many in the SBC ranks; local and national policies that stand against blacks; institutions, such as segregation academies, that offend blacks; and Confederate battle flags that "perpetuate racial superiority and stereotypes and foster racial animosity." He admonishes Southern Baptists to "stand firm and speak out against questionable solutions to serious social and economic problems," such as more prisons, leg irons, and capital punishment as the solution to crime. He writes: "I applaud Southern Baptists for attacking individual and systemic racism and committing themselves to 'eradicate racism in all its forms from Southern Baptist life and ministry.' For more than a century we've been complaining that racism was systemic, but were ignored and told we're crazy. Such a pledge is a start and if it is healing and makes you feel better, fine. But leave the political statements for politicians. It is time for those extremely conservative Baptist leaders to do more than sit back and feel good and say, 'See what we've done': They have got to lead their flock in the daunting tasks of implementing the pledge."[29]

Specifically, what struck some African American journalists as incongruent was that Southern Baptist conservatives had passed a resolution calling for racial reconciliation and justice but stood opposed to virtually all government policies aimed at ending racial injustice. As Bill Maxwell writes: "And, paradoxically, today's Southern Baptist Convention is the same organization that is supporting the Republicans' cynical attack on affirmative action, and racism still makes affirmative action necessary. If Southern Baptists are serious about atoning for their historical sins, how can they also join Republicans in destroying affirmative action—the one federal program that modestly attempts to redress some of the wrongs of discrimination?" He urged Southern Baptist conservatives to support affirmative action and to see that racial justice was as much a moral issue as abortion.[30]

William Singleton III tells of two incidents at the convention in Atlanta that illustrate the need for more than a resolution. While speaking to a group of Tennessee preachers, he jokingly commended the preachers for picking a great place to live. One of the them responded, "You picked it, I was born there." While Singleton could not be sure, he and some others with whom he shared the story believed this was a racist comment having to do with his Tennessee ancestors picking cotton. The second incident came when a white friend asked him honestly to explain why it was important for black people to be called African Americans and black Christians. "I don't think we should be African Americans or European Americans, but

Americans," this person said to Singleton. "I don't think we should be considered black Christians or white Christians, but just Christians." Singleton interpreted this as an honest attempt to understand, and the friend seemed to seriously consider Singleton's answer, which was that God created different racial groups, so who are we to deny their importance? Singleton uses these experiences to illustrate that there was hope but still a long way to go on race. He concludes by writing: "The Southern Baptist Convention effectively said it wants to enter a new era of race relations by issuing its apology to blacks. Let us hope it doesn't take another 150 years for the spirit of that resolution to be fulfilled."[31] Like the others, well-known African American columnist Carl Rowan also stressed that the SBC resolution tied the past to the present. He called on Southern Baptists to do what the presidents of some elite southern universities had done—that is, create an affirmative action program to reach out to the "great-grandchildren of slaves" to offer them opportunity.[32]

At some point, SBC conservatives who like Land want to be out front and progressive on the race issue may find that desire colliding head on with their overall conservatism. One does not have to believe that conservatives are really all closet racists to note that in contemporary American politics it has been virtually impossible to be conservative and still out front on the race issue. The basic conservative argument is that government power can only do the negative task of eliminating barriers but cannot effectively and positively address the issues of racial injustice. Those must be remedied, the conservative argument goes, by the free market and a level playing field. African American columnists were attempting to show Southern Baptist conservatives that their acknowledgment of the on-going effect of past sins means essentially that, while the playing field may now be even, there are many who are so hamstrung by past injustice that they need a little positive help just to get into the game. This has been the point made by some African American scholars who acknowledge that they benefited from affirmative action.

Response to the racial reconciliation resolution was mixed from African American religious leaders outside the SBC. Calvin Butts III, who pastored the forty-five-hundred-member Abyssinian Baptist Church in Harlem, New York, praised the resolution, saying, "If there's a fitting response to the 'Letter from Birmingham Jail,' this is it." Less enthusiastic, but nevertheless positive, was Arlee Griffin Jr., who pastored the four-thousand-member Berean Missionary Baptist Church in Brooklyn and served as the historian for the Progressive National Baptist Convention. Reminding that Southern Baptists have a "long history and legacy to overcome," he said, "It is only when one's request for forgiveness is reflected in a change of attitude and actions that the victim can then believe that the request for forgiveness is authentic."[33] Other African American pastors and leaders were more critical. Amos C. Brown of the Third Baptist Church in San Francisco responded, "It's pretty late in the day for Southern Baptists to finally come around to admit that their forebears were wrong for supporting slavery." He said that Southern Baptists will need to show "the fruits of repentance" before African Americans will accept them. Caesar A. W. Clark of Dallas was even more direct, accusing Southern Baptists of sheep stealing. "Southern Baptists have been working overtime to win National Baptists," he said while pointing out that there was a widespread perception among African Americans that the SBC was trying to recruit National Baptist congregations into the denomination.[34]

McCall understood why so many African American religious leaders outside the SBC were suspicious of the resolution. Many have had experiences in the past where they sought the help of Southern Baptists in ameliorating racial tension but were rebuffed or ignored. He cited the example of Birmingham pastor Nelson Smith who had been part of Martin Luther King Jr.'s entourage. On numerous occasions during the Civil Rights era, he went to Southern Baptists to ask for support in breaking down racial barriers, but in most cases he was turned down. Those types of experiences, McCall has said, are hard to forget. This led to questions concerning the motives of the resolution. Still, McCall contrasts that view with his own as a former SBC insider. He saw the resolution as a sincere effort to move the convention forward on the issue of race.[35]

Coolness toward the resolution was not confined to African Americans outside the denomination. When asked in 1999 to recall his response to the statement, Southern Seminary professor T. Vaughn Walker said: "Personally, I think it's just a resolution. It's better than nothing, but it's not anything that made me jump up and down and shout." For Walker, the issue should be less about resolutions and more about change. He wants to see African Americans on some of the boards of seminaries and colleges and holding significant positions in the denomination. When asked five years after the resolution if that was happening, he responded soberly, "It's at a snail's pace," and then, as evidence, pointed to the fact that for a time after Timothy Johnson and Robert Smith left Southern Seminary in the mid-

1990s, Walker and Leroy Gainy of Golden Gate Baptist Theological Seminary were the only African American professors in any of the six Southern Baptist seminaries. (Actually, there was one other.)[36] While acknowledging that it was sometimes difficult for SBC seminaries to match the salaries of black pastors who were qualified to teach, Walker pointed out that Southern Seminary itself had graduated nine black Ph.D.'s during his time at the school. Some have been outstanding scholars, Walker said, yet there has not been a real effort to bring them on board.[37]

Like McCall, Walker also understood why the resolution was "not received as anything meaningful among the historic black Baptist denominations." In his view, Frost and other African Americans who are singly aligned with the SBC are not taken seriously by National Baptists. "They are seen as those who have sold out," according to Walker, a view echoed by McCall and others. Walker contrasts those like himself who are dually aligned with the National Baptists and the SBC with those like Frost who are solely Southern Baptist. "The black community sees me as one of them here [at Southern]" and not as a Southern Baptist who happens to also be in a black church. It is that credibility in the black community, Walker believes, that attracts African American students into his D.Min. program at Southern; they know he is not going to try to indoctrinate them with white SBC conservatism. As for a resolution passed by the predominately white and historically racist SBC, African Americans outside the denomination were understandably not impressed.[38]

Even the ardently Southern Baptist Frost registered mild disappointment that the race resolution was not presented to leaders of the National Baptist Convention. Still, he is stung by the response of National Baptists. "I understood it, but I was hurt that some were not willing to accept the possibility of a change of heart." He especially rejects the sheep-stealing charge.[39]

For the most scathing critique of the race resolution either within or outside the SBC, one can turn to former Southern Seminary professor Timothy James Johnson Jr. In 1999 he recalled his reaction when the resolution was announced. "It's like Hitler apologizing for what he had done to the Jews and Himmler accepting his apology." Given his own experiences at Southern (to be discussed below), which he believes were a direct result of racism, Johnson is highly skeptical about any move Southern Baptists might make toward racial reconciliation. Moreover, from his perspective, the whole South's perception of race is that Americans have dealt with it, so now we can move on. The primary problem is a lack of biblical restitution accompanying the resolution of apology. Talk is cheap, Johnson argues, the resolution cost Southern Baptists nothing. He believes the apology would have some meaning if the SBC backed it up with several million dollars for the United Negro College Fund or the Center for Racial Reconciliation.[40]

In addition to serving as a professor of social work at Roberts Wesleyan College outside Rochester, New York, Johnson pastors a Southern Baptist church that is roughly 60 percent black and 40 percent white. He is the church's first African American pastor. When the congregation first called him about serving as interim pastor, he was so bitter about his experience at Southern Seminary that he replied, "I don't want to ever see another Southern Baptist as long as I live." Nevertheless, he started interim work and then became pastor. The difference, he found, was that there is not a culture of Southern Baptists in New York State. Johnson's brother pastors a church in Philadelphia that is dually aligned with the SBC and a black Baptist denomination. Like most such churches, Johnson says, his brother's congregation was attracted to the SBC because of its resources. Like the National Baptists Walker cited, Johnson believes that his brother's church would think the race resolution "ridiculous."[41]

Johnson also sees the race issue among Baptists, as well as others, as a liberal-conservative issue. Just before he went on the faculty at Southern in the early 1990s, he attended one of Richard Land's Christian Life Commission seminars on race. Johnson claims that the black leadership in the SBC would say privately that all the talk about race was merely going through the motions and that nothing would come of it. Liberals, in Johnson's view, tend to get involved and are much more willing to journey with the oppressed. Conservatives will not get in the trenches, but they talk a good game. That being his view, Johnson perceives the whole race issue in the SBC as being "product driven." The fastest growing groups in the denomination are people of color. They are where the future of the SBC is, and that, Johnson believes, is why SBC conservatives are courting blacks. He would hate to think that this was all there was to the issue, but Johnson believes nevertheless that the evidence suggests exactly that.[42] At the time the resolution was passed, even Land acknowledged that since 1980, virtually all the growth in the SBC had been multiethnic.[43]

Five years after the resolution, many have asked if there has been progress. The numbers suggest there has. As reported in 1995, an estimated twelve hundred predominately black congregations were in the SBC with roughly 800,000 African American members; Land put the figure of individuals at

500,000 African Americans and 300,000 Latino and Asian Americans. By 1999, the number of predominately black congregations was reported to be twenty-eight hundred.[44] Beyond the numbers, the answer varies depending on who one asks. As different as they are from one another, Frost and Walker in 1999 did share a concern for the lack of African American representation within the leadership ranks of the SBC. Frost emphasizes that he had been close to the movers and shakers of the SBC and never felt any racism. The one challenge, however, is the lack of representation that often leads to ignorance of the issues from a black perspective. He has been in situations where he had to stop and ask the "black question" because no one else at a particular meeting was capable of seeing things that way. He compares his situation to that of black reporters in presidential press conferences and tells how he used to cringe when one would get the floor for a question because Frost knew what the black reporter was going to do. One time, Frost asked a friend of his, "Why does the black reporter always have to ask the black question?" His friend responded that if the reporter fails to do so, the question would not get asked at all. Frost finds himself experiencing that in the SBC. He wants to deal with issues that others just fail to even consider. So, even though he might have something to say about many topics, he ends up having to play the part of the black reporter because no one else can and has to raise the racial issues or they will not be addressed at all. He compares this to the experiences of women: "It's not that they're being put down; it's just that they're not being considered."[45]

Frost counters Walker, however, emphasizing that there have been efforts to increase African American representation. At least three of the seminary presidents, including Mohler and Patterson, have asked Frost to give them lists of potential seminary professors who are black. The problem is, according to Frost, that most of the qualified people are pastoring and making more money doing that than the seminaries could pay them. In many situations it would be a drastic cut in pay for one to leave the pastorate for a faculty position at a seminary. McCall has made the related point that the pastor model is revered far more in the African American community than the scholar model. For this reason, in addition to pay, African Americans with doctorates still prefer the ministry over being full-time professors. So the seminaries are going to the bivocational route, in which pastors can come and do some teaching without giving up their congregations.[46]

In the summer of 2000, McCall gave a qualified "yes" to the question of whether there had been progress since the 1995 resolution. He mentioned appointments on the North American Mission Board and also cited what was happening in several state conventions and local associations, where African Americans were increasingly visible in positions of leadership. While acknowledging that there are certainly areas where Southern Baptists have not done so well lately on the issue of race, he emphasized that "Around the nation we can find those places where there are exceptional and exciting things being done by Southern Baptists."[47]

African Americans who are involved with Southern Baptists at the state and associational levels corroborate McCall's view that the SBC is making progress with race matters. Sid Smith, the director of the African American Ministries Division for the Florida Baptist Convention, is very positive about the work of Southern Baptists in African American communities, especially in evangelism. He calls the SBC conservative movement "cutting edge" regarding race and views the proliferation of African American churches in the SBC as one of the great stories in contemporary church history. As evidence he points out that there was only one African American SBC church in 1951 but nearly three thousand by the turn of the century. The increase has come through the dual affiliation movement first, then, more recently, through efforts to plant singly aligned African American Southern Baptist churches.[48]

Two Kinds of African American Southern Baptists

Most dually aligned churches are National Baptist congregations that have affiliated with the SBC. Churches in this category became aligned with Southern Baptists for the resources that the denomination has to offer, because of key leaders who recruited them, and because of the influence of black pastors already in the SBC. The denominational emphasis in recent years, though, has been on church planting in African American communities under the auspices of the North American Mission Board, often in conjunction with state convention agencies. In Florida, for example, out of a total of one million Southern Baptists, there were in 2000 an estimated eighty thousand African Americans, most of them in the four hundred predominately black SBC churches in the state. In Smith's view, which is supported by compelling evidence, the SBC has quietly become the most ethnically diverse denomination in the United States today. In making this case, he cites the work of C. Peter Wagner, a church-growth expert at Fuller Theological Seminary, who wrote in 1986: "At the top of the list in ethnic ministries in the United States are the Southern Baptists. . . . Southern Baptists are the most ethnically diverse denomination, worshiping in 87 languages in more than 4,600 language-culture congregations every Sunday."[49] While Wagner pointed to the vast variety of ethnic and language missions that Southern Baptists had developed under moderate auspices, Smith argues that the emphasis on black church starts has taken place largely since conservatives consolidated their control of the denomination in the late 1980s.[50]

Smith, like Frost, is a singly aligned African American Southern Baptist, unlike Walker, Johnson, and others who are or have been historically dually aligned with Southern Baptists and one of the black Baptist denominations. "I am a *Southern* Baptist," avers Smith, as opposed to being a National, Northern, or some other kind. His early experiences with Southern Baptists were positive from the beginning. In the early 1960s, he was mistakenly admitted to the University of Corpus Christi, Texas. The school at that time was still segregated and did not know Smith was African American. As the board of trustees deliberated over whether to let him enroll, thereby desegregating the school forever, the pastor of First Baptist Church, Corpus Christi informed the board that he had been authorized by his church members, many of whom were wealthy, to say they stood ready to withdraw their support for the university if Smith were not admitted. As Smith tells the story with a chuckle, the Lord was thereby able to move the hearts of the trustees. During his second year of college, the National Baptist church he attended in Corpus Christi was admitted into the local association of Southern Baptist churches. Also while a student in college, Smith became involved with the (Southern) Baptist Student Union on campus, and he has identified himself as a Southern Baptist ever since. He has spent virtually all of his career in ministry on the staff of SBC agencies, first in a field position with the Home Mission Board and then in Nashville with the Sunday School Board before moving to the Florida Baptist Convention. This is not to say that he never encountered racism in SBC life. Smith attended Golden Gate Baptist Theological Seminary in San Francisco partly because Southwestern Seminary in Fort Worth, the logical choice of Texas Baptists, had a policy barring African Americans from living on campus.

Like Smith, McCall also had very positive early experiences with Southern Baptists. Raised in western Pennsylvania, he attended Simmons Bible College in Kentucky, not knowing that it had lost its accreditation. He left after one year and went to the University of Louisville. In 1954 he was accepted by the Baptist Student Union on the Louisville campus. Noticing only that he had put Baptist as his preference on his enrollment profile, they recruited him. There was an attempt by the local Baptist association to force those who were not Southern Baptists to leave the BSU, a thinly veiled attempt to get rid of McCall and the other black students. But the student union stood by the African Americans and said that if they were forced to leave because they were not Southern Baptists, then the BSU would dissolve. This had a profound effect on McCall, and he, like Smith, earned his M.Div. degree at a Southern Baptist seminary (Southern Seminary for McCall) and has been singly aligned with the SBC ever since.[51]

McCall and Smith also share the distinction, along with T. Vaughn Walker and some others, of having careers in SBC institutions that spanned both the moderate and conservative regimes. This is possible, they point out, because the SBC controversy was not a black issue. McCall has said that African Americans were given something of an exemption on many matters, especially those that are political. In other words, they could get by in the conservative movement with views that might be unacceptable for a white Southern Baptist. Smith uses the analogy of the historic Texas battle at the Alamo, where at least one African American left before the fighting commenced, realizing that it was not his fight. Likewise, Smith believes, African Americans in the SBC did not feel a need to take a side in the controversy, and conservatives granted them McCall's exemption, never requiring them to declare themselves. By analogy, Smith cites the example of preaching. Black preachers in the SBC are not expected to preach like their white counterparts. So too in politics, they are not expected to have the same views as whites. In summing up the tendency of African American Southern Baptists to be different in many ways from white Southern Baptists, Smith says, "We do not expect African American churches to be mirrors of white churches." The same can be said for individuals. African American Southern Baptists can be more politically and socially liberal than whites so long as they remain theologically conservative.[52]

Still, McCall is much less active in the denomination than he was when moderates were in control. Of all African Americans in the SBC, he was the one with the highest profile and most powerful position under moderate leadership. In 1968 he became the first African American to serve on the staff of an SBC agency, going to the Missions Division of the Home Mission Board under Hugo Culpepper, who had been McCall's missions professor at Southern Seminary. He headed up the Department of Negro

Work, which became the Department of Work with National Baptists, then the Department of Black Church Relations, and finally the Division of Black Church Planting and Growth. In all, McCall was at the Home Mission Board from 1968–91, during which time he earned his doctor of ministry degree at Emory University.

In addition to McCall's long tenure in the SBC under moderates, he also served as the president of the Southern Seminary Alumni Association when the Carver School debacle took place in 1995. In that capacity he had to express alumni concern to President Mohler. The meeting did not go well. This, combined with his career as a moderate insider, made him even more suspect in the eyes of conservatives. It is no secret among the SBC conservatives that those who did not support their goals with a high level of dedication have had difficulty finding or retaining positions in the denomination. McCall's preference for moderate leadership and his opposition to what Mohler did at his alma mater may have made it nearly impossible for him to work in conjunction with the conservatives, whereas other African Americans were in positions that actually allowed them to sit out the controversy. It appears that McCall is one of the few African Americans for whom the black exemption is no longer operative.

McCall rarely attends SBC convention meetings largely because he simply does not know or does not relate to the new conservative leadership. The new SBC is not his SBC. An alternative explanation, however, is that being on the outs with conservatives may simply be a matter of McCall having moved from a position in the denomination to becoming a pastor. This is Smith's read on his friend's situation. He attributes McCall's status as something of an outsider to his leaving national leadership to take a pastorate and having to concentrate on his own church and local association. In this interpretation, McCall simply moved out of the denomination's power structure at about the time the conservatives consolidated their control. That being the case, McCall simply fell out of the national network. Smith, as a Florida denominational leader, continues to feel quite at home with the conservatives, as do a growing number of African American pastors.[53] It should be noted, however, that McCall holds high status in the history of African American Southern Baptists and is considered the pioneer. In 2000 he was the first recipient of an award created in his honor by the African American Denominational Servants Network. The Emmanuel L. McCall Award for Denominational Service is now given annually by the organization.

Other African American Southern Baptists have found the SBC attractive because of its efficient programmatic approach to church planting and church growth. Pastor Fred Luter was an associate pastor of a National Baptist church in New Orleans until the mid-1980s, when he heard that the Franklin Avenue Baptist Church was in need of a pastor. He was moved by the description of Franklin Avenue as a hurting church, dying because of white flight to the suburbs. He became a candidate there, and the congregation subsequently called him as its pastor. The white members who were leaving the city gave the church building to the African American congregants who were moving into the structure. When this happened, the church came under the auspices of the Home Mission Board for a few years, then became autonomous in 1988. Luter had never had any previous experience with Southern Baptists, but he was very impressed with the support he saw from the denomination and the organizational structure that the SBC Home Mission Board used to advance home missions. From 1986 to 2000, Franklin Avenue Baptist Church grew from sixty-five members to more than six thousand.

In the early years of his foray into Southern Baptist life, Luter's relationship with National Baptists was strained. He recalls being called an "Uncle Tom" for his move into a predominately white denomination. Luter's experience in this respect is consistent with Smith's and McCall's view that National Baptist leaders are not very well informed about the progress the SBC has made and often find it hard to fathom how African Americans could get involved in the SBC. The perception that he had somehow sold out to a white denomination bothered Luter at first, but over time he became convinced that he was just doing the work God called him to, and he believes that his National Baptist friends have come to accept that as well. His relationship with National Baptists was much better by 2000 than it had been in the early years. Luter sums up his reasons for making the change simply. "I was impressed with their heart for missions."[54]

Like Luter, Elroy Barber crossed over to the SBC and became singly aligned. Originally from a National Baptist background, during the mid-1980s he was doing prison ministry when the head of church planting for the Florida Baptist Convention approached him about starting a ministry in Fort Lauderdale. Barber was impressed with the SBC's organizational apparatus. Why start from scratch when the SBC had a well-developed method for planting churches, he later recalled reasoning. Barber saw in action what scholar C. Peter Wagner has discovered in his studies of church-growth in the United States: "The Southern Baptist Home Mission Board in Atlanta is, to my knowledge, the most sophisticated agency for starting new churches in the United States," Wagner wrote in 1979.[55] After successfully planting the church in Fort Lauderdale, Reverend Barber later became pastor of Westside Baptist Church in Hollywood, Florida. Most significantly for the visibility of African Americans in Southern Baptist life, Barber was eventually elected president of the Florida Baptist Convention. Like Smith, he believes that the SBC is on the cutting edge with regard to race relations. The denomination is not moving fast enough for some, he acknowledges, but it is moving too fast for others. In his view, the most important point is that it is moving, and in the right direction.[56]

Frost, who has figured so prominently in the African American Southern Baptist scene, has a similar story that predates Barber's and Luter's association with Southern Baptists. He grew up in a National Baptist church and shortly after graduation from college was licensed to preach in that denomination. He served three years as interim pastor of a black Presbyterian Church in Youngstown, Ohio. John Tatum, a graduate of Southwestern Seminary, went to Youngstown and planted a Home Mission church called New Rising Star Baptist. As Tatum pastored the congregation through its infancy, he also groomed Frost to take his place. In 1983 Frost stepped in as pastor a week after Tatum's departure. The church became autonomous and now thrives with a large congregation, a new physical plant, and Open Door Christian Academy, which educates roughly fifty students from grades one through six. Like Barber, Frost served as the president of his state convention for two terms in the early 1990s.[57]

While there are many churches and pastors who remain dually aligned with the National Baptists and the SBC, the trend is toward the model pioneered by McCall, Smith, and a few others who have been solely Southern Baptist. There is a growing number of African American pastors like Frost, Luter, and Barber who either never had ties with National Baptists or who have loosened or severed those ties. Together, these singly aligned Southern Baptists band together in the African American Fellowship of the SBC, which meets at Southern Baptist Convention meetings each summer.

AFRICAN AMERICAN FACULTY IN THE SEMINARIES

While a growing number of African Americans and African American pastors find the SBC an attractive alternative to the historic black Baptist denominations, getting African Americans into leadership positions in the

SBC remains a challenge. This is especially so in the seminaries, where there have been a very small number of black professors on the faculties. It is, therefore, instructive to evaluate their experiences in an attempt to discern the kind of progress or lack thereof the denomination is making with regard to race.

T. Vaughn Walker is arguably the most successful African American Southern Baptist academic, success being determined by his ability to thrive on the faculty of a Southern Baptist seminary. Originally from Virginia, he attended Hampton University and Eastern Illinois University for his bachelors and masters degrees, then earned a Ph.D. in general education from Oregon State University. In between his masters and doctoral work, he taught and coached in public schools. After receiving his doctorate, he joined the faculty at the University of Missouri in 1979 in the area of sports psychology, which had been his area of doctoral emphasis. While teaching at Missouri, he felt a call to the ministry and began pastoring a rural church outside of Columbia. In 1984 he moved to Louisville and enrolled at Southern Seminary, also taking a pastor's position in a dually aligned church in town. When he graduated from Southern with the M.Div. degree, he began to teach courses in black church studies in the Carver School of Social Work, then in 1993 he moved over to the School of Theology. Walker eventually became chair of the Department of Black Church Studies and holder of the WMU (Women's Missionary Union) Chair of Christian Ministries.[58]

Walker is one of the few faculty members whose tenure at Southern spans the moderate and conservative eras. Having been hired by the moderates but tenured by the conservatives, he is a survivor. For the most part, this was not a problem for Walker theologically. He is conservative on most important points. After Mohler became president, however, it took considerably more than basic theological conservatism to gain tenure at Southern. Specifically, one had to pass the litmus test that included opposition to women in pulpit ministry. Walker interpreted the new view as being that faculty cannot affirm women as senior pastors. When he came up for tenure, he explained to the conservative trustees that he does not see ordination as being equivalent to senior pastor status. As a professor, he is at Southern to teach students; if the seminary accepts students, he will teach them. His personal conviction about women pastors does not interfere with what he does in the classroom. "I understand the seminary's position. And my understanding of headship probably in some ways is in accord with that. But, I have an ethical position with women pastors. As a local pastor I'm going to respect another pastor. If another congregation chooses to call a woman as their pastor, I respect their right to do that. Whether I would or would not is not the issue." Going into the late stages of his tenure review, Walker did not know if he would be accepted by the trustees. "But, [my position] seemed to squeak me by." It helped, Walker believes, that the black church sees ordination differently than do traditional Southern Baptist churches. Moreover, at the time he was tenured, Walker's church had never ordained a woman, even though there were ordained women on its staff.[59]

During Walker's time at Southern, there has always been verbal support for hiring African Americans. Both the Honeycutt and Mohler administrations recognized that African American students need black mentors. Many African American students left the seminary when conservatives took over, not because they believed the new leaders were too conservative theologically, but because they feared that Southern was going to become a "Falwell, Criswell, Ronald Reagan, Republican-type of institution." Walker sometimes jokes that the real difference between the old and new Southern Seminary is that it has moved from being a Democratic to a Republican institution. "That's a gross generalization," he says, but African American students were genuinely concerned about how they were going to be treated by the new regime. The problem was not theological but political, for many African American students were afraid that they were going to be indoctrinated into a conservative Republican agenda. All this gave Walker a greater determination to ride through the storm in an attempt to be a pastor and mentor for the African American students who did stay.[60]

Walker also had another motivation for riding through the storm rather than leaving, and that was his church, First Gethsemane Baptist. Since his becoming pastor, the church has grown from 125 to 1,200 members, with forty associate pastors on the staff. It is a tri-aligned church—National Baptist, Southern Baptist, and American Baptist—but it is mainly a National Baptist congregation. In order to continue in Louisville as both a professor and pastor, Walker needed to find a way to stay on the faculty at Southern, and this was probably easier for him than for white moderate professors. As he has said, from the perspective of an African American, things are not that different at Southern now from what they were before except that the personnel have changed. He never fully fit the mold of a Southern Baptist moderate, and he does not quite fit the mold of an SBC conservative either. His situation was unique when he began and still is. This helps him understand the foot dragging in hiring more African Americans at Southern and other SBC seminaries. The conservative leadership wants to be sure that its new hires are fully supportive of Mohler and the conservative program. Walker acknowledges that conservatives can never be sure where African Americans are going to be theologically or, even more so, politically. Theologically conservative African Americans are likely to be far to the political left of white Southern Baptist conservatives. In his own case, Walker cites the death penalty as one example. While he can support it theologically, he opposes it in its present form because of the racial disparity in the sentence's application.[61]

Even more significant than the death penalty, however, is the issue of affirmative action. It almost goes without saying that virtually no white Southern Baptist conservative supports affirmative action, while most black Southern Baptists do. "I'm for affirmative action," Walker says. "I think we need affirmative action. I don't think it's anti-white. I think it's pro-people." He acknowledges that this is one difference between himself and white Southern Baptist conservatives. To illustrate his position, Walker uses an analogy from his days as a basketball player. When he was young, he got to where he could play the game very well on the court at his home, which had a dirt surface and a crooked basket. When people came to his home, he was a terror. But when he got into the gym at school to try out for the team, it was a different story. The goals were regulation height. He was on another person's court. "It's sort of like saying, 'Everything is equal now. Let's all play on the same court.' . . . But, I had been playing on this other court all these years. You just can't say overnight that I'm on the same court with you and everything is now equal. We have to have some remedies to balance the scales. Just saying 'equal opportunity' is not a remedy, as far as I'm concerned. That is not to imply that I think you should give anyone who is unqualified a position. I don't agree with that. But, I believe there are competent people who are qualified and we need to decide who sets the standard."[62]

For support of his position, Walker cites research done by one of his former colleagues at the University of Missouri dealing with standardized tests like the Graduate Records Exam. Of the African Americans who were earning doctoral degrees in the 1970s, at the time of the study, most had GRE scores too low to qualify at the institution where they were teaching, yet all had superior grades. The research determined that the only factor that was an accurate predictor of success for black candidates was grade-point average. In the D.Min. program that Walker oversees, he has eliminated test scores as a criterion for admission. While the program was too young in

1999 to yet have graduated anyone, twelve African Americans were making progress toward doctoral degrees. Walker makes this point forcefully: If Southern Baptist seminaries will make the effort, they can attract and train well-qualified African Americans, but thus far it has not been a priority. As Walker puts the case: "The issue for Southern Baptists and for the Southern Baptist Convention and for Southern Seminary is this: We have really not arrived until a student can come here, black or white, and be a serious candidate for any vacant church that comes. It's when the white church will call a black pastor and vice versa that we have arrived." But for Walker, this is a leadership issue first. When churches will diversify their staffs by including men, women, and people of color, that communicates that all are welcome. "I don't see that as the case [now], and I'm afraid I don't see that happening anytime soon." As for his own seminary, "The test for Southern is when we have some openings, will we really stretch and find competent African American scholars to come? And will we trust them to teach some things that the SBC may not be totally comfortable with."[63]

If Walker's experience represents the best-case scenario for an African American Southern Baptist scholar, and if, as has been argued, he believes things are not progressing quickly enough, it will come as no surprise that those whose experiences have been less positive will be even more pessimistic. Timothy James Johnson's experience is quite possibly the worst of any of the African American scholars in the SBC. Born in 1944, Johnson grew up in what he calls pre–civil rights Philadelphia—integrated neighborhoods, but predominately black; integrated schools, but not integrated life. He grew up in a National Baptist church that would later become part of the Progressive Baptist Convention when that group split from the National Baptists. He found his identity in the historic black church. "Without the black church, I wouldn't be doing what I am now," Johnson has said.[64]

Johnson attended the Philadelphia College of the Bible, where he studied social work with Charles Yardley Furness, father of Janet Furness Spressart and founder of the first social work program at a Christian college. After completing a masters degree in social work at the University of Pennsylvania, Johnson served on the faculty of Eastern College, an evangelical Baptist institution outside of Philadelphia, from 1980 to 1991. In 1990 Diana Garland and founding dean Anne Davis began to recruit Johnson for the faculty of the Carver School of Social Work at Southern. Although reluctant to give up his tenured position at Eastern and to go to the South, Johnson found the lure of the Carver School irresistible and accepted the position. By this time he was writing his dissertation at Temple University, and he had an up-front sabbatical to get as deeply into that work as possible before commencing teaching at Southern. Moreover, he also went to Southern with a promise that once his Ph.D. was in hand, he would begin the tenure review process.

Johnson arrived at Southern in the fall of 1991, the "last days of Camelot," as he recalls it. Roy Honeycutt was still president, and both he and Davis believed that Johnson's Afrocentric perspective would be an asset at Southern. While Johnson experienced some tension with a few white students, which he attributes to their not being accustomed to having a black professor, the real problems developed between himself and the administration. By the time Johnson had completed his dissertation and was thereby eligible for tenure review, Honeycutt was gone, Al Mohler was president, David Dockery was dean of the faculty, and Garland dean of the Carver School. None of these administrators had been party to the original agreement concerning Johnson's tenure-track status. When he inquired as to when his tenure review would begin, the new administration informed him that he would be given an eighteen-month contract, which Johnson considered "the kiss of death." As Garland recalled it, the administration told her that the institution was doing away with tenure, hence the rebuff of Johnson. Garland believed this and began to work to get Johnson a three-year contract, which was the best she believed was going to be possible for any faculty at Southern. Still, Garland and Johnson's relationship deteriorated as she attempted to work with the new administration. She believed she was acting in good faith, while Johnson believed he was being singled out because of his Afrocentric views and because Garland was unwilling to fight for him. Clearly, Johnson's perspective, which had been considered a strength when Honeycutt was president and Davis the dean of the Carver School, was now a liability under the Mohler administration. Johnson became bitter and disillusioned, then he eventually recognized that he could not harbor such feelings and function happily. Even after Garland informed him that he would be offered a three-year contract, Johnson continued to look for a position elsewhere. In the fall of 1994, he began teaching at Roberts Wesleyan College.

Garland recalls Johnson's situation as her single greatest regret from the years that she was dean of the Carver School, a regret stemming from her believing that the seminary was doing away with tenure and not singling out Johnson for denial.[65] Ironically, it was when Garland tried to fill Johnson's position with David Sherwood that the Southern debacle ensued, leading to the demise of the Carver School. Following that, Spressart and Sherwood would join Johnson at Roberts Wesleyan. Johnson recalls that sometime after the demise of Carver, Garland apologized for not backing him more forthrightly.[66]

Johnson's own view some five years after his leaving Southern is that the primary problem was the inability of students and administration to accept even his mildly Afrocentric perspective. As for the difference between moderates and conservatives at the seminary, he was not there long enough under the conservatives to get a sense that they were any worse than the moderates. As a result of his experiences, Johnson continues to be rather wary of all southerners on the race question. He believes most of them just could not break through the southern niceness to even acknowledge discomfort and injustice, let alone the presence of racism. "That's one thing about southerners," Johnson declares, "they're always going to put that polite front on. That paternalism is there. It's designed to hide a whole lot of things. And you're not going to talk about racism because it's not nice to talk about racism. . . . Racism is never dealt with openly in a system like that. You can't even acknowledge that it exists."[67]

Was it racism that did in Johnson at Southern Seminary, or was it his theological and political views? While conservative and evangelical for the most part, Johnson claims to be radical politically. Moreover, he is not conservative in his handling of the Bible, for example arguing for the "Africanity of scripture," by which he highlights that much of what happened in biblical life was African. His dissertation was on the Afrocentricity of the black church, and he says he can see God anthropomorphically with a black face, much as whites see Him with a white face. On the issue of sexual preference, Johnson believes that the first issue is not what an individual's sexual orientation is, but "what do you do with Christ?" "I can fellowship with anyone if they're trusting [Christ] for salvation," he claims.[68] At a seminary that refuses to hire professors who are not solidly opposed to women in pulpit ministry, and in a denomination that has called for a boycott of Disney partly because the corporation extends health benefits to gay partners of employees, Johnson's views are clearly not acceptable.

So how does he answer this challenge: "Professor Johnson, it was not racism that got you at Southern, it was just that your theology, while broadly evangelical, just didn't fit, and that's why they got rid of you." Johnson's reply is that no one ever asked him about his theology. When he came onto the faculty, there was only one stipulation: that he join a Southern Baptist church. The moderate administration assumed that he was where he needed to be, and when the conservatives came to power, they never asked either. He is convinced that what the administration knew of his theology came from complaints made by students who were not prepared for even his mildly Afrocentric perspective, and those complaints were filtered through a conservative board of trustees that then pressured the new administration to deny him a tenure-track slot.[69] Perhaps the fear was not so much that Johnson's skin was black, but that his views were. There was always the risk that he would embarrass Southern Seminary by asking the black question.

Within the SBC seminaries, there is at least one African American who represents the whole package of what the white SBC leadership is looking for in its faculty. R. Logan Carson is senior professor of Christian theology at Southeastern Seminary in Wake Forest, North Carolina, and brings to his position both theological and political conservatism. Born in 1932 in the mountains of western North Carolina, Carson was converted in a black Baptist church in 1948, then decided as a sophomore in college that he wanted to teach. With a bachelor of divinity from Hartford Theological Seminary, a masters degree from Louisville Presbyterian Seminary, and a doctorate from Drew University, Carson joined the faculty at Gardner-Webb University in the early 1970s and stayed for twenty-one years; Gardner-Webb is affiliated with the Baptist State Convention of North Carolina. In 1989 Carson's secretary left Gardner-Webb and went to work at Southeastern. There she began to lobby the administration to bring Carson onto the faculty. She recruited Gardner-Webb graduates who were studying at the seminary to sign a letter urging the school to consider hiring Carson. Paige Patterson became president of Southeastern in 1992, and Carson's secretary continued her efforts with the new administration. Within a short time, Patterson grew interested and brought Carson to Southeastern for an interview that eventually resulted in his hiring for the fall of 1994.[70]

Carson's experience as an African American Southern Baptist is unique in that he is blind. Having overcome both racial prejudice and the difficulties associated with blindness, Carson believes that hard work is the answer to disabilities of any kind. He remembers a teacher he had at the North Carolina School for the Blind who told him, "You may be blind, but don't act blind." She taught him to overcome obstacles instead of fixating on them. Carson did and expects others to do the same. He has attempted to pass on to his own students his belief that they can individually overcome all obstacles. Some African American students at Gardner-Webb thought he would give them a break because he was black. "Some of the black students thought I was not being a brother because I wouldn't let them have special attention or wouldn't wink at them missing class," he recalls. These personal experiences reflect Carson's larger views of affirmative action. While not necessarily opposing the concept, he believes its time has passed. "Affirmative action had its day, but now it's time when you've got to get out there. . . . These students have to get out there and compete." Indeed, Carson's overall political philosophy is overtly conservative. "I'm even a Republican," he says. "I've always liked their philosophy." He says that he grew up in a conservative part of North Carolina and that those views must have rubbed off on him, but he also agrees that having overcome both racial prejudice and a major disability tends to shape his belief that others can also overcome prejudice without the aid of affirmative action.[71]

In addition to his nearly thirty-year career in teaching at Southern Baptist institutions, Carson has since 1974 also pastored churches, and most of this work, like that of Vaughn Walker, has been in National Baptist churches. In fact, the congregation he has led since going to Southeastern is not even dually aligned with Southern Baptists. Even so, as he has traveled and preached revivals, he has done so in more Southern Baptist than black churches. All this makes Carson very difficult to categorize. It may be that, whereas Walker is viewed as a National Baptist who happens to teach in a Southern Baptist seminary, Carson is a Southern Baptist professor who happens to pastor a National Baptist church. This is not necessarily the way Carson would prefer things. Indeed, his longtime dream has been to teach in one of the historically black colleges, but this has yet to work out for him; he suspects that he may be too conservative for them. Most black colleges have "gone liberal," in his view. Carson is somewhat wary and critical of black Baptist churches as well, for he believes they are not into mission work as they should be. He says that they need to move beyond the yearning to just have a good time with gospel music and think about those out there who need to be brought in.[72]

Oddly, one thing that Carson and Walker have in common is that neither was invited to participate in the drafting of the racial reconciliation resolution of 1995. For Carson, this may have been merely because he had just joined the faculty at Southeastern when the move for a resolution began. He had, however, been at Gardner-Webb for two decades prior, and he had been brought to Southeastern by Patterson, one of the prime movers and shakers in the SBC conservative movement, so he certainly was known in the denomination. Yet ignoring Walker and Carson was in some ways logical because neither had much interest in the statement, even if for very different reasons—Walker because he believes so much more than a mere resolution is needed, and Carson because the race issue looms so low on his issue barometer. Where race is central for the teaching and scholarship of Walker and Johnson, it seems to be peripheral and incidental to Carson's concerns as a Southern Baptist professor and revival preacher. Carson does not even know the other African American Southern Baptist seminary professors. He is just not in the same loop.

Nevertheless, as a Southern Baptist African American, Carson has experienced some racial prejudice. He has been invited by white Southern Baptist pastors to preach in churches, then uninvited once the congregation learns that he is black. He also shares with Walker the concern that more African Americans gain positions of leadership and visibility within the SBC and seems somewhat puzzled that he has never been asked to appear in any capacity at a Southern Baptist Convention meeting. Like other African Americans affiliated with the SBC, Carson believes that Southern Baptists must show African Americans that they are wanted, not just for their numbers, but for the gifts they have that can be utilized in the denomination's work. Moreover, while Carson fully supports the denomination's efforts to evangelize in urban minority centers, he also believes that individual congregations that want to dually align with black Baptists should be allowed to do so.[73]

The mixed success in the seminaries notwithstanding, Sid Smith still emphasizes the positive. He cites what he believes is the significant progress that has taken place on the issue of race in the SBC. As for the seminaries, he points out that before 1979, when the conservatives began to take over the denomination, there were no black professors, but by 2000 all the seminaries had at least one. Moreover, at least two of the seminaries now have programs in black studies. Smith also notes that most of the conservative SBC presidents have had significant numbers of African American members in their own churches. He used Jerry Vines's church in Jacksonville, Florida, as an example: out of the more than twenty thousand members, four thousand are black. Smith also relates the story of when Adrian Rogers's church, Bellevue Baptist outside of Memphis, voted to integrate many years ago. Rogers allegedly told the congregation after the vote that he was glad at the outcome because had the vote gone the other way, he would have resigned. Smith acknowledges that while there is not widespread African American representation in these churches, there is, nevertheless, an openness and inclusiveness. As evidence of racial progress, he points out that the one African American vice president of a major denominational agency, the International Mission Board, has been appointed under conservative rule and that fifteen state conventions have elected black presidents. Most national agencies have black-oriented programs with African American staff, and most of the agency boards have African American representation. Echoing what Paige Patterson has said, Smith believes it is plausible that by 2005 the SBC will have a minority president. He believes that increasingly, especially at the state level, African Americans will move into roles that have nothing to do with race. Already in South Carolina, he emphasizes, the state convention has named an African American as head of church planting—not black-church relations or church planting of black congregations, but all church planting was in 2000 under the leadership of an African American.[74]

For Smith, this is just indicative of a larger trend whereby Southern Baptist churches are becoming increasingly integrated. The pace may be too slow for some, but he clearly likes the trajectory. Furthermore, he makes an explicit connection between racial progress and conservative theology, which, he argues, puts an emphasis on evangelism of all people regardless of color. There is a mandate to evangelize all people; it is not an option.

CONCLUSION

Race is the one issue where Southern Baptist conservatives want to be progressive and the only one about which they talk progressive. The race reconciliation resolution of 1995 is a significant achievement for the SBC. Still, conservatives have trouble getting into the progressive trenches because they are dug in too deeply on the other side of the battle lines they have drawn in American culture. The SBC conservative experience with race illustrates that once people adopt the culture-war model and then declare themselves combatants for the traditional right, it becomes difficult to stand with progressives on any other issue, including race. This is because it is nearly impossible to stand in an alliance with those forces that one has declared the enemy. Southern Baptist conservatives are by no means the only group on the right or the left to do this, but according to the model they have chosen, the culture is at war. For them, it is not a series of battles with shifting alliances—it is not a fluid situation. Rather, a secular and hostile progressive culture is running roughshod over people of faith, and it must be resisted at every turn. The only option for SBC conservatives is to attempt to win converts among people of color, which is itself a commendable goal. As for the fight for justice, the race issue requires SBC conservatives to leave their own side of the culture war and take up positions with the other side, and they have not found a way to do this politically. They lobby the state on all sorts of culture-war issues, but what could they possibly support politically that would put them in a league with Civil Rights activists, most of whom are in the Democratic Party?

Conclusion

Given that each of the chapters of this book has its own conclusion, what appears here will include only brief observations, most of them rather tentative. It is quite early in the history of the SBC conservative movement to draw anything but provisional conclusions. That being the case, this work is intended to start, not complete, a historiographical process. Certainly, historians fifty years from now will have a clearer picture.

The first observation is that in one sense, Southern Baptist conservatives have become fully American. Whereas once Southern Baptists identified with southern culture and were largely defined regionally, SBC conservatives now define themselves against the broader national culture. They recognize that the South as Zion, as Rufus Spain called it, has largely passed from history. At the same time, however, they still retain at least one very southern feature, for they interpret social, cultural, and political developments in the United States as part of a religious drama. This has been a consistent feature of southern life that was accentuated following the Civil War, when southerners had to make sense of their great loss. In discussing the work of southern historians such as Charles Reagan Wilson and his influential book *Baptized in Blood: The Religion of the Lost Cause, 1865–1920*, Bill Leonard has summed up nicely what the post–Civil War situation called for: "In the aftermath of defeat and the humiliation of Reconstruction, southern religionists set themselves to the task of remythologizing their place in the divine plan and restoring faith in the ultimate victory of their spiritual, if not their political, cause."[1]

There is a sense in which Southern Baptist conservatives at the outset of the twenty-first century are remythologizing the whole of American culture, not as a Christian entity, but rather the opposite, as a culture that has ceased to be broadly Christian and relatively intact. Myth, as used here, has to do with the story people develop as a way of making sense of their situation. The story that has become central for SBC conservatives is one of a culture that was once whole and good that has become fractured and decadent. As for the South, it is no longer set apart as more intact than the rest of the country but instead has been fully integrated into the larger nation to the detriment of the region. This is largely unspoken. As readers will no doubt observe, SBC conservatives simply do not talk much about a distinctive South. Their focus is on the United States. The South may have stayed intact longer than the North, but this is no longer so. Within this larger American culture, however, Southern Baptist conservatives are still remythologizing their own place in the divine plan of restoration.

A second observation is that Southern Baptist conservatives are not only less southern than their predecessors but they are also less tribal. There is a sense in which Southern Baptist identity has historically been in large part clannish, at least in a cultural sense. Eminent historian of the South Sam Hill has referred to this as a sort of cultural ethnicity so pronounced and developed that it is virtually impossible to become fully Southern Baptist if one were not reared in the tradition. Only with great difficulty, if at all, can one come from the outside and become fully part of the group. In contrast to this, Southern Baptist conservatives seek to fashion an identity that is more confessional than tribal. As was argued in chapter one, this confessional identity is largely neoevangelical, and the shift to a confessional identity is one of the things that made the SBC controversy so painful for many moderates. Eventually coming to the conclusion that they simply could no longer identify with the theological or cultural program the conservatives were able to put in place required many moderates to forego their identity as Southern Baptists. For many of them, the conservative movement became the theological equivalent of an ethnic cleansing. One does not have to be around Southern Baptist moderates long to hear the stories and actually feel the pain that the controversy, with its attendant shift in identity, caused.

Still, however, this alteration of identity is not complete and may never be. Southern Baptists who happen to support the conservative theological and cultural agenda can continue being what they have always been and can scarcely imagine ever ceasing to be—Southern Baptist. Others who are in positions to ignore the cultural agenda, African American Southern Baptists and converts from outside the South, for example, can with greater ease than was the case before conservative control become more fully Southern Baptist because they identify with the confessional identity even while not sharing the cultural ethnicity. Unlike SBC moderates, these new Southern Baptists have nothing to lose and a confessional identity to gain. It remains to be seen if they can become fully Southern Baptist in comparison to conservatives who were born and reared in the denomination. Perhaps the tribal identity or cultural ethnicity will continue, but the conservative leadership would like to replace it with a confessional identity, and if the recent growth of the denomination outside the white South is any indication, they seem to have succeeded at least in part.[2]

A third consideration is somewhat related to this shift. Just as the refashioning of the Southern Baptist identity confessionally required that conservatives take control of the denomination, so it was that they had to control the denomination in order to remake its public persona. Moderates who controlled the SBC into the 1980s and desired to promote the Grand Compromise projected a sense of tolerance that downplayed serious theological disagreement. Relative harmony within the denomination was matched by a desire for harmony between the convention and its host culture, the South. Conservatives, by contrast, because they desire a confessional identity, needed a theological debate in order to force a crisis within the denomination. Similarly, they also needed to end the harmony between the SBC and its host culture, which for them was the nation, not the region. Simply put, conservatives could not afford to continue as gadflies on the right wing of the denomination, as the progressives were apparently willing to do on the left.[3] Rather, they had to take control of the SBC and drive the moderates from positions of influence in order to create a new and very different posture diametrically opposed to the dominant institutions of American culture. Whether or not conservatives were aware from the outset of their campaign in the late 1970s that they would need full control is a question that certainly has not been settled by this book. What does seem clear, however, is that while SBC conservatives spoke for several years about wanting parity within the denomination, their cultural program would never have allowed it. They had to control the SBC from top to bottom in order to enter the national culture war as they desired. It would have been impossible for the denomination to identify with traditionalists while having within it many leaders who were progressives who opposed the culture-war model altogether.

Fourth, just as Southern Baptist conservatives have retained something of their southernness as they have largely begun to think of themselves as part of the broader American evangelical community, so they have recaptured the Baptist tradition of dissent that was lost when the denomination dominated the South. Perhaps a better way of putting the point is that they have continued to exercise their half of David Stricklin's "genealogy of dissent" in cultural matters. No longer able to define themselves against opponents within their denomination, as they did before 1979, conservatives now must exercise their dissent against American culture. Southern Baptist conservatives at the beginning of the twenty-first century are setting out to interpret their situation religiously, but they have set for themselves a very different task than Southern Baptists from the late nineteenth century. Whereas their forerunners set out to build and maintain their region's culture, Southern Baptist conservatives have taken on the mantle of cultural resistance, not so much to protect the South but to engage the broader American society in hopes of stemming the tide of decay.

When it comes to prospects for winning their culture war, SBC conservatives cannot afford to be as triumphal as their moderate forebears often were. Sometimes they sound as if the crisis in America is so deep that all is nearly lost, but they remain determined nevertheless to bear what they believe is a prophetic countercultural witness against the forces of secularism. This is easiest on issues having to do with gender, where they can stand four-square against the dominant egalitarianism of American society. By contrast, on the issue of race they find themselves in the uneasy position of standing with the forces of secular progressivism. On a range of other questions in between they find their allies among evangelicals, traditional Roman Catholics, and other types of culturally conservative theists. They stand willing to make tactical alliances with any and all groups that espouse traditional, antisecularist views, but they retain the old Southern Baptist desire to lead and control all endeavors in which they are active. In one sense, when it comes to prospects for actually winning over American culture, they are more chastened than moderates in the mid-twentieth century, who could afford to take cultural dominance in the South for granted. When it comes to declarations of cultural warfare, however, they can be every bit as bombastic as the Southern Baptist preacher who declared in 1948 that his denomination was "the last hope, the fairest hope, the only hope" for the evangelization of the world.[4] The issues today include both evangelization and social transformation. Southern Baptist conservatives are not sure that the culture can be transformed, but if it is to be, they are pretty sure they are the ones who can do it.

Fifth, it is an open question and largely a matter of perception as to whether conservatives are correct in their description of an American culture gone secular, decadent, and hostile to all things religious. It appears, however, that to maintain such an interpretation is to overlook many features of recent American history. While there is hostility aplenty in many quarters, one does not have to be a mainstream nonevangelical "going with the cultural flow" to disagree with conservatives, as Land maintains is the case. Just to choose one example as a counter to the generally gloomy cultural prognosis conservatives maintain, the presidential election of 2000 serves well. Both candidates that year, Gov. George W. Bush and Vice President Al Gore, touted their born-again status seemingly at every whistle stop. Then, as if the heads of the two tickets failed to provide enough religion, Democratic vice-presidential candidate Joseph Lieberman, an Orthodox Jew, outdid them both in presenting a forceful argument for the integration of religion and public policy. While there were many examples of hostility to these expressions of public faith, examples that on the one hand would seem to confirm the SBC conservative argument, the campaign season was on the other hand Rawlsian liberalism's worst nightmare. The candidates simply ignored the Rawlsian argument that comprehensive doctrines should be confined to the private sphere and that public positions should be based only on secular criteria widely shared by all in America's diverse public square. Indeed, Richard Neuhaus's "naked public square" seemed well clothed, if not overly dressed.

Moreover, the influence that SBC conservatives and those from the larger Christian Right have carved out within the Republican Party seem to also temper the kind of cultural portrait that SBC conservatives paint. To point once again to the SBC's chief lobbyist, Richard Land, it seems almost disingenuous to walk the halls of Congress, testify before committee after committee, and rub shoulders with some of the most politically powerful personalities in the United States all the while claiming there is little or no room for religious influence in American public life.

Finally, it appears, at least to this author, that at this early stage in the interpretation of the SBC conservative movement, the cultural program is the glue that is holding conservatives together. One might argue that during the controversy inerrancy served that purpose. The battle for inerrancy is won, however, and still revivalist preachers such as Adrian Rogers, Calvinist theologians such as Al Mohler and Timothy George, pietistic expositors such as Paige Patterson, and public activists like Land continue to live together in relative harmony. There are widespread fault lines, but the SBC conservative movement seems to be maturing and not breaking apart. It is as if these leaders with their varied and at times oppositional theologies do not have time to battle each other because they are too busy saving America, if not saving sinners. How long this will be the case is hard to tell. At the moment, however, it seems that sojourning uneasily in Babylon is enough to keep SBC conservatives together.

Notes

Introduction

1. Rufus B. Spain, *At Ease in Zion: Social History of Southern Baptists, 1865–1900* (Nashville: Vanderbilt University Press, 1967), 213–14.

2. Quoted in Bill Leonard, *God's Last and Only Hope: The Fragmentation of the Southern Baptist Convention* (Grand Rapids, Mich.: Eerdmans, 1990), 3.

3. See Leonard, *God's Last and Only Hope*, 15; and Nancy Ammerman, *Baptist Battles: Social Change and Religious Conflict in the Southern Baptist Convention* (New Brunswick, N.J.: Rutgers University Press, 1990). Ammerman's second chapter is entitled "From English Dissent to Southern Establishment."

4. While there is a consensus among scholars that the South has changed dramatically, especially since World War II, there remains a healthy debate as to how much the region has lost its distinctiveness. As early as 1960, C. Vann Woodward wondered if there was not coming a time when it will be difficult for southerners to say what it means to be southern. See C. Vann Woodward, *The Burden of Southern History* (Baton Rouge: Louisiana State University Press, 1960), 3. For an opposing view, see Charles Roland, "The Ever-Vanishing South," *Journal of Southern History* 48 (Feb. 1982). See also Leonard, *God's Last and Only Hope*, 16–17.

5. David Morgan, *The New Crusades, the New Holy Land: Conflict in the Southern Baptist Convention* (Tuscaloosa: University of Alabama Press, 1996), 46.

6. David Stricklin, *A Genealogy of Dissent: Southern Baptist Protest in the Twentieth Century* (Lexington: University Press of Kentucky, 1999).

7. Grant Wacker, *Augustus H. Strong and the Dilemma of Historical Consciousness* (Macon, Ga.: Mercer University Press, 1985), 17. George Marsden writes, "This is not an exhaustive definition, but it is economical and carefully framed." *Understanding Evangelicalism and Fundamentalism* (Grand Rapids, Mich.: Eerdmans, 1991), 65 n. 7.

8. Leonard, *God's Last and Only Hope*, 6; Samuel S. Hill Jr., "Fundamentalism

in the South," in *Perspectives in Churchmanship,* ed. David M. Scholer (Macon, Ga.: Mercer University Press, 1986), 49–52.

9. Leonard, *God's Last and Only Hope,* 29, 38.

10. Ammerman, *Baptist Battles,* 74–75.

11. Leonard, *God's Last and Only Hope,* 8; James Davison Hunter, *Evangelicalism: The Coming Generation* (Chicago: University of Chicago Press, 1987), 21.

12. Quoted in Morgan, *New Crusades,* 43–44.

13. Ammerman, *Baptist Battles,* 80.

14. Walter B. Shurden and Randy Shepley, eds. *Going for the Jugular: A Documentary History of the SBC Holy War* (Macon, Ga.: Mercer University Press, 1996), xii.

15. Actually the presidency is open every year, but there has been a longstanding tradition of reelecting a president for a second one-year term.

1. MOVING OFF THE PLANTATION

1. See Stricklin, *Genealogy of Dissent,* especially chap. 6, "The 'Return' of Southern Baptist Fundamentalists: The Other Dissenters." See also Leonard, *God's Last and Only Hope,* for his discussion of the Grand Compromise, whereby moderates, until the 1980s, were able to keep the left and the right at bay in order to avoid conflict and maintain a consensus on missions. Other works to consult for an understanding of the Southern Baptist controversy are Ammerman, *Baptist Battles;* and, for the most up-to-date history, Morgan, *New Crusades.*

2. James Leo Garrett Jr., E. Glenn Hinson, and James E. Tull, *Are Southern Baptists Evangelicals?* (Macon, Ga.: Mercer University Press, 1983), 87.

3. Ibid., 104–5. For a discussion of Landmarkism, see H. Leon McBeth, *The Baptist Heritage: Four Centuries of Baptist Witness* (Nashville: Broadman, 1987), 446–47; and Walter B. Shurden, *Not a Silent People: Controversies That Have Shaped Southern Baptists* (Macon, Ga.: Smyth and Helwys, 1995), 9–17.

4. See, for example, Wacker, *Augustus H. Strong,* 17. George Marsden, usually considered a leading authority on fundamentalists and evangelicals, writes, "This is not an exhaustive definition, but it is economical and carefully framed." *Understanding Evangelicalism and Fundamentalism,* 65 n. 7.

5. Garrett, Hinson, and Tull, *Are Southern Baptists Evangelicals?,* 165, 166.

6. Ibid., 167, 141.

7. This statement can be found in Kenneth L. Woodward et al., "Born Again! The Year of the Evangelicals," *Newsweek,* 25 Oct. 1976, 76; and is quoted in full in Joel Carpenter, "Is 'Evangelical' a Yankee Word?: Relations between Northern Evangelicals and the Southern Baptist Convention in the Twentieth Century," in *Southern Baptists and American Evangelicals: The Conversation Continues,* ed. David S. Dockery (Nashville: Broadman and Holman, 1993), 78. Garrett, Hinson, and Tull also quote and critique the statement in *Are Southern Baptists Evangelicals?* 119.

8. H. Leon McBeth, "Baptist or Evangelical: One Southern Baptist's Perspec-

tive," in *Southern Baptists and American Evangelicals: The Conversation Continues,* ed. David S. Dockery (Nashville: Broadman and Holman, 1993), 76.

9. See Barry Hankins, *God's Rascal: J. Frank Norris and the Beginnings of Southern Fundamentalism* (Lexington: University Press of Kentucky, 1996).

10. See George Marsden, "The Evangelical Denomination," in *Evangelicalism and Modern America,* ed. George Marsden (Grand Rapids, Mich.: Eerdmans, 1984), xiv. Marsden lists Southern Baptists with others "who are hardly part of the card-carrying evangelical fellowship, even though they may certainly be evangelicals in the broader sense" (xv).

11. Mark Noll, Nathan Hatch, and George Marsden, *The Search for Christian America,* exp. ed. (Colorado Springs: Helmers and Howard, 1989), 145. While this reference bears the names of all three authors, I am here attributing the "heirs of fundamentalism" idea primarily to Marsden because it is carried through in his other works as well. See *Reforming Fundamentalism: Fuller Theological Seminary and the New Evangelicalism* (Grand Rapids, Mich.: Eerdmans, 1987). Also, in Marsden, "The Evangelical Denomination," xiv, he writes, "Typically, those who have the strongest sense of being 'evangelicals' are persons with directly fundamentalist background, although persons from other traditions—Pentecostal, holiness, Reformed, Anabaptist, and others—often are deeply involved as well." The idea that evangelicals are somehow fundamentalists in disguise has seeped into the minds of many moderate Southern Baptists and then reemerged in only slightly altered form. As the assistant editor of a state Baptist newspaper once remarked to me, "Evangelicalism is just cleaned up fundamentalism."

12. McBeth, "Baptist or Evangelical," 69.

13. Leonard I. Sweet, "The Evangelical Tradition in America," in *The Evangelical Tradition in America,* ed. Leonard I. Sweet (Macon, Ga.: Mercer University Press, 1984), 85 n. 306. Sweet did not say what he viewed as strange about the book.

14. For example, Marsden has written recently: "Southern Baptists sometimes raise the question of whether they are evangelicals. Most other people do not raise this question because either they do not know what an evangelical is or they do know and think it obvious that many Southern Baptists qualify." "Contemporary American Evangelicalism," in *Southern Baptists and American Evangelicals: The Conversation Continues,* ed. David S. Dockery (Nashville: Broadman and Holman, 1993), 27. In another chapter of this same book, Northern Baptist scholar Stanley Grenz confesses that prior to being confronted with the question, "I had never entertained the thought that Southern Baptists could be anything but evangelicals." "Baptist and Evangelical: One Northern Baptist's Perspective," 52. Also typical of this view is Cullen Murphy, "Protestantism and the Evangelicals," *The Wilson Quarterly* 5:4 (autumn 1981): 111. Murphy here calls the Southern Baptists "America's strongest evangelical movement." Only the most persnickety would quibble with such a statement.

15. Joel Carpenter, *Revive Us Again: The Reawakening of American Fundamentalism* (New York: Oxford University Press, 1997), 141–60; Marsden, "The Evangelical

Denomination," vii–xix. Marsden wrote: "So with the possible exception of this extreme position [fundamentalist separatism], evangelicalism is a transdenominational movement in which many people, in various ways, feel at home. . . . The structure is somewhat like that of the feudal system of the Middle Ages. It is made up of superficially friendly, somewhat competitive empires built up by evangelical leaders competing for the same audience, but all professing allegiance to the same king" (xiv).

16. Cited in Carpenter, "Is 'Evangelical' a Yankee Word?" 96.

17. William Hendricks quoted in Robert C. Ballance Jr., "Next Generation of Ministers Looking beyond Denominational Lines," *Baptists Today,* Dec. 1998, 3.

18. The standard history of fundamentalism is still George Marsden, *Fundamentalism and American Culture: The Shaping of Twentieth-Century Evangelicalism* (New York: Oxford University Press, 1980). Marsden traces the development of neo-evangelicalism in his book *Reforming Fundamentalism.* For the most recent and thorough interpretation of fundamentalism during its realignment and institution-building phase of the 1930s and 1940s, see Carpenter, *Revive Us Again.* For the most recent interpretation of the Scopes trial and the way it was interpreted in the 1930s, see Edward Larson, *Summer for the Gods: The Scopes Trial and America's Continuing Debate over Science and Religion* (New York: Basic Books, 1997).

19. D. M. Roark, "Carl F. H. Henry," in *Dictionary of Christianity in America* (Downers Grove, Ill.: InterVarsity, 1990), 520–21.

20. See: Michael Hamilton, "The Dissatisfaction of Francis Schaeffer," *Christianity Today,* 3 Mar. 1997. The cover title for this issue was "Our Saint Francis." For two examples of evangelical intellectuals who credit Schaeffer as a positive influence while pointing out that his analysis was skewed, see Mark Noll, "Getting the Facts Straight," *TRI (Rutherford Institute),* Mar. 1993, 10–11; and Ronald Wells, "Francis Schaeffer's Jeremiad: A Review Article," *TSF Bulletin,* Sept.–Oct. 1984, 20–23. Wells's article was originally published in *The Reformed Journal* 32 (May 1982); he then responded to some criticisms of that article in *The Reformed Journal* 33 (May 1983). In his *Christianity Today* piece, Hamilton sums up these "dissatisfactions" by writing, "Even in his more careful early work [before "How Shall We Then Live?"], Schaeffer ranged so widely over disciplines and broad periods of time that specialists could not help noticing embarrassing errors of detail and facile oversimplifications" (28).

21. Richard D. Land, interview by author, 1 Apr. 1997.

22. Ibid. See also Hamilton, "Dissatisfaction of Francis Schaeffer," 30.

23. Carl F. H. Henry, *The Uneasy Conscience of Modern Fundamentalism* (Grand Rapids, Mich.: Eerdmans, 1947).

24. Richard D. Land, "Is Democracy Doomed?," *Light,* Jan.–Feb. 1996, 2.

25. Richard D. Land, "Will It Be Faith in Practice?," in *Christians in the Public Square: Faith in Practice?* ed. Richard D. Land and Lee Hollaway (Nashville: ERLC Publications, 1996), 2. Henry's book is *Has Democracy Had Its Day?* (Nashville: ERLC Publications, 1996).

26. Land, interview by author, 1 Apr. 1997.

27. Growing up as a northern evangelical, I can attest personally to the attraction Schaeffer had for any young person who was interested in serious Christian intellectual activity. After hearing of him in the late 1970s, I read one of his books, then read them all. In addition to citing the shortcomings of Schaeffer's analysis, Hamilton's *Christianity Today* article also includes testimonials to the positive effect Schaeffer had on young evangelical intellectuals. "Dissatisfaction of Francis Schaeffer," 28.

I can also attest personally to the deep disappointment many felt when Schaeffer threw in his lot with Jerry Falwell, the Moral Majority, and the New Religious Right. As Hamilton describes this part of Schaeffer's career, "The countercultural Francis Schaeffer seemed [to many in the countercultural generation] to have disappeared" (29).

28. R. Albert Mohler, interview by author, 5 Aug. 1997.

29. Ibid.

30. Ibid.

31. For an extended discussion of this, see Barry Hankins, "Southern Baptists and Northern Evangelicals: Cultural Factors and the Nature of Religious Alliances," *Religion and American Culture: A Journal of Interpretation* 7 (summer 1997): 271–98.

32. Mohler, interview by author, 5 Aug. 1997.

33. *Battle for the Minds*, produced by PBS, video library, Southern Seminary video library, videocassette.

34. Roy Honeycutt, interview by author, 5 Sept. 2000.

35. Mohler, interview by author, 5 Aug. 1997. Charles Scalise was the student-author of the paper under consideration that day. Charles Scalise to author (e-mail), 2 Mar. 2001.

36. Mohler, interview by author, 5 Aug. 1997.

37. Honeycutt, interview by author.

38. Timothy George, interview by author, 24 July 1998.

39. Ibid.

40. See note 20 above.

41. My own experiences corroborate this. When I want to use Schaeffer as an example of evangelical thinking, I almost always have to explain to my southern students who he was. With evangelicals from outside the South who come to Baylor to do graduate work, this is never the case.

42. George, interview by author. While there is no recent published biography of Ockenga, he is covered extensively in Carpenter, *Revive Us Again*, and Marsden, *Reforming Fundamentalism*. See also John M. Adams, "The Making of a New-Evangelical Statesman: The Case of Harold John Ockenga" (Ph.D. diss., Baylor University, 1994).

43. George, interview by author. See George, "The Southern Baptist Wars: What Can We Learn from the Conservative Victory?" *Christianity Today*, 9 Mar. 1992; and George, "Passing the Southern Baptist Torch," *Christianity Today*, 15 May 1995.

44. Mohler, interview by author, 5 Aug. 1997.

45. George, interview by author.

46. Mark Coppenger, interview by author, 18 June 1998.

47. Ibid.

48. See Harold Lindsell, *The Battle for the Bible* (Grand Rapids, Mich.: Zondervan, 1976), 89–105. The chapter is entitled simply "The Southern Baptist Convention" and is sandwiched in between a chapter on the Lutheran Church Missouri Synod, where inerrancy was upheld, and Fuller Theological Seminary, where it was denied. Lindsell had been a founding professor at Fuller and lamented the loss of the inerrancy requirement there. David Morgan shows that inerrancy was by 1969 already a concern of some SBC conservatives, so it would be erroneous to assert that Lindsell's book created concern over it in Southern Baptist circles. See Morgan, *New Crusades,* 47.

49. Coppenger, interview by author.

50. Ibid.

51. Ibid.

52. Leonard, *God's Last and Only Hope,* 29–39.

53. Coppenger, interview by author. The argument that conservative churches were more successful in evangelism was a standard charge made by the right wing. Conservative journalist and historian James Hefley touted this line in his five-volume series on the controversy, *The Truth in Crisis* (Dallas: Clarion Publications; Hannibal, Mo.: Hannibal Books, 1986–90). Hefley records the conservative charge and what he calls the moderate "excuses" for why their churches baptize fewer people (1:19).

While Hefley took at face value the claim that conservative church baptisms were proof of the superiority of their position, historian Claude Howe Jr. points out that at the same time conservatives trumpeted the growth of conservative churches as proof of God's blessing, they attacked the SBC seminaries that were experiencing unprecedented growth. Howe wrote caustically: "If the blessings of God were to be identified with success as in the churches, then his hand must be upon the seminaries. But, of course, logic and consistency are never virtues in a controversy, so the sustained criticisms continued." "From Houston to Dallas: Recent Controversy in the Southern Baptist Convention," *The Controversy in the Southern Baptist Convention: A Special Issue of the Theological Educator* (New Orleans: Faculty of the New Orleans Baptist Theological Seminary, 1985), 40–41; Howe's article was reprinted in *The Theological Educator* 41 (spring 1990). In the reprint the quote can be found on page 88.

54. Coppenger, interview by author.

55. Clifton Allen, ed. *The Broadman Bible Commentary,* vol. 3 by M. Pierce Matheney Jr. and Roy L. Honeycutt Jr. (Nashville: Broadman, 1970), 241–42.

56. Allen, *Broadman Bible Commentary,* vol. 3, Matheney and Honeycutt, 242.

57. Coppenger, interview by author.

58. Allen, *Broadman Bible Commentary,* vol. 3, Matheney and Honeycutt, 208.

See also C. F. Keil and F. Delitzsch, *Biblical Commentary on the Old Testament* (Grand Rapids, Mich.: Eerdmans, 1950), 236–37.

59. Coppenger, interview by author.

60. Ibid.

61. Adrian Rogers, interview by author, 18 Aug. 1997; James Draper Jr., interview by author, 2 June 1997.

62. Paul Pressler, "It Happened at Princeton," *The Baptist Student*, Apr. 1952, 6–8.

63. Coppenger, interview by author.

64. A prime example of this was the 1987 inerrancy conference at the Ridgecrest Retreat in North Carolina. See *The Proceedings of the Conference on Biblical Inerrancy, 1987* (Nashville: Broadman, 1987).

65. Coppenger, interview by author.

66. Mark Noll, "A Brief History of Inerrancy, Mostly in America," in *Proceedings of the Conference on Biblical Inerrancy, 1987*, 22.

67. See Hankins, *God's Rascal*.

2. "THE WAR OF THE WORLDS"

1. James Davison Hunter, *Culture Wars: The Struggle to Define America* (New York: Basic Books, 1991), 44–45.

2. Rhys H. Williams, ed., *Culture War in American Politics: Critical Reviews of a Popular Myth* (New York: Aldine de Gruyter, 1997).

3. Jeremy Rabkin, "The Culture War That Isn't," *Policy Review*, Aug.–Sept. 1999, <http://www.heritage.org/policyreview/aug99/rabkin.html>.

4. In my interviews with them, conservatives such as Mohler, Land, and Patterson all stress how right they believe the moderates were who took a stand against racial segregation. H. Richard Niebuhr's classic articulation of the relationship of Christian faith and culture is *Christ and Culture* (New York: Harper and Row, 1951). For a recent critique of Niebuhr's position, see Glen H. Stassen, Diane M. Yeager, and John Howard Yoder, *Authentic Transformation: A New Vision of Christ and Culture* (Nashville: Abingdon, 1996).

5. Mohler, interview by author, 5 Aug. 1997.

6. Ibid. On the issue of inerrancy, Nancy Ammerman's research supports Mohler's view that grassroots congregants believed in inerrancy, however they defined it. Her surveys in 1985 showed that 85 percent of Southern Baptists "agreed" or "strongly agreed" that the Scriptures are "the inerrant word of God, accurate in every detail." It should be noted, however, that fewer than half of the inerrantists insisted on a literal reading of the Genesis creation stories. See Ammerman, *Baptist Battles*, 74–75.

7. Mohler, interview by author, 5 Aug. 1997.

8. Paige Patterson, interview by author, 20 May 1997.

9. See William Martin, *With God on Our Side: The Rise of the Religious Right in*

America (New York: Broadway Books, 1996), 193–94, 201. Martin tells how Paul Weyrich, Howard Phillips, Ed McAteer, and Robert Billings met with Jerry Falwell in May 1979 and came up with the idea of the Moral Majority. Abortion was at the top of the agenda.

10. See chapter 6 for a full discussion of abortion. A recent sociological study revealed that evangelical activists in what could be called the Christian left differ substantially from those of the Christian right on every political issue except abortion. Views as to when abortions should be permitted were very similar in the evangelical left and the Christian Right. See: Charles F. Hall, "The Christian Left: Who Are They and How Are They Different from the Christian Right?" *Review of Religious Research* 39 (Sept. 1997): 34.

11. R. Albert Mohler, "The Struggle over Gender," tape 13 of *War of the Worlds: The Struggle for the Nation's Soul,* Christian Life Commission Annual Seminar, Southeastern Baptist Theological Seminary, 1995. I have not been able to find this charge in a published work, but I can attest personally that among moderates there was speculation about Mohler's emphasis on homosexuality. Given that there were and are so few Southern Baptists of any stripe who affirm the homosexual lifestyle, it seemed to many of us on the faculties of various Baptist schools out of proportion to make that issue part of the hiring criteria at Southern.

12. R. Albert Mohler, "Unchanging Truths and Our Changing World," *The Tie* 62 (winter 1994), inside cover. *The Tie* is the slick-backed Southern Seminary alumni magazine. Mohler writes a regular column that appears on the inside cover of each issue.

13. Allan Bloom, *The Closing of the American Mind* (New York: Simon and Schuster, 1987), 25 quoted in Mohler, "Unchanging Truths." This is the first sentence of Bloom's introduction to the book.

14. R. Albert Mohler, "Ministry Is Stranger Than It Used to Be: The Challenge of Postmodernism," *The Tie* 65 (spring 1997): 4. This title is a play on Walter Truett Anderson's book on postmodernism, *Reality Isn't What It Used to Be* (San Francisco: Harper and Row, 1990). Mohler cites Anderson.

15. Quoted in Mohler, "Ministry Is Stranger Than It Use to Be," 6.

16. Ibid.

17. Ibid., 6–7.

18. Ibid., 7. See also Mohler, "Transforming Culture: Christian Truth Confronts Post-Christian America," *The Tie* 64 (summer 1996): 2–5.

19. R. Albert Mohler, "What Mean These Stones?" *The Tie* 63 (summer 1995): 24.

20. R. Albert Mohler, "The Lessons of History," *The Tie* 63 (spring 1995): 13.

21. On Mohler's sense of the displacement of southern culture, see Mohler, "Keeping Faith in a Faithless Age: The Church as the Moral Minority," *The Tie* 63 (spring 1995): inside cover.

22. "Up and Comers: Fifty Evangelical Leaders 40 and Under," *Christianity Today,* 11 Nov. 1996, 22

23. Mohler, interview by author, 5 Aug. 1997.

24. Ibid. For Kuyper, see Irving Hexham, "Abraham Kuyper," in *Evangelical Dictionary of Theology*, ed. Walter A. Elwell (Grand Rapids, Mich.: Baker Book House, 1984), 616; and Frank Vandenberg, *Abraham Kuyper* (Grand Rapids, Mich.: Eerdmans, 1960).

25. James Bratt, "Abraham Kuyper, American History, and the Tensions of Neo-Calvinism," in *Sharing the Reformed Tradition: The Dutch–North American Exchange, 1846–1996*, ed. George Harinck and Hans Krabbendam (Amsterdam: VU Uitgeverij, 1996), 106.

26. Mohler, interview by author, 5 Aug. 1997.

27. Mohler here speaks very loosely of Geneva in the sense of it being a Christian community, not a theocracy, as some would view the reference. As will be discussed elsewhere, Mohler had little sympathy with Reconstructionist theology that would seek to reinstitute Old Testament law in the United States.

28. R. Albert Mohler, "Leadership and Change" (interview), *The Tie* 63 (fall 1995): 17.

29. Richard John Neuhaus, *The Naked Public Square: Religion and Democracy in America* (Grand Rapids, Mich.: Eerdmans, 1984).

30. For a helpful discussion of Neuhaus and fellow neoconservative Michael Novak, see James Skillen, *The Scattered Voice: Christians at Odds in the Public Square* (Edmonton, Alberta: Canadian Institute for Law, Theology, and Public Policy, 1996), 75–96. Skillen's chapter is primarily on Neuhaus and Novak and entitled "Sophisticated Neo-Conservatives."

31. Mohler, interview by author, 5 Aug. 1997.

32. Paige Patterson, interview by author.

33. Timothy George, interview by author, 24 July 1998.

34. Paige Patterson, "War of the Worlds: A Perennial Battle," tape 15 of *The War of the Worlds: The Struggle for the Nation's Soul*, Christian Life Commission Annual Seminar, Southeastern Baptist Theological Seminary, 1995.

35. Timothy George, "Between Pacifism and Coercion: The English Baptist Doctrine of Religious Toleration," *Mennonite Quarterly Review* 58 (Jan. 1984): 47.

36. Land, interview by author, 1 Apr. 1997.

37. Richard D. Land, "Salt and Light" (abridged version of Land's installation address), *Light*, July–Sept. 1989, 4. See also Land, "The Struggle for the Right to Be Involved," tape 9 of *The War of the Worlds: The Struggle for the Nation's Soul*, Christian Life Commission Annual Seminar, Southeastern Baptist Theological Seminary, 1995.

38. Land, "Salt and Light," 2.

39. Richard D. Land, "Responses," in *Disciples and Democracy: Religious Conservatives and the Future of American Politics*, ed. Michael Cromartie (Grand Rapids, Mich.: Eerdmans; and Washington, D.C.: Ethics and Public Policy Center, 1994), 99, 100–101.

40. See John Whitehead, *Religious Apartheid: The Separation of Religion from Public Life* (Chicago: Moody Press, 1994). See also Neuhaus, *Naked Public Square*. It

should be noted that Carter's book, *The Culture of Disbelief: How American Law and Politics Trivialize Religious Devotion* (New York: Basic Books, 1993), is not merely a restatement of Neuhaus's naked-public-square thesis. Rather, Carter explicitly differentiates his view of the "trivialization of religion" from the view that religion is excluded from public life (51). Carter acknowledges that there is religion aplenty in public life. He contends, however, that it is usually treated as a "hobby" that should not seriously influence any important public matter.

41. Land, interview by author, 1 Apr. 1997. Land's position on religion and public schools will be covered in more detail in chapter 5.

42. Land, "Struggle for the Right to Be Involved."

43. Land, interview by author, 1 Apr. 1997.

44. "Epistemological Modesty: An Interview with Peter Berger," *Christian Century*, 29 Oct. 1997, 974.

45. See Stephen V. Monsma and Oliver Thomas, *Church-State Relations: A Debate*, Crossroads Monograph Series on Faith and Pubic Policy, vol. 1, no. 16 (Wynnewood, Pa.: Crossroads, 1997), 33–35.

46. "Epistemological Modesty," 974. Berger's phrase "antiseptically free of religious symbols" is one of Mohler's preferred descriptions of American culture.

47. See Richard D. Land, "Persecution of Christians," *Light*, May–June 1996. Land has addressed the issue of religious persecution in foreign lands before a subcommittee of the U.S. House of Representatives Committee on International Relations.

48. Barrett Duke, "Religious Liberty: But Not for Christians," The Ethics and Religious Liberty Commission, <www.erlc.com/Sundays/1997/Sermons/97s-rliberty. htm>, 17 Nov. 1997, 1.

49. Clifford Goldstein, "Shatter the Silence," *Liberty*, March–Apr. 1998, 30.

50. Jeff Taylor, "Hollow Cries," *Liberty*, Jan.–Feb. 1998, 27.

51. Douglas Laycock, "Continuity and Change in the Threat to Religious Liberty: The Reformation Era and the Late Twentieth Century," *Minnesota Law Review* 80 (May 1996): 1047–1102.

52. Land, "Struggle for the Right to Be Involved."

53. *Proceedings of the 1980 Christian Life Commission Seminar on Ethical Issues for the Eighties*, Roosevelt Hotel, New York City, Mar. 24–26, 1980.

54. See *Proceedings of the 1976 Christian Life Commission Seminar; Proceedings of the 1978 Christian Life Commission Seminar; Proceedings of the 1979 Christian Life Commission Seminar*. The published proceedings of these and other CLC seminars can be found in the Roberts Library at Southwestern Baptist Theological Seminary, Fort Worth, Texas.

55. Land, interview by author, 1 Apr. 1997.

56. Land, "Will It Be Faith in Practice?" 3.

57. Ibid.

58. See, for example, Stephanie Coontz, *The Way We Never Were: American Families and the Nostalgia Trap* (New York: Basic Books, 1992), 35.

59. James Draper Jr., *Authority: The Critical Issue for Southern Baptists* (Old Tappan, N.J.: Fleming H. Revell, 1984), 20.

60. James T. Draper and Forrest Watson, *If the Foundations Be Destroyed* (Nashville: Oliver Nelson, 1984).

61. Ibid., 86, 86–87, 23, 25.

62. Mark Noll, Nathan Hatch, and George Marsden, *The Search for Christian America*, exp. ed. (Colorado Springs: Helmers and Howard, 1989).

63. Draper and Watson, *If the Foundations*, 19, 12, 3 (last quotation on 12).

64. Mohler, interview by author, 5 Aug. 1997; Land, interview by author, 1 Apr. 1997.

65. Draper and Watson, *If the Foundations*, 1, 169.

66. Ibid., 67.

67. Ibid., 103, 101.

68. Ibid., 101.

69. Timothy Smith, *Revivalism and Social Reform in Mid-Nineteenth-Century America* (Nashville: Abingdon, 1957), 40 (emphasis mine).

70. Draper, interview by author.

71. Randall Balmer, "Churchgoing: Bellevue Baptist Church near Memphis," *Christian Century*, 5 May 1993, 484. This was part of a series of articles resulting from Balmer's travels to the sanctuaries considered "great churches" in 1950.

72. *Reflections of the Savior: A Silver Anniversary Celebration* (Cordova, Tenn.: Bellevue Baptist Church, 1997); Balmer, "Churchgoing," 485.

73. Quoted in Balmer, "Churchgoing," 485.

74. Rogers, interview by author. Rogers made this statement without notes on a Monday morning while sitting in his office. I could not help but think that this was a frequently used sermon excerpt.

75. Ibid.

76. Adrian Rogers, *Bring Back the Glory* (Atlanta: Walk through the Bible Ministries, 1996), 7, 9.

77. Quote in ibid., 11.

78. Rob Boston, "Consumer Alert: WallBuilders Shoddy Workmanship," *Church and State*, July–Aug. 1996, 13. For more on Barton's errors and distortions, see Rob Boston, "Sects, Lies, and Videotape"; and "David Barton's Bad History," *Church and State*, Apr. 1993, 8–11. For Barton's best known book, see *The Myth of Separation: What Is the Correct Relationship between Church and State?* (Aledo, Tex.: WallBuilders, 1989). After the flap over the erroneous quotes, the book was updated with the title *Original Intent*. WallBuilders comes from a passage in the Book of Nehemiah, chapter 2, that speaks of rebuilding the walls of Jerusalem. The name is ironic and sometimes confusing, given that Barton attacks the "wall of separation" between church and state.

79. Rogers, *Bring Back the Glory*, 56. The two cases were *Reid* v. *VanHoven* (1965) and *DeSpain* v. *Cobb County* (1967). Rogers claimed erroneously that the Supreme Court ruled against lunchtime prayer by an individual student and group nonsec-

tarian prayer by kindergartners respectively. The kindergarten prayer in question was "We thank you for the flowers sweet, we thank you for the food we eat, we thank you for the birds that sing, we thank you for everything." For examples of Barton's conflation of "Supreme Court" and "court," see Boston, "David Barton's Bad History," 12.

80. Morris Chapman, interview by author, 16 June 1998.

81. Quoted in Marsden, *Fundamentalism and American Culture,* 38.

82. Chapman, interview by author.

83. "The End of Democracy?: The Judicial Usurpation of Politics," *First Things* 67 (Nov. 1996): 18.

84. Robert Bork, "An Illegitimate Regime?" *First Things* 69 (Jan. 1997): 2 (correspondence).

85. Gertrude Himmelfarb, "An Illegitimate Regime?" *First Things* 69 (Jan. 1997): 2 (correspondence); and Walter Berns, "An Illegitimate Regime?" *First Things* 69 (Jan. 1997): 2–3 (correspondence).

86. Rogers, interview by author.

87. Land, interview by author, 1 Apr. 1997. See Charles Colson, "Kingdoms in Conflict," *First Things* 67 (Nov. 1996): 34–38.

88. Patterson, interview by author.

89. Mohler, interview by author, 5 Aug. 1997.

90. George, interview by author.

3. From CHRISTIANITY TODAY to WORLD MAGAZINE

1. See Leonard I. Sweet, ed., *The Evangelical Tradition in America* (Macon, Ga.: Mercer University Press, 1984); Marsden, *Understanding Fundamentalism and Evangelicalism;* Marsden, ed., *Evangelicalism and Modern America* (Grand Rapids, Mich.: Eerdmans, 1984); Randall Balmer, *Mine Eyes Have Seen the Glory: A Journey into the Evangelical Subculture in America,* exp. ed. (New York: Oxford University Press, 1993); Samuel S. Hill, *One Name but Several Faces: Variety in Popular Christian Denominations in Southern History* (Athens: University of Georgia Press, 1996); and Samuel S. Hill, ed., *Varieties of Southern Religious Experience* (Baton Rouge : Louisiana State University Press, 1988).

2. McBeth, *The Baptist Heritage,* 445–46. See also William Wright Barnes, *The Southern Baptist Convention, 1845–1953* (Nashville: Broadman, 1954), 120–39. For a brief discussion of how the denomination came to control the seminary more completely in 1927, see Robert Baker, *The Southern Baptist Convention and Its People, 1607–1972* (Nashville: Broadman, 1974), 435–37. See also William E. Ellis, *A Man of Books and a Man of the People: E. Y. Mullins and the Crisis of Moderate Southern Baptist Leadership* (Macon, Ga.: Mercer University Press, 1985), 107–23.

3. I am indebted to both Tim Weber and David Gushee for this analytical framework. Timothy Weber, interview by author, 19 May 1998; and David Gushee, interview by author, 16 June 1999.

4. "Covenant Renewal between Trustees, Faculty, and Administration," the Southern Baptist Theological Seminary, adopted by the seminary faculty, 28 Mar. 1991, adopted by the Board of Trustees, 8 April 1991, 3, 4, 5.

5. Timothy P. Weber, *Living in the Shadow of the Second Coming: American Premillennialism, 1875–1925* (New York: Oxford University Press, 1979); Weber, interview by author.

6. Weber, interview by author. Southern Seminary would eventually work out a Covenant of Commitment, whereby moderate faculty would be allowed to stay on, while new faculty would be required to subscribe to inerrancy and possibly other tenets of theology as well. This would allow for an evolutionary process in which moderates would be phased out of the seminary. The evolutionary process was then sped along with buyout offers for tenured faculty. See Bill J. Leonard, "Seminary Crackdown," *Christian Century,* 10 May 1995, 500-501.

7. Bill Wolfe, "Baptist Trustees Approve 5 Teachers for Seminary, Disapprove of Views," *Louisville Courier Journal,* 30 Apr. 1992. n.p.

8. Weber, interview by author. Weber jokes that he would have put his own ratio at about 82 percent.

9. Ibid.

10. Timothy Weber, "Evangelicalism North and South," *Review and Expositer* 92 (1995): 308.

11. The information on the search process at Southern circulates off the record in various Southern Baptist circles, both moderate and conservative.

12. "Up and Comers," 22.

13. Gushee, interview by author.

14. Mark Coppenger, "Who Then?" *SBC Life,* June–July 1994, 17.

15. R. Albert Mohler, interview by author, 13 Aug. 1999.

16. After our August 1999 interview, Mohler and I discussed this in more detail, and he did seem to leave open the possibility that prior to his coming to Southern, there was a period when the vision for the seminary was less than clear. The main point he would stress is that there was never an explicit policy from the trustees to make Southern moderately evangelical. For his part, Dockery prefers not to talk about the Southern situation at this time.

17. Mohler, interview by author, 13 Aug. 1999. Mohler made the point about his own hiring himself.

18. See George H. Shriver, ed., *Dictionary of Heresy Trials in American Christianity* (Westport, Conn.: Greenwood, 1997), 242–51.

19. Diana R. Garland, "When Professional Ethics and Religious Politics Conflict: A Case Study," *Social Work and Christianity* 26 (spring 1999): 63, 64. See also David Sherwood, "Editorial: A Funny Thing Happened on the Way to the Seminary," *Social Work and Christianity* 22 (fall 1995): 80.

20. See also Leslie Scanlon, "Dean at Baptist Seminary Forced to Quit," *Louisville Courier Journal,* 21 Mar. 1995, A1, A9. An article in the *Courier Journal* the next day covered Garland's version. She said she had not resigned but had been fired. See

Mark McCormick, "Dean Says Seminary Fired Her from Post," *Louisville Courier Journal,* 22 Mar. 1995, A1, A9. Garland's story is clearly the correct version, though it is possible that Mohler believed that she had acquiesced when he asked for her resignation during their meeting on 20 March. In a letter dated that day, Garland laid out her concerns to Mohler and stated explicitly that while she had planned to resign that day, "[I] decided to defer my decision to resign until I could invite other advocates for Carver School . . . to work through this crisis with me to save Carver School of Church Social Work." Diana R. Garland to Dr. R. Albert Mohler, 20 Mar. 1995, 2–3, copy in author's possession. That letter was in Mohler's office by 9:00 A.M. on 20 March. Diana Garland, conversation with author, 26 May 1999.

Subsequent to her dismissal, Garland's attorneys wrote a formal request that Mohler retract his statement that she had resigned. In a written reply, Mohler's attorneys claimed that the president had, in fact, understood Garland to have resigned during their meeting on 20 March. Herbert L. Segal to R. Albert Mohler, 29 Mar. 1995, 1; and M. Stephen Pitt to Herbert L. Segal, 14 Apr. 1995, 1, copies of both in author's possession.

For going public with Mohler's secret hiring criteria, Garland was named the recipient of the 1996 Jack Otis Whistleblower Award by the National Association of Social Workers. See Mark Wingfield, "Garland to Presbyterian Seminary; Named 'Whistle Blower,'" *Kentucky Western Recorder,* 28 May 1996, 2. This article also covers Garland's temporary position at Louisville Presbyterian Seminary.

21. Mohler, interview by author, 13 Aug. 1999.

22. Between 1992, when Weber was hired, and 1996, a year after the Carver crisis, Southern lost forty-two of its sixty-six fulltime tenure-track faculty. Three of the forty-two were scholars who had been hired since Mohler became president, but this was still prior to Weber's own departure. See Mark Wingfield, "Seminary Has Lost 59 Percent of Faculty since 1992," *Kentucky Western Recorder,* 28 May 1996, 2. When I interviewed Weber in May 1998, he had heard that the number of faculty departures had reached fifty-two out of roughly seventy.

23. Mohler, interview by author, 13 Aug. 1999.

24. Weber, interview by author.

25. Jack Harwell, "Reactions around Country Criticize Mohler for Firing Diana Garland at Southern Seminary's Carver School," *Baptists Today,* 20 Apr. 1995, 3.

26. David A. Sherwood to Dr. Albert Mohler, 3 Apr. 1995, copy in author's possession; Art Toalston, "Seminary Controversy Continues over Mohler's Dismissal of Dean," Baptist press release, 23 Mar. 1995. For a brief published version of Sherwood's own story, see "Editorial: A Funny Thing Happened on the Way to the Seminary," 79–84.

27. Faculty of the Southern Baptist Theological Seminary, "A Resolution of Support for the Carver School of Church Social Work," 5 Apr. 1995, copy in author's possession.

28. "A Report of Spiritual Distress on the Part of the Faculty of the Southern Baptist Theological Seminary," 5 Apr. 1995, copy in author's possession.

29. Mohler, interview by author, 13 Aug. 1999.

30. Weber, interview by author; Carey Newman, interview by author, 11 Aug. 1999.

31. Richard D. White, "What's Really Going on at Southern Seminary?" *Western Recorder*, 18 Apr. 1995, 6.

32. Weber, interview by author; Newman, interview by author.

33. Weber, interview by author.

34. Quoted in Mark Wingfield, "Faced with Crisis, Trustees Stand by Their Man," *Kentucky Western Recorder*, 25 Apr. 1995.

35. David Sherwood, interview by author, 24 June 1999.

36. Ibid.

37. This is my own impression of Sherwood after having spent time both in his home and office. I have found no one who would challenge this characterization.

38. Sherwood, interview by author.

39. Ibid.

40. Janet Furness Spressart, interview by author, 24 June 1999.

41. Ibid.

42. Ibid. This faculty meeting took place seven to ten days before the student-faculty meeting of 20 March 1995, when Garland went public with Mohler's criteria.

43. Janet Furness Spressart, "Statement to ATS/SACS/CSWE Site Team," 9 Nov. 1995, 2, copy in author's possession.

44. Spressart, interview by author.

45. Spressart, "Statement to ATS/SACS/CSWE Site Team," 4.

46. Spressart, interview by author.

47. David Gushee to author (e-mail), 3 Jan. 2000.

48. All the biographical background information on Gushee is based on Gushee, interview by author.

49. Gushee, interview by author.

50. David Gushee, "The Tragedy of Christian Lovelessness," ABC Annual Meeting, 29 Apr. 1995, Scottsburg; sermon manuscript copy in author's possession.

51. David Gushee, "Learning again the Way of Love," *Prism*, May–June 1997, 15. *Prism* was called the *ESA Advocate* when Gushee was editor.

52. Gushee, interview by author.

53. Ibid.

54. Newman, interview by author.

55. Gushee, interview by author.

56. Gushee to author, 3 Jan. 2000.

57. See "Up and Comers," 30.

58. Gushee, "Learning again the Way of Love," 12, 15.

59. Gushee to author, 3 Jan. 2000.

60. Newman, interview by author.

61. Ibid.

62. Ibid.

63. Ibid.
64. Ibid.
65. Ibid.
66. Mohler, interview by author, 13 Aug. 1999.
67. This somewhat subjective measure is based on impressions from the interviews I have done. When discussing the Black Wednesday faculty meeting, all those interviewed point to Weber and Chancellor as the ones who took the lead in articulating what the rest of the faculty were feeling. Newman goes so far as to say that the holdover moderates did not even know how to fight for Garland and that the new evangelical Covenant faculty were the ones who took up the challenge. Newman, interview by author.
68. Newman, interview by author.
69. Mohler, interview by author, 13 Aug. 1999.
70. Weber, interview by author.
71. Ibid. On this point, see Weber, "Evangelicalism North and South."
72. Weber, interview by author.
73. Ibid.

4. THE SEARCH FOR A USEABLE PAST

1. Paige Patterson, interview by author, 20 May 1997.
2. Hunter, *Culture Wars,* 44.
3. Richard Land, interview by author, 1 Apr. 1997.
4. Timothy George, interview by author, 24 Aug. 1998.
5. Laurie Goodstein, "Religious Right, Frustrated, Trying New Tactic on G.O.P.," *The New York Times,* 23 Mar. 1998, 12.
6. Gary Parker, "Confusing Trends in Baptist Life," *Baptists Today,* 24 Sept. 1998, 26.
7. Land, interview by author, 16 June 1998; J. Bradley Creed, "John Leland, American Prophet of Religious Individualism," (Ph.D. diss., Southwestern Baptist Theological Seminary, 1986), 45–46.
8. See, for example, J. Brent Walker, "Coalitions a Necessity to Get Things Done in Washington," *Report from the Capital,* 13 Oct. 1998, 3. While generally defending the BJC practice of entering into coalitions on specific issues with groups that do not share Baptist theology, Walker was possibly making a veiled reference to Land's *New York Times* quote when he wrote, "If [the coalition] is more like a marriage partnership or formal alliance—such as the relationship we have with participating Baptist bodies—then we insist upon a confluence of beliefs, values and assumptions."
9. Among the many places where Criswell's statement has been cited are Richard Pierard, "Separation of Church and State: Figment of an Infidel's Imagination?" in *Faith and Freedom: A Tribute to Franklin H. Littell,* ed. Richard Libowitz (New York: Pergamon, 1987), 143; and Richard V. Pierard, "Religion and the 1984 Election Campaign," *Review of Religious Research* 27(1985): 104–5.

10. Cecil E. Sherman, "An Overview of the Moderate Movement," in *The Struggle for the Soul of the SBC: Moderate Responses to the Fundamentalists Movement*, ed. Walter B. Shurden (Macon, Ga.: Mercer University Press, 1993), 34–35. Sherman emerged in the 1980s as the most important leader of the moderate counterattack once it became clear that conservatives were taking control of the SBC.

11. Paige Patterson, interview by author.

12. Draper, interview by author.

13. Leonard, *God's Last and Only Hope*, 139; Morgan, *New Crusades*, 60–63.

14. Rogers, interview by author.

15. Mohler, interview by author, 5 Aug. 1997; George, interview by author.

16. Rob Boston, *The Most Dangerous Man in America? Pat Robertson and the Rise of the Christian Coalition* (Amherst, N.Y.: Prometheus Books, 1996), 70.

17. Mohler, interview by author, 5 Aug. 1997.

18. Paige Patterson, interview by author.

19. Gary North and Gary DeMar, *Christian Reconstruction: What It Is, What It Isn't* (Tyler, Tex. : Institute for Christian Economics, 1991).

20. Baptists Committed to the Southern Baptist Convention, "Struggle for the Baptist Soul," Southern Baptist Archives, Nashville.

21. "Book and Tape Catalog," Dominion Press, Fort Worth, Tex., Southern Baptist Archives, Nashville.

22. Paul Pressler, interview by Gary North, 1987 (Fort Worth: Dominion Tapes, 1988). There is a transcript of this interview in Dennis Ray Wiles, "Factors Contributing to the Resurgence of Fundamentalism in the Southern Baptist Convention, 1979–1990" (Ph.D. diss., Southern Baptist Theological Seminary, 1992), 287–319. North's book on the Presbyterian controversy is *Crossed Fingers: How the Liberals Captured the Presbyterian Church* (Tyler, Tex.: Institute for Christian Economics, 1996), xvi (quote). In the footnote, North writes, "Paul Pressler and Paige Patterson deserve far more than this footnote for what they engineered, 1977–1990."

23. Draper and Watson, *If the Foundations*, v.

24. Draper, interview by author.

25. Mohler, interview by author, 5 Aug. 1997. The recent book that confirmed Mohler's view of Calvin is Robert Kingdon, *Adultery and Divorce in Calvin's Geneva* (Cambridge: Harvard University Press, 1995). Kingdon shows that while Geneva did execute adulterers in extreme cases, this was done as a matter of public order and morality, not on the basis of a Levitical theocracy.

26. George, interview by author.

27. Rogers, interview by author. George also emphasizes that he is not a theonomist and that his premillennialism is inconsistent with that position.

28. John Muether, "The Theonomic Attraction," in *Theonomy: A Reformed Critique*, ed. William S. Barker and W. Robert Godfrey (Grand Rapids, Mich.: Academie Books, 1990), 249–50.

29. Robertson was quoted in 1987 as saying, "I admire many of these (Reconstruction) teachings because they are in line with Scripture. But others I cannot accept because they do not correspond with the biblical view of the sinful nature of

mankind or the necessity of the second coming of Christ." See Rodney Clapp, "Democracy as Heresy," *Christianity Today*, 29 Feb. 1987, 21. According to one author, Robertson fired professor Herbert Titus from the Regent University School of Law because of Titus's "strict dominion views." See Alec Foege, *The Empire God Built: Inside Pat Robertson's Media Machine* (New York: John Wiley and Sons, 1996), 176. Harvard theologian Harvey Cox has argued that Robertson has moved from a premillennial to a postmillennial view, though not full-blown Reconstructionism. See Harvey Cox, "The Warring Visions of the Religious Right," *The Atlantic Monthly*, Nov. 1995, 59–69; he cites Bruce Barron, *Heaven on Earth? The Social and Political Agendas of Dominion Theology* (Grand Rapids, Mich.: Zondervan, 1992), which has a chapter on Robertson and Regent University. Barron believes that Robertson holds a moderating position that avoids full-blown Reconstructionism. A solid, though dated, biography of Robertson is David Edwin Harrell Jr., *Pat Robertson: A Personal, Religious, and Political Portrait* (San Francisco: Harper and Row, 1987). Most of the televangelist's alleged postmillennial and Reconstructionist tendencies have surfaced since Harrell's book appeared.

30. Land, interview by author, 1 Apr. 1997; Mohler, interview by author, 5 Aug. 1997.

31. Paige Patterson, interview by author.

32. See Hunter, *Culture Wars*, 135–58 (chap. entitled "The Discourse of Adversaries").

33. James Dunn, panel discussion, Lilly Fellows Program in the Humanities and Arts, Baylor University, 19 Oct. 1997.

34. Mohler, interview by author, 5 Aug. 1997.

35. Ibid.

36. George Marsden, *The Soul of the University* (New York: Oxford University Press, 1994), 435–36.

37. See: George Marsden, *Religion and American Culture* (New York: Harcourt Brace Jovanovich, 1990), 6. He writes: "So the story of religion in American culture is not that of a simple move from the religious to the secular. Rather, it is the story of the repositioning of the religious and the secular in an emerging modern society. This repositioning may have momentous implications for the culture as a whole. Yet religious communities may flourish better than ever."

38. Mohler, interview by author, 5 Aug. 1997.

39. George, interview by author. In our session, George said he could not fully accept any of Niebuhr's five types. When I characterized his views as "Christ-transforming-culture with an Anabaptist bias," he agreed that was accurate.

40. George, interview by author.

41. Land, interview by author, 1 Apr. 1997.

42. Ibid.

43. Ibid.

44. Land, "Responses," 103.

45. This is almost exactly how James Draper Jr. puts it. Draper, interview by author.

46. Land, "Responses," 103.

47. Ibid., 101.

48. *Ronald W. Rosenberger* v. *Rector and Visitors of the University of Virginia* 115 Sup. Ct. 2510 (1995).

49. Carl Esbeck, "Five Views of Church-State Relations in Contemporary American Thought," *Brigham Young University Law Review* no. 2 (1986): 371–404.

50. James Dunn, "Christian Citizenship and Political Advocacy," address at the Lilly Fellows program "The City of God Revisited: Church and State in the Twenty-First Century," Baylor University, 18 Oct. 1997.

51. Sherman, "Overview of the Moderate Movement," 34.

52. Draper and Watson, *If the Foundations*, 99, 98, 100. Emphasis in the original.

53. Ibid.

54. See as examples Barton, *Myth of Separation;* and David Barton, *Original Intent: The Courts, The Constitution, and Religion* (Aledo, Tex.: WallBuilders, 1997).

55. Draper, interview by author.

56. William McLoughlin, *Isaac Backus on Church, State, and Calvinism: Pamphlets, 1754–1789* (Cambridge: Harvard University Press, Belknap Press, 1968), 50–51, 436. Stanley Grenz challenges McLoughlin's assessment of the Backus quote in his book (based on his dissertation), *Isaac Backus: Puritan and Baptist* (Macon, Ga.: Mercer University Press, 1983), 175–76. Grenz argues that Backus cited the test oath favorably only because it was an improvement over the days when officeholders had to swear to both Christ and the king of England. He points out, moreover, that some lines later Backus wrote, "our Divine Lord and the great apostle of the Gentiles explicitly renounced any judicial power over the world by virtue of their religion" (Grenz, 175; McLoughlin, 437). Grenz's view, however, seems difficult to reconcile with the actual wording chosen by Backus who wrote, "For the following reasons convince me that God has now set before us an open door for equal Christian liberty." Reason three was, "No man can take a seat in our legislature till he solemnly declares 'I believe the Christian religion'"; he does not say that legislators have *only* to swear to the Christian faith and not the king. There is nothing whatsoever about the absence of a kingly oath being what makes this test oath commendable.

57. McLoughlin, *Isaac Backus on Church, State, and Calvinism*, 51 n. 33.

58. Edwin S. Gaustad, "The Backus-Leland Tradition," *Foundations* 2 (Apr. 1959): 134.

59. Creed, "John Leland, American Prophet of Religious Individualism," 202.

60. Gaustad, "Backus-Leland Tradition," 140.

61. McLoughlin, *Isaac Backus on Church, State, and Calvinism*, 51 n. 33.

62. Gaustad, "Backus-Leland Tradition," 145, 133.

63. Edwin S. Gaustad, "Religious Liberty: Baptists and Some Fine Distinctions," *American Baptist Quarterly* 6 (Dec. 1987): 220, 222, 223.

64. Steven H. Fennell, "Harmony or High Wall: A Comparison of the Views of John Leland and Isaac Backus Concerning Church-State Relations," (Th.M. thesis, Southeastern Baptist Theological Seminary, 1989), 106–8, 112.

65. Richard D. Land, interview by author, 16 June 1998.

66. For examples see Joseph M. Dawson, *Baptists and the American Republic* (Nashville: Broadman, 1956); T. B. Maston, *Isaac Backus: Pioneer of Religious Liberty* (Rochester, N.Y.: American Baptist Historical Society, 1962); Robert Baker, "Baptists and Religious Liberty in the Revolutionary Era," in *The Lord's Free People*, ed. W. R. Estep (Fort Worth, Tex.: Southwestern Baptist Theological Seminary, 1976), 75–85. William R. Estep, *Revolution within the Revolution* (Grand Rapids, Mich.: Eerdmans, 1990). Dawson views Backus as the successor of Roger Williams and John Clarke. Like Gaustad, Estep analyzes the differences between Backus and Leland, noting that the former was not as consistent as Roger Williams. Leland, however, represents the truer, more mature aspect of the Baptist tradition that had more influence on the new nation (Estep, 117). Estep tends to see Leland's work as a logical extension of Backus's (Estep, 111).

67. James Dunn, "The Baptist Vision of Religious Liberty," 34; and Walter B. Shurden, "How We Got That Way," 18; both in *Reclaiming the Baptist Vision: Religious Liberty*, ed. Walter B. Shurden (Macon, Ga.: Smyth and Helwys, 1997).

68. William McLoughlin, "Isaac Backus and Separation of Church and State," in *The Marrow of American Divinity*, ed. Peter Hoffer (New York: Garland, 1988), 222–23; the essay was originally published in *The American Historical Review* 73 (1968): 1392–1413.

69. C. C. Goen, "Baptists and Church-State Issues in the Twentieth Century," in *Modern American Protestantism and Its World: Historical Articles on Protestantism in American Life*, vol. 3, *Civil Religion, Church and State*, ed. Martin Marty (New York: K. G. Saur, 1992), 109, 111; the essay was originally published in *American Baptist Quarterly* 6 (Dec. 1987): 226–53.

70. Coppenger, interview by author; and George, interview by author.

71. William McLoughlin, *New England Dissent 1630–1833: The Baptists and Separation of Church and State* (Cambridge: Harvard University Press, 1971), 1:605, 606; McLoughlin, "Isaac Backus and Separation of Church and State," 230. See also: Joe L. Coker, "Sweet Harmony vs. Strict Separation: Recognizing the Distinctions between Isaac Backus and John Leland," *American Baptist Quarterly* 16 (Sept. 1997): 241–48.

72. Sherman, "Overview of the Moderate Movement," 35.

73. Melissa Rogers, "Baptists and the Establishment Clause: Our Commitment and Challenge," in *Baptists in the Balance: The Tension between Freedom and Responsibility*, ed. Everett C. Goodwin (Valley Forge, Pa.: Judson, 1997), 291–305. When she wrote this article, Rogers was counsel for the Baptist Joint Committee.

74. George, "Between Pacifism and Coercion," 39, 49.

75. McLoughlin, *Isaac Backus on Church, State, and Calvinism*, 50–51. Backus's support for a religious test for office is cited in Draper and Watson, *If the Foundations*, 99. On the next page they say Backus went too far in supporting government-paid missionaries. It is not clear that he actually supported state aid for missionaries, but some Massachusetts Baptists did.

76. William Henry Brackney, *The Baptists* (New York: Greenwood, 1988), 105.

77. For a representative moderate view that separation of church and state is a means toward the goal of religious liberty, see Derek H. Davis, ed., *The Separation of Church and State Defended: Selected Writings of James E. Wood Jr.* (Waco, Tex.: J. M. Dawson Institute of Church-State Studies, 1995), 27–28. It should be noted that Wood's view differs from those who say that the Establishment Clause is subservient to the Free Exercise Clause, as if the former were a means to the latter.

78. Bill Leonard, "Southern Baptists and the Separation of Church and State," *Review and Expositor* 83 (spring 1986): 195.

5. Using a Useable Past

1. Edwin S. Gaustad, "Colonial Religion and Liberty of Conscience," in *The Virginia Statute for Religious Freedom: Its Evolution and Consequences in American History*, ed. Merril D. Peterson and Robert C. Vaughan (New York: Cambridge University Press, 1988), 23.

2. Coker, "Sweet Harmony vs. Strict Separation," 248; McLoughlin, "Isaac Backus and Separation of Church and State," 222.

3. McLoughlin, "Isaac Backus and Separation of Church and State," 222–23, 230 (quote on 230).

4. Land, interview by author, 1 Apr. 1997; Richard D. Land, "A Baptist's View of Prayer in Schools," Critical Issues Pamphlet (Nashville: Southern Baptist Christian Life Commission, 1995), 11.

5. Ira C. Lupu, "Reconstructing the Establishment Clause: The Case against Discretionary Accommodation of Religion," *University of Pennsylvania Law Review* 140 (1991): 559.

6. Michael McConnell, "Accommodation of Religion: An Update and a Response to the Critics," *The George Washington Law Review* 60 (Mar. 1992): 687, 686.

7. For a helpful discussion of various church-state positions, see Esbeck, "Five Views of Church-State Relations," 371–404. For an article specifically addressing Southern Baptists, see Robert Linder, "Shall the Accommodationists Win? Religious Liberty in the Balance in the Closing Decades of the Twentieth Century," *Southwestern Journal of Theology* 36, no. 3 (summer 1994): 37–44.

8. *Rosenberger* v. *University of Virginia*.

9. Lupu, "Reconstructing the Establishment Clause," 557. Cases where accommodationist principles have won the day include *Corporation of the Presiding Bishop of the Church of Jesus Christ of Latter-Day Saints* v. *Amos* 483 U.S. 327 (1987), and *Texas Monthly* v. *Bullock* 489 U.S. 1 (1989). Other cases in which nonpreferentialism, equal access, or other accommodationist principles have been at work include *Wallace* v. *Jaffree* 472 U.S. 38(1985); *Rosenberger* v. *University of Virginia;* and *Lambs Chapel* v. *Center Moriches Union Free School District* 508 U.S. 384 (1993). In *Wallace,* a moment-of-silence law in Alabama was struck down, but the Supreme Court stipulated that other such provisions might pass muster if framed with proper intent. Also, Justice

William Rehnquist's dissent in *Wallace* can be considered a classic articulation of the accommodationist position.

10. Quoted in Jay Grelen, "Ripping down RFRA," *World* 12–19 July 1997, 19.

11. See *Employment Division, Department of Human Resources of Oregon* v. *Smith* 494 U.S. 872 (1990). This case can be found in Robert T. Miller and Ronald B. Flowers, eds., *Toward Benevolent Neutrality: Church, State, and the Supreme Court*, 5th ed. (Waco, Tex.: Baylor University Press, 1996), 709.

12. *City of Boerne* v. *P. F. Flores* 521 U.S. 507 (1997). The text of this case can also be found in *Journal of Church and State* 39 (autumn 1997): 846.

13. *The Baptist Faith and Message*, sec. 17, "Religious Liberty" (Nashville: The Sunday School Board of the Southern Baptist Convention, 1963), 19.

14. *Rosenberger* v. *University of Virginia*, 25. The Court writes, "The course of action [excluding a Christian periodical from access to university funds provided for other student magazines] was a denial of the right of free speech and would risk fostering a pervasive bias or hostility to religion, which could undermine the very neutrality the Establishment Clause requires."

15. Paige Patterson, interview by author.

16. Rogers, interview by author.

17. Wayne Flynt, *Alabama Baptists: Southern Baptists in the Heart of Dixie* (Tuscaloosa: University of Alabama Press, 1998), 543. Flynt says that a survey of the 1978 SBC meeting revealed that three-fourths of the 23,000 messengers were on either denominational or church payrolls.

18. "Resolution No. 11—On the First Amendment," *Annual of the Southern Baptist Convention* (Nashville: Southern Baptist Convention, 1969), 76.

19. "Resolution No. 8—On Voluntary Prayer," *Annual of the Southern Baptist Convention* (Nashville: Southern Baptist Convention, 1971), 78; "Resolution No. 2— Religious Liberty," *Annual of the Southern Baptist Convention* (Nashville: Southern Baptist Convention, 1964), 80. The constitutional amendment proposed in Congress at the time of the 1964 SBC resolution was often called the Becker amendment, named after its primary sponsor.

20. Quoted in "Resolutions Stir Heated Debate among Messengers," *Texas Baptist Standard*, 27 May 1964, 10.

21. See, for example, Wayne Flynt's discussion of Baptist responses to the Becker and Dirksen amendments in Alabama in the 1960s. There, elite Baptist leaders seem to have played a key role in convincing most of the state's U.S. representatives to vote against Becker. A barrage of criticism then issued forth from grassroots Baptists who feared the secularization of the schools. When the Dirksen amendment followed Becker, the editor of the newspaper *Alabama Baptist* backed away from the issue, noting that there were Baptists on both sides of the prayer in schools debate. *Alabama Baptists*, 490–91.

22. "Resolution No. 13—On Voluntary Prayer in Public Schools," *Annual of the Southern Baptist Convention* (Nashville: Southern Baptist Convention, 1980), 49.

23. Bill Moyers, *God and Politics: The Battle for the Bible* (Princeton, N.J.: Films for the Humanities, 1994), videocassette.

24. "Resolution No. 9—On Prayer in Schools," *Annual of the Southern Baptist Convention* (Nashville: Southern Baptist Convention, 1982), 58.

25. "Resolution No. 6—On the First Amendment and Religious Liberty," *Annual of the Southern Baptist Convention* (Nashville: Southern Baptist Convention, 1986), 75.

26. "Resolution No. 5—On Free Exercise in Public Schools," *Annual of the Southern Baptist Convention* (Nashville: Southern Baptist Convention, 1992), 88.

27. Flynt, *Alabama Baptists*, 578.

28. Rogers, interview by author.

29. Land, "A Baptist's View of Prayer in Schools," 11–13. Land does not mention the earth-goddess Gaea in this pamphlet, but he used it as a further example in our April 1997 interview.

30. A 1997 Gallup poll on religious preference showed that 58 percent of Americans cite Protestant as their religious preference and 25 cite Roman Catholic; 3 percent preferred Judaism. See Princeton Religion Research Center, "Latest Religious Preferences," *Emerging Trends* 19 (Mar. 1997): 3.

31. Land, "A Baptist's View of Prayer in Schools," 12.

32. See Jay P. Dolan, *The American Catholic Experience: A History from Colonial Times to the Present* (Garden City, N.Y.: Doubleday, 1985), 270–71.

33. See Robert T. Handy, *Undermined Establishment: Church-State Relations in America, 1880–1920* (Princeton, N.J.: Princeton University Press, 1991), 47. Here, Handy quotes Robert H. Keller Jr., "[N]ot until American Catholicism began to grow in size did 'strict separation' become a Protestant constitutional doctrine." See Keller, *American Protestantism and United States Indian Policy, 1869–1882* (Lincoln: University of Nebraska Press, 1983), 214. Handy then adds: "[This doctrine] was a response to the mounting challenge to Protestant power. Attitudes of many Catholic [*sic*] and Protestants, hardened in this period of intense school controversy, persisted well into the next century. The conceptual wall of separation between church and state had been raised higher in many minds."

34. Glenn L. Archer, "Freedom in Schools," *Texas Baptist Standard*, 13 May 1959, 11.

35. C. Stanley Lowell, "Battle of the Century," *Texas Baptist Standard*, 12 Apr. 1958, 6, 7.

36. Joseph M. Dawson, "Temptations of the Churches," *Texas Baptist Standard*, 23 July 1955, 6. See also Walker L. Knight, "POAU Reveals Texas Violations," *Texas Baptist Standard*, 20 May 1954, 3.

37. Flynt, *Alabama Baptists*, 486.

38. Ibid., 578.

39. "Resolution No. 6—Public and Private Education," *Annual of the Southern Baptist Convention* (Nashville: Southern Baptist Convention, 1970), 79.

40. "Resolution No. 9—On Parental Choice on Education," *Annual of the Southern Baptist Convention* (Nashville: Southern Baptist Convention, 1996), 96.

41. Land, interview by author, 1 Apr. 1997.

42. "Light from the Capital: CLC Supports Inclusion of Religious Schools in Program," *Light,* Mar.–Apr. 1996, 14.

43. Land, interview by author, 1 Apr. 1997.

44. Rogers, interview by author; Draper, interview by author.

45. Joseph L. Conn, "Armed and Dangerous?" *Church and State* 50 (Mar. 1997): 9.

46. See most recently *Capitol Square Review and Advisory Board* v. *Vincent J. Pinette, Donnie A. Carr, and Knights of the Ku Klux Klan,* 115 Sup. Ct. 2440 (1995), commonly referred to as *Capitol Square* v. *Pinette;* Miller and Flowers, *Toward Benevolent Neutrality,* 218. Other cases dealing with private religious exercise or displays on public property are *Widmar* v. *Vincent* 454 U.S. 263 (1981); *Lynch* v. *Donnelly* 465 U.S. 668 (1984); and *Allegheny County* v. *ACLU of Pittsburgh* 492 U.S. 573 (1989).

47. For a concise history of the first draft of the Istook amendment, see Derek Davis, "Editorial: Assessing the Proposed Religious Equality Amendment," *Journal of Church and State* 37 (summer 1995): 493–508.

48. Quoted in ibid., 494.

49. "Resolution No. 5—On a Constitutional Amendment Regarding Prayer and Religious Expression," *Annual of the Southern Baptist Convention* (Nashville: Southern Baptist Convention, 1995), 93. A copy of this resolution can also be found in *Light,* Sept.–Oct. 1995, 13.

50. *Baptist Faith and Message,* sec. 17, p. 19.

51. Land, interview by author, 1 Apr. 1997.

52. See *Report from the Capital,* 6 May 1997, 1.

53. Richard Land and Will Dodson, "A Summary Analysis of Rep. Ernest Istook's Proposed Constitutional Amendment" (unpublished paper, copy in author's possession). Emphasis in the original. This was a three-page statement that resembled, and may have been, a press release. Land and Patterson both made a point of telling me, as a good-natured ribbing, that Istook is a Baylor graduate.

54. Anticipating the *Boerne* decision, Land asked rhetorically in the months leading up to the case what the position of the BJC might be if RFRA were overturned.

55. Mohler, interview by author, 5 Aug. 1997.

56. Another SBC conservative related this to me off the record.

57. Land and Dodson, "Summary Analysis." The words in parentheses are Land and Dodson's.

58. Land, interview by author, 1 Apr. 1997. Separationists reject the notion that they are concerned with the Establishment Clause to the detriment of free exercise. Wood, for example, has argued that the two clauses are equally necessary to achieve religious liberty. See James E. Wood Jr., "Editorial: Separation Vis-à-vis Accommodation: A New Direction in American Church-State Relations?" *Journal of Church and State* 31 (spring 1989): 202.

59. Paige Patterson, "My Vision for the Twenty-first Century SBC," *Review and Expositor* 88 (winter 1991): 48. This notion that the Free Exercise Clause has been unattended in recent years is pervasive among accommodationists. See, for example, Richard John Neuhaus, "A New Order of Religious Freedom," *The George Washington Law Review* 60 (Mar. 1992): 627–28. Here, Neuhaus writes: "In recent history, especially in the last four decades, the priority of free exercise has been dangerously obscured. . . . One gets the distinct impression from some constitutional scholars and, all too often, from the courts that avoiding establishment is the end to which free exercise is something of a nuisance."

60. Ira C. Lupu, "The Trouble with Accommodation," *The George Washington Law Review* 60 (Mar. 1992): 780.

61. Land, "Will It Be Faith in Practice?" 3; "Struggle for the Right to Be Involved"; and interview by author, 1 Apr. 1997.

62. Matt. 22:21 New American Standard Version (1977).

63. Walter B. Shurden, "How We Got We That Way," in *Reclaiming the Baptist Vision*, 2.

6. No One Has Been Shot Yet

1. James Davison Hunter, *Before the Shooting Begins: Searching for Democracy in America's Culture War* (New York: Free Press, 1994), 13.

2. John Rawls, *A Theory of Justice* (Cambridge: Harvard University Press, 1971), 213.

3. See John Rawls, *Political Liberalism* (New York: Columbia University Press, 1993).

4. Rawls, *A Theory of Justice*, 12.

5. For an argument that religious people should find secular reasons for the positions they advocate in the public square, and for a critique of that position from a Christian Reformed perspective, see Robert Audi and Nicolas Wolterstorff, *Religion in the Public Square: The Place of Religious Convictions in Political Debate* (Lanham, Md.: Rowman and Littlefield, 1997).

6. Oran P. Smith, *The Rise of Baptist Republicanism* (New York: New York University Press, 1997), 90.

7. See James Guth, "Southern Baptists and the New Right," in *Religion in American Politics*, ed., Charles W. Dunn (Washington D.C.: CQ Press, 1989), 177–90; and Guth, "The Politics of Preachers: Southern Baptist Ministers and Christian Right Activism," in *New Christian Politics*, ed. David G. Bromley and Anson Shupe (Macon, Ga.: Mercer University Press, 1984), 235–49.

8. Smith, *Rise of Baptist Republicanism*, 91.

9. Quoted in Laurie Lattimore, "Campolo a Biblical 'Conservative,' but His Views Controversial," *Texas Baptists Committed Newsletter*, June 1997, 11. This article was circulated by the Alabama Baptist Press and originally appeared in the *Alabama Baptist*.

10. Guth, "Southern Baptists and the New Right," 180. Guth writes, "Not surprisingly, Moral Majority activists [among SBC ministers] and opponents [of the Moral Majority] tend to focus on different issues: the former concentrate on Israel, homosexuality, school prayer, and pornography, while the latter show more concern for hunger and poverty, economic issues, environmental concerns, and civil rights."

11. "Abortion Decision: Death Blow?" *Christianity Today*, 16 Feb. 1973, 48.

12. James Draper, who was at one time a Criswell associate, reads the statement as evidence that hardly anyone in the SBC had given abortion much thought before 1973. Draper, interview by author, 2 June 1997.

13. Press release, Baptists Committed to the SBC, 1986, Southern Baptist Archives, Nashville. It was also widely reported in state Baptist newspapers.

14. Toby Druin, "Patterson, Reporter Differ on Hiring Story," *Texas Baptist Standard*, 9 July 1986, 5.

15. Land, interview by author, 16 June 1998.

16. Kenneth Hayes, "Baptists Oppose Legalized Abortions," *Kentucky Western Recorder*, 9 May 1970, 7. Later that year another VIEWpoll found that majorities of 60–70 percent favored legalized abortions when the mental or physical health of the woman was threatened, when there was clear deformity of the unborn fetus, or in pregnancies resulting from rape or incest. See "Abortion Law Revisions Favored," *Kentucky Western Recorder*, 19 Sept. 1970, 10.

17. Quoted in Ray Waddle, "S. Baptists Ban Speakers Backing Abortion Rights," *The Tennessean*, 9 Mar. 1990, 4A. For the details of this survey, see Nancy T. Ammerman, "Organizational Conflict in the Southern Baptist Convention," in *Secularization and Fundamentalism Reconsidered*, vol. 3, *Religion and the Political Order*, ed. Jeffrey K. Hadden and Anson Shupe (New York: Paragon House, 1986), 133–51.

18. Smith, *Rise of Baptist Republicanism*, 160.

19. *Issues and Answers: Abortion* (Nashville: Christian Life Commission, n.d.), 5.

20. "Abortion Issue: A Baptist Ethicist Shares His Insights (Interview with Foy Valentine)," *Light*, Mar. 1985, 9.

21. Ibid.

22. Druin, "Patterson, Reporter Differ on Hiring Story," 5.

23. Dan McGee, "The Abortion Debate: Recognizing All the Issues," *Therefore: The Newsletter of the Texas Baptist Christian Life Commission*, spring 1986, 3. The article was originally an address to the 1986 statewide workshop of the Texas CLC.

24. Cecil Sherman, "The Idea of Being Baptist," *Light*, May 1983, 3–4 (quotes on 4), 2–3.

25. James E. Wood Jr., "Religious Liberty and Abortion Rights," *Report from the Capital* 29 (Jan. 1974): 2.

26. A written affidavit in the case *Jane Doe et al* v. *Helen O'Bannon*, Civil Action 81-0555, Class Action, U.S. District Court for the Eastern District of Pennsylvania, 6.

27. Ibid., 6, 7.

28. Simmons quoted in "Abortion Issue Shifts," *Texas Baptist Standard,* 8 Sept. 1976, 17.

29. Mohler, interview by author, 5 Aug. 1997. My own experience studying with James Wood at Baylor in the early 1980s is similar to Mohler's at Southern. In Wood's seminars he frequently broached the abortion issue in a variety of contexts, always advocating the pro-choice position.

30. Paul D. Simmons, "A Theological Response to Fundamentalism on the Abortion Issue," vertical file, "Abortion—Baptists" folder, J. M. Dawson Institute of Church-State Studies, 1, 29. This lecture was later published in adapted form using the same title in *Church and Society,* 71 (Mar.–Apr. 1981): 22–35. For another reference to the biblical and religious liberty arguments, see Simmons, "Bioethical Issues in Christian Perspective," *Light,* Mar.–Apr. 1983, 5.

31. Simmons, "Theological Response to Fundamentalism on the Abortion Issue," 29.

32. Ibid., 30, 33.

33. Gushee to author (e-mail), 3 Jan. 2000. Gushee remembers Simmons's classroom discussions on abortion to be more biblical than Rawlsian.

34. Simmons, "Bioethical Issues in Christian Perspective," 5.

35. Gushee to author, 3 Jan. 2000.

36. Paul Simmons, "Religious Liberty and the Abortion Debate," *Journal of Church and State* 32 (summer 1990): 577.

37. Ibid., 572–73 575, 577. Simmons reiterated these points, in light of a more recent U.S. Supreme Court decision, in "Religious Liberty and Abortion Policy: *Casey* as 'Catch-22,'" *Journal of Church and State* 42 (winter 2000): 69–88. In this article he urged the Court to consider abortion a religious right protected by the First Amendment. He also once again used Rawls to argue that law should not be based on metaphysical constructs.

38. Simmons, "Religious Liberty and the Abortion Debate," 583, 584.

39. "Resolution No. 4—On Abortion," *Annual* (1971), 72.

40. Wood, "Religious Liberty and Abortion Rights," 2; Timothy George, "Southern Baptist Heritage of Life," in *Life at Risk: The Crisis in Medical Ethics,* ed. Richard D. Land and Louis A. Moore (Nashville: Broadman and Holman, 1995), 83.

41. George, "Southern Baptist Heritage of Life," 83.

42. *Annual of the Southern Baptist Convention* (Nashville: Southern Baptist Convention, 1976), 57–58.

43. The words "limited role of government" were often interpreted to mean opposition to any constitutional amendment prohibiting abortion. See "Abortion Change Loses," *Texas Baptist Standard,* 23 June 1976, 9.

44. "Resolution No. 13—Abortion," *Annual of the Southern Baptist Convention* (Nashville: Southern Baptist Convention, 1977), 53.

45. *Annual of the Southern Baptist Convention* (Nashville: Southern Baptist Convention, 1979), 50.

46. "Resolution No. 10—On Abortion," *Annual* (1980), 48–49.

47. David Briggs, "Southern Baptists Urge Abortion Limits," *Las Vegas Review Journal,* 16 June 1989.

48. Robert Parham, "Abortion: Some Common Ground," *Light,* Oct. 1986, 9–10. The Christian Life Commission was still under moderate control in 1986 but would not be for long.

49. James L. Franklin, "Baptists and Abortions," *Boston Globe,* 7 July 1980, 6.

50. U.S. Congress, House, "Extension of Remarks," *Congressional Record,* 96th Cong., 2d sess., 26 June 1980, E3258. Ashbrook must have meant to say "the absurdity of the pro-life movement as a Catholic Bishop's plot." This is the only way I can make sense of his statement.

51. Franklin, "Baptists and Abortions," 6.

52. McAteer and Wood quoted in ibid.

53. Baptist colleges and universities, such as Baylor, are under the auspices of their state conventions, not the SBC. Wood (when he was at Baylor) as well as McGee, therefore, were not denominational employees as were agency heads and seminary professors like Valentine and Simmons respectively.

54. See "Christian Life Commission Announces New Resources for Sanctity of Human Life Sunday, January 18, 1987," *Light,* Nov.–Dec. 1986, 12.As for pamphlets, see "Special 1986 Atlanta Convention Edition: Do You Know the Facts about Abortion-on-Demand?" vertical file, "Abortion—Baptists" folder, J. M. Dawson Institute of Church-State Studies. James Draper Jr. told me that in the early 1980s his church, First Baptist, Euless, was using the Schaeffer films to mobilize congregants on the abortion issue. Draper, interview by author.

55. Larry Baker, "Reflections," *Light,* Nov.–Dec. 1987, 2; "Abortion: A Challenge for Baptists," *Light,* Nov.–Dec. 1987, 4–6, 16.

56. Quoted in Ray Waddle, "Besieged Baptist Director Sought as Pastor," *The Tennessean,* 12 May 1988, 3B.

57. David Morgan recounts the transition from Valentine to Baker to Land in *New Crusades,* 108–14. A similar account is given by Grady C. Cothen, former president of the Baptist Sunday School Board, in his book, *What Happened to the Southern Baptist Convention?* (Macon, Ga.: Smyth and Helwys, 1993), 350–56.

58. See respectively *Florida Baptist Witness,* 1 Mar. 1990; *Baptist New Mexican,* 10 Mar. 1990; *Baptist True Union* (Maryland/Delaware), 15 Feb. 1990; and *North Carolina Biblical Recorder,* 17 Feb. 1990. Among the other state or area Baptist newspapers opposing the defunding were the *Texas Baptist Standard, South Carolina Baptist Courier, Northwest Witness, Virginia Religious Herald, Arkansas Baptist, Tennessee Baptist and Reflector, Mississippi Baptist Record, Ohio Baptist Messenger, Kentucky Western Recorder.* There may have been others.

59. For a discussion of the defunding of the BJC, see Morgan, *New Crusades,* 108–14; See also Ammerman, *Baptist Battles,* 238–42.

60. Paige Patterson, interview by author.

61. Ray Waddle, "Abortion View Checked before Honor Awarded," *The Tennessean*, 15 Sept. 1989, 1A.

62. Quoted in Waddle, "S. Baptists Ban Speakers Holding 'Pro-Choice' Views," 4A.

63. "Religious Liberty Bill before Congress Highlights Differences among Baptists," *SBC Today* 9, no. 14, 26 July 1991, 1.

64. Ibid.

65. Michael Whitehead, interview by author, 19 June 1998.

66. *Annual of the Southern Baptist Convention* (Nashville: Southern Baptist Convention, 1991), 75.

67. Mohler, interview by author, 5 Aug. 1997.

68. "The Nashville Statement of Conscience: Why the Killing of Abortion Doctors is Wrong" (copy in author's possession), secs. 3.8, 5.10.

69. George, "Southern Baptist Heritage of Life," 89, 95, 93.

70. Quoted in ibid., 92.

71. "For Faith and Family," 16 Feb. 1998, Southern Baptist Ethics and Religious Liberty Commission. Tape in author's possession.

72. Gushee, interview by author.

73. "For Faith and Family"; Land, interview by author, 1 Apr. 1997.

74. "The Nashville Statement of Conscience," sec. 5.12.

75. Ibid., 5.14, 5.15.

76. Paige Patterson, interview by author.

77. *Baptist Faith and Message*, Article 18, "The Family."

78. Land, interview by author, 16 June 1998.

79. George, "Southern Baptist Heritage of Life," 84.

80. Mohler, interview by author, 5 Aug. 1997.

81. George, "Southern Baptist Heritage of Life," 86, 87 (emphasis in original).

82. Audi and Wolterstorff, *Religion in the Public Square*, 63, 105.

83. James Dunn, panel discussion, Lilly Fellows Program, Baylor University, 18 Oct. 1997.

7. Graciously Submissive

1. Harry Leon McBeth, "The Role of Women in Southern Baptist History," *Baptist History and Heritage* 12 (Jan. 1977): 25.

2. Betty DeBerg, *Ungodly Women: Gender and the First Wave of American Fundamentalism* (Minneapolis: Fortress, 1990).

3. Mark Chaves, *Ordaining Women: Culture and Conflict in Religious Organizations* (Cambridge: Harvard University Press, 1997), 6.

4. Susan M. Shaw and Tisa Lewis, "'Once There Was a Camelot': Women Doctoral Graduates of the Southern Baptist Theological Seminary, 1982–1992, Talk about the Seminary, the Fundamentalist Takeover, and Their Lives since SBTS,"

Review and Expositor 95 (1998): 404. See McBeth, "Role of Women in Southern Baptist History," 18. McBeth reported that in 1970 women composed only 10.5 percent of the faculties of all Southern Baptist seminaries and 1.3 percent of the trustees. Four of the six seminaries had no women trustees.

5. Shaw and Lewis, "'Once There Was a Camelot,'" 408.

6. Ibid., 408, 418, 404.

7. Quoted in McBeth, "Role of Women in Southern Baptist History," 22.

8. Shaw and Lewis, "'Once There Was a Camelot,'" 410.

9. Ibid., 419, 421 (quote on 421).

10. Ibid., 411.

11. Ibid., 412.

12. McBeth, "Role of Women in Southern Baptist History," 18, 23.

13. Ibid., 25. McBeth here quotes C. R. Daley, the editor of the *Western Recorder.* See C. R. Daley, "Current Trends among Southern Baptists," *Western Recorder,* 5 Aug. 1976, 2, for the prediction that the trickle of ordination would become a stream. For a good sociological "guesstimate" as to the number of ordained women by the early 1980s, see Sarah Frances Anders, "Women in Ministry: The Distaff of the Church in Action," *Review and Expositor* 80 (summer 1983): 30. Anders points out that there was no central registry of ordained women because, for Baptists, ordination is a matter for local congregations. Anders continued to track the increase in ordained SBC women into the 1990s as the figure rose to over three hundred. Still, one must remember that there were by 1999 about forty thousand SBC churches.

14. Jann Aldredge Clanton, "Why I Believe Southern Baptist Churches Should Ordain Women," *Baptist History and Heritage* 23 (July 1988): 50. The addresses of Clanton and Dorothy Patterson (which will be discussed below) can be viewed on videocassette. See Southern Baptist Historical Association, "Annual Meeting, 27 April 1988," video library, Southern Baptist Historical Library and Archives, Nashville, videocassette.

15. Clanton, "Why I Believe Southern Baptist Churches Should Ordain Women," 51.

16. Ibid., 52.

17. Charles Talbert, "Biblical Criticism's Role: The Pauline View of Women as a Case in Point," in *The Unfettered Word: Southern Baptists Confront the Authority-Inerrancy Question,* ed. Robison James (Waco, Tex.: Word Books, 1987), 64–65. See also Charles Talbert, *Reading Corinthians: A Literary and Theological Commentary on 1 and 2 Corinthians* (New York: Crossroad, 1987), 91–95. See also David W. Odell-Scott, "Let the Women Speak in Church: An Egalitarian Interpretation of I Cor. 14:33b–36," *Biblical Theology Bulletin* 13 (1983): 90–93.

18. Talbert, "Biblical Criticism's Role," 66–67.

19. Clanton, "Why I Believe Southern Baptist Churches Should Ordain Women," 53.

20. Talbert, "Biblical Criticism's Role," 68–69 (quote on 69).

21. Clanton, "Why I Believe Southern Baptist Churches Should Ordain Women," 53.

22. Ibid., 53–54.

23. Dorothy Patterson, interview by author, 8 June 1999.

24. The addresses by Clanton and Patterson were covered by the local press. See Ray Waddle, "Debaters Cross Swords over Ordination of Baptist Women," *The Tennessean*, 28 Apr. 1988, 1A, 4A. Patterson's response to this particular question is covered on page 4A.

25. Dorothy Kelley Patterson, "Why I Believe Southern Baptist Churches Should Not Ordain Women," *Baptist History and Heritage* 23 (July 1988): 56, 62.

26. Donald W. Dayton and Lucille Sider Dayton, "Women as Preachers: Evangelical Precedents," *Christianity Today* 19 (23 May 1975): 4–7.

27. Patterson, "Why I Believe Southern Baptist Churches Should Not Ordain Women," 58.

28. Ibid., 58, 59.

29. Ibid., 59, 60.

30. Ibid., 60–61.

31. Ibid., 61.

32. H. Leon McBeth, "Perspectives on Women in Baptist Life," *Baptist History and Heritage* 22 (July 1987): 9

33. Patterson, "Why I Believe Southern Baptist Churches Should Not Ordain Women," 62.

34. Southern Baptist Historical Association, "Annual Meeting, 27 April 1988," videocassette.

35. Ibid.

36. James J. Thompson Jr., *Tried as by Fire: Southern Baptists and the Controversy of the Twenties* (Macon, Ga.: Mercer University Press, 1982), 101–36; Ellis, *A Man of Books*, 189–98; Hankins, *God's Rascal*, 40–41.

37. McBeth, *The Baptist Heritage*, 679. For Elliott's own story see Ralph Elliott, *The Genesis Controversy and Continuity in Southern Baptist Chaos: A Eulogy for a Great Tradition* (Macon, Ga.: Mercer University Press, 1992).

38. The motion read as follows: "That the President of the Southern Baptist Convention appoint a committee to review the *Baptist Faith and Message* of May 9, 1963, for the primary purpose of adding an Article on The Family, and to bring the amendment to the next convention for approval." See "Report of the Baptist Faith and Message Study Committee to the Southern Baptist Convention," 9 June 1998. This document was printed and distributed widely at the 1998 convention and to media.

39. The discussion of the mechanics of the meeting is based on Dorothy Patterson, interview by author.

40. Dorothy Patterson, interview by author; Land, interview by author, 16 June 1998.

41. "Report of the Baptist Faith and Message Study Committee."

42. Jim Jones, "Baptists Take Stand on Role of Wives," *Fort Worth Star Telegram*, 10 June 1999, 13.

43. Dorothy Patterson, interview by author.

44. Richard Land first told me that Patterson wrote the commentary. In fact, he claimed that she did most of the "heavy lifting" in the whole process. Land, interview by author, 16 June 1998. Patterson herself confirmed to me that she wrote the first draft of the commentary but emphasized that the committee made revisions. Dorothy Patterson, interview by author. For the concept of complementarianism and the word "complement," see "Report of the Baptist Faith and Message Study Committee," 3.

45. Dorothy Patterson, interview by author.

46. Land, interview by author, 16 June 1998.

47. "Report of the Baptist Faith and Message Study Committee," 2, 4.

48. Dorothy Patterson, interview by author.

49. Gustav Niebuhr, "Southern Baptists Declare Wife Should 'Submit' to Her Husband," *The New York Times*, 10 June 1998, A1.

50. *Larry King Live*, 12 June 1999, video library, Southern Baptist Theological Seminary Library, videotape copy. See also Bob Allen, "Mohler Defends Family Statement on National TV," *Texas Baptist Standard*, 1 July 1998, 3.

51. Land, interview by author, 16 June 1998.

52. Diana Butler Bass, "Southern Baptists Take Scripture Out of Context," *Baptists Today*, 25 June 1998, 3.

53. Peter Steinfels, "Beliefs," *The New York Times*, 13 June 1998.

54. Gary Wills, "Baptists' Woman-bashing Theologically off the Mark," *Chicago Sun Times*, 13 June 1998.

55. Ibid. The scripture quote is from the New International Version.

56. Quoted in Steinfels, "Beliefs."

57. Ibid.

58. Quoted in Stuart Vincent, "Baptists Draw Fire for Policy," *Melville (N.Y.) Newsday*, 11 June 1998.

59. *CBS News Saturday Morning*, 13 June 1998, video library, Southern Baptist Theological Seminary, videotape copy.

60. Stan Hastey, "Southern Baptists and Women: The Real Issue," *Baptists Today*, 23 July 1998, 28.

61. Ibid.

62. Marv Knox, "Fellowship Declines to Debate SBC," *Texas Baptist Standard*, 8 July 1998, 1, 6 (Vestal quotes on 6).

63. Mark Wingfield, "Sexes Marked by 'Biblical Equality,' Texas Baptists Resolve," *Texas Baptist Standard*, 18 Nov. 1998, 6; Wingfield, "BGCT Affirms 1963 Doctrinal Statement," *Texas Baptist Standard*, 17 Nov. 1999, 1. See also "Submission Rejected," *Christianity Today*, 6 Dec. 1999, 27.

64. "Evangelical Leaders Back SBC Statement," *Texas Baptist Standard*, 29 July 1998, 3.

65. See *Baptist Faith and Message*, article 5, "God's Purpose of Grace," 12, which reads in part, "Those whom God has accepted in Christ, and sanctified by His Spirit, will never fall away from the state of grace, but shall persevere to the end."

66. Edward E. Plowman, "Beyond the Pews," *World*, 27 June 1998, 19.

67. John Kennedy, "Patterson's Election Seals Conservative Control," *Christianity Today*, 13 July 1998, 21.

68. Dorothy Patterson, interview by author.

69. Morris Chapman, interview by author, 16 June 1998.

70. "Submission Rejected."

71. "Men, Women, and Biblical Equality," Christians for Biblical Equality, Inner Grove Heights, Minn., n.d. The statement appeared as an advertisement in *Christianity Today*, 9 Apr. 1990, 36–37. As of early 2000, an updated version with names of signatories could be accessed at <www.cbeinternational.org/state.htm>.

72. Ibid.

73. Information on the Council on Biblical Manhood and Womanhood, including "The Danvers Statement," which outlines the rationale, purpose, and affirmations of the organization, can be found online at <www.cbmw.org/index.html>.

74. This claim is based on a meticulous study of William L. Lumpkin, *Baptist Confessions of Faith* (Valley Forge, Pa.: Judson, 1969). There are several confessions that mention marriage as an ordinance of God, but none specify gender roles. There is at least one Baptist confession that mentions deacons as both men and women, "A Declaration of Faith of English People Remaining at Amsterdam in Holland" (1611) (Lumpkin, 121). The "Somerset Confession" (1656) of the Particular Baptists instructs to the contrary, "The women in the church to learn in silence, and in all subjection," but then item 10 of the same article says, "Submitting one to another in the Lord" (Lumpkin, 210). "Propositions and Conclusions" (1612) states, "Christ hath set in his outward church the vocations of master and servant, parents and children, husband and wife" (Lumpkin, 139). This could be interpreted to mean that servants submit to slaves, children to parents, and wives to husbands, but it does not actually stipulate such. Interestingly, the "Russian Baptist Confession" (of the Evangelical Christian Brotherhood), which was written in the 1940s, includes the statement "domination in marriage from either side should not exist" (Lumpkin, 431–32).

75. *Larry King Live*, 12 June 1998.

76. *CBS News Saturday Morning*, 13 June 1998.

77. Land, interview by author, 16 June 1998.

78. Gayle White, "Baptists to Consider Adopting Statement on Marriage, Family," *Atlanta Constitution*, 30 May 1998.

79. Chapman, interview by author.

80. Mohler, interview by author, 5 Aug. 1997.

81. Ibid.

82. Moyers, *God and Politics.*

83. Shaw and Lewis, "'Once There Was a Camelot,'" 410-11.

84. Quoted in Margaret Lamberts Bendroth, "Fundamentalism and Femininity: Points of Encounter between Religious Conservatives and Women, 1919-1935," *Church History* 61 (June 1992): 227. Bendroth here cites "Taking the Bible 'Literally,'" *Moody Bible Institute Magazine* 23 (1923): 191-92.

85. Quoted in Bendroth, "Fundamentalism and Femininity," 227. Bendroth cites William Bell Riley, "Women in the Ministry," *Christian Fundamentalist* 1 (May 1928): 21.

86. See William Vance Trollinger Jr., *God's Empire: William Bell Riley and Midwestern Fundamentalism* (Madison: University of Wisconsin Press, 1990), 104-5. On the decline in opportunities for women evangelical preachers between the wars, see Janette Hassey, *No Time for Silence: Evangelical Women in Public Ministry around the Turn of the Century* (Grand Rapids, Mich.: Zondervan, 1986). See also Margaret Lamberts Bendroth, *Fundamentalism and Gender: 1875 to the Present* (New Haven, Conn.: Yale University Press, 1993).

87. The "Faculty Questionnaire" (copy in author's possession) can be most easily accessed at the Midwestern Baptist Theological Seminary website, <www.MBTS.edu/facquest.cfm>.

88. See Midwestern Baptist Theological Seminary website, <www.MBTS.edu>.

89. Coppenger, interview by author. See also Midwestern Baptist Theological Seminary website.

90. Numbers supplied by the Midwestern Baptist Theological Seminary Registrar's Office for female M.Div. graduates are as follows: 1986—5, 1988—4, 1990—8, 1991—6, and 1996—8.

91. See Midwestern Baptist Theological Seminary website.

92. Dorothy Patterson, interview by author.

93. Mohler, interview by author, 13 Aug. 1999.

94. George, interview by author.

95. Toby Druin, "Southwestern Profs to Sign New Statement," *Texas Baptist Standard,* 14 Oct. 1998, 3.

96. Quoted in Bob Allen, "Mark Coppenger Calls Women Preachers 'Affront to Home and Family,'" *Texas Baptist Standard,* 23 May 1996, 8.

97. Ibid.

98. Coppenger, interview by author.

99. Bob Allen, "Coppenger Confesses His Anger," *Texas Baptist Standard,* 4 Aug. 1999, 3; Bob Allen, "Coppenger Fired at Midwestern," *Texas Baptist Standard,* 22 Sept. 1999, 3.

100. Chris Burritt, "Around the South," *Atlanta Journal,* 4 May 1997, A14.

101. McBeth, "Role of Women in Southern Baptist History," 12-13, 14. The SBC amended its constitution again in 1918 to allow women messengers.

102. DeBerg, *Ungodly Women,* 153.

103. Bendroth, "Fundamentalism and Femininity," 223.

8. Conservatives Can Be Progressive Too

1. McBeth, *The Baptist Heritage*, 381. The following brief history of the formation of the SBC is taken largely from McBeth. See also Baker, *Southern Baptist Convention and Its People*, 153–69.

2. Cited in McBeth, 387.

3. E. Luther Copeland, *The Southern Baptist Convention and the Judgment of History* (Lanham, Md.: University Press of America, 1995)

4. Charles Marsh, *God's Long Summer: Stories of Faith and Civil Rights* (Princeton, N.J.: Princeton University Press, 1997), 82–115.

5. Quoted in Leonard, *God's Last and Only Hope*, 22.

6. Stricklin, *Genealogy of Dissent.*

7. John Lee Eighmy, *Churches in Cultural Captivity: A History of the Social Attitudes of Southern Baptists* (1972; reprint, Knoxville: University of Tennessee Press, 1987), 190.

8. Gayle White, "'A Great Day,' Black Pastors Agree," *Atlanta Journal Constitution*, 21 June 1995. Land was quoted in this article as saying that he had made racial reconciliation a condition of his taking the directorship of the CLC.

9. Briggs, "Southern Baptists Urge Abortion Limits." This was an Associated Press article that was also carried in the *Washington Post*, 17 June 1989. The article concerned various resolutions passed at the 1989 convention meeting, one of which had to do with race, and referred to Caine's statement, which had occurred the previous autumn.

10. Gushee, interview by author.

11. This brief synopsis has been pieced together from Gushee, interview by author; Gary Frost, interview by author, 14 Oct. 1999; and Emmanuel McCall, interview by author, 12 June 2000.

12. John Dart, "Christians Say Prayers of Atonement for Past Sins," *Fort Lauderdale Sun-Sentinel*, 24 June 1995, 7D.

13. Judith Lynn Howard, "Baptists Apologize for Racism," *Dallas Morning News*, 21 June 1995, 1A.

14. Mohler, interview by author, 13 Aug. 1999.

15. John Dart, "Christian Say Prayers of Atonement," 1D, 7D.

16. John Dart, "Book's Tales May be Inspiring Repentance," *Fort Lauderdale Sun-Sentinel*, 24 June 1995, 7D.

17. Frost, interview by author.

18. Quoted in Jim Jones, "Baptists Take First Step," *Fort Worth Star-Telegram*, 25 June 1995.

19. Frost, interview by author; Gushee, interview by author. McCall, interview by author.

20. Gushee, interview by author.

21. McCall, interview by author.

22. Frost, interview by author.

23. Anonymous delegate and Frost quoted in Judith Lynn Howard, "Baptists Apologize for Racism," *Dallas Morning News,* 21 June 1995, 1A.

24. Frost, interview by author. Ephesians 4:32 New American Standard Version reads, "And be kind to one another, tender-hearted, forgiving each other, just as God in Christ also has forgiven you."

25. "Resolution No. 1—On Racial Reconciliation on the 150th Anniversary of the Southern Baptist Convention," *Annual* (1995), 80.

26. Ibid., 81.

27. Deborah Mathis, "Southern Baptists Take Vital First Step," *Knoxville News-Sentinel,* 25 June 1995.

28. Les Payne, "Late Regrets about Slavery," *New York Newsday,* 25 June 1995.

29. Paul Delaney, "Baptists' Apology Accepted, So Let the Healing Begin," *Birmingham News,* 25 June 1995, 1C, 4C.

30. Bill Maxwell, "Baptists' Apologies Are Right," *St. Petersburg Times,* 25 June 1995, 1D, 8D (quotes).

31. William C. Singleton III, "A Real Dialogue about Race Is Needed," *Birmingham News,* 24 June 1995.

32. Carl Rowan, "Southern Baptists Face Sin of Racism," *Denver Post,* 25 June 1995.

33. Butts and Griffin quoted in Gustav Niebuhr, "Baptist Group Votes to Repent Stand on Slaves," *The New York Times,* 21 June 1995.

34. Brown and Clark quoted in "Racist No More? Black Leaders Ask," *Christianity Today,* 14 Aug. 1995, 53.

35. McCall, interview by author.

36. T. Vaughn Walker, interview by author, 11 Aug. 1999. Walker was here forgetting Logan Carson, who went on the faculty at Southeastern in the early 1990s. By 2000, both New Orleans and Southwestern also had African American professors, which meant that all six seminaries had African American representation on their faculties.

37. Ibid.

38. Ibid.

39. Frost, interview by author.

40. Timothy James Johnson, interview by author, 15 Oct. 1999.

41. Ibid.

42. Ibid.

43. See Greg Garrison, "Southern Baptists Repent over Racism," *Birmingham News,* 21 June 1995, 10A; Mary Otto, "Southern Baptists Repent Racist Past," *Akron Beacon Journal,* 21 June 1995, A4; and "Southern Baptists Plan Churches in Inner Cities," *Nashville Tennessean,* 16 June 1999, 15A.

44. See Garrison, "Southern Baptists Repent over Racism," 10A; Otto, "Southern Baptists Repent Racist Past," A4; and "Southern Baptists Plan Churches in Inner Cities," 15A.

45. Frost, interview by author.

46. Ibid.; McCall, interview by author.

47. McCall, interview by author.

48. Sidney Smith, interview by author, 6 June 2000.

49. C. Peter Wagner, "A Vision for Evangelizing the Real America," *International Bulletin of Missionary Research* (Apr. 1986): 62. Wagner listed the following groups in California alone that worshipped in their native languages in Southern Baptist churches or missions: American Indian, Cambodian, Laotian, Thai, Chinese (several dialects), Estonian, Filipino, Hebrew, Hungarian, Indonesian, Italian, Japanese, Korean, Arabic, Egyptian, Afghan, Pakistani, Russian, Slavic, Ukrainian, Spanish, and Vietnamese.

50. Smith, interview by author.

51. McCall, interview by author.

52. Smith, interview by author.

53. McCall, interview by author; Smith, interview by author.

54. Fred Luter, conversation with author, 6 June 2000.

55. C. Peter Wagner, *Our Kind of People: The Ethical Dimensions of Church Growth in America* (Atlanta: John Knox Press, 1979), 11.

56. Elroy Barber, conversation with author, 6 June 2000.

57. Frost, interview by author.

58. Walker, interview by author.

59. Ibid.

60. Ibid.

61. Ibid.

62. Ibid.

63. Ibid.

64. Johnson, interview by author.

65. Diana Garland, conversation with author, 6 June 2000.

66. Johnson, interview by author.

67. Ibid.

68. Ibid.

69. Ibid.

70. R. Logan Carson, interview by author, 23 May 2000.

71. Ibid.

72. Ibid.

73. Ibid.

74. Smith, interview by author.

Conclusion

1. Leonard, *God's Last and Only Hope*, 13. See Charles Reagan Wilson, *Baptized in Blood: The Religion of the Lost Cause, 1865–1920* (Athens: University of Georgia Press).

2. While this analysis is the product of conversations with many individuals, including Samuel S. Hill, most recently Al Mohler addressed the topic at a conference at Southern Baptist Seminary, 13–15 Feb. 2001.

3. See Stricklin, *Genealogy of Dissent.*

4. See Leonard, *God's Last and Only Hope,* 2.

Bibliography

PRIMARY MATERIAL

Annual of the Southern Baptist Convention. Nashville: Southern Baptist Convention, 1964.
———. Nashville: Southern Baptist Convention, 1969.
———. Nashville: Southern Baptist Convention, 1970.
———. Nashville: Southern Baptist Convention, 1971.
———. Nashville: Southern Baptist Convention, 1976.
———. Nashville: Southern Baptist Convention, 1977.
———. Nashville: Southern Baptist Convention, 1979.
———. Nashville: Southern Baptist Convention, 1980.
———. Nashville: Southern Baptist Convention, 1982.
———. Nashville: Southern Baptist Convention, 1986.
———. Nashville: Southern Baptist Convention, 1991.
———. Nashville: Southern Baptist Convention, 1992.
———. Nashville: Southern Baptist Convention, 1995.
———. Nashville: Southern Baptist Convention, 1996.
Baptists Committed to the Southern Baptist Convention. "Struggle for the Baptist Soul." Southern Baptist Archives, Nashville.
The Baptist Faith and Message. Nashville: The Sunday School Board of the Southern Baptist Convention, 1963.
CBS News Saturday Morning, 13 June 1998. Video library, Southern Baptist Theological Seminary. Videocassette copy.
Christians for Biblical Equality. "Men, Women and Biblical Equality." Advertisement in *Christianity Today*, 9 April 1990, 36–37.
Clanton, Jann Aldredge. "Why I Believe Southern Baptist Churches Should Ordain Women." *Baptist History and Heritage* 23 (July 1988): 50–55.
Coppenger, Mark. "Who Then?" *SBC Life*, June–July 1994, 17.
"Covenant Renewal between Trustees, Faculty, and Administration." The Southern

Baptist Theological Seminary. Adopted by the seminary faculty, 28 March 1991. Adopted by the Board of Trustees, 8 April 1991. Copy in author's possession.

Draper, James T., Jr. *Authority: The Critical Issue for Southern Baptists.* Old Tappan, N.J.: Fleming H. Revell, 1984.

Draper, James T., Jr., and Forrest Watson. *If the Foundations Be Destroyed.* Nashville: Oliver Nelson, 1984.

Dunn, James. "The Baptist Vision of Religious Liberty." In *Reclaiming the Baptist Vision: Religious Liberty,* edited by Walter B. Shurden. Macon, Ga.: Smyth and Helwys, 1997.

———. "Christian Citizenship and Political Advocacy." Address at the Lilly Fellows Program, "The City of God Revisited: Church and State in the Twenty-First Century," Baylor University, 18 October 1997.

———. Panel discussion, Lilly Fellows Program in the Humanities and Arts, Baylor University, 19 October 1997.

Faculty of the Southern Baptist Theological Seminary. "A Resolution of Support for the Carver School of Church Social Work." 5 April 1995. Copy in author's possession.

"For Faith and Family." Radio broadcast, 16 February 1998. Southern Baptist Ethics and Religious Liberty Commission. Audiocassette in author's possession.

Garland, Diana R. "When Professional Ethics and Religious Politics Conflict: A Case Study." *Social Work and Christianity* 26 (spring 1999): 60–75.

George, Timothy. "Between Pacifism and Coercion: The English Baptist Doctrine of Religious Toleration." *Mennonite Quarterly Review* 58 (January 1984): 30–49.

———. "The Southern Baptist Wars: What Can We Learn from the Conservative Victory?" *Christianity Today,* 9 March 1992, 24–27.

———. "Passing the Southern Baptist Torch." *Christianity Today,* 15 May 1995, 32–34.

———. "Southern Baptist Heritage of Life." In *Life at Risk: The Crisis in Medical Ethics,* edited by Richard D. Land and Louis A. Moore. Nashville: Broadman and Holman, 1995.

Gushee, David. "The Tragedy of Christian Lovelessness." ABC Annual Meeting, 29 April 1995, Scottsburg. Sermon manuscript copy in author's possession.

———. "Learning again the Way of Love." *Prism,* May–June 1997, 15.

Issues and Answers: Abortion. Nashville: Christian Life Commission, n.d.

Land, Richard D. "Salt and Light" (abridged version of Land's installation address). *Light,* July–September 1989, 4.

———. "Responses." In *Disciples and Democracy: Religious Conservatives and the Future of American Politics,* edited by Michael Cromartie. Grand Rapids, Mich.: Eerdmans; and Washington, D.C.: Ethics and Public Policy Center, 1994.

———. "A Baptist's View of Prayer in Schools." Critical Issues Pamphlet. Nashville: Southern Baptist Christian Life Commission, 1995.

———. "The Struggle for the Right to Be Involved." Tape 9 of *The War of the Worlds: The Struggle for the Nation's Soul.* Christian Life Commission Annual Seminar, Southeastern Baptist Theological Seminary, 1995.

———. "Is Democracy Doomed?" *Light,* January–February 1996, 2.

———. "Persecution of Christians." *Light,* May–June 1996.

———. "Will It Be Faith in Practice?" In *Christians in the Public Square: Faith in Practice?* edited by Richard D. Land and Lee Hollaway. Nashville: Southern Baptist Ethics and Religious Liberty Commission, 1996.

Land, Richard D., and Will Dodson. "A Summary Analysis of Rep. Ernest Istook's Proposed Constitutional Amendment." Copy in author's possession.

Larry King Live, 12 June 1999. Southern Baptist Theological Seminary Library. Videocassette copy.

Mohler, R. Albert. "Unchanging Truths and Our Changing World." *The Tie* 62 (winter 1994), inside cover.

———. "Keeping Faith in a Faithless Age: The Church as the Moral Minority." *The Tie* 63 (spring 1995): inside cover.

———. "The Lessons of History." *The Tie* 63 (spring 1995): 13.

———. "What Mean These Stones?" *The Tie* 63 (summer 1995): 24.

———. "Transforming Culture: Christian Truth confronts Post-Christian America." *The Tie* 64 (summer 1996): 2–5.

———. "Leadership and Change" (interview). *The Tie* 63 (fall 1995): 17.

———. "The Struggle over Gender." Tape 13 of *War of the Worlds: The Struggle for the Nation's Soul.* Christian Life Commission Annual Seminar, Southeastern Baptist Theological Seminary, 1995.

———. "Ministry Is Stranger Than It Used to Be: The Challenge of Postmodernism." *The Tie* 65 (spring 1997).

Patterson, Dorothy Kelley. "Why I Believe Southern Baptist Churches Should Not Ordain Women." *Baptist History and Heritage* 23 (July 1988): 56–62.

Patterson, Paige. "My Vision for the Twenty-first Century SBC." *Review and Expositor* 88 (winter 1991): 37–52.

———. "War of the Worlds: A Perennial Battle." Tape 15 of *The War of the Worlds: The Struggle for the Nation's Soul.* Christian Life Commission Annual Seminar, Southeastern Baptist Theological Seminary, 1995.

Pressler, Paul. "It Happened at Princeton." *The Baptist Student,* April 1952, 6–8.

Proceedings of the Conference on Biblical Inerrancy, 1987. Nashville: Broadman, 1987.

Proceedings of the 1980 Christian Life Commission Seminar on Ethical Issues for the Eighties. Roosevelt Hotel, New York City, March 24–26, 1980.

Report of the Baptist Faith and Message Study Committee to the Southern Baptist Convention," 9 June 1998. Copy in author's possession.

"A Report of Spiritual Distress on the Part of the Faculty of the Southern Baptist Theological Seminary," 5 April 1995. Copy in author's possession.

Rogers, Adrian. *Bring Back the Glory.* Atlanta: Walk through the Bible Ministries, 1996.

Rogers, Melissa. "Baptists and the Establishment Clause: Our Commitment and Challenge." In *Baptists in the Balance: The Tension between Freedom and Responsibility,* edited by Everett C. Goodwin. Valley Forge, Pa.: Judson, 1997.

Sherwood, David. "Editorial: A Funny Thing Happened on the Way to the Seminary." *Social Work and Christianity* 22 (fall 1995): 79–84.

Simmons, Paul D. "A Theological Response to Fundamentalism on the Abortion Issue." Vertical file, "Abortion—Baptists" folder, J. M. Dawson Institute of Church-State Studies.

Spressart, Janet Furness. "Statement to ATS/SACS/CSWE Site Team," 9 November 1995. Copy in author's possession.

Southern Baptists for Life. "Special 1986 Atlanta Convention Edition: Do You Know the Facts About Abortion-On-Demand?" Copy in folder "Abortion—Baptists," vertical file, J. M. Dawson Institute of Church-State Studies, Baylor University, Waco, Texas.

Southern Baptist Historical Association. "Annual Meeting, 27 April 1988." Video library, Southern Baptist Historical Library and Archives, Nashville. Videocassette.

Toalston, Art. "Seminary Controversy Continues over Mohler's Dismissal of Dean." Baptist Press Release, 23 March 1995.

INTERVIEWS, CONVERSATIONS, AND CORRESPONDENCE

Barber, Elroy. Conversation with author, 6 June 2000.

Carson, R. Logan. Interview by author, 23 May 2000.

Chapman, Morris. Interview by author, 16 June 1998.

Coppenger, Mark. Interview by author, 18 June 1998.

Draper, James, Jr. Interview by author, 2 June 1997.

Frost, Gary. Interview by author, 14 October 1999.

Garland, Diana R. Letter to Dr. R. Albert Mohler, 20 March 1995. Photocopy in author's possession.

———. Conversation with author, 26 May 1999.

———. Conversation with author, 6 June 2000.

George, Timothy. Interview by author, 24 July 1998.

Gushee, David. Interview by author, 16 June 1999.

———. Correspondence with author (e-mail), 3 January 2000.

Honeycutt, Roy. Interview by author, 5 September 2000.

Johnson, Timothy James. Interview by author, 15 October 1999.

Land, Richard D. Interview by author, 1 April 1997.

———. Interview by author, 16 June 1998.

Luter, Fred. Conversation with author, 6 June 2000.

McCall, Emmanuel. Interview by author, 12 June 2000.

Mohler, R. Albert. Interview by author, 5 August 1997.

———. Interview by author, 13 August 1999.

Newman, Carey. Interview by author, 11 August 1999.

Patterson, Dorothy. Interview by author, 8 June 1999.

Patterson, Paige. Interview by author, 20 May 1997.

Pitt, M. Stephen. Letter to Herbert L. Segal, 14 April 1995. Photocopy in author's possession.

Pressler, Paul. Interview by Gary North, 1987. Fort Worth: Dominion Tapes, 1988.

Rogers, Adrian. Interview by author, 18 August 1997.

Scalise, Charles. Correspondence with author (e-mail), 2 March 2001.

Segal, Herbert L. Letter to R. Albert Mohler, 29 March 1995. Photocopy in author's possession.

Sherwood, David A. Letter to Dr. Albert Mohler, 3 April 1995. Photocopy in author's possession.

———. Interview by author, 24 June 1999.

Smith, Sidney. Interview by author, 6 June 2000.

Spressart, Janet Furness. Interview by author, 24 June 1999.

Weber, Timothy. Interview by author, 19 May 1998.

Whitehead, Michael. Interview by author, 19 June 1998.

COURT CASES

Capitol Square Review and Advisory Board v. *Vincent J. Pinette, Donnie A. Carr, and Knights of the Ku Klux Klan.* 115 Sup. Ct. 2440 (1995).

City of Boerne v. *P. F. Flores.* 521 U.S. 507 (1997). The text of this case can be found in *Journal of Church and State* 39 (autumn 1997): 846–72.

Doe, Jane, et al. v. *Helen O'Bannon.* Civil Action 81-0555, Class Action. U.S. District Court for the Eastern District of Pennsylvania.

Employment Division, Department of Human Resources of Oregon v. *Smith.* 494 U.S. 872 (1990).

Rosenberger, Ronald W. v. *Rector and Visitors of the University of Virginia.* 115 Sup. Ct. 2510 (1995).

SECONDARY MATERIAL

"Abortion: A Challenge for Baptists." *Light,* November/December 1987, 4–6, 16.

"Abortion Change Loses." *Texas Baptist Standard,* 23 June 1976, 9.

"Abortion Decision: Death Blow?" *Christianity Today,* 16 February 1973, 48.

"Abortion Issue: A Baptist Ethicist Shares His Insights (Interview with Foy Valentine)." *Light,* March 1985, 9.

"Abortion Issue Shifts." *Texas Baptist Standard,* 8 September 1976, 17.

"Abortion Law Revisions Favored." *Kentucky Western Recorder,* 19 September 1970, 10.

Adams, John M. "The Making of a New-Evangelical Statesman: The Case of Harold John Ockenga." Ph.D. diss., Baylor University, 1994.

Allen, Bob. "Mark Coppenger Calls Women Preachers 'Affront to Home and Family.'" *Texas Baptist Standard,* 23 May 1996, 8.

———. "Mohler Defends Family Statement on National TV." *Texas Baptist Standard,* 1 July 1998, 3.

———. "Coppenger Confesses His Anger," *Texas Baptist Standard,* 4 August 1999, 3.

———. "Coppenger Fired at Midwestern." *Texas Baptist Standard,* 22 September 1999, 3.

Allen, Clifton, ed. *The Broadman Bible Commentary.* Nashville: Broadman, 1970.

Anders, Sarah Frances. "Women in Ministry: The Distaff of the Church in Action." *Review and Expositor* 80 (summer 1983): 427–36.

Anderson, Walter Truett. *Reality Isn't What It Used to Be.* San Francisco: Harper and Row, 1990.

Ammerman, Nancy T. "Organizational Conflict in the Southern Baptist Convention." In *Secularization and Fundamentalism Reconsidered,* vol. 3, *Religion and the Political Order,* edited by Jeffrey K. Hadden and Anson Shupe. New York: Paragon House, 1986.

———. *Baptist Battles: Social Change and Religious Conflict in The Southern Baptist Convention.* New Brunswick, N.J.: Rutgers University Press, 1990.

Archer, Glenn L. "Freedom in Schools." *Texas Baptist Standard,* 13 May 1959, 11.

Audi, Robert, and Nicolas Wolterstorff. *Religion in the Public Square: The Place of Religious Convictions in Political Debate.* Lanham, Md.: Rowman and Littlefield, 1997.

Baker, Larry. "Reflections." *Light,* November/December 1987, 2.

Baker, Robert. *The Southern Baptist Convention and Its People, 1607–1972.* Nashville: Broadman, 1974.

———. "Baptists and Religious Liberty in the Revolutionary Era." In *The Lord's Free People,* edited by W. R. Estep. Fort Worth: Southwestern Baptist Theological Seminary, 1976.

Ballance, Robert C., Jr. "Next Generation of Ministers Looking beyond Denominational Lines." *Baptists Today,* December 1998, 3.

Balmer, Randall. "Churchgoing: Bellevue Baptist Church near Memphis." *Christian Century,* 5 May 1993, 484–88.

———. *Mine Eyes Have Seen the Glory: A Journey into the Evangelical Subculture in America.* Exp. ed. New York: Oxford University Press, 1993.

Barnes, William Wright. *The Southern Baptist Convention, 1845–1953.* Nashville: Broadman, 1954.

Barron, Bruce. *Heaven on Earth? The Social and Political Agendas of Dominion Theology.* Grand Rapids, Mich.: Zondervan, 1992.

Barton, David. *The Myth of Separation: What Is the Correct Relationship between Church and State?* Aledo, Tex.: WallBuilders, 1989.

———. *Original Intent: The Courts, the Constitution, and Religion.* Aledo, Tex.: WallBuilders, 1997.

Bass, Diana Butler. "Southern Baptists Take Scripture Out of Context." *Baptists Today,* 25 June 1998, 3.

Bendroth, Margaret Lamberts. "Fundamentalism and Femininity: Points of Encounter between Religious Conservatives and Women, 1919–1935." *Church History* 61 (June 1992): 221–33.

———. *Fundamentalism and Gender: 1875 to the Present.* New Haven, Conn.: Yale University Press, 1993.

Berns, Walter. "An Illegitimate Regime?" *First Things* 69 (January 1997): 2–3 (correspondence).

Bloom, Allan. *The Closing of the American Mind.* New York: Simon and Schuster, 1987.

Bork, Robert. "An Illegitimate Regime?" *First Things* 69 (January 1997): 2 (correspondence).

Boston, Rob. "David Barton's Bad History." *Church and State,* April 1993.

———. "Sects, Lies, and Videotape." *Church and State,* April 1993.

———. "Consumer Alert: WallBuilders Shoddy Workmanship." *Church and State,* July/August 1996, 13.

———. *The Most Dangerous Man in America? Pat Robertson and the Rise of the Christian Coalition.* Amherst, N.Y.: Prometheus Books, 1996.

Brackney, William Henry. *The Baptists.* New York: Greenwood, 1988.

Bratt, James. "Abraham Kuyper, American History, and the Tensions of Neo-Calvinism." In *Sharing the Reformed Tradition: The Dutch–North American Exchange, 1846–1996,* edited by George Harinck and Hans Krabbendam. Amsterdam: VU Uitgeverij, 1996.

Briggs, David. "Southern Baptists Urge Abortion Limits." *Las Vegas Review Journal,* 16 June 1989.

Burritt, Chris. "Around the South." *Atlanta Journal,* 4 May 1997, A14.

Carpenter, Joel. "Is 'Evangelical' a Yankee Word? Relations between Northern Evangelicals and the Southern Baptist Convention in the Twentieth Century." In *Southern Baptists and American Evangelicals: The Conversation Continues,* edited by David S. Dockery. Nashville: Broadman and Holman, 1993.

———. *Revive Us Again: The Reawakening of American Fundamentalism.* New York: Oxford University Press, 1997.

Carter, Stephen J. *The Culture of Disbelief: How American Law and Politics Trivialize Religious Devotion.* New York: Basic Books, 1993.

Chaves, Mark. *Ordaining Women: Culture and Conflict in Religious Organizations.* Cambridge: Harvard University Press, 1997.

"Christian Life Commission Announces New Resources for Sanctity of Human Life, Sunday, 18 January 1987." *Light,* November/December 1986, 12.

Clapp, Rodney. "Democracy as Heresy." *Christianity Today,* 29 February 1987, 17–23.

Coker, Joe L. "Sweet Harmony vs. Strict Separation: Recognizing the Distinctions between Isaac Backus and John Leland." *American Baptist Quarterly* 16 (September 1997): 241–48.

Colson, Charles. "Kingdoms in Conflict." *First Things* 67 (November 1996): 34–38.

Conn, Joseph L. "Armed and Dangerous?" *Church and State* 50 (March 1997): 9.

Coontz, Stephanie. *The Way We Never Were: American Families and the Nostalgia Trap.* New York: Basic Books, 1992.

Copeland, E. Luther. *The Southern Baptist Convention and the Judgment of History.* Lanham, Md.: University Press of America, 1995.

Cothen, Grady C. *What Happened to the Southern Baptist Convention?* Macon, Ga.: Smyth and Helwys, 1993.

Creed, J. Bradley. "John Leland, American Prophet of Religious Individualism." Ph.D. diss., Southwestern Baptist Theological Seminary, 1986.

Daley, C. R. "Current Trends among Southern Baptists." *Western Recorder,* 5 August 1976.

Dart, John. "Christians Say Prayers of Atonement for Past Sins." *Fort Lauderdale Sun-Sentinel,* 24 June 1995, 7D.

Davis, Derek H. "Editorial: Assessing the Proposed Religious Equality Amendment." *Journal of Church and State* 37 (summer 1995): 493–508.

———, ed. *The Separation of Church and State Defended: Selected Writings of James E. Wood Jr.* Waco, Tex.: J. M. Dawson Institute of Church-State Studies, 1995.

Dawson, Joseph M. "Temptations of the Churches." *Texas Baptist Standard,* 23 July 1955, 6.

———. *Baptists and the American Republic.* Nashville: Broadman, 1956.

Dayton, Donald W., and Lucille Sider Dayton. "Women as Preachers: Evangelical Precedents." *Christianity Today* 19 (23 May 1975): 4–7.

DeBerg, Betty. *Ungodly Women: Gender and the First Wave of American Fundamentalism.* Minneapolis: Fortress, 1990.

Delaney, Paul. "Baptists' Apology Accepted, So Let the Healing Begin." *Birmingham News,* 25 June 1995, 1C, 4C.

Dolan, Jay P. *The American Catholic Experience: A History from Colonial Times to the Present.* Garden City, N.Y.: Doubleday, 1985.

Druin, Toby. "Southwestern Profs to Sign New Statement." *Texas Baptist Standard,* 14 October 1998.

Duke, Barrett. "Religious Liberty: But Not for Christians." The Ethics and Religious Liberty Commission, <www.erlc.com/Sundays/1997/Sermons/97s-rliberty. htm>, 17 November 1997.

Eighmy, John Lee. *Churches in Cultural Captivity: A History of the Social Attitudes of Southern Baptists.* 1972. Reprint, Knoxville: University of Tennessee Press, 1987.

Elliott, Ralph. *The Genesis Controversy and Continuity in Southern Baptist Chaos: A Eulogy for a Great Tradition.* Macon, Ga.: Mercer University Press, 1992.

Ellis, William E. *A Man of Books and a Man of the People: E. Y. Mullins and the Crisis of Moderate Southern Baptist Leadership.* Macon, Ga.: Mercer University Press, 1985.

"The End of Democracy? The Judicial Usurpation of Politics." *First Things* 67 (November 1996): 18.

"Epistemological Modesty: An Interview with Peter Berger." *Christian Century,* 29 October 1997, 972–75, 978.

Esbeck, Carl. "Five Views of Church-State Relations in Contemporary American Thought." *Brigham Young University Law Review,* no. 2 (1986): 371–404.

Estep, William R. *Revolution within the Revolution.* Grand Rapids, Mich.: Eerdmans, 1990.

"Evangelical Leaders Back SBC Statement." *Texas Baptist Standard,* 29 July 1998, 3.

Fennell, Steven H. "Harmony or High Wall: A Comparison of the Views of John Leland and Isaac Backus Concerning Church-State Relations." Th.M. thesis, Southeastern Baptist Theological Seminary, 1989.

Flynt, Wayne. *Alabama Baptists: Southern Baptists in the Heart of Dixie.* Tuscaloosa: University of Alabama Press, 1998.

Foege, Alec. *The Empire God Built: Inside Pat Robertson's Media Machine.* New York: John Wiley and Sons, 1996.

Franklin, James L. "Baptists and Abortions." *Boston Globe,* 7 July 1980, 6.

Garrett, James Leo, Jr., E. Glenn Hinson, and James E. Tull. *Are Southern Baptists Evangelicals?* Macon, Ga.: Mercer University Press, 1983.

Garrison, Greg. "Southern Baptists Repent over Racism." *Birmingham News,* 21 June 1995, 10A.

Gaustad, Edwin S. "The Backus-Leland Tradition." *Foundations* 2 (April 1959): 131–52.

———. "Religious Liberty: Baptists and Some Fine Distinctions." *American Baptist Quarterly* 6 (December 1987): 215–25.

———. "Colonial Religion and Liberty of Conscience." In *The Virginia Statute for Religious Freedom: Its Evolution and Consequences in American History,* edited by Merrill D. Peterson and Robert C. Vaughan. New York: Cambridge University Press, 1988.

Goen, C. C. "Baptists and Church-State Issues in the Twentieth Century." In *Modern American Protestantism and Its World: Historical Articles on Protestantism in American Life,* vol. 3, *Civil Religion, Church, and State,* edited by Martin Marty. New York: K. G. Saur, 1992.

Goldstein, Clifford. "Shatter the Silence." *Liberty,* March–Apr. 1998, 18–19.

Goodstein, Laurie. "Religious Right, Frustrated, Trying New Tactic on G.O.P." *The New York Times,* 23 March 1998, 12.

Grelen, Jay. "Ripping down RFRA." *World,* 12–19 July 1997, 19.

Grenz, Stanley. *Isaac Backus: Puritan and Baptist.* Macon, Ga.: Mercer University Press, 1983.

———. "Baptist and Evangelical: One Northern Baptist's Perspective." In *Southern Baptists and American Evangelicals: The Conversation Continues,* edited by David S. Dockery. Nashville: Broadman and Holman, 1993.

Guth, James. "The Politics of Preachers: Southern Baptist Ministers and Christian Right Activism." In *New Christian Politics,* David G. Bromley and Anson Shupe. Macon, Ga.: Mercer University Press, 1984.

———. "Southern Baptists and the New Right." In *Religion in American Politics,* edited by Charles W. Dunn. Washington D.C.: CQ Press, 1989.

Hall, Charles F. "The Christian Left: Who Are They and How Are They Different from the Christian Right?" *Review of Religious Research* 39 (September 1997): 27–45.

Hamilton, Michael. "The Dissatisfaction of Francis Schaeffer." *Christianity Today,* 3 March 1997, 22–30.

Handy, Robert T. *Undermined Establishment: Church-State Relations in America, 1880–1920.* Princeton, N.J.: Princeton University Press, 1991.

Hankins, Barry. *God's Rascal: J. Frank Norris and the Beginnings of Southern Fundamentalism.* Lexington: University Press of Kentucky, 1996.

————. "Southern Baptists and Northern Evangelicals: Cultural Factors and the Nature of Religious Alliances." *Religion and American Culture: A Journal of Interpretation* 7 (summer 1997): 271–98.

Harrell, David Edwin, Jr. *Pat Robertson: A Personal, Religious, and Political Portrait.* San Francisco: Harper and Row, 1987.

Harwell, Jack. "Reactions around Country Criticize Mohler for Firing Diana Garland at Southern Seminary's Carver School." *Baptists Today,* 20 April 1995, 3.

Hassey, Janette. *No Time for Silence: Evangelical Women in Public Ministry around the Turn of the Century.* Grand Rapids, Mich.: Zondervan, 1986.

Hastey, Stan. "Southern Baptists and Women: The Real Issue." *Baptists Today,* 23 July 1998, 28.

Hayes, Kenneth. "Baptists Oppose Legalized Abortions." *Kentucky Western Recorder,* 9 May 1970, 7.

Hefley, James. *The Truth in Crisis.* 5 vols. Dallas: Clarion Publications; and Hannibal, Mo.: Hannibal Books, 1986–1990.

Henry, Carl F. H. *The Uneasy Conscience of Modern Fundamentalism.* Grand Rapids, Mich.: Eerdmans, 1947.

————. *Has Democracy Had Its Day?* Nashville: Southern Baptist Ethics and Religious Liberty Commission, 1996.

Hexham, Irving. "Abraham Kuyper." In *Evangelical Dictionary of Theology,* edited by Walter A. Elwell. Grand Rapids, Mich.: Baker Book House, 1984.

Hill, Samuel S., Jr. "Fundamentalism in the South." In *Perspectives in Churchmanship,* edited by David M. Scholer. Macon, Ga.: Mercer University Press, 1986.

————. *One Name but Several Faces: Variety in Popular Christian Denominations in Southern History.* Athens: University of Georgia Press, 1996.

————, ed. *Varieties of Southern Religious Experience.* Baton Rouge: Louisiana State University Press, 1988.

Himmelfarb, Gertrude. "An Illegitimate Regime?" *First Things* 69 (January 1997): 2 (correspondence).

Howard, Judith Lynn. "Baptists Apologize for Racism." *Dallas Morning News,* 21 June 1995, 1A.

Howe, Claude L., Jr. "From Houston to Dallas: Recent Controversy in the Southern Baptist Convention." In *The Controversy in the Southern Baptist Convention: A Special Issue of* The Theological Educator. New Orleans: Faculty of the New Orleans Baptist Theological Seminary, 1985. Reprinted in *The Theological Educator* 41 (spring 1990).

Hunter, James Davison. *Evangelicalism: The Coming Generation.* Chicago: University of Chicago Press, 1987.

————. *Culture Wars: The Struggle to Define America.* New York: Basic Books, 1991.

————. *Before the Shooting Begins: Searching for Democracy in America's Culture War.* New York: Free Press, 1994.

Jones, Jim. "Baptists Take First Step." *Fort Worth Star-Telegram,* 25 June 1995.

————. "Baptists Take Stand on Role of Wives." *Fort Worth Star Telegram,* 10 June 1999, 13.

Keil, C. F., and F. Delitzsch. *Biblical Commentary on the Old Testament.* Grand Rapids, Mich.: Eerdmans, 1950.

Keller, Robert H., Jr. *American Protestantism and United States Indian Policy, 1869–1882.* Lincoln: University of Nebraska Press, 1983.

Kennedy, John. "Patterson's Election Seals Conservative Control." *Christianity Today,* 13 July 1998, 21.

Kingdon, Robert. *Adultery and Divorce in Calvin's Geneva.* Cambridge: Harvard University Press, 1995.

Knight, Walker L. "POAU Reveals Texas Violations." *Texas Baptist Standard,* 20 May 1954, 3.

Knox, Marv. "Fellowship Declines to Debate SBC." *Texas Baptist Standard,* 8 July 1998.

Larson, Edward. *Summer for the Gods: The Scopes Trial and America's Continuing Debate over Science and Religion.* New York: Basic Books, 1997.

Lattimore, Laurie. "Campolo a Biblical 'Conservative,' but His Views Controversial." *Texas Baptists Committed Newsletter,* June 1997, 11.

Laycock, Douglas. "Continuity and Change in the Threat to Religious Liberty: The Reformation Era and the Late Twentieth Century." *Minnesota Law Review* 80 (May 1996): 1047–1102.

Leonard, Bill. "Southern Baptists and the Separation of Church and State." *Review and Expositor* 83 (spring 1986): 195–207.

———. *God's Last and Only Hope: The Fragmentation of the Southern Baptist Convention.* Grand Rapids, Mich.: Eerdmans, 1990.

———. "Seminary Crackdown." *Christian Century,* 10 May 1995, 500–501.

"Light from the Capital: CLC Supports Inclusion of Religious Schools in Program." *Light,* March–April 1996, 14.

Linder, Robert. "Shall the Accommodationists Win? Religious Liberty in the Balance in the Closing Decades of the Twentieth Century." *Southwestern Journal of Theology* 36, no. 3 (summer 1994): 37–44.

Lindsell, Harold. *The Battle for the Bible.* Grand Rapids, Mich.: Zondervan, 1976.

Lowell, C. Stanley. "Battle of the Century." *Texas Baptist Standard,* 12 April 1958, 6.

Lumpkin, William L. *Baptist Confessions of Faith.* Valley Forge, Pa.: Judson, 1969.

Lupu, Ira C. "Reconstructing the Establishment Clause: The Case against Discretionary Accommodation of Religion." *University of Pennsylvania Law Review* 140 (1991): 555–612.

———. "The Trouble with Accommodation." *The George Washington Law Review* 60 (March 1992): 743–81.

Marsden, George. *Fundamentalism and American Culture: The Shaping of Twentieth-Century Evangelicalism.* New York: Oxford University Press, 1980.

———. "The Evangelical Denomination." In *Evangelicalism and Modern America,* edited by George Marsden. Grand Rapids, Mich.: Eerdmans, 1984.

———. *Reforming Fundamentalism: Fuller Theological Seminary and the New Evangelicalism.* Grand Rapids, Mich.: Eerdmans, 1987.

———. *Religion and American Culture.* New York: Harcourt Brace Jovanovich, 1990.

———. *Understanding Evangelicalism and Fundamentalism.* Grand Rapids, Mich.: Eerdmans, 1991.

———. "Contemporary American Evangelicalism." In *Southern Baptists and American Evangelicals: The Conversation Continues,* edited by David S. Dockery. Nashville: Broadman and Holman, 1993.

———. *The Soul of the University.* New York: Oxford University Press, 1994.

Marsh, Charles. *God's Long Summer: Stories of Faith and Civil Rights.* Princeton, N.J.: Princeton University Press, 1997.

Martin, William. *With God on Our Side: The Rise of the Religious Right in America.* New York: Broadway Books, 1996.

Maston, T. B. *Isaac Backus: Pioneer of Religious Liberty.* Rochester, N.Y.: American Baptist Historical Society, 1962.

Mathis, Deborah. "Southern Baptists Take Vital First Step." *Knoxville News-Sentinel,* 25 June 1995.

Maxwell, Bill. "Baptists' Apologies Are Right." *St. Petersburg Times,* 25 June 1995, 1D, 8D.

McBeth, Harry Leon. "The Role of Women in Southern Baptist History." *Baptist History and Heritage* 12 (January 1977): 3–25.

———. "Perspectives on Women in Baptist Life." *Baptist History and Heritage* 22 (July 1987): 4–11.

———. *The Baptist Heritage: Four Centuries of Baptist Witness.* Nashville: Broadman, 1987.

———. "Baptist or Evangelical: One Southern Baptist's Perspective." In *Southern Baptists and American Evangelicals: The Conversation Continues,* edited by David S. Dockery. Nashville: Broadman and Holman, 1993.

McConnell, Michael. "Accommodation of Religion: An Update and a Response to the Critics." *The George Washington Law Review* 60 (March 1992): 685–742.

McCormick, Mark. "Dean Says Seminary Fired Her from Post." *Louisville Courier Journal,* 22 March 1995, A1, A9.

McGee, Dan. "The Abortion Debate: Recognizing All the Issues." *Therefore: The Newsletter of the Texas Baptist Christian Life Commission,* spring 1986, 3.

McLoughlin, William. *Isaac Backus on Church, State, and Calvinism: Pamphlets, 1754–1789.* Cambridge: Harvard University Press, Belknap Press, 1968.

———. *New England Dissent 1630–1833: The Baptists and Separation of Church and State.* Cambridge: Harvard University Press, 1971.

———. "Isaac Backus and Separation of Church and State." In *The Marrow of American Divinity,* edited by Peter Hoffer. New York: Garland, 1988.

Miller, Robert T., and Ronald B. Flowers, eds. *Toward Benevolent Neutrality: Church, State, and the Supreme Court.* 5th ed. Waco, Tex.: Baylor University Press, 1996.

Monsma, Stephen V., and Oliver Thomas. *Church-State Relations: A Debate.* Crossroads Monograph Series on Faith and Pubic Policy, vol. 1, no. 16. Wynnewood, Pa.: Crossroads, 1997.

Morgan, David. *The New Crusades, the New Holy Land: Conflict in the Southern Baptist Convention, 1969–1991.* Tuscaloosa: University of Alabama Press, 1996.

Moyers, Bill. *God and Politics: The Battle for the Bible.* Princeton, N.J.: Films for the Humanities, 1994. Videocassette.

Murphy, Cullen. "Protestantism and the Evangelicals." *The Wilson Quarterly* 5:4 (autumn 1981): 105–16.

Neuhaus, Richard John. *The Naked Public Square: Religion and Democracy in America.* Grand Rapids, Mich.: Eerdmans, 1984.

———. "A New Order of Religious Freedom." *The George Washington Law Review* 60 (March 1992): 627–28.

Niebuhr, Gustav. "Baptist Group Votes to Repent Stand on Slaves." *The New York Times,* 21 June 1995.

———. "Southern Baptists Declare Wife Should 'Submit' to Her Husband." *The New York Times,* 10 June 1998, A1.

Niebuhr, H. Richard. *Christ and Culture.* New York: Harper and Row, 1951.

Noll, Mark. "Getting the Facts Straight." *TRI (Rutherford Institute),* March 1993.

Noll, Mark, Nathan Hatch, and George Marsden. *The Search for Christian America.* Exp. ed. Colorado Springs: Helmers and Howard, 1989.

North, Gary. *Crossed Fingers: How the Liberals Captured the Presbyterian Church.* Tyler, Tex.: Institute for Christian Economics, 1996.

North, Gary, and Gary DeMar. *Christian Reconstruction: What It Is, What It Isn't.* Tyler, Tex.: Institute for Christian Economics, 1991.

Odell-Scott, David W. "Let the Women Speak in Church: An Egalitarian Interpretation of I Cor. 14:33b-36." *Biblical Theology Bulletin* 13 (1983): 90–93.

Otto, Mary. "Southern Baptists Repent Racist Past." *Akron Beacon Journal,* 21 June 1995, A4.

Parham, Robert. "Abortion: Some Common Ground." *Light,* October 1986, 9–10.

Parker, Gary. "Confusing Trends in Baptist Life." *Baptists Today,* 24 September 1998, 26.

"Patterson, Reporter Differ on Hiring Story." *Texas Baptist Standard,* 9 July 1986, 5.

Payne, Les. "Late Regrets about Slavery." *New York Newsday,* 25 June 1995.

Pierard, Richard V. "Religion and the 1984 Election Campaign." *Review of Religious Research* 27 (1985): 104–5.

———. "Separation of Church and State: Figment of an Infidel's Imagination?" In *Faith and Freedom: A Tribute to Franklin H. Littell,* edited by Richard Libowitz. New York: Pergamon, 1987.

Plowman, Edward E. "Beyond the Pews." *World,* 27 June 1998, 19.

Princeton Religion Research Center. "Latest Religious Preferences." *Emerging Trends* 19 (March 1997): 3.

Rabkin, Jeremy. "The Culture War That Isn't." *Policy Review,* August–September 1999, <http://www.heritage.org/policyreview/aug99/rabkin.html>.

"Racist No More? Black Leaders Ask." *Christianity Today,* 14 August 1995, 53.

Rawls, John. *A Theory of Justice.* Cambridge: Harvard University Press, 1971.

———. *Political Liberalism.* New York: Columbia University Press, 1993.

Reflections of the Savior: A Silver Anniversary Celebration. Cordova, Tenn.: Bellevue Baptist Church, 1997.

"Religious Liberty Bill before Congress Highlights Differences among Baptists." *SBC Today,* 9:14, 26 July 1991, 1.

"Resolutions Stir Heated Debate among Messengers." *Texas Baptist Standard,* 27 May 1964, 10.

Roark, D. M. "Carl F. H. Henry." In *Dictionary of Christianity in America,* edited by Daniel G. Reid et al. Downers Grove, Ill.: InterVarsity, 1990.

Roland, Charles. "The Ever-Vanishing South." *Journal of Southern History* 48 (February 1982): 3–20.

Rowan, Carl. "Southern Baptists Face Sin of Racism." *Denver Post,* 25 June 1995.

Scanlon, Leslie. "Dean at Baptist Seminary Forced to Quit." *Louisville Courier Journal,* 21 March 1995, A1, A9.

Shaw, Susan M., and Tisa Lewis. "'Once There Was a Camelot': Women Doctoral Graduates of the Southern Baptist Theological Seminary, 1982–1992, Talk about the Seminary, the Fundamentalist Takeover, and Their Lives since SBTS." *Review and Expositor* 95 (1998): 397–423.

Sherman, Cecil E. "The Idea of Being Baptist." *Light,* May 1983, 2–4.

———. "An Overview of the Moderate Movement." In *The Struggle for the Soul of the SBC: Moderate Responses to the Fundamentalists Movement,* edited by Walter B. Shurden. Macon, Ga.: Mercer University Press, 1993.

Shriver, George H., ed. *Dictionary of Heresy Trials in American Christianity.* Westport, Conn.: Greenwood, 1997.

Shurden, Walter B. *Not a Silent People: Controversies That Have Shaped Southern Baptists.* Macon, Ga.: Smyth and Helwys, 1995.

———, and Randy Shepley, eds. *Going for the Jugular: A Documentary History of the SBC Holy War.* Macon, Ga.: Mercer University Press, 1996.

———, ed. *Reclaiming the Baptist Vision: Religious Liberty.* Macon, Ga.: Smyth and Helwys, 1997.

Simmons, Paul D. "Bioethical Issues in Christian Perspective." *Light,* March–April 1983, 5.

———. "Religious Liberty and the Abortion Debate." *Journal of Church and State* 32 (summer 1990): 567–84.

———. "Religious Liberty and Abortion Policy: *Casey* as 'Catch-22.'" *Journal of Church and State* 42 (winter 2000): 69–88.

Singleton, William C., III. "A Real Dialogue about Race Is Needed." *Birmingham News,* 24 June 1995.

Skillen, James. *The Scattered Voice: Christians at Odds in the Public Square.* Edmonton, Alberta: Canadian Institute for Law, Theology, and Public Policy, 1996.

Smith, Oran P. *The Rise of Baptist Republicanism.* New York: New York University Press, 1997.

Smith, Timothy. *Revivalism and Social Reform in Mid-Nineteenth-Century America.* Nashville: Abingdon, 1957.

"Southern Baptists Plan Churches in Inner Cities." *Nashville Tennessean,* 16 June 1999, 15A.

Spain, Rufus B. *At Ease in Zion: Social History of Southern Baptists, 1865–1900.* Nashville: Vanderbilt University Press, 1967.

Stassen, Glen H., Diane M. Yeager, and John Howard Yoder. *Authentic Transformation: A New Vision of Christ and Culture.* Nashville: Abingdon, 1996.

Steinfels, Peter. "Beliefs." *The New York Times,* 13 June 1998.

Stricklin, David. *A Genealogy of Dissent: Southern Baptist Protest in the Twentieth Century.* Lexington: University Press of Kentucky, 1999.

"Submission Rejected." *Christianity Today,* 6 December 1999, 27.

Sweet, Leonard I. "The Evangelical Tradition in America." In *The Evangelical Tradition in America,* edited by Leonard I. Sweet. Macon, Ga.: Mercer University Press, 1984.

Talbert Charles. "Biblical Criticism's Role: The Pauline View of Women as a Case in Point." In *The Unfettered Word: Southern Baptists Confront the Authority-Inerrancy Question,* edited by Robison James. Waco, Tex.: Word Books, 1987.

———. *Reading Corinthians: A Literary and Theological Commentary on 1 and 2 Corinthians.* New York: Crossroad, 1987.

Taylor, Jeff. "Hollow Cries." *Liberty,* January–February 1998, 27.

Thompson, James J., Jr. *Tried as by Fire: Southern Baptists and the Controversy of the Twenties.* Macon, Ga.: Mercer University Press. 1982.

Trollinger, William Vance, Jr. *God's Empire: William Bell Riley and Midwestern Fundamentalism.* Madison: University of Wisconsin Press, 1990.

"Up and Comers: Fifty Evangelical Leaders 40 and Under." *Christianity Today,* 11 November 1996, 22.

Vandenberg, Frank. *Abraham Kuyper.* Grand Rapids, Mich.: Eerdmans, 1960.

Vincent, Stuart. "Baptists Draw Fire for Policy." *Melville (N.Y.) Newsday,* 11 June 1998.

Wacker, Grant. *Augustus H. Strong and the Dilemma of Historical Consciousness.* Macon, Ga.: Mercer University Press, 1985.

Waddle, Ray. "Debaters Cross Swords over Ordination of Baptist Women." *The Tennessean,* 28 April 1988, 1A, 4A.

———. "Besieged Baptist Director Sought as Pastor." *The Tennessean* 12 May 1988, 3B.

———. "Abortion View Checked before Honor Awarded." *The Tennessean,* 15 September 1989, 1A.

———. "S. Baptists Ban Speakers Holding 'Pro-Choice' Views." *The Tennessean,* 9 March 1990, 4A.

Wagner, C. Peter. *Our Kind of People: The Ethical Dimensions of Church Growth in America.* Atlanta, Ga.: John Knox Press, 1979.

———. "A Vision for Evangelizing the Real America." *International Bulletin of Missionary Research* (April 1986): 59–64.

Walker, J. Brent. "Coalitions a Necessity to Get Things Done in Washington." *Report from the Capital,* 13 October 1998, 3.

Weber, Timothy P. *Living in the Shadow of the Second Coming: American Premillennialism, 1875–1925.* New York: Oxford University Press, 1979.

———. "Evangelicalism North and South." *Review and Expositor* 92 (1995): 299–317.

Wells, Ronald. "Francis Schaeffer's Jeremiad: A Review Article." *TSF Bulletin,* September–October 1984, 20–23.

White, Gayle. "'A Great Day,' Black Pastors Agree." *Atlanta Journal Constitution,* 21 June 1995.

———. "Baptists to Consider Adopting Statement on Marriage, Family." *Atlanta Constitution,* 30 May 1998.

White, Richard D. "What's Really Going on at Southern Seminary?" *Western Recorder,* 18 April 1995, 6.

Whitehead, John. *Religious Apartheid: The Separation of Religion From Public Life.* Chicago: Moody, 1994.

Wiles, Dennis Ray. "Factors Contributing to the Resurgence of Fundamentalism in the Southern Baptist Convention, 1979–1990." Ph.D. diss., Southern Baptist Theological Seminary, 1992.

Williams, Rhys H., ed. *Culture War in American Politics: Critical Reviews of a Popular Myth.* New York: Aldine de Gruyter, 1997.

Wills, Gary. "Baptists' Woman-bashing Theologically off the Mark." *Chicago Sun Times,* 13 June 1998.

Wilson, Charles Reagan. *Baptized in Blood: The Religion of the Lost Cause, 1865–1920.* Athens: University of Georgia Press.

Wingfield, Mark. "Faced with Crisis, Trustees Stand by Their Man." *Kentucky Western Recorder,* 25 April 1995.

———. "Garland to Presbyterian Seminary; Named 'Whistle Blower.'" *Kentucky Western Recorder,* 28 May 1996, 2.

———. "Seminary Has Lost 59 Percent of Faculty since 1992." *Kentucky Western Recorder,* 28 May 1996, 2.

———. "Sexes Marked by 'Biblical Equality,' Texas Baptists Resolve." *Texas Baptist Standard,* 18 November 1998, 6.

———. "BGCT Affirms 1963 Doctrinal Statement." *Texas Baptist Standard,* 17 November 1999, 1.

Wolfe, Bill. "Baptist Trustees Approve 5 Teachers for Seminary, Disapprove of Views." *Louisville Courier Journal,* 30 April 1992, n.p.

Wood, James E., Jr. "Religious Liberty and Abortion Rights." *Report from the Capital* 29 (January 1974): 2.

———. "Editorial: Separation Vis-à-Vis Accommodation: A New Direction in American Church-State Relations?" *Journal of Church and State* 31 (spring 1989): 202.

Woodward, C. Vann. *The Burden of Southern History.* Baton Rouge: Louisiana State University Press, 1960.

Woodward, Kenneth L., et al. "Born Again! The Year of the Evangelicals." *Newsweek,* 25 October 1976, 76.

Index